NEW EUROPE IN THE

Elena
summer '01

New Europe in Transition

Edited by Peter J. Anderson, Georg Wiessala and
Christopher Williams

CONTINUUM
London and New York

Continuum
The Tower Building, 11 York Road, London SE1 7NX
370 Lexington Avenue, New York, NY 10017-6503

First published 2000

British Library Cataloguing-in-Publication Data
A catalogue record of this book is available from the British Library.

ISBN 0-8264-4779-1 (hardback)
0-8264-4780-5 (paperback)

Typeset by YHT Ltd, London

Printed and bound in Great Britain by Creative Print and Design Wales, Ebbw Vale

Contents

Tables

Contributors

Editors

Peter J. Anderson is Senior Lecturer in European Studies and International Relations, Department of Languages and International Studies, University of Central Lancashire, Preston. He has taught previously at the Universities of Lancaster and Southampton. He has special interests in foreign policy, international relations, environmental politics, the European Union and the UK media. His published works in English include *The Global Politics of Power, Justice and Death* (1996), for Routledge, and *Insulting the Public? The British Press and the European Union* (with Tony Weymouth) (1999), for Longman. He is working currently on the role of NATO in Kosovo.

Georg Wiessala, a trained lawyer, is Senior Lecturer in European Studies, Department of Languages and International Studies, University of Central Lancashire, Preston. He has major research interests in the areas of European integration, external relations of the EU, national identities, European law and Europe–Asia relations. His recent publications include *The European Union – Annual Review of Activities 1997* (edited, 1998) and articles in the journals *Europe*, *German Politics*, *Debatte*, *The Journal of Area Studies and World Affairs.* He is a regular contributor to European conferences in the UK, continental Europe and the Asia Pacific. He is currently working on *The European Union and Asia* for UACES/Sheffield University Press.

Christopher Williams is Reader in Russian Studies, Department of Languages and International Studies, University of Central Lancashire. He has taught previously at the University of Cork. He has particular research interests in Russian and Soviet social policy and sociology; youth in Russia; contemporary Russian politics; and right-wing extremism and nationalism in Russia and East-Central Europe in the post Cold War era. His publications include articles in *Journal of Communist Studies and Transition Politics*, *Revolutionary Russia*, *Irish Slavonic Studies*, *Journal of Urban History*, *Sociology of Health and Illness* and *Sotsiologicheskie issledovaniya.* His recently published books include *AIDS in Post-communist Russia and the Successor States* (1995), *Young People in Post-communist Russia and Eastern Europe* (edited, 1995), *Russian Society in Transition* (edited, 1996), *Ethnicity and Nationalism in Russia, the CIS and the Baltic States* (edited, 1999) and *Ethnicity and Nationalism in East-Central Europe and the Balkans* (edited, 1999). He is currently completing *Growing Up in a Risk Society: A Sociological Analysis of Russian Youth* (with Vladimir Chuprov and Julia Zubok). He is a consultant for the Canadian immigration authorities on asylum rights for the sexual minorities. Since 1998 he has been Secretary of the British Association of Slavonic and East European Studies.

Other contributors

Geoffrey Edwards is Jean Monnet Chairholder, Director of the Institute for International Relations and affiliated to Pembroke College, Cambridge.

Jack Hampson is Senior Lecturer in Social Policy, Department of Social Work, Faculty of Health, University of Central Lancashire, Preston.

Robert Harmsen is Lecturer in the Institute for European Studies, Queen's University, Belfast.

Karen Henderson is Lecturer in the Department of Politics, University of Leicester.

Neil Hughes is Principal Lecturer, Department of Modern Economics, Nottingham Trent University.

Joanna McKay is Senior Lecturer, Department of Languages and Politics, Nottingham Trent University.

Frands S. Pedersen is a PhD candidate in the Department of Languages and International Studies, University of Central Lancashire, Preston.

Philippa Sherrington is Lecturer in the Department of Politics, University of Warwick.

Simona Talani is Lecturer in the Department of Economics, London School of Economics.

Alastair H. Thomas is Professor of Nordic Politics, Department of Languages and International Studies, University of Central Lancashire, Preston.

David Travers is Lecturer in the Department of Politics and International Relations, University of Lancaster.

Preface and acknowledgements

Although the co-editors made the final selection of material and edited all contributions, we have made no attempt to impose particular political ideologies on the individual contributors and have limited intentionally our requirements with regard to chapter structure and content. Instead contributions are based on specialist knowledge of a specific topic, with two sole provisos: that country study contributors should address questions that they believe to be central to the social, political and economic dimensions of their chosen states; and that all contributors should address the core themes of globalization and threats to democracy, unless they are not relevant to their chapter focus. As a result what follows is a wide diversity of opinions. This we hope will increase interest in the book as well as augment its intrinsic value. This book is also based on the firm premise that there are very few existing studies offering distinguished social scientists the opportunity to make their research findings on trends in the New Europe known to a wider audience.

It is hoped that this survey of selected EU member states, Russia and East European countries and key international organizations operative within the continent will enable scholars in all parts of the New Europe and beyond to gain a greater understanding of the problems and futures of different parts of Europe in the twenty-first century.

We wish to thank all contributors for their co-operation in producing this book, in particular for revising and updating their chapters. Thanks to Saleel Nurbhai for his work as the project researcher. Special thanks also go to Caroline Wintersgill and Continuum for invaluable editorial and technical expertise.

Peter Anderson
Georg Wiessala
Christopher Williams

Department of Languages and International Studies
University of Central Lancashire Preston
January 2000

Introduction

Peter J. Anderson, Georg Wiessala and Christopher Williams

The question of 'What is Europe?' confronts, and at times vexes, all scholars who use the term. The answer could most effectively be described as being dependent on where one sits. Many current European issues continue to demonstrate that citizens of, for example, the successor states of the former Soviet Union, or Turkey, do not necessarily share the same definition or understanding of Europe as residents of Belgium or France. It is, in short, not possible as yet to produce a definition of Europe or to draw boundaries with which all of the affected peoples agree.

Our approach, made complex by this dilemma, has, however, been simplified by one important fact: the vast diversity of the European continent means that it is not possible to include all of its states, or even most of them, within a single volume such as this. We have therefore had to be highly selective, and have chosen a representational sample of those states and organizations that constitute, or sit within or between *the major poles of power* that currently dominate the continent of Europe – Russia, the (European Union) EU and NATO (complications of overlap between the latter two will be addressed in relevant chapters). This does not mean that all of our contributors have a single definition of Europe. They do not. But what is true is that all subscribe to the view that included within the text is a representative selection of the contents of the core of the new, post-Cold War Europe.

The particular selection of states, organizations and thematic areas can be explained as follows: the sample of EU states is designed to ensure that there is adequate representation of small, large and medium-sized states, including two very different incumbents of the Presidency of the Council of Ministers in 2000. It includes also rich and poor states and those in between, together with states from North, South and Central Europe. As far as the EU itself is concerned, given the limits to the book's size, a representative sample of key current and ongoing issues and policy areas has been selected for analysis to give a feel of the quintessence of this now most significantly evolving institution at the beginning of a new century. The main focus is on EU institutions, law, external relations, and the Union's social dimension, together with its relationship to the fundamental question of European identity. There is no specific chapter on the EU's economics dimension. This aspect is woven throughout the chapters on individual countries and is covered significantly in Chapter 1.

The book's coverage on Eastern Europe too is constrained by space, so we had to be selective. There is considerable coverage of Russia, with one chapter mainly on its political and social dimensions, and another containing detailed analysis of the country's economic predicament. A sample of key Eastern and Central European states is then analysed in the context of a chapter on the eastern enlargement of the

EU and within the overall chapter on the transition economies. The role the United Nations plays in Europe is examined, with particular reference to Eastern Europe. Finally, NATO and the OSCE are analysed in their capacity as organizations that include members from both Eastern and Western Europe.

Woven through all of the above are a series of core aims and themes. These are, first, to identify a selection of the most interesting and important political and other questions confronting the major levels of European society currently, together with those likely to persist into, or to arise in, the near future of the twenty-first century. The second aim is to analyse these in terms of their likely impact on those affected by them and any dilemmas they might create. An attempt will then be made, wherever feasible, to estimate the likelihood of such problems being resolved and to identify ways in which this might occur.

Two concepts at the heart of contemporary Europe, *globalization* and *democracy*, will run as a *leitmotiv*, a continuous theme, throughout the book. It seems to us that in a year which is going to see in a new, reform-oriented Intergovernmental Conference (IGC), seeking to reshape an ever more outwardly active Union, those are the overarching concerns which matter most. The cumulative corollary of the above will be to produce a picture of key representational dimensions of Europe in all of its current, rich complexity. This will play a crucial role in helping students of European Studies and Politics to approach and understand something of the range and intricacy of the subject matter with which they are dealing.

PART I

The Global Context

CHAPTER ONE

Globalization and Democracy in Europe

Peter J. Anderson

Globalization

Globalization earns its place as one of the key concepts to be addressed, where relevant, throughout this book, on several crucial grounds. First, it has been cited by critics of the EU, such as Jamieson, as one of the factors that makes such bodies, with their focus on continuing regionally based processes of integration, out of step with global reality (Jamieson, 1993). Second, it has been suggested also that globalization is damaging seriously the ability of European and other states to continue to lay any meaningful claim to sovereignty, whether or not they are part of the EU (Anderson, P.J., 1996: Chapters 3, 4; Dicken, 1998: 3). Third, it is argued that globalization is a process that is creating an economic environment that is increasingly complex and unpredictable and therefore more difficult for European and other states, and the business organizations at their heart, to manage.[1] Fourth, it has been strongly argued that globalization is making traditional forms of democracy in Europe and elsewhere increasingly deficient (McGrew, 1997). Fifth, it has been argued that globalization is a mask to cover what is really a process of imperialism (Parker, B., 1998: 33–5) promoted by the large multinational corporations in the West and Japan, and which is primarily a vehicle for US expansionism. Sixth, it has been contended that globalization is undermining national (Giddens, 1999) and regional identities. Finally, it has been argued that globalization is making people all over the world aware of the UN-driven idea of universal human rights in a manner that was not previously the case and which challenges fundamental tenets of the traditional notion of state sovereignty (Evans, 1997: Chapter 6). The implications for Europe most recently have been demonstrated by the successful calls from the people of Kosovo for NATO intervention against the Serbs.

In short, whether it is a 'mask' for other processes or not, globalization is important because it has been alleged to be striking at the heart of key elements of European society – at the relevance or otherwise of the EU, at the viability of state sovereignty and liberal democracy in both Eastern and Western Europe, and at the ability or otherwise of those managing the multiple, interwoven layers of European economic activity to do so in a coherent and stable manner. For all of these reasons, and for others that will emerge during the course of the book, globalization has to be addressed as a major concern.

But it is not only the threats which globalization is alleged to pose which make it of interest. It is argued also to be creating a variety of new opportunities for European and other societies, whether these lie in the ease and efficiency of communication for business, media and social purposes, as with the internet, or through the alleged decrease in the likelihood of war between the major powers in Europe, Asia and the Americas as globalizing forces cause them to become ever more closely intertwined economically. The opportunities as well as the threats which globalization creates for European societies will be discussed therefore.

However, because globalization is such a vast topic, it will not be possible to look at every single way in which it is relevant to the chapters which follow. That would require a separate book in itself. Instead, in chapters to which the concept is relevant, each author will illustrate briefly but effectively one or more of the dimensions of globalization (such as those outlined above) that seem to them to be the most important to their chapter in the context of their overall discussion. There will also be an initial analysis of the concept's role in the new Europe in this chapter. By these means, *something of the central role which globalization now plays in European life* will be illustrated and analysed, even if it is not possible in a book concerned with many additional issues to give the concept *comprehensive* coverage.

With the above comments kept firmly in mind, it is necessary to consider how globalization can be defined for the purposes of this book. Before this can be done adequately, however, it is desirable briefly to demonstrate something of the range of competing definitions of the concept that is available and then to evaluate the extent to which pre-existing versions might be helpful in producing the core definition to be used throughout the chapters which follow. What will be done also, where relevant, is to elaborate briefly on some of the views of precisely what globalization involves that are attached to those definitions. The multidisciplinary literature on globalization is now simply too vast for all of it to be examined here, so what follows is a representative sample of the available definitions chosen specifically for their illustrative appropriateness in the context of this analysis.

Defining globalization

For the specific purposes of this chapter it has been decided to compare definitions of globalization offered by Peter Dicken, James H. Mittelman, Barbara Parker, Charlotte Bretherton, Peter Anderson, Anthony McGrew, Paul Q. Hirst and GrahameThompson. These have been selected for their ability to illustrate, individually and collectively, the key dimensions of the concept of globalization that have been identified in the mainstream literature. They will form the foundation on which the definition of globalization to be used in this book will be built.

Dicken's view

One way in which Dicken defines globalization involves comparing it to and distinguishing it from 'internationalization'. He states that:

> Internationalisation processes involve the simple extension of economic activities across international boundaries. It is, essentially, a quantitative process which leads to a more extensive geographical pattern of economic activity ... Globalisation processes are qualitatively different from internationalisation processes. They involve not merely the geographical extension of economic activity across national boundaries but also –

> and more importantly – the functional integration of such internationally dispersed activities. (Dicken, 1998: 5)

He goes on to stress that this integration is not geographically or temporally uniform:

> globalisation is a complex set of processes which operate very unevenly in both time and space. What we see 'on the ground', at various geographical scales, is primarily the outcome of the interaction between two major sets of institutions – transnational corporations and states – set within the context of a volatile technological environment. (Dicken, 1998: xiv)

Mittelman's perspective

Mittelman adopts a different slant on the globalization concept. He states that:

> With the move towards a post-hegemonic order, there emerged a series of structural changes in the global political economy, a period known as globalisation. Understood historically, these shifts entail not only an intensification of previous patterns (e.g. from cross-national lending to the hyper mobility of finance capital) but also a quantum transformation of a system lacking the saving power of effective means of regulation. In this sense, globalisation constitutes a dialectic of continuities and discontinuities. (Mittelman, 1996: 231)

He sees globalization as being: 'encoded with the values of economic liberalism – the inevitability of progress and ultimately a market utopia' (Mittelman, 1996: 231). In short,

> globalisation is a coalescence of varied transnational processes and domestic structures, allowing the economy, politics, culture, and ideology of one country to penetrate another. Driven by changing modes of competition, globalisation compresses the time and space aspects of social relations. In short, globalisation is a market-induced, not a policy-led, process. (Mittelman, 1996: 232)

Parker's definition

Parker notes that:

> globalisation is defined broadly as increased permeability of traditional boundaries of almost every kind, including physical borders such as time and space, nation states and economies, industries and organizations and less tangible borders such as cultural norms or assumptions about 'how we do things around here'. (Parker, B. 1998: 6–7)

She observes that globalization can occur both from above and from below. From above it is:

> consolidation of business and political power to create a powerful and abusive 'New World Order' ... and many conclude it is consolidation of power among already powerful business and government interests ... nations and organizations with economic and political power will pool their clout to advance their common economic interests by disseminating consumerism worldwide. (Parker, B., 1998: 33)

Globalization from below can arise as the result of the activities of social and communal forces. Such activities are generally of a voluntary nature and are not driven primarily by the interests of such forces, and are pursued in the hope of furthering human rights and transnational social justice (Parker, B., 1998: 36).

Parker notes that one of the concerns that has been expressed about the New World Order version of globalization is that it can become a new name for imperialism (Parker, B., 1998: 33-5).

Bretherton's definition

For Bretherton: 'globalisation suggests a significant intensification of global connectedness and a consciousness of that intensification, with a corresponding diminution in the significance of territorial boundaries and state structures' (Bretherton and Ponton, 1996: 3).

Bretherton's attempt to define globalization is one of the most lucid and even-handed available within the literature and is worthy of as detailed a summary as is possible in a book with the necessarily broad and multiple aims that drive this one. She sees technology as a crucial and necessary enabling factor within globalization, but notes that: 'Nevertheless its impacts are both uneven and mixed. Thus technology can enhance the ability of states to control ... their citizens, while simultaneously contributing to the reduction of government autonomy in the economic sphere.'

While new technologies 'are used to facilitate global cooperation, they may equally serve to emphasize cultural divisions. Ultimately, economic and political considerations influence the choice and spread of technologies' (Bretherton and Ponton, 1996: 5–6).

Economic globalization 'implies more than the extensive reach of capital: it implies the existence of a unified global economy which has a dynamic beyond the interaction of separate domestic economies' (Bretherton and Ponton, 1996: 6).

She sees arguments relating to this aspect of the concept focusing principally upon the globalization of production and of finance. This in turn relates to the strategies and activities of multinational business corporations and relies substantially upon technological innovation and the ownership of knowledge (Bretherton and Ponton, 1996: 6).

However, Bretherton is careful to stress that these kinds of globalization have had and are having uneven effects, particularly with regard to their impact within the developed and the under-developed world. She notes that while moves towards a globalized economy have been significant, 'they do not represent the whole picture. Global production strategies coexist with traditional international trade and with localized production' (Bretherton and Ponton, 1996: 7). For her, there are two other key types of globalization. Political globalization refers to 'a growing tendency for issues to be perceived as global in scope, and hence requiring global solutions: and to the development of international organizations and global institutions which attempt to address such issues' (Bretherton and Ponton, 1996: 8). The globalization of ideas is an area of concern where the focus is on 'the extent to which ideas concerning social, economic and political relationships have become global in scope: and second, the potential emergence of a cosmopolitan culture' (Bretherton and Ponton, 1996: 10).

For some, globalization is a powerful means of spreading and facilitating the dominance of Western ideas. However, Bretherton notes that 'the dissemination of ideas, whether they reflect western or cosmopolitan values, does not imply their acceptance: indeed reaction to new ideas can range from complete assimilation to outright rejection' (Bretherton and Ponton, 1996: 12).

Bearing all of the above in mind, globalization is:

> a set of overlapping processes that are neither inexorable nor irreversible: the impact of which varies in intensity and is highly differentiated in effect. Simply put – globalisation is an uncertain process which affects some people more than others: it also produces winners and losers. (Bretherton and Ponton, 1996: 5)

Anderson's view

Anderson fills in a few of the gaps that Bretherton does not. However, cautioned by the loose way that the term globalization has come to be used and by the variety of different meanings that have become attached to the single term, he prefers to re-title his understanding of the fundamentals involved as global interfusion. Global interfusion processes, he argues, can involve the interfusing of one or more of several things. These include:

> (1) the economies or part or entire sectors of the economies of two or more states: or (2) of the values and practices of one society with those of another: or (3), directly or indirectly, formally or informally, of states' people and their interests with a variety of power structures beyond their individual boundaries: or (4) of problems in one part of the world relating to anything from pollution to religion with the fund of human concern in another: or (5) of attitudes or concerns in one state with those in others. The extent to which factors fuse will vary greatly according to specific circumstances. (Anderson, P.J., 1996: 19)

According to Anderson, global interfusion can occur via four main process types. First, it can be the result of the growing subversion of the values of many states and nations by the values of other societies transferred by global economic mechanisms and/or the media. Second, it can be the consequence of:

> a continuing process whereby more and more decisions affecting any one large or small state and its people, that were taken previously by that state or firms within it, are now being made by or in other states, or by other types of international actor partially or wholly outside of that state's control. (Anderson, P.J., 1996: 20)

Third, global interfusion can be the result also of a process whereby crises, decisions and issues increasingly are becoming global in their impact as a result of the revolution in communications and technology. Fourth, it can be the result of ideologies of an interfusing nature, such as economic liberalism, being taken up by governments which have the necessary power to spread them across the globe (Anderson, P.J., 1996: 20–1).

Like Bretherton, Anderson is not convinced that the continuing advance of globalization/global interfusion is an inevitable process. He argues that the extent to which it progresses ultimately is dependent upon such things as the competition between economic ideological prescriptions and the interests behind them (he points out that there is no iron law that states that economic liberalism will remain the dominant global economic force forever) and the strength of such things as nationalist backlashes (Anderson, P.J., 1996: 80).

McGrew's definition

For McGrew, globalization can be defined as growing global interconnectedness. He sees it as having a number of distinctive attributes:

> Firstly, it implies that social, political and economic activities are becoming 'stretched' across national frontiers such that events, decisions and activities in one part of the

> world come to have immediate significance for individuals and communities in distant parts of the globe ... Secondly, globalisation involves an intensification, or increasing density, in the flows and patterns of interaction or interconnectedness which transcend the states and societies which constitute the modern world system ... Thirdly, the growing extensity and intensity of global interactions is associated with a deepening enmeshment of the local and the global so that the distinction between what is internal and what is external is increasingly blurred. Fourthly, growing interconnectedness generates a host of transnational problems, from the proliferation of weapons of mass destruction to global trafficking in narcotics, which cannot be resolved by the action of individual governments but only through multilateral or international cooperation ... Fifthly, the density and intensity of patterns of global and transnational interconnectedness weave ever tighter and more complex webs of relations between the states, international institutions, communities, non-governmental organizations and multinational corporations which make up the global system generating systemic constraints upon all their activities and their autonomy. (McGrew, 1997: 7)

McGrew *et al.* in this edited volume (McGrew, 1997) consider the views of those who are sceptical about the globalization process in some detail. There is not room to do the same in this brief chapter, so, in addition to the previous mention of such cautious voices as Bretherton and Anderson, one of the most respected and influential of the sceptical accounts, that of Hirst and Thompson, will be referred to here as a 'representative highpoint' of the overall sceptical side of the globalization debate.

Hirst and Thompson's viewpoint

Where economics is concerned, Hirst and Thompson are deeply suspicious of the whole globalization premise. For the purposes of their overall argument, they define an ideal type of a globalized economy. They state that:

> In such a global system distinct national economies are subsumed and rearticulated into the system by international processes and transactions ... The international economic system becomes autonomized and socially disembedded, as markets and production become truly global ... In such a globalized economy the problem ... for public authorities is how to construct policies that coordinate and integrate their regulatory efforts in order to cope with the systematic interdependence between their economic actors. (Hirst and Thompson, 1996: 10)

However, they argue strongly that such an ideal type, or indeed many other forms of globalization beloved of globalization analysts, do not as yet exist. They state that: '... such internationalisation as has occurred ... is well short of dissolving distinct national economies in the major advanced industrial countries or of preventing the development of new forms of economic governance at the national and international levels' (Hirst and Thompson, 1996: 4).

Equally, they argue that the claim of the most enthusiastic of globalization theorists that the globalization process is one that is beyond regulation is nonsense, and that all that has changed is the potential sources and means of governance. In short, 'It does not follow ... that economic relations at both international and national levels are beyond "governance", that is, means of regulation and control. The agencies of governance are less likely to be nation states or their officials' (Hirst and Thompson, 1996: 199). They see the EU as one of the key new emerging agencies of governance (Hirst and Thompson, 1996: 200).

This is a theme that will be returned to in the section on threats to democracy in this chapter. For the moment, it can simply be noted that, while it may be possible to define globalization as a concept and for broadly common understandings of the term to emerge, one should not presume that all analysts in the field of global politics and economics agree that globalization as yet exists in the 'real world' or that, if it does, it is progressing as rapidly as some suggest. Neither should it be presumed that all analysts have the same views as to the actual or likely impact of globalization processes. This means that the reader should not be surprised if subsequent chapters present considerably varied accounts of the importance of globalization with regard to the various topic areas they discuss.

The chosen definition

At this point, having surveyed a sample range of some of the most prominent and commonly used understandings of globalization, it is necessary to decide what kind of definition is most appropriate for this book and its needs. Given the many purposes of the book, and the consequent fact that there is only a limited amount of time and space that each author can devote to globalization, the preference obviously must be for a definition that says the most about the commonly accepted essence of the concept in the fewest possible words. In this respect, the McGrew definition would seem to be the most promising candidate. However, this particular offering is a little too brief for the simple reason that 'growing interconnectedness' is a notion that, on its own, does not convey the strong sense of subversiveness (of state sovereignty) that is present within most definitions of globalization. It is only when McGrew's more detailed elaborations of the concept are considered as well that this dimension of its meaning becomes clearly enough visible. Explicit or implicit within the root of most definitions of the term is the idea that it involves a *significant* intensification of global interconnectedness, and of the definitions considered here, only that of Bretherton captures this and its implications explicitly, fully and concisely enough to justify its usage as the core of the definition of the term to be used in this book. Accordingly, her definition, that globalization, 'suggests a significant intensification of global connectedness and a consciousness of that intensification, with a corresponding diminution in the significance of territorial boundaries and state structures' is the one that will be used, after only minor modification, whenever globalization is addressed within subsequent chapters. The modification that is required is as a result of the emphasis which she and other analysts (Dicken, for example) place on the unevenness of the impact of globalization across the globe, with some parts of the planet being touched by it in a much smaller way than others. It takes the form of the insertion of four words into the above definition, so that, for the purposes of this book, globalization suggests a significant *although as yet uneven* intensification of global connectedness and a consciousness of that intensification, with a corresponding diminution in the significance of territorial boundaries and state structures.

This is not to say that all of the rest of the material summarized here, that by Parker, Mittelman, Dicken, Anderson, McGrew, Hirst and Thompson and Bretherton herself, will be discarded (Bretherton's view that globalization is not irreversible, for example, needs to be kept in mind even though, for reasons of conciseness, it has not been incorporated in the chosen definition – the same is true of allegations that globalization is simply another name for imperialism). On the contrary, that material was chosen deliberately to elaborate and illustrate something of the richness of the globalization concept and attendant processes and to summarize some of the key means by which mainstream analysts argue globalization occurs or does not occur in global society. The intention is that this will provide an illumination of the depth of the concept that the reader will be able to keep in mind when engaging with the various ways in which each author in this study employs the necessarily brief core definition adopted for use in their chapters. The various authors similarly will use these elaborations as reference points when indicating the distinctive features (i.e. those which are additional to those contained within the core definition) of the particular kinds of globalization they are examining.

The impact of globalization on Europe

The activities of multinational business corporations

As was suggested in the introduction to this chapter, globalization, in the sense defined above, can be seen to impact directly upon Europe in a number of ways. For example, and perhaps most obviously, there are the continuing globalizing activities of multinational business corporations. During 1998–99, for example, Europe and the USA, and the global manufacturing and sales operations in which each is involved, *became even more closely linked economically* through the joining together of Daimler-Benz of Germany and Chrysler of the USA and then of Ford of the USA and Volvo Cars of Sweden.

While the book is being written there is a considerable controversy raging in the UK media as the result of the attempts of the American Monsanto Corporation to persuade a significantly hostile British public to warm to the idea of genetically modified organisms for use within foodstuffs on sale in UK shops. The activities of Monsanto and other US companies have already resulted in such organisms (GMOs) finding their way into processed foods on British supermarket shelves without consumers being told or consulted in the case of many products. *The controversy has raised serious questions of how European citizens can effectively protect the perceived integrity of something as crucial as what they eat* when huge global corporations have acquired control of so much of the world's food chain, including their own.

A threat to democracy and an uncontrollable process?

The Monsanto issue has been cast also in the light of a *threat to democracy* in so far as people have begun to see the matter as one more example of power over their daily lives being taken out of their hands as a result of the globalization process of which multinationals are a part. The discourse of the UK press, for example, including its readers' letters columns during the period of the controversy, carried a clear suggestion that the New Labour Prime Minister and other key decision-makers were much more inclined to listen to global multinationals such as Monsanto than the voters, to whom and for whom they were theoretically responsible.

The period 1998/99 was notable also for the number of occasions on which a key actor within the EU, the British government, claimed that *significant aspects of economic events were outside its control in a 'globalized' world.* It was referring to such things as the freedom and rapidity with which, for example, investment funds are able to move around the globe, with often only scant or no regard for localized concerns as to the consequences of this. European governments and economic interests in general became deeply concerned during parts of 1998 that the economic turmoil then affecting Asia and Russia and later Brazil would spread into the Western European heartlands as a result of the economic web of the globalized economy, bringing with it a global contagion of economic panic and recession.

What the British and other EU governments did not tell their voters was that, because of the scale, attractiveness and diversity of the market which the EU represents, arguably it can, if it achieves sufficient internal agreement on such matters, severely constrain the manner in which global corporations and several other key globalizing forces are able to operate within the boundaries of its member states. From this point of view the impact of globalization upon entities such as the EU or the USA is not self-determining – these actors are so large that they have the bargaining leverage to greatly affect its shape and content if they so choose – a point, as was noted earlier, that has already been made strongly with regard to the EU by Hirst and Thompson.

Equally, the limited extent to which EU members have chosen to try and limit the influence of globalizing forces could be argued to have played a significant role in leading eleven member states to sign up for the new European single currency, the euro, during spring 1998. The volatile global currency markets which have been one of the main factors pushing EU leaders towards what they believe to be the greater safety of a common currency are in part their own creation through their contributions to the liberalization of global financial markets and the abandonment of exchange controls. In short, in some of its key aspects, globalization could be argued to travel on the back of particular ideologies, and shades of ideologies, and of those powerful enough to implement them. Thinking back to our earlier coverage of Hirst and Thompson and of Bretherton's ideas, *it must be noted that there are strong grounds for concluding that globalization is not in its entirety an uncontrollable or irreversible process.*

The information revolution

The most visible current symbol of the information revolution in Europe is the internet. It is a symbol also of the speed and the power of globalization. It permits the creation of new kinds of regional and global social, academic, political and professional communities on a scale that simply was not possible previously. On the one hand, theoretically it offers European economies and societies a powerful new means of growing more closely together. On the other, it has the potential, under appropriate conditions, of helping make the idea of European society obsolete in favour of a new, all-encompassing notion of global society. The picture initially looks startlingly impressive: 'The internet is the fastest-growing communication tool ever invented. Ten years ago only 100,000 computers were connected to the net: today there are 36m PCs online with 150m users' (Denny, 1999: 23). However, the great planetary communications tool is not quite as global as it first appears: 'Most internet users live in the west, and 30 per cent have a university degree. The US has more computers than the rest of the world combined' (Denny, 1999: 23).

This is a phenomenon which is American-led, with Europe not even present as an equal partner. This fact has serious implications for Europe's economic and technological future. Furthermore, income and education are crucial factors in gaining admission to the most advanced levels of the global information revolution. Even within the supposed 'rich man's club' of the EU there are bands of society living in what, by Western standards, is dire poverty. For such people it is difficult enough to provide decent housing and a healthy diet for themselves and their children without even beginning to think of the expense of being attached to something as exotic as the world wide web. This is true within parts of Britain, Italy, Greece and Portugal, to name but four relevant member states. The globalization of information that comes with the spread of the new computer technologies is therefore (thinking back to Bretherton) *uneven* in its impact across the world and within Europe. As far as Europe is concerned, this unevenness threatens to further disadvantage and exclude the poorer members of society if the trend towards knowledge- and ideas-based economies continues to progress significantly. The internet may be bringing the information 'haves' closer together in Europe and the wider world, at least in the sense of greater ease of communication, but so far its positive impact on the 'have-nots' is extremely limited.

The much-proclaimed culturally and socially integrative aspects of the internet need to be treated with caution. While it is undoubtedly a forum in which passports become irrelevant and within which people can converse on equal terms across Europe and, indeed, across the globe, it can not *in itself* necessarily create the reality of a truly European or global community which is strong enough to supersede feelings of national community and identity. Perhaps the best example of this is in the USA, where, despite the fact that the country contains the largest number of internet users, there is no visible sign of the traditionally strong sense of American national identity and of American cultural preferences breaking down in favour of something more global. Furthermore, the internet can be used specifically to try and block or undermine particular feelings of regional or global community. For example, it can be and is used by various nationalist or far right racist groups to communicate more effectively with existing and potential members. American Nazis have found it particularly useful. Finally, as pointed out above, while the internet undoubtedly has grown extremely fast, it still involves only a small proportion of Europe and the world's population, and it is difficult to build a sense of regional or global community on such a limited basis.

While the internet *is* an important dimension of globalization in the context of both Europe and the wider world in a number of respects, it is advisable not to overestimate its impact to date and not to assume that that impact will be entirely positive in the way that its most enthusiastic advocates seem to do.

The preceding aspects of globalization are only some of those that potentially could be raised in the context of Europe. It is not possible to look at the entire range of contenders due to space limitations, but those that have been examined here are some of the most important and together provide a useful indicative insight into the role of globalization within the new Europe.

The great debate and its impact on this book

To return to an important point made earlier in this chapter which cannot be overemphasized, it is essential to realize that there is no consensus amongst academic experts on the precise impact of globalization on either Europe or the world, or on its inevitability, or indeed on the causal factors that lie behind it. The most that can be said is that there is widespread agreement that globalization currently is a highly important force helping shape European and other societies. Given this fact, while a single definition of globalization will be used in the chapters which follow, it would be unreasonable of the editors to impose any one view of the importance of globalization within the present and the foreseeable future on the various contributors to the book. Each therefore will be left to make their own judgement as appropriate to the subject matter of their particular chapters.

Threats to democracy

A second major theme running across virtually all of the chapters in the book is that of threats to democracy within Europe. Given that the general concept of democracy is far more widely understood than globalization, our intention here is not to engage in any great definitional debate, but simply to put forward well-established understandings of the term that the editors found most particularly suited to the purposes of this book.

Defining democracy

Given that there is a range of different democratic models operative across Europe, the intention here is to provide a concise overall summary of their broad characteristics. Threats to democracy identified within subsequent chapters therefore are taken to be threats to one or more of the broad models outlined below.

Parliamentary democracy[2] requires, first, that the government is politically responsible to the assembly and, second, that the government is representative of public opinion, but is only indirectly responsible to the electorate.

(a) The majoritarian model of parliamentary democracy logically derives from the principle of concentrating political power in the hands of the majority, usually in the form of the leadership elite of a tightly disciplined party that holds the majority of seats in parliament. This majority is generally the result of an electoral system that allocates a disproportionately large share of parliamentary seats to the party having a plurality of votes. A majoritarian executive is mainly constrained by the prospect of a parliamentary election, but it may also be constrained by the idea that it should keep to the policies on which it was elected: this idea has been elaborated as the doctrine of an electoral mandate.

(b) The consensual model of parliamentary democracy is characterized by majority-restraining elements which include proportional representation, a multi-party system which reflects the main cleavages in society, executive power-sharing (often in cabinet coalitions), and a written constitution that constrains the executive by securing minority representation, permitting a minority veto, separating and dispersing power, and which often includes federal or decentralized structures.[3]

Most states across Europe approximate more or less to these models, with the UK as the clearest majoritarian example, and Switzerland, Belgium, Finland, the French Fourth Republic, the Netherlands and Italy as good examples of the consensual model. The main problematical state with regard to all of the above, is Russia, which, as Chris Williams' chapter will demonstrate, is best thought of as a transitional democracy. It would be difficult at the moment to classify it as a parliamentary democracy, given the considerable concentration of power in the hands of the presidency.

It is important to stress that none of the above should be taken as signifying any assumption that democracy, even in its ideal form, is a perfect mode of governance in an ethical sense. That is the subject matter for a debate which requires rather more space than is available here.

Conclusion

Some alleged threats to democracy, arising from globalization, have been discussed already. The range of literature on other potential threats is simply too large for any comprehensive coverage to be attempted here, given the overall aims of the project. Contributors will therefore focus on those potential threats to democracy which they believe to be the most serious with regard to the subject matter of their particular chapters. Some overall observations on the state of democracy within the new Europe will be made at the end of the book.

It is now necessary to begin our journey through a representational sample of the problems and prospects of Europe at the beginning of the twenty-first century.

Notes

1. See, for example, Giddens, A., 'New World Without End', abridged version of the first of the 1999 Reith Lectures published in the *Observer*, 11 April 1999.
2. This system summary was kindly provided by Alastair Thomas in place of a rather unwieldy original definition of democracy.
3. See, for example, Almond and Bingham Powell, 1978; Lijphart, 1984; and Verney, 1959, 1979.

PART II

The European Union in Transition

Pre-Note: The Interwoven Economics Dimension

To facilitate inclusion of all of the topics covered in this book, the economics dimension of the EU has been interwoven in chapters in other sections, principally in those on individual member states (where readers will find the EMU discussed in, for example, the chapters on Portugal, Italy and Britain), globalization and democracy and eastern enlargement.

Peter J. Anderson, Georg Wiessala and Christopher Williams

CHAPTER TWO

Institutions and Issues

Philippa Sherrington

While Europe means far more than simply the European Union (EU),[1] the ever-increasing impact of the EU upon the political and economic lives of European citizens is undeniable. In the post-Cold War order, these two terms are becoming increasingly synonymous. The current clamour to join the EU signifies the relative historical success of the EU in promoting political and economic stability and ensuring some measure of security. Concurrently, existing member states of the EU have further committed themselves to the overarching goals of European integration. The majority have taken a tangible step in promoting this through signing up to and launching a single currency with the stated longer-term aim of Economic and Monetary Union (EMU). A passive observer could easily be fooled into believing that European integration is in a healthy state.

The development of integration in Europe has proceeded at a steady pace since its inception by the Schuman Plan in 1950. Successive enlargements have increased membership from six to fifteen states, policy competences have deepened, the internal market is almost complete, and all this has been facilitated by member state governments working through the institutions of the EU. However, the EU is now at a critical juncture, a victim of its own success perhaps, but also because of a changed European context. With each previous enlargement of the EU, commentators debated whether the EU could absorb the impact of increased membership without damaging the pace of integration. The reality was such that despite particular difficulties, or the coincidence of external events, the EU adjusted and survived. The conditions now are markedly different. It is not simply a question of numbers, although the scale of future enlargement is daunting. It is this combined with the shifting context of globalization, the problems of integration in the 'new' Europe, the ability of EU structures to sustain effective policy-making, and the natural growing awareness, but also questioning, of the EU by its citizens. Such a cocktail of fundamental issues challenges the existing modes of operation of the EU and the nature of any further deepening of the integration process.

This opening chapter of Part II does not seek to address all these issues, but concentrates on those that are considered to be of particular resonance. The main focus is upon the key institutional questions facing the EU, and it assesses the moves that are being made to resolve these issues in a manner that is acceptable to all member states. The latter part of this chapter raises some of the broader issues confronting the EU, acting as an introduction for the more detailed analysis of EU economic and foreign policy, and enlargement, provided in subsequent chapters.

The EU's institutional machinery

The structure and mechanics of EU policy-making are fundamental to the success of European integration. The original architects, Jean Monnet and Robert Schuman, clearly stressed that without effective machinery there would be no EU (as practice has demonstrated). In striving for better, more efficient and effective policy-making at the supranational level, the EU has been in a perpetual state of institutional reform. Formal treaty revisions to the role and structure of the key decision-making institutions, as well as informal adaptations agreed by member states, have created a complex structure, and by no means a perfect machine. Issues of accountability and transparency remain on the agenda.

However, despite an awareness of the latter fact on the part of the member states, the Treaty of Amsterdam, 1997, failed to adequately prepare the EU for the future as the key institutional issues were left unresolved. Despite setting up the 1996–97 Intergovernmental Conference (IGC) to address structural arrangements for an enlarged EU, member states backtracked when it came to formalizing agreement in the Treaty. The further extension of the co-decision procedure may have enhanced the formal role of the European Parliament (EP) in EU policy-making, but the more pressing issues of efficiency and effectiveness were left open. The 'institutional status-quo would hurt less – at least in the short run – than making what some of them perceived as painful adaptations' (Devuyst, 1998: 626).

The Protocol on institutional reform attached to the Amsterdam Treaty suggested that enlargement negotiations would be dependent on some resolution of these questions by existing member states. The debate has since stumbled from one European Council meeting to another, and predictably little ground has been made on the trade-off between limiting the future size of the Commission and the adjustment of voting mechanisms in the Council. Conclusions adopted at the Helsinki Council, December 1999, have ended some of this uncertainty by stating that the IGC on institutional reform should be completed by December 2000, thus opening the door to new members in 2003. However, 'a firm political commitment to make every effort to' does not exude a high degree of confidence that this objective will be reached (see Council of the European Union, 1999).

An issue of numbers

There appear to be two concerns within the current institutional reforms that are not necessarily compatible. On the one hand, member states are striving to ensure that the efficiency of the Community method is sustained in an enlarged EU. Numbers clearly matter. However, any adjustment will naturally affect existing member states' capacity to wield influence within the formal EU structures. While the informal processes and negotiations are just as, but arguably even more, significant in EU policy-making terms, the other preoccupation is formal representation. Each member state government has to be seen by its domestic audience to be holding on to its power in the main EU institutions, and has an obvious desire to do so to maintain influence within EU policy-making structures. The Amsterdam Protocol on institutional reform states that each member state will only be permitted one Commissioner, providing that the re-weighting of votes in the Council compensates those who would sacrifice having an additional Commissioner. This is a formal admission that national representation in the Commission matters, a political reality known to commentators and practitioners alike but a facet of the EU's operation that is denied in the Treaties by the required oath of allegiance that Commissioners take. More importantly, the linking of these two issues has opened significant tensions between large and small member states. Duff sees this as a highly politicized cleavage which has the potential to divide member states further (1997: 134). Clearly, the fact that little progress has been made, and that the Helsinki Council conclusions make little reference to the discussions, indicates the difficulties in reconciling these two major concerns.

Although it is now readily agreed that the member states prefer a consensual approach to their work within the Council, qualified majority voting is relevant and is likely to be of greater significance in an enlarged EU (Hayes-Renshaw and Wallace, 1997; Kerremans, 1998; Nugent, 1999). The knowledge that a vote could be taken in the Council has ensured some measure of institutional efficiency over recent years. Without a workable and credible voting mechanism, the value of the threat of the vote will be undermined. In the future enlarged EU, an increase in the number of member states, different policy priorities, and the enhancement of the 'North–South–East' and 'rich–poor' cleavages mean that it may be more difficult to reach consensus and physical voting could be increasingly required. The voting thresholds were organized in such a way that an acceptable balance of power was ensured between the large and smaller member states, conceptualized by Kerremans as capacity and control (1998: 87–109). The allocation of votes was based on a loose approximation of size, enabling coalitions to protect against the dominance of one or more of the larger member states. The difficulty for the Council of the future is that the existing mechanism for allocating votes would result in the over-representation of smaller states and thus call into question the representative nature of Council decisions.

Member states have agreed that change needs to occur, either through a re-weighting of the votes or by the introduction of a dual majority system. France has made it abundantly clear that it will not accept the latter as this would give Germany greater voting power. Spain argued that its agreement on accession to have two Commissioners, but less votes in the Council than the other large member states, would no longer be acceptable. The Dutch proposal to re-weight the votes in favour of the larger member states in exchange for surrendering the Commission angered Belgium, primarily because the Netherlands gave itself two more votes than Belgium in this suggested scenario. The delicate balance of voting power in the Council is more politicized than ever. The potential for the frequent use of qualified majority voting should not be over-stated. For the immediate post-enlargement years, new members will have less political manoeuvrability, and the culture of EU policy-making will not significantly alter. The transition years may actually establish informal coalitions that will circumvent formal voting practices. However, a solution still needs to be found to the weighting of votes that will maintain an acceptable balance of power within the Council for all member states.

Administrative efficiency

While the numbers issues dominate discussions at present, and clearly have the potential to delay enlargement and reduce policy-making efficacy if a solution remains elusive, there are also more specific operational concerns that need to be addressed. These have been on the agenda for some time, but impending enlargement has forced member states to enter into a more systematic review. The forced resignation of the Commission in March 1999 has seriously undermined its own political credibility and that of the EU in general. The Commission has always been the target for public scrutiny, and a scapegoat for member state governments trying to justify less favourable policy decisions to their electorate. The complete fiasco that resulted from the allegations of financial misconduct did little to improve perceptions of the EU. However, in some ways, the events of early 1999 have actually speeded up the process of internal reform of the Commission, and may assist in addressing the legitimacy crisis. Questions dealing with the role, structure and organizational mechanisms of the Commission are certainly not new, but did not gain political urgency until the mid-1990s and the appointment of the Santer Commission. Delors, as Cini points out, was well aware of the pressures for internal reform but was 'able to sideline and ignore them' (1996: 199). Santer, in a bid to assert his own presidential identity, placed institutional reform high on his presidential agenda. The start of discussions on the future institutional shape of an enlarged EU may have forced him to do so, but at least issues of financial and personnel management, institutional accountability and efficiency were finally being discussed. Some managerial reorganization was achieved but reform was not instituted to the extent set out in the agenda.

The new Commission under the Presidency of Romano Prodi, appointed in the summer of 1999, is explicitly charged with forcing the pace of administrative reform. A new Directorate has been set up to facilitate this, and there is a high degree of consensus between member states that changes should be implemented as quickly as possible. At the time of writing, the reform programme is yet to be released, but is likely to contain proposals to generate more effective internal management of the Commission. If implemented, such reform may help to enhance internal efficiency and improve external accountability of the Commission. Improving the internal management of the Commission may be enough to absorb the extension of the administrative machinery as a result of enlargement. The belief seems to be that such mechanisms will also be sufficient in the short to medium term to improve transparency and induce greater public confidence in the Commission. A more direct accountability to the European electorate is not on the agenda at present. Whether such reform as the above is adequate remains to be seen.

Legislative capability in the Council

Although the Helsinki Council failed to make crucial progress on the weighting of votes in the Council, member states approved recommendations for reform of some Council working mechanisms (Council of the European Union, 1999). Given the authority and crucial role of the Council in EU policy-making, member states are being forced to examine existing operational practices if an enlarged Council is to function as effectively as it can do. Arguably, one of the most important issues, and a recurrent theme in Council history, is reform of the Presidency. The Presidency is not only responsible for the daily management of Council affairs; it acts as a mediator in council negotiations. It is also a crucial means for promoting national interests. The extent to which this latter aim is achieved is constrained by a variety of factors and there is a danger in over-emphasizing the ability of the Presidency to be successful in this regard (Hayes-Renshaw and Wallace, 1997: 145–6). Nevertheless, the opportunity exists, and this has been heavily guarded by member states.

Successive enlargements have raised the question of whether the efficiency of Council business and the abilities of the Presidency are undermined by a less frequent rotation between member states, and the inexperience of new member states. Revision of rotational arrangements has ensured that the sequence of member states balances out large and small, old and new, and this will be added to when the first wave of new members from Central Europe accede to the EU. The appointment of the High Representative for Common Foreign and Security Policy matters has relieved some of the burden on the Presidency. However, there is still concern that enlargement will reduce the efficacy of the Presidency. Among many suggestions, proposals have been made to shift the Presidency to a troika arrangement, or have team Presidencies according to portfolios.

At the Helsinki Council in December 1999, member states approved a report that maintains the existing formula (Council of the European Union, 1999). The proposal permits the incoming Presidency to assist the current Presidency in its administrative workload, but without challenging its overall responsibility and authority. Such an arrangement may slightly strengthen existing troika practices aimed at sustaining some coherence and continuity between Presidencies in an enlarged Council. Clearly, member states remain reluctant to reduce their opportunity to influence policy-making through the Presidency. It acts as a mechanism for demonstrating to the electorate that national interests are being protected and therefore legitimizes EU participation. The essential feature of the Presidency has been that it works, and satisfies member states. In the medium term though, the experience of enlargement may challenge this.

For the future success of the EU, the institutional machinery needs to be able to cope with a growing policy agenda and to provide some clear direction for the development of the European project. Already we have seen a streamlining of the Commission Directorates as a means of generating more organizational efficiency. At Helsinki, the European Council agreed to limit the number of sectoral councils to 15, with no new councils, unless agreed by member state Foreign Ministers. The organization of the General Affairs Council agenda is also to be improved so that the European Council can deal more with policy direction than with conflict resolution on specific policy proposals (Council of the European Union, 1999). The aim in setting up the regularized European Council meetings was to provide policy leadership. Increasingly the Heads of State or Government have found themselves having to deal with specific proposals that failed to be resolved lower down the Council hierarchy. These will be difficult arrangements to adhere to but are essential to future policy-making efficiency.

Generating institutional appeal

Much of the discussion on the EU's institutional legitimacy has focused on the development of the EP to provide direct accountability to its citizens. The view has been that extending the powers of the EP will generate greater acceptance of, and support for, the EU as the EP offers a democratic and legitimate mechanism for the representation of citizens' interests. The introduction of the cooperation procedure, and the subsequent development of co-decision, have increased EP legislative input, and the Treaty of Amsterdam has resulted in the EP becoming a co-legislator in some, albeit limited, policy areas. This is having little effect upon the public appeal of and identity with the European endeavour. The referenda on the Maastricht Treaty in Denmark and France are often cited as signifying a turning point in the history of European integration (Anderson, C., 1995). Given that it was no longer a readily accepted elite-driven process, governments across the EU were forced to respond to increased questioning of the EU by their citizens. This can be seen as natural and predictable, given the growing impact of the EU on member states, and a consequent demand by affected citizens to know more about what was going on. However, it is also the case that public support for the EU has steadily declined during the 1990s, from an average of 70 per cent in 1990, to 49 per cent in 1999 (European Commission, 1999a). Even the EP flexing its political muscle against the Commission, which brought about the demise of the Santer Commission in 1999, had only a limited impact. Turnout in EP elections three months later was the lowest in history (49 per cent compared with 57 per cent in 1994). Although EP elections are second-order and so often a judgement upon national governments, it is clear that EU citizens are reluctant to engage with the EP, and therefore other means of addressing the EU's legitimacy must be found. Generating support and a measure of identity through supranational institutions does not seem to reduce the alienation that citizens have with EU policy processes.

Managing the future policy agenda

The decline in support for European integration is probably more a result of an opaque policy agenda than institutional accountability problems. While the EU is currently pursuing identifiable policy objectives, its future direction is less clear. Moreover, the success of current policy goals is not guaranteed. The changing context of Europe, and the demand that the EU respond to this by opening its doors, has created some of this uncertainty. However, hesitancy about the direction of European integration was emerging before 1989. Member states were locked into a process with the signing of the Single European Act that required further IGCs on EMU and political union. The resultant Maastricht Treaty set a legal precedent by allowing the UK and Denmark to opt out of a commitment to EMU, and brought into question the issue of whether further political union was desirable or attainable.

At a policy specific level, the EU has been muddling through the 1990s. The main objective for those committed to the EMU project was to ensure its launch. The fudging of the convergence criteria may prove to be economically costly, but was seen as a necessary political expense. Strategies for competitiveness and employment were developed to help improve the economic framework in which EMU is to function. In addition, member state governments used all of this to try to generate appeal for EMU. In putting forward proposals for policy reform, Agenda 2000, with its emphasis on the budgetary implications of sustaining the Common Agricultural

Policy (CAP) and the structural funds in an enlarged EU, has led to new tensions between existing states as to the cost of EU membership and enlargement.

The direction and nature of further integration has never been predetermined but some longer-term strategy has always existed. The question of whether European integration holds the political resonance and imperatives of the past has to be sufficiently addressed if public support for the EU is to increase. The issue of European security has accentuated differences between member states as to the nature of the EU as an organization and whether it should be engaging in the formulation of a credible and enforceable foreign policy. Until recently, European integration has also proceeded at a pace acceptable to all those involved. The ability of current members to opt out and the certainty that new members will not be in a position to engage in all areas of EU policy integration is fast becoming the accepted working pattern for the future EU. This raises significant practical institutional issues as to how coherent policy decisions are to be reached, and introduces an EU 'West Lothian' question.

Conclusion

The task facing member states is unprecedented and considerable. If European integration is to be sustained, member states not only need to ensure that the institutional machinery works effectively, but have to define the future policy agenda more adequately. Institutional reform has always been a reactive process, and it is likely that only the experience of enlargement will generate the pressure for real structural adjustment. The political climate of Europe is still full of great uncertainty and prevents its states from being able to define their goals for the future EU. Despite such fundamental challenges, the EU will continue. One of the enduring characteristics of the EU has been its ability to absorb change, transform itself and survive.

Note

1. While legal distinctions remain between European Community and European Union, the term EU will be used for simplicity, except in those cases where it is historically correct to use EC.

CHAPTER THREE

Legal Features and Challenges of the European Union

Georg Wiessala

Introduction: EU Law in the age of globalization

While the many facets of globalization are analysed in Chapter 1 of this book, this chapter shows that globalization also possesses a legal dimension of many layers. It forms the background for a global pluralism of laws. This complex network of legal relationships is worldwide in scope and reveals itself as both fragmented and interconnected (Maher, June 1998: 237–54). Within this normative network, both the European legal order and national laws link up and play their part. In Europe, different legal systems share the same space. The European Community (EC), which possesses wide-ranging legal personality (Article 210 EC) and treaty-making capacity, and the European Union (EU), which does not, represent perhaps one of the most unique legal orders in the world. Moreover, the existence and further evolution of European Law and a European Court of Justice (ECJ) challenge many conventional legal systems and perceptions. The definition of EU Law as a self-defining legal order is an unusual one. European Law calls into question much of the traditional discourse about law, by disconnecting issues of state, sovereignty, identity, power and law. The EU has transformed itself into an assembly of states which, like no other international institution in existence, is pervaded and shaped by law, the observance of which is presided over by a Court.

Questions of the functions of this Court as a motor of integration in Europe, and issues arising from its relationship with national courts, through the vehicle of preliminary rulings in Article 234 of the EC Treaty, form an important part of this chapter on the legal dimension of the EU. As the title of this chapter suggests, however, the perspective of this investigation is somewhat wider than a summary of the ECJ and EU legal principles. This means that it is sometimes at the expense of detail. The current and future 'Constitution' of the EU, encompassing issues such as legal structure, enlargement and current attempts at reform and 'constitution-building', represent another aspect of this chapter. A third concern will be with Human Rights and their possible codification by the EU. These three main areas will be complemented by a somewhat shorter look at current issues affecting EU Law and at law, identity and exclusion, a topic dealing as much with national identity and culture as with legal issues. Specialized areas of EU Law, the legal characteristics of Economic and Monetary Union (EMU), the euro and of the Freedom of Movement rules are referred to only when they are relevant to the understanding of the context.

The prominence and impact of legal issues

The legal dimension of the EU continues to be the subject of a public debate which is often as intense as it is erratic. The failures of the Treaty of Amsterdam in the area of reform and the low turnout during the June 1999 European Parliament (EP) elections, the demise of the old Commission in March 1999 and the ongoing reform efforts of the new President, Romano Prodi, are just four of the more prominent events which have re-emphasized the crisis the Union is in. These and other current developments have brought to the fore renewed criticism regarding legitimacy and the continuing existence of a perceived '*democratic deficit*' in the EU. This works on three levels: individual, often extraordinary and much publicized cases, the current background of attempts at EU reform, and, most generally, the overall debate about the desirable future course of the Union. Issues, ranging from transfer fees in football, EU Directives on metric weighing or Britain's anti-rabies laws to the minimum wage, the 48-hour week, French or German politicians playing for time over the beef ban or the updating of the 1990 Biotechnology Directive (90/220), have all in recent months brought European Law and European courts more into the limelight, often in a haphazard way, unconnected to current EU developments or general legal perceptions or debates. But this discourse about the rights of the EU to interfere and the use of its legal system has long found its way to the 'inside' of EU governance.

The drafting of a Third 'Wise Men's Report', under the direction of former Belgian PM Jean-Luc Dehaene, the calls for more legal powers for the new European Anti-Fraud Office (OLAF) and, above all, the preparations for the 2000 Intergovernmental Conference (IGC) all continue to demonstrate the degree to which legal and constitutional issues still top EU agendas. On the IGC issue alone, just how much scope the IGC talks will have to assume remains a bone of contention, with proponents of a 'minimalist' solution versus the 'maximalists'. While the former concentrate on the topics left over after the June 1997 Amsterdam summit, i.e. the size of the Commission, qualified majority voting (QMV) and re-weighting of votes, the latter, among them Michel Barnier, the new 'IGC Commissioner', and Jean-Luc Dehaene, advocate much more comprehensive Treaty changes, discussion of an EU Constitution, defence issues, reform of the ECJ and a wider, constitutional approach to the Union and its legal system.

On a more general level, divergent interpretations of federalism and the tension between the principles of intergovernmentalism and supranationalism form the background to a wider legal-political debate about the future of the Union. Subsidiarity and flexibility as new legal precepts of EU governance and the reduction in the procedures of EU legislation, from a plethora to only a handful, have underscored the stronger role of the EP in policy and thought leadership under its new President Nicole Fontaine. Plans aiming at the further widening of the EP's powers of co-decision and the breaking up of any remaining legislative monopoly of the Commission have reinvigorated the debate about the law and constitution of the Union. Inside the EU, some of the 90 Recommendations of the Second Report of the Committee of Wise Men, published in September 1999, have a legal target. Recommendations 2, 3, 17, 29, 42, 59, among others, aim at a clearer hierarchy of Community acts and their enforcement, at transparency, auditing and the swifter prosecution of offences. These findings, together with those of the First Report of the Committee of Independent Experts, also in 1999, have reinforced the institutional linkages between the Commission and the EP, stressing the responsibility of the former towards the latter.

Recent initiatives in the area of Justice and Home Affairs have helped to propel Community Law into the limelight. The statements of a more assertive EP on legal harmonization are important and have led to a more discerning public debate. Discussions about the desirability of further legal coordination in the EU, in the form of, for instance, the abolition of extradition, have received much impetus from the EP's pronouncements on a future 'Common European Judicial Area' (European Parliament, Working Document, 1998). The immigration chapter of the Amsterdam Treaty and its new 'Area of Freedom, Security and Justice', as well as the Pinochet case and British proposals for a 'Eurowarrant', may have been the sources feeding this concept. But it was only during the second half of 1999 that these were taken further. The Extraordinary European Council on Justice and Home Affairs (JHA) in Tampere (Finland) on 15 and 16 October 1999 contained the idea of the EU as a common legal area. The 'Tampere Milestones', the conclusions of the summit, reasserted Human Rights, laid the foundations for the 'communitarization' of asylum and immigration policy and addressed trans-border crime. The summit took place against the background of UK resistance to a 'European Legal System' and the creation of a European Public Prosecutor, recommended by the Second Wise Men's Report (European Commission, *The Week in Europe*, 16 September 1999). These and related legal matters, such as privacy protection or the Schengen Information System (SIS), have led to a reassessment of Civil and Human Rights issues and to renewed calls for a Europe-wide 'Charter of Rights', which since the Helsinki summit in late 1999, has moved up the ladder of EU priorities.

But it is three other strands in EU development that have redirected public attention towards European Law and the role of the ECJ in particular: first, the vociferous efforts of the Finnish incumbents, in the second half of 1999, to push the case for more EU reform, openness and transparency, and, second, the complex vetting into office of the new Commission by the EP which was completed in October 1999. Last but not least, the coming into being of the third stage of EMU on 1 January 1999, of the Amsterdam Treaty on 1 May 1999 and of rights to initiate proceedings, conferred on the new European Central Bank (ECB), have been responsible for a further increase in litigation originating in financial and JHA provisions. Thus, in 1998, 485 cases were commenced before the ECJ and 238 before the Court of First Instance (CFI). The Court seems to be approaching the limit of its functional capacity. The high political priority of both the Amsterdam Treaty and the euro (€) projects have made the work of the ECJ and the CFI harder, but also more visible. This is a development that was only to be expected. It will continue in other priority areas, such as enlargement, Regional Policies or the Common Foreign and Security Policy (CFSP).

European Law and public awareness

In spite of these complex contemporary developments, a recognition of legal issues in Europe and a fuller understanding of what the Commission calls the 'every-day reality' of European Law, its tangible impact on the lives of all European citizens, continue to be low among Europeans. Across the Union, a large number of individuals are either ignorant of, or fail to utilize, their rights and liberties under EC or EU Law. In late 1999, one-third of citizens across the 15 EU member states (EU-15) had never heard of the existence of the ECJ. The important reform initiative by the Court's President G.C. Rodríguez Iglesias (European Court of Justice, 1999) and the swearing in of Ireland's Fidelma Macken as the Court's first female judge in October 1999 went largely unnoticed by press and public alike. Of those who are roughly familiar with the Court, only a thin majority of 57 per cent rated the Court's role as 'important'. Perhaps it is this lack of information, combined with widespread ignorance of the practical relevance of the Court, that results in only 44 per cent of people in the EU-15, and just 30 per cent in the UK, placing their trust in the institution (European Commission, 1999a: 13, 47, 49, 51).

This appears particularly salient in Britain, where awareness of how directly EU Law impinges on citizens' routine activities is still low. Furthermore, prejudice about an 'interfering' 'Brussels bureaucracy' and a 'biased' ECJ continues to survive and is perpetuated by sections of the political parties and a largely euro-ignorant popular press which is often more hostile than informative (Anderson and Weymouth, 1999). This is all the more surprising as it is the case that the ECJ far from always interprets European legal rules in a 'Brussels-friendly' way. Even a superficial look at the case statistics reveals that the (UK) Government either prevails straight away, or at least has its arguments taken on board, in more cases than is generally assumed. Moreover, against the background of a general improvement in the level of implementation, the rate of transposition of EU Law into UK Law continues to be high. In the last few years, it has, for example, consistently been higher than German rates of transposition. In 1998, 94.7 per cent of national measures required to implement EU directives into UK Law had been taken by the UK Government by 31 December 1997. This compares with only 93.6 per cent for Germany and France and 91.8 per cent for Belgium, seat of many of the EU's institutions. The figures for 1997 are 94.19 per cent (UK), 93.94 per cent (Germany), 91.93 per cent (France) and 92.68 per cent (Belgium) respectively (Laffan, 1998: 159; 1999: 185). It appears that in the UK, there is a significant gap between stronger awareness of European Law on the one hand and government compliance with its rules on the other. A more detailed investigation of the nature and effect of European Law, its sources and foundations and the courts which develop it and put it into practice, will go some way towards closing this 'information gap'. By facilitating understanding, it may also begin to serve the more far-reaching purpose of critical analysis and identification, which both appear as important criteria of any modern European citizenship.

The *acquis communautaire* and the ECJ

Values and goals which have been present at the heart of the formation of the EU have found expression in the EC Treaty Preamble of 'an ever closer union among the peoples of Europe' and in the Union's common policies and other tasks (Articles 2, 3, 3a). These values have contributed to the basis for the EU's legal body and identity. Peace and security, fundamental rights, unity, justice and equality form a part of those values. Together with the safeguarding of free movement, social cohesion and new concepts of constitutionalism and European citizenship, the realization of those *leitmotivs* is part of a continuing effort to create a Union with comprehensive legal achievements.

The *acquis communautaire*, codified in Articles B and C of the Treaty of European Union (TEU), constitutes the essence of the hitherto achieved EU legal dimension. It binds old and new member states, governments and citizens alike. EU Law and its legitimacy, it has often been said, is born of the member states, depends on them, rests on a wide-ranging transfer of sovereignty and ultimately feeds from the principle of loyalty to the Community, enshrined in Article 5. But the legal reality of the EU has another dimension. It provides primary and secondary sources of autonomous law. These comprise the Founding Treaties, any International Agreements the Union enters into, institutional law, such as Directives, Regulations or 'soft-law', and the more ambivalent 'general principles of law', for instance the ideas of subsidiarity or proportionality, which have been articulated by the ECJ. The blanket clause of 'general principles' has, until Maastricht and Amsterdam, formed the main lever for Human Rights Law and other extraneous areas, which were not originally built into the Treaties of Paris and Rome. Law therefore has at least a two-fold meaning for the EU: first, it forms the bedrock for the institutions and the achievement of the EU's objectives and common policies and, second, it has a dimension which reaches out and forms part and parcel of the citizens' daily lives. This duality has found expression in a complex system of justiciability of European Law, which includes legal protection and the judicial control of the legality of the actions of EU institutions, member states or individuals. (See for instance Articles 155, 164, 169, 173, 175, 234, 184 or 215.)

The ECJ and its satellite, the CFI, are the 'Guardians' of this European legal order, not unlike the way in which the European Commission is the appointed Guardian of the Treaties (Article 155). Charged in Article 220 with ensuring respect for the implementation and interpretation of EU Law, the Court, in particular, can be seen as one of the most prolific international courts, dealing with legal problems anywhere in the triangle formed by the member states, the EU institutions and the citizens of Europe. But the ECJ is much more than this; in one of the earliest (1962) academic treatments of the Court, it takes the author only half a page to forecast:

> There can be little doubt that the present Court now responsible for interpreting all three constitutive treaties, all of which are concerned with closer European integration, will seize the opportunity to strengthen such efforts towards integration by the unity of its jurisprudence in interpretation and its formulation of a EU Law. (McMahon, 1962: 1)

This idea has been formulated again and again over the years and was put into practice by an increasingly self-conscious Court, which has proved to be a powerful instrument of integration, setting, with its case-law, the milestones of the uniqueness of the EU legal system.

It did so mostly by means of combining elements of both the Continental, written statutory law and the Anglo-American case-law traditions. If one were to attempt an overall weighing of this *mélange*, it would probably be more accurate to say that there is a stronger flavour of civilian, written law than there is of Common Law thinking. In spite of this, Common Law traditions of adherence to precedent and the application of the *stare decisis* doctrine play an increasingly important part in EU Law as a dynamic and – most importantly – a self-perpetuating legal order. The resulting body of law which is both a legal system in its own right and a part of the legal systems of the member states, is unprecedented anywhere else in the world.

The nature and some fundamentals of European Law

The status of EU Law which is, in the above sense, both independent and penetrative, has given the ECJ the opportunity to delineate some powerful principles which can only be hinted at here. Thus, European Law possesses supremacy and takes precedence over conflicting national law, even national Constitutions or Human Rights provisions. It has the power to automatically render conflicting national law inapplicable. It has to be uniformly applied and given full effect by courts in all member states. In recent years, EU Law has expanded its rules of decentralized enforcement, given rise to direct rights and duties of individuals and empowered more citizens to take a state to court for failure to give full effect to the European legal system. New rules on the liability of states towards citizens, and a system of fines and sanctions in case of the non-implementation of EU Law, have provided powerful incentives for states to comply with the system. But these new state liability rules, in particular, have sometimes also led to inaction or shunning of responsibility on the part of member states, and occasionally, during Intergovernmental Conferences (IGCs) and elsewhere, there have been calls for a curtailing of the ECJ's powers.

Those precepts, or doctrines, of the primacy of EU Law, its direct applicability and its direct effect on individuals and member states are, in no small measure, attributable to the ECJ's integrative jurisdiction over decades: some of the most basic cases are: *Van Gend en Loos v. Nederlandse Administratie der Belastingen*, case 26/62 [1963] ECR 1; [1963] CMLR 105; *Costa v. ENEL*, case 6/64 [1964] ECR 585; [1964] CMLR 425; *Amministrazione delle Finanze dello Stato v. Simmenthal SpA*, case 106/77 [1978] ECR 629; [1978] 3 CMLR 263; *Internationale Handelsgesellschaft GmbH v. Einfuhr-und Vorratsstelle für Getreide und Futtermittel*, case 11/70 [1970] ECR 1125; [1970] CMLR 255; *R. v. Secretary of State, ex parte Factortame* (No. 1) [1989] 2 WLR 997; *R. v. Secretary of State, ex parte Factortame* (No. 2), case C-213/89 [1990] ECR I-2433; [1990] 3 CMLR 867 (European Court); *Van Duyn v. Home Office*, case 41/74 [1974] ECR 1337; [1975] 1 CMLR 1; *Francovich v. Italian Republic*, cases C6/90 and C9/90 [1993] 2 CMLR 66. The integrative approach to jurisdiction can be seen in the area of justiciability of EU Law, i.e. its subjection to full legal scrutiny in many forms, and in the other legal precepts which define contemporary European Law.

A constitution for the EU

Traditional scholarship has often approached the question of the nature of a Constitution by a process of elimination or categorization. Depending on one's intellectual persuasion, different elements have been declared, either individually or cumulatively, to form the essence of a Constitution. The 'formal quality or organization of a body', a 'more substantive legal order', the 'inclusiveness of a body of human rights' or simply a 'written fundamental document', are all examples of the use of the attribute 'Constitution'. There can be little doubt that in all of the above, more generalized, meanings, the EU has been seen as having – or being – a Constitution. But if one focuses the legal lens a little more precisely, Constitutions invariably emerge as texts which, by means of norms of a supreme nature, define the conditions and exercise of political power or function as normative rules conditioning the relationship between government in all its forms and the public (Dehousse, 1998: 67; Finer, Bogdanor and Ruden, 1995: 1). Notwithstanding political utopias, it remains on the whole unsatisfactory to bring the EU into total congruence with a nation-state and a national Constitution as a kind of 'birth certificate' for a nation-state. However, there are a number of compelling reasons in favour of the existence, or at least emergence, of a 'European Constitution'. A wide, contextual view is helpful in this area, and the European Constitution has to be understood as an unfinished one and furthermore as one that continues to draw inspiration from many sources. Like its British counterpart, the European Constitution is located within a broad, historical, economic, political and legal context. It is subject to constant change and comprises more than one unified document or overriding 'supreme law'. A 'Constitution' in the context of a Union encompassing 15 member states, with ambitions to enlarge even further in the future, has to rest on a multitude of general legal and cultural aspects. Some of these are, for example, embodied in different theories of integration, a prevailing culture of consensus, the significance of lobbying and *ad hoc* compromise, the importance of negotiation or the recognition that the member states, acting in the Council of Ministers, continue to be in charge of the Treaties. Against this background, a constitutional culture, the elements of a constitution and the processes of further constitutionalization, or constitution-building, can be identified as parts of the emerging EU Constitution (Snyder, 1998: 53, 72, 139, 154/5).

Within this framework, the Treaties of Paris (1951), Rome (1957) and subsequent amendments through the Single European Act (1987), the Schengen Agreements, the Maastricht (1991) and Amsterdam (1997) Treaties are more than merely legal symbols of European integration. They also form integral parts of the European Constitution. Legal precepts, such as legitimacy and accountability, adjudication and liability, flexibility and subsidiarity, intergovernmentalism and supranationalism further define the features of this emerging Constitution. In a political context, successive enlargements of the EU, its network of external relations, its institutional design, its competencies or the increasingly important provisions on Human Rights are vital political keys to the Union Constitution. EMU, the Stability and Growth Pact and the introduction of the euro – because of the high priority attached to these 'historical' projects – have served to highlight the often neglected economic side of the European Constitution. Moreover, moral aims, values and directions and consensus on unification and integration are less tangible, but no less important parts of the Constitution.

The 'constitutionalization' of the European legal order

If all these, from a legal perspective, contribute to the formation of a common legal ethos and background to the legal system in the EU, the case-law of the ECJ must not be forgotten. The Court mirrors the incremental growth of the Community as a whole. It has contributed a number of elements to the formation of an EU

Constitution and to its explanation and interpretation. Its view of the Founding Treaties as the 'basic constitutional chart of the Community' (case 294/83: *Parti écologiste 'Les Verts' v. Parliament* [1986] ECR 1339), was the point of departure for a constitutional 'programme'. The ECJ 'constitutionalized' the Treaties and thus transformed international agreements into a 'Constitution' for the future Europe. In the words of a seminal US analysis from the early 1980s: 'Tucked away in the fairyland Duchy of Luxembourg and blessed, until recently, with benign neglect by the powers that be and the mass media, the Court of Justice of the European Communities has fashioned a constitutional framework for a federal-type structure in Europe' (Stein, 1981: 1–27).

The media glare has become brighter since then, and the use of the label 'federal' has certainly received wider and, on the whole, more discerning treatment, but the kernel of truth in this statement still holds true. The expansion of doctrines such as supremacy and direct effect or the rulings on state liability or individual rights have contributed to the evolution of EU Law as a 'new legal order of international law' (*Van Gend en Loos v. Netherlands*, case 26/62 [1963] ECR 1; [1963] CMLR 105), for the benefit of which the member states have relinquished some of their sovereignty, although national views about the extent of this differ widely.

Judicial politics and integration

The legislative and interpretative power of the ECJ and its function as a source of EU Law, leading to a progressive 'legalization' and 'constitutionalization' of the Community order, have already been stressed. The contribution the ECJ has made to the process of integration is indeed considerable. It could, however, never be an exclusively legal and interpretational contribution; the ECJ has also developed into a uniquely successful judicial organ for reasons other than legal or jurisdictional ones. Successive judgements of the ECJ have provided consistent evidence of a Court that has conceived of itself as the engine, the vehicle of integration, a facilitator of homogenization of the emerging European legal order. The visionary project of integration, through the instrument of the Court, has become progressively more driven by Law.

But the concept of Law in an EU context has to be wider. In this image the Court evolves into a central political actor in the Community institutional system. This view tends to neglect other approaches which conceive of the Law as an over-arching and objective normative order, or as a moral order or as an institution which in turn binds the Courts (Armstrong, 1998: 155–74). The realization that 'the law may be insulated, but it is not isolated' (Slaughter-Burley, 1993: 393), has led to intense research on the Court and its more political functions, intentions and effects. Apart from being described as a 'constitution-maker' or a 'protector of rights', the Court continues to be identified as a 'catalyst' or 'engine' of integration, disintegration or even equilibrium. These labels are widely accepted, but are perhaps less important than the key question of whose vehicle it is: that of democratically legitimized authority or of political pressure groups. This and the dilemma of a reduction in the 'democratic deficit' in the EU is what lies hidden behind the irony of statements like: 'The European Court of Justice is not a political actor at all; it is "merely" protecting the Community from ruin' (Kuper, R., 1998: 38). The ECJ is also an institutional player and as such has a function in the decision-making processes of the Community, as a final arbiter and supervisor of EU Law. But beyond that, enhanced tendencies towards 'judicial activism' or 'judicial policy-making' have made the Court's role much more contentious than in the first few decades of its existence.

Theories emphasizing an ECJ which is more involved in disputes of a political nature and concepts of the Court as an 'integrator through law' show that it has become far removed from traditional concepts of separation of powers. This development of a more interdependent relationship between law, politics and integration is not surprising. This trend has its roots in Eurosclerosis and the crises of the Community in the 1960s and 1970s. Since then, the quest for legal uniformity and the idea of integration by law has revived neo-functionalist theories, and models of the ECJ as a more interventionist political actor have become more popular. The legal aspects of economic integration, the Single Market Project, and the enforcement of the freedom of movement principles have continued to provide evidence of a Court that interferes, defines and re-defines agendas, promotes and facilitates concepts, manages and provides justifications. Such 'juridification' of the EU policy process has greatly prejudiced the Community legal system. It has shaped the relationship of the Court with other EU institutions, member state governments, companies or individuals. The potentially destabilizing phenomenon of 'strategic litigation' by individuals or companies is only one of the consequences of this, but it illustrates a scenario where decision-making is increasingly being shifted away, hijacked, one is almost tempted to say, from the political to the judicial arena.

This is not only true on the Community stage but has its reach into national politics: the Court's political role and leverage on the domestic politics and agendas of the member states has been explained by political pressures, enthusiasm for integration or the impossibility for any judge to be, in a paraphrase of Rousseau's words, *un être inanimé*, a totally neutral being, a mere 'mouthpiece' of the law. Even though the Court's legal reasoning has often been closer to the Commission than to the member states, the latter's interests are not without importance. Interest analysis provides a powerful tool when seeking to explain the ECJ's judicial activism. This is particularly true, for instance, of the member states' interest in a non-disruption of the Community as a whole, in the *pacta sunt servanda* rule or in economic aspects, such as the mutual recognition of goods principle, achieved through rulings such as *Cassis de Dijon* (*Rewe-Zentral AG v. Bundesmonopolverwaltung für Branntwein* (*Cassis de Dijon* case): case 120/78 [1979] ECR 649; [1979] 3 CMLR 337).

The interface of Article 234

The reception and administration of EC Law by means of the Preliminary Ruling Procedure of Article 234 (the old Article 177) makes national courts indispensable interlocutors of the ECJ. Against the background of a generally mounting caseload, referrals to the ECJ for preliminary rulings rose by some 10 per cent in 1998, as compared with 1997, and by more than 85 per cent, compared with 1990. They now account for more than 50 per cent of the new cases (264 out of 485) (European Commission, DG X, 1999). Moreover, Article 234 provides a way of enhancing national incentives to abide by EU Law and an important channel for legal challenges brought by individuals. There are traces, however, of an ambivalent and almost paradoxical development in this area: a considerable resistance towards European rules on the part of governments or the highest national courts has persistently gone hand in hand with a willing acceptance of European Law by the lower courts in national judiciaries. If one only considered the national courts of last instance as an example, a picture would emerge in which important issues related to the translation of EU Law doctrines into national law are far from being sufficiently resolved. The cumbersome, ambiguous and often convoluted rulings of the *Bundesverfassungsgericht* (Everson, 1998: 389–410), on the Maastricht Treaty (see BVerfGE, 155 (1989), English translation in [1994] 1 CMLR 57 and 2 BvR 2134/92 or 2159; *Juristenzeitung* 1993, 1100), or its judgements on EMU and national judicial control are only the latest examples of this continuing doctrinal stand-off.

Lower courts, by contrast, have consistently given fast and comprehensive effect to EU Law and have thus been a vehicle of its further advancement. Irrespective of the question whether this involves them more, they continue to be gateways, interfacing with the ECJ and exerting what has been termed a strong 'pull' towards compliance with European Law (Weiler, 1993: 422). This continuing discrepancy between resistance by higher courts and acceptance by lower ones has traditionally been explained in terms of procedure, awareness, status and loyalty. But it also has a great deal to do with the empowerment of lower courts and, consequently, the stakes individuals can hold in EU Law.

Citizenship and the place of Human Rights

Although it remains difficult fully to identify in the EU the political preconditions of full legitimacy and democratic representation, which are normally associated with a nation-state, the idea of citizenship is not alien to the EU. The general principles of EU Law, such as direct effect or supremacy of Community Law, in opening legal avenues for individuals have not only formed part of the EU institution; but have also contributed to the idea of an emerging 'European' citizenry. The formative power of institutions, the increased clout of the EP and the identity-building impact of 'European' symbols, such as the euro, flags, youth orchestras or anthems, have further enlarged this point. However, not unlike some other aspects of EU Law, the idea of 'European' citizenship is closely connected with aspects of national identity, nationalism or national boundaries. But while it may be possible to conceive of a European citizenry in general, the idea of European citizenship continues to give rise to the metaphor of a Union whose parts do not yet quite add up. In the case of the EU, a collective sense of belonging, or '*affectio societatis*' is often indeterminate, under-developed and vague, in spite of a flag, a currency, an anthem and an emerging European Constitution. There is still the problem of a chasm between individuals' empowerment and their rights, as legally defined subjects of the law, the generation of a more 'European' loyalty and a sense of a common future. In the case of welfare provisions, the first Danish 'no' in the Maastricht referendum provided a revealing example for this. Participation in the EU policy process and awareness of rights, welfare and duties in European Law may be keys to a better understanding of what it means to be European. The 1998 'Citizens First' initiative and other information campaigns have indeed gone a long way towards providing some hard evidence for this. However, processes and initiatives will have to be accompanied by a more substantial re-examination of European citizenship, particularly in times of continuing ethnic strife, the reawakening of nationalisms on Europe's boundaries and ambitious plans for further enlargement to the East.

The Maastricht Treaty introduced the idea of an EU citizenship. It further provided a more substantive legal basis for citizenship (Articles 8 to 8d), predicating on member state nationality and homing in on the areas of civic and political European citizenship. The concept arrived at in Maastricht entailed new voting rights for municipal and EP elections, a system of consular protection in non-member states and enhanced statutory provision regarding some fundamental rights and national identities (Article F1 and 2 TEU). However, the legal protection mainly applied to European nationals living in *other* member states, i.e. between 5 and 6 million people, or less than 2 per cent of the European population. These were narrow citizenship rules, which had to be interpreted, widened and amended by the Amsterdam Treaty and, in particular, the case-law of the ECJ. Several Commission Communications focus on the freedoms of movement (for people, goods, services and money), especially on the fundamental right to free personal movement and permissible restrictions to it, on grounds of public policy, security or health. The significance of the most recent communication (at the time of writing), adopted by the Commission in July 1999, lies in the fact that, against the background of public debates about cases of expulsions and criminal convictions, it probably makes the most explicit reference available in recent times to Union citizenship and the requirement of respect for Human Rights. It is no surprise that the issue of Rights and their protection therefore loomed large in the Cologne, Tampere and Helsinki summits in 1999. These issues continue to inform debates during the 2000 IGC.

But Human Rights provisions are otherwise scattered throughout the EC Treaty and concentrate on anti-discrimination rules or commercial freedoms of movement arising from the Single Market (for instance, in Articles 6, 9, 48, 52, 59, 73b or 119). This situation has made the development of Human Rights law one of the most practical examples of judicial activism by the ECJ. The Maastricht Treaty has gone beyond that and has achieved more than occasional references to the UN Declaration of 1948, the two Covenants of 1966, the Organization for Economic Cooperation and Development or the Council of Europe. The latter's Convention for the Protection of Human Rights and Fundamental Freedoms (ECHR), of 4 November 1950, now rules the behaviour of the Union. The Convention has been signed by 41 member states (as of 28 October 1998), including Russia, and has been incorporated into EU Law as a 'general principle' and hence a source of the law by Article F of the TEU. But although all member states have incorporated the Convention into domestic law, the debate about the desirablity and implications of an accession by the EU as a whole rages on, reflected recently in the debates about a comprehensive European 'Bill of Rights'. The relevant piece of UK legislation is the Human Rights Act 1998, which received Royal Assent on 9 November 1998. But in spite of this, the debate about the desirability and implications of an accession by the EU as a whole rages on, reflected recently in the debates about a comprehensive 'European Bill of Rights' (Harris, O'Boyle and Warbrick, 1995: 27/8). Arguably the most significant of the innovations of the new Treaty of Amsterdam in 1997 was to further solidify new EU competencies in the areas of Human Rights and Civil Liberties (Duff, 1997: 8). Supported by Mary Robinson, the UN Commissioner for

Human Rights, the Treaty has made respect for Human Rights a part of its preamble and a membership criterion for the EU. Moreover, it has introduced the use of punitive sanctions, such as the suspension of voting and other rights, for member states found to be in breach of Human Rights (see, for example, Articles F1 and 236 Treaty of Amsterdam). The Treaty also added some religious, social and sex equality aspects of Human Rights protection.

In addition to this, on 10 December 1998, in the year of the 50th anniversary of the UN Declaration of Human Rights (UNDHR), the EU adopted its own new Human Rights Declaration. In May 1999, the Council deliberated on further steps towards an 'EU Charter of Fundamental Rights', to underpin European citizenship. The process was taken further by the Germans, who made the entrenchment of Human Rights one of their Presidency priorities during the June 1999 Cologne summit, which concluded an otherwise lacklustre term in the first half of 1999. The German promotion of a European Charter or 'Catalogue' of Human Rights has received much praise. But in spite of the Annex to the Tampere Conclusions, setting out its *Composition, Method of Work and Practical Arrangements*, the process suffers from disagreements over membership in the relevant bodies. The underlying concept can be traced back to two strands: the ECHR, of November 1950, in its function as a 'nascent European Bill of Rights', and the 50th anniversary, in 1999, of the German Constitution, the Basic Law. This Basic Law (*Grundgesetz*) contains a comprehensive catalogue of Human Rights and civil liberties.

Despite the Commission's 'Citizens First' campaign, and even though Human Rights are now more safely anchored in EU Law, many issues remain disturbingly unsettled and the forceful rhetoric of the Union on Human Rights matters is, more often than not, insufficiently matched by legal reality. The work on the EU Human Rights Charter has run into difficulties over the thorny issue of who should make up the membership of the drafting committee. While reform of the Council of Europe as the original Human Rights body and of both the Strasbourg and Luxembourg Courts appears to be an ongoing process, the tension between European Law, politics and the national identities of member states and individuals has not been exhaustively resolved. Several examples may serve to illustrate this issue: in its external and trade relations, the lack of a truly coherent EU Human Rights policy has recently been illustrated by the arguments over the inclusion of 'Good Governance' or 'Human Rights' clauses in all new agreements. This policy has sparked heated rows with the African, Caribbean and Pacific (ACP) countries, but also with developed countries, such as Australia or New Zealand. Moreover, as the EP and organizations such as Amnesty International keep stating, finger-pointing in Human Rights matters is neither accurate nor useful, for Human Rights abuses also exist within the borders of the EU and range from abortion-related issues in Ireland to police brutality towards foreigners in Germany. Moreover, immigration and asylum matters are a constant and persistent reminder of this, in the face of mounting racism and xenophobia throughout the new Europe. During 1997, the EU's official 'Year Against Racism', there was, in fact, a further increase in the restrictions placed on the rights of asylum seekers in EU member states. These problems are compounded by internal EU divisions, for example over UN Human Rights Resolutions concerning states such as China, institutional inertia, an increased lack of EU funding for Human Rights bodies and non-governmental organizations (NGOs), and continuing foot-dragging on the issue of Monitoring Agencies or a dedicated Human Rights Commissioner for the new Commission.

Rights and the danger of exclusion

Some issues related to the Schengen Agreements and immigration are, since the Treaty of Amsterdam, in the process of being brought into the 'central' pillar of the EU. It is hoped that this will result in augmented efficiency, increased majority voting and a much-needed control of this area by the ECJ. While this may in itself be a good thing, this, and new plans of EU member states to recognize each other's asylum decisions, illustrate an important problem which concerns Human Rights issues and European Law in equal measure. This concerns law in its including or excluding functions, and, to exaggerate only slightly, the role of legal rules in determining who is inside the 'Fortress Europe' and who is not. The term 'morality' of European Law remains the most accurate analytical term for this critique. It has been pointed out that the four Freedom of Movement rules of Articles 48–73(h), in only encompassing workers, the self-employed or service providers, continue to invite the interpretation that the freedom of movement is only free so long as it does not cost money (Ward, 1996: 149). In the case of non-EC nationals, the image is a stark one: these individuals in particular have felt the Community's legal incompleteness and the effects of marginalization in this area and suffer from increasing racism, xenophobia, exclusion and poverty which transforms them into 'a kind of Community sub-species' (Ward, 1997: 85).

Conclusion and future prospects

The grand project of enlargement has been propelled forward by the implementation of the 'regatta' principle and the Commission's recommendations of 13 October 1999 to double to 12 the number of countries the EU will open accession negotiations with. An increase in the number of member states by 2006 is becoming a more tangible reality. The contradiction of European Law acting as an alienating agent on the one hand and an integrating force on the other, and the resulting effect of the projection of a more pronounced 'otherness' and experience of exclusion towards the outside, versus enhanced efforts at harmonization on the inside, will have to be addressed by both legal and policy measures in the near future. In a post-modern and post-national world, European Law can fulfil more than an identity-building function on a supranational scale: it can certainly contribute to a wider, more socially-oriented concept of citizenship, solidarity, participation and benefit. It will further dilute the citizenship–nationality link which still prevails among most of Europe's peoples, and is often at the source of major conflicts. Whether it is possible to create a kind of national identity without nationalism may be open to further debate and academic research, but most concur that, as concepts of identity are slowly changing, so the law has to evolve.

Accompanied by a steady increase in its caseload, the ECJ has seen its role as an instigator of judicial politics and a motor of political integration further strengthened. This has happened especially in the relationship between the member states and the Community, as the new rules on state liability and fines have illustrated.

Other fields of judicial activism, combined with the consolidation and slow evolution of EC/EU Law as a whole, have been the priority areas of EMU, the four Freedom of Movement rules, the euro and Human Rights. These, together with Competition Law, the scrutiny of national Procedural Law, Sex Equality Law and a number of discrimination and intellectual property cases have contained significant new developments in the European Court's jurisdiction over the last few years. Through the important gateways provided by Article 234, these developments will continue, in the twenty-first century, to radiate into national legislation and jurisdiction and will enhance the legitimizing, enforcing and empowering aspects of European Law. The characterization that both ECJ and CFI have 'moved things along gently' is very much to the point in this context (Foster, 1998: 132).

On the negative side, this method of working provides the underlying reason for longer delays in the arrival of cases at the ECJ. Preliminary ruling procedures, for instance, can now take between two and three years. Delays like this and the structural imbalance between the increase in the volume of cases in the ECJ and the institution's capacity to dispose of them, are inexorably calling for an overhaul of the system in an overall climate of willingness towards reform. In his report to the Council of Justice Ministers of 28 May 1999, the ECJ's President, G.C. Rodríguez Iglesias, identified fast-track routes, filtering mechanisms and the subjection of the preliminary ruling procedure to more subsidiarity and decentralization, as some potential responses to congestion. He also acknowledged the need for the recruitment of more judges as a consequence of further Eastern enlargement. These measures will necessitate amendments, for instance to the Court's Rules of Procedure (Articles 225, 245) and to the treatment of staff cases. It is largely on the successful implementation of these and other measures that the future of the ECJ as a court of last instance and a court with an additional constitutional brief depends.

The evolution of European Law through the case law of the ECJ and new developments in Human and Civic Rights will form new contributories to the emerging European Constitution and will enrich its diversity and nature. The area of Human Rights is a legal and political example of further 'constitutionalization' in the EU. By means of the Maastricht and Amsterdam Treaties, Human Rights are now accessible, in an unprecedented way, to political agendas and judicial review. There is little doubt that questions of inclusion and participation, but also social and economic matters, are going to constitute a sharper lens for European Law. The current discussions about a 'European Human Rights Charter', to complement social or employment ones, is a welcome development, because it will enhance awareness of the uniqueness of the Union's legal system and of the values on which it is built.

CHAPTER FOUR

The Global Reach of the European Union

Georg Wiessala

> As long as there is neither an existential threat, nor an existential foe, institutions do not really matter and so Europe tends to enjoy the luxury of eclecticism – pushing the EC/WEU without eschewing NATO, trying to expand the CSCE and calling for the UN, as in the case of Yugoslavia, when discretion is the better part of valour ... Yet when threats and foes materialise again, the Europeans will behave as nations have always done. They will listen to their national interests, look for like-minded partners, and launch an enterprise capable of deterrence and defence.
>
> Lodge, 1993: 267

Introduction: the external context of the European Union

The European Union (EU) is not a 'superstate'. It is not even a state. Consequently, it does not have external relations similar to those of a state. It has no legal personality but only a shadowy collective one and has as yet fostered little identity amongst its citizens. But it is more than a marketplace. With regard to its external affairs it is more than a 'paper tiger' (Gasteyger, 1997: 94–108; Ginsberg, 1999: 429), and many observers agree that it continues to play an active international role, irrespective of internal ways of decision-making and whether or not it is sufficiently prepared for it. In his European Parliament (EP) hearing, Chris Patten, the new External Affairs Commissioner, spoke of the 'moral imperative' of the EU to 'extend its borders of civil society, democracy and prosperity as far and as fast as it can within the European continent, in line with the Union's leading economic and commercial status in the world'.

From these words two general phenomena can be inferred: first, the EU has, at last, acquired a more distinct international identity and has emerged as a significant worldwide force to be reckoned with, playing a number of roles. And second, its performance, formal or otherwise, on the world stage is impressively varied for a body that is not a state. The global importance and impact of the political Union created at Maastricht may have grown out of, but is in many ways different from, the era of Europe's colonial past or the outward reach of the European Economic Community (EEC) as an international trader or provider of development aid. A brief survey of selected areas of EU external activity will reveal the global nature of the Union's external relations and allow a glimpse at its global reach and at the way the Union is continuously attempting to prioritize, as well as to define and balance its international partnerships. For this purpose, it has developed a hierarchical network of agreements, ranging from Association and Partnership and Cooperation Agreements to Free Trade Agreements and Human Rights provisions. These are complemented by international agreements and 'structured dialogue' with states or groups of states.

EU interaction with Central and Eastern Europe, through Europe Agreements (Articles 228, 238), a pre-accession strategy and entry negotiations with Central and Eastern European countries, the Baltic states and Cyprus, forms the roadmap for the next enlargement of the EU. The Union aims to cooperate with Turkey, on the basis of an Association Agreement dating back to 1963 and a contentious Customs Union. EU cooperation with Russia takes place within the framework of the 1997 Partnership and Cooperation Agreement (PCA). Ukraine and the Newly Independent States (NIS) of the former Soviet Union are further partners for the EU, the latter mainly through Partnership and Cooperation Agreements (PCAs) and the TACIS programme (giving technical assistance to the Commonwealth of Independent States and Mongolia).

But in spite of the priority of eastern enlargement, EU external relations do not end there. The Union also attempts to safeguard stability, trade and development in Europe's 'near-abroad' of the Maghreb and Mashreq (North African and South East Mediterranean) states. Generally, policy towards the Mediterranean area is part of the 'Barcelona process' and the Mediterranean Association Agreements. The policy has evolved during three Euro-Mediterranean conferences (from 1995 to 1999) so far.

On a more global scale, these areas of activity are complemented by a partnership with the USA, which has been known to be made fraught by 'banana wars' and other trade disputes, but has been injected with new energy by a stronger EU–US Transatlantic Agenda since 1995. Equally, EU relations with Australia have been put on a firmer footing by the 1997 Joint Declaration, and ties with both New Zealand and Canada have gone through a similar process of consolidation.

These relations are increasingly balanced by an emerging EU strategy towards states in East, South and Southeast Asia, culminating in the ASEM (Asia-Europe-Meeting) process, which has seen summits in Bangkok (1995) and London (1998) thus far. This 'New Asia Strategy' builds on existing links, for example with the Korean Peninsula Energy Development Organisation (KEDO) and the Association of Southeast Asian nations (ASEAN). However, it comprises a number of significant new declarations and policy papers on Japan, Korea, China and Hong Kong, both before and after the 1997 handover (Wiessala, 1999a: 96–112).

In addition to this, the EU has recently established a new framework convention to succeed Lomé IV, regularizing its complex relationship with the 71 African, Caribbean and Pacific (ACP) states. Moreover, the last two years of the twentieth century saw important changes in the association and citizenship rules regarding the EU's farflung Overseas Countries and Territories. The EU's Development and Aid policies are set for fundamental change at the time of writing. As Lomé IV expired in February 2000, the structure of the Union's aid funding has come under review in its entirety. April 2000 has seen the first-ever EU–Africa summit. The nascent EU–Latin American dialogue, conducted largely through the Southern Common Market (MERCOSUR) and the San José, Andean Pact and Rio groups of Latin American countries, was given a boost, in 1999, by the first-ever inter-regional summit meeting in Rio de Janeiro, which laid the foundation stone for a more institutionalized dialogue.

In addition to dealing with states or groups of states, the EU is an active player in many multilateral fora, such as the European Free Trade Association (EFTA) and its umbrella, the European Economic Area (EEA), the G8 and the Organisation for Security and Cooperation in Europe (OSCE, formerly CSCE). With regard to the United Nations (UN), the EU, even though it is not a member, has observer status. The Union is also associated with or represented in the activities of the International Monetary Fund (IMF), the World Bank (IBRD), the Council of Europe, the European Bank for Reconstruction and Development (EBRD), and the World Trade Organisation (WTO), which is about to begin (at the time of writing) what promises to be a complex new round of talks in Seattle from November 1999.

The acquisition of the external

The picture painted above, was, of course, not always as all-encompassing as this. From the 1970s, a voluntary European Political Cooperation (EPC) and contractual arrangements with states, groups of states, international organizations and non-governmental organizations (NGOs) in almost every part of the globe began to add a political dimension to the EU's traditional trade relationships. This broke new and unprecedented ground for a Community which Jean Monnet – visionary and advocate of a *moral Europe* as he was – would perhaps have found difficult to predict in his time. The founder-Treaties of Paris (1951) and Rome (1957), with the exception, perhaps, of the Common Commercial Policy (CCP) and the 1968 Customs Union, did not envisage an external direction for European policy.

But commerce and trade, external relations in the meaning of those original Treaties, revealed themselves, more often than not, as being interdependent with and closely linked to political events. Following trade and aid, the ambition and practice of EU external activities had to expand in tandem with the development of international affairs which were often in crisis. Invariably, all the member states, as well as the Union's institutions, had to become a part of this. Apart from the CCP and numerous bilateral and multilateral agreements, the EU external dimension soon included a humanitarian aspect. Political change on the EC's southern and eastern borders from the 1970s to the 1990s soon necessitated additional association or enlargement policies. This process continues to evolve, as shown by the development of the pre-accession strategy towards Central and Eastern Europe. It has promoted EPC to a firmer Common Foreign and Security Policy (CFSP).

But if the foundation Treaties did not contain an external dimension to speak of, because the drafters believed this to lie solely in the domain of national law, sovereignty and identity, then it may be added that the shadows of this thinking continue to haunt today's EU. A further shifting of foreign relations to the supranational, 'Community' pillar, 'communitarization' of this area, in order to make it open to majority voting and the scrutiny of the European Court of Justice (ECJ), often stumbles and falls precisely on the grounds of continued national sensitivities, jealousies and guarded interests, especially among the larger member states. As much as the image appeals, the sum does not always appear as more than its individual parts. In parallel to this, and in terms of its geopolitical and international importance, the EU has often seen its hand forced by events which simply demanded a single, credible European voice to join the international concert, particularly the voice of the USA. Speaking with such a functionally logical *single voice* has been vociferously advocated, even by otherwise reluctant partners like the UK, whose Government, for example, stressed the concept in the Foreign Office White Paper for the 1996 Intergovernmental Conference (IGC), and many times since. Unity on the world stage has near-unanimously been seen as constituting an added value for the Union in foreign relations. But in practice, such harmony has often proved elusive for the relevant decision-makers or has occurred with less success than was anticipated. The famous model of a 'credibility-expectations paradox' in the field of EU external relations, in which the Union lacks actorship and is seen as a 'panacea, a cross between Father Christmas and the 7th Cavalry' (Hill, 1993: 322; Holland, 1995: 555–72), unable to match mounting external pressures with its own means, resources or possibilities, continues to be a pertinent description of this situation.

This chapter is concerned with the EU's international role and external policies. The traditional way of conceptualizing external actorship distinguishes between national foreign policy, EPC or CFSP and, in a wider sense, the external relations of the Union. The chapter deliberately retains these categories and places a particular emphasis on the two latter aspects. It investigates the contention that an externally active EU amounts to more than the combined foreign policies of its 15 member states. The assessment starts with current issues, as far as they are relevant for EU external affairs. Kosovo and Eastern enlargement have been emphasized, because these events either have a priority that cannot be overlooked in this context, or they push back the hitherto agreed frontiers of the EU's external reach and provide significant indicators for a development that has been characterized as an extended *diplomatic* role of the Union. The present attempts to redress what is widely seen as a *democratic deficit* and the anti-fraud measures, dealing with the legacy of a discredited former Commission, as a new one takes office, form another part of the investigation. Again, this holds true in so far as these internal developments are impacting upon external matters. The development and representation of the CFSP as a branch of external relations constitutes an important part of this chapter and is included on the grounds of the changes to this area, brought about by the Treaties of Maastricht and Amsterdam and because of the 1999 events inside the Commission, culminating in the White Paper on Reform of March 2000.

This structure means that important areas of the EU's external relations had to be either left out completely or only briefly referred to. These include Trade, Commercial, Development, parts of Defence Policy and the important field of Human Rights policy. Moreover, I have placed more emphasis on certain foreign policy actors, such as the Council Presidency and its associated supporting groups, to the detriment of the Commission or the EP. References to those institutions mainly appear in an indirect way, for example in connection with appointments of new staff, the significance of reforms or the June 1999 elections to the EP.

The external impact of reform

The position of the EU in the wider world and the way it appears and acts towards the outside has long been the subject of intense debates in both the political and the diplomatic arenas and in economic and academic circles. External relations and the Foreign and Security Policy of the post-Amsterdam political Union continue to be under close public scrutiny, in times of crises in the executive of the Union and against the background of worldwide financial turmoil and ethnic war on the EU's Balkan doorstep. The Kosovo war of 1998/99 has had a perceptible impact on public opinion in this respect. The *Eurobarometer* survey of July 1999 shows that in the majority of the 15 member states, support for a Common Defence Policy and a Common Security Policy was lower than in the autumn of 1998. But seen as a key issue of concern to the EU-15, a Common Defence and Security Policy and a Common Foreign Policy continue to enjoy high levels of public support (71 per cent and 63 per cent respectively). This means that more European citizens back these policies than are in favour of the euro (€) as the Single Currency, following its introduction on 1 January 1999 (European Commission, 1999a: 57/8). Against the backdrop of globalization (see Chapter 1), the concept of 'a strong Europe, open to the world' and a Common Foreign and Security Policy figure strongly in the 1999 Work Programme of the Commission.

It has become almost commonplace to refer to the present (at the time of writing – the year 2000) as a watershed period for the EU. While this may be true for certain areas of its activities, including external relations, it is perhaps more accurate to speak of the present as a time of limited transition (Edwards and Wiessala, 1999: 1). Important issues of democratic legitimacy, political responsibility, accountability and the project of thorough internal reform of the EU continue to be raised supranationally, from within the new Commission, and by a number of old and new bodies and committees. Apart from a restoration of confidence of European citizens in the European institutions, by means of more openness and transparency, the Finnish incumbents of the second half of 1999 elevated the *coherent and comprehensive development of external relations, in line with a cross-pillar approach*, to priority status during their term of office. This throws a much more glaring spotlight on questions such as the Union's reactions to fraud in its own ranks and to an increased level of public criticism. It has made the need for, and the future potential of, an internally overhauled EU much more imminent.

But the reform debate necessarily contributes to a reassessment of the external role, the competencies and the behaviour of a new EU which finds itself compelled to act and react on a much more demanding scale than ever before. In this sense, it is appropriate to talk of a 'global Europe' (Piening, 1997; Bretherton and Vogler, 1999). Invariably, internal affairs have an external dimension; problems and change on the inside alter perceptions and ultimately influence actions and priorities of the EU on the outside. The difficulties, in mid-1999, in renegotiating the Lomé IV Convention, are a case in point: if some of the 71 ACP states refused to accept the inclusion of principles of *good governance* in the new convention and instead pointed a finger back to the demise of the last Commission, mired in allegations of sleaze, fraud and mismanagement for much of 1999, then this is only one example of the strong linkages between internal reform and external consequences and policies.

Internal integration and external matters have been described as two sides of the same coin. The relevance of this process of *externalization*, already evident in the 1987 Single European Act (SEA), the euro (Glöckler, 1997: 187–206), or the 'historic opportunity' presented by AGENDA 2000 and Eastern enlargement, is thrown into further relief by current developments. Staff reorganization at the Commission, in particular the appointments of Chris Patten and Günter Verheugen as new

Commissioners for External Affairs and Enlargement respectively, are mirrored by the creation of the new position of Vice-President for Internal Reform, filled by Neil Kinnock. It seems important now that any reservations about overlapping portfolios and the resulting inefficiency, which so heavily burdened the old Santer Commission, are being met more efficiently this time by the reforms introduced by the new President Romano Prodi.

Romano Prodi's blueprints for change at the level of the Union executive can be summed up in the words: centralisation, consolidation, closer coordination and codes of conduct. Within this framework, a number of reform initiatives will impact on the Union's external relations. The implementation of Prodi's programme on closer internal coordination aims to ensure more consistency and effectiveness of the Commission's actions. The objectives of this 'streamlining' are to make certain that priorities are put into practice and are 'rigorously implemented at every level'. No doubt in an effort to counteract public perceptions about a limp and hesitant EU when it comes to external relations, the Secretariat-General's function as coordinator, facilitator and neutral actor in regard to the activities of the Directorates-General has been given a much-needed boost.

New personnel, wide-ranging reform of staff rules and a reshaping of structure, portfolios, departments and cabinets are a long overdue attempt to invest the Commission with new integrity, following its downfall in March 1999. These initiatives are complemented by new regulations concerning the inauguration of at least five Standing Groups of Commissioners in the medium to long term. These will be in the areas of: Growth, Competitiveness and Employment, Equal Opportunities, Internal Reform, Inter-institutional Relations and External Relations. Apart from internal reform, one of these key groups concerns external relations. If put into practice, the concept of enhanced group coordination inside the Commission not only constitutes a reaction to past strife, inconsistencies and delays, but also contains a number of potential gains for the conduct and organization of external affairs. The EU's Common Foreign Policy, as a matter of *common* interest, will increase in cohesiveness and credibility; the traditional perception of it as mainly responsive and reactive will shift to proactive, provided that relevant Commissioners are offered a recognized opportunity for an early input into policy initiatives, the formulation of new priorities and the preparation of discussions in Commission plenary sessions. The reform targets inherent in the appointment of new Commissioners, the improved coordination of their actions and enhanced cooperation on a group level make good management sense if, as is planned, they go hand in hand with a clearer delineation of overall responsibilities.

Whether initiatives, such as a revamped Fraud Prevention Office, the *Designing the New Commission* blueprint or the second report on 'management culture' provided by the Committee of Independent Experts under André Middelhoek (in September 1999) really amount to a revolution in the EU, is open to debate. The reform plans have, however, been cautiously welcomed by an EP that is very much changed in political composition and more powerful and vigilant than ever before. The new chair of the EP's Committee on Foreign Affairs, Human Rights and Defence Policy, Elmar Brok (Germany, EPP), will prove to be a considerable force to reckon with in EU foreign policy. So will Javier Solana, ex-NATO Secretary General and newly appointed Foreign Policy Representative. What exactly the relationship will be between these powerful external policy actors, Chris Patten, Günter Verheugen and Javier Solana, and how great the new Foreign Affairs Commissioner's risk is of having his decisions questioned and challenged by the new High Representative of the CFSP is, at present open to question. Nevertheless, there is now, to use the famous Kissinger metaphor of 25 years ago, 'someone to speak to on the telephone' on foreign policy matters. Many hope that wires are not being crossed and overlapping of competencies will not again lead to inertia and political standstill in external affairs. This was exactly what so often made the Union seem an economic heavyweight but a political lightweight.

Enlargement, Kosovo and the new diplomatic role for the EU

Since the inception of the European Communities in the Treaties of Paris (1951) and Rome (1957) and during the first thirty years of its development, this unique body has been lacking political weight commensurate with its ascendance as an economic superpower and its activities in trade, commerce or development. Is it justified to describe this as a 'glaring imbalance' (Dinan, 1999: 483)? External or foreign policy-related competencies have indeed only been acquired very slowly, through a pattern of incremental, rather than linear, growth and *ad hoc* consensus, coupled with gradual expansion, using Treaty provisions (Lodge, 1993: 228–51). The move from EEC to EPC and its successor, today's CFSP, demonstrates an important development: it shows how the Union, a uniquely 'civilian power' in the famous words of F. Duchêne, has evolved into a much more outwardly active and involved grouping on the world stage, based on its values. This has no doubt contributed to the evolution of the Union into a body *sui generis*, a design in its own right, a 'putative superpower'. More careful analysts have spoken of the EU's 'emerging – but not sought after – status as an international power in the making, or of a 'world community which has been increasingly willing to let the EU wear the clothes of a major actor' (Lodge, 1993: 227; Laursen, 1991: 747–59; McGoldrick, 1997: 210). The Union has been driven to deepen this position through its own agendas and priorities, particularly in regard to Central and Eastern Europe, and by external events and developments which have required the EU, if not always to speak *una voce*, then at least to react in a politically credible way and to provide an outwardly visible sign of its power, reflecting its economic weight and population size.

Some general remarks relating to the modified state of the EU as an external player are required at this point. They derive mainly from three parallel and recent developments. Firstly, the external dimension of the new Agenda 2000 blueprint, which Tony Blair has incompletely described as being about 'enlargement, enlargement, enlargement'; secondly, the implications of the Kosovo war on the status of the changing Union; and thirdly, the new diplomatic force the EU has acquired and is representing with increased confidence in global affairs.

Widening of the Union as an external goal, by means of the Agenda 2000 project (Galloway, 1999: 9–35) and the related budgetary ringfencing, has been driven forward by the Commission's recommendations of 13 October 1999, to begin negotiations with another group of six states. The success of enlargement, as envisaged by the Commission's 'regatta' approach, may represent the export of capitalist values and may raise many questions about asymmetries of benefit, but it is also inextricably linked to profound institutional reform. The constituent elements of what the Union calls its 'triple challenge' of widening, deepening and reform are in many ways interdependent. Therefore, the IGC of 2000 on reform has already had a much wider and more diverse agenda than was expected by many observers. The EU, it seems, is pulled, with a rare and powerful immediacy and an ever-increasing speed, in two directions at the same time. It has gone through two enlargements, two amendments of the Treaties and two budgetary packages in the last decade alone. This has provided a powerful impetus for further budgetary and institutional overhaul and a reform of the EU's external relations. Their further development into a fully-fledged, coherent, credible and operational foreign policy has now been envisaged by the architects of Agenda 2000.

Amsterdam and the euro have set the scene: the Treaty of Amsterdam has ensured that there is already an EU with new and more efficient CFSP mechanisms and tools, by adding, for example, 'common strategies' and a case-by-case-flexibility in the shape of 'constructive abstentions' to the existing Maastricht arsenal. The Treaty on European Union (TEU) had already introduced the Common Defence Policy into the EU toolset. Furthermore, Maastricht had provided for some, mainly reactive, external tools, such as 'common positions', 'joint actions' and 'common statements', which, by and large, formed the *acquis politique* and delineated the scope of possible foreign policy commitments of the EU in the early 1990s (Nugent, 1999: 451–5). The EU's policies towards Libya, Haiti, Rwanda, Burundi, Nigeria and Ukraine have constituted prominent cases of 'common positions', whereas the promotion of the Stability Pact in Central and Eastern Europe and policies on the Middle East Peace Process, the organization and supervision of elections in Palestine, South Africa and Russia or the administration of the town of Mostar have provided examples of 'joint actions'. In addition to Maastricht and its successor, the Treaty of Amsterdam, the 1999 German Presidency explicitly sought a further 'communitarization' of the CFSP. The euro offers the chance of both monetary identity and currency unity and is expected to further the Union's potential to be a recognized global financial authority. There is only a small and consistent step left between an EU capable of speaking with a common foreign voice and paying with common money, to one encompassing its eastern half, acting on the basis of its own military identity and achieving much more coherence in its overall diplomatic and external relations.

The rationale and, arguably, ultimate justification for the great project of eastern enlargement, apart from political, economic, security and cultural considerations, largely derives from the changed external environment for the EU. This eventually leads to and rests on the need for an augmentation of the EU's status, image and profile in the world. Numerous initiatives and policy papers re-emphasize that point, both in respect to Eastern Europe and the wider world. Outside the Central and Eastern European countries, a more recent example of this is provided by the EU's new Strategy Papers redefining its relationship with the People's Republic of China. Both the 1995 basic document and a 1998 summary and update refer to 'EU presence and profile' as one of the five important key elements of the policy. Similar formulations can be found elsewhere. The underlying need of the EU to reinvent itself, to be more respected, more counted on as a body with global power, becomes clear in and beyond phrases such as 'historic opportunity', 'milestone', 'historic compromise' and 'Marshall

Plan'. This illustrates the overall future target of a Union that sets about adapting, developing and reforming itself with great implications for the outside world.

The war in Kosovo has provided the last straw. Since its end, or since the violence turned from one set of victims to another, questions of enlargement, civil protection, peaceful conflict-settlement and related issues of status and international standing of the EU have been brought to the fore in an unprecedented way. The conflict, the latest instalment in a series of wars in the former Yugoslavia, has, much more than its predecessors, made a considerable difference for everyone involved. But has the war delayed or accelerated eastern enlargement of the EU? Both case-scenarios have been convincingly argued in the applicant states and within the EU institutions. It is perhaps better to argue on a more general level that it contained much potential to alter the framework, manner and speed with which the EU eventually expands and deals with the CEE applicants.

The argument that follows on from these developments is that, for everybody involved, enlargement has moved irreversibly from a technicality to a much more pressing geo-political reality. This will impinge on the image of the EU as an external power in at least two ways: first, a new dimension of divisiveness has been added to an enlargement process which, many observers argue, is already suffering from overload, asymmetry, too much competitive bidding and an uneven distribution of benefit. Second, the need for the EU to rethink a membership in the region of 30, complete with the requisite internal adjustments, has become crucial, if Europe does not want to risk what Dietrich von Kyaw, retiring German EU Ambassador, has called 'imperial overstretch and withering away'.

For the press and many other observers Kosovo has demonstrated the EU's continuing inferiority and weakness when compared to the USA. With the American diplomatic and military shadow looming overwhelmingly large, the EU again failed to operate a Common Foreign and Security Policy. This is the latest episode in a series of challenges and disasters over the last decade. However, a closer look reveals something more remarkable. The strength with which the EU has displayed unity in military and other institutionalized cooperation, trade sanctions, and political declarations has become more pronounced, coherent and much more noticeable this time.

In this context, the Cologne summit, at the end of an otherwise lacklustre German Presidency in the first half of 1999, amounted to something of a turning point for the EU's external dimension and a considerable advancement for a Common Defence Policy, which had been foreshadowed by provisions (Article J.4) in the 1991 Maastricht Treaty. The meeting showcased a Union basking in the success of bringing a peace deal with Milosevic closer to reality. 'Peace was brought about by the European Union', participants stated, and special envoys Martti Ahtisaari and Viktor Chernomyrdin and the host, German Chancellor Gerhard Schröder, made similarly enthusiastic noises. A newly self-confident EU took the credit for winning what was lauded as an external political breakthrough. This was widely hailed as being a big step closer to a new diplomatically mature nature of the Union. It was certainly in marked contrast to European indecision and inactivity which had characterized the war in Bosnia.

Carried by the impetus of these events, and the continuing initiative by French President Jacques Chirac and Tony Blair, the political leaders in Cologne had no choice but to go further in the advancement of a stronger Common Security and Defence policy. The construction, by a target date of late 2000, of a stronger military infrastructure of the EU, in tandem with a new European security identity, is a huge step forward, although it will still operate under a NATO umbrella and falls way short of anything like a Common European Army. In parallel to this, at its 50th Anniversary Washington summit, NATO member states had already agreed unanimously to a more independent European defence and security capacity and to 'arrangements for ready access by the EU to the collective assets and capabilities of the Alliance, for operations in which NATO as a whole is not engaged militarily'. As was to be expected, the ambiguity of this formulation attracted US criticism of the EU acting outside, instead of in tandem with, the Alliance. Regardless of the need to iron out formulations, this concept constitutes a departure to wholly new shores. It incorporates an unprecedented NATO commitment to enable the EU to use NATO equipment for EU missions.

These developments sounded the death-knell for the Western European Union (WEU), also presided over by Germany in the first half of 1999. The largely marginalized defence arm of the EU has, for a long time, led an almost dormant existence, although it was, to a degree, revitalized by the Petersberg Declaration in 1992. Following this short lease of life, the organization's peacekeeping, humanitarian and crisis management capabilities are now supposed to be incorporated into the EU. How both experience and assets which the WEU has acquired as a 'link organization' between NATO and EU are going to be used in a constructive and cooperative manner in future conflicts, remains, however, open to dispute (Duke, 1996: 167–90).

If many questions in this area remain open, there are even more uncertainties surrounding the role and future functions of Javier Solana, ex-head of NATO, now (at the time of writing) making the changeover to the EU as its first Foreign Policy Representative. This position was envisaged by the Amsterdam Treaty and could be filled as soon as the Treaty was ratified by all member states on 1 May 1999. Supported by a Policy Planning and Early Warning Unit (PPEWU), Solana's high-profile appointment has raised eyebrows on both sides of the Atlantic, but it will undoubtedly also augment the EU's external position and profile.

Economic giant and political pygmy?

It has been argued that 'the world does not yet quite know what to make of the European Union, in large part because the European Union does not yet quite know what to make of itself' (McCormick, 1999: 202). The evolution of the EU as a 'non-state' (Nugent, 1999: 446) – its development from civilian orientation to a body with an external voice – has been a direct response to the emergence of a new world disorder, new conflicts, and ever faster and more complex global change. If the Union's change towards more active and pronounced external relations can be characterized as incremental, this holds particularly true in the area of the Common Foreign and Security Policy (CFSP). The acquisition of CFSP competencies and a related identity only partially derives from the 1992 and 1995 European Councils in Lisbon and Madrid. While these meetings provided some of the blueprints, earlier initiatives had already paved the way from informality to institutionalization and an increased 'Brusselsization' of foreign affairs matters, by means of which member states begin to pool and expand their joint foreign activities in Brussels.

In the beginning, the embryonic and 'extra-treaty' EPC of the 1970s began to have consequences for a Community with expanding economic clout. For neo-functionalists, this seemed a logical, almost inevitable, 'spillover' of European integration into other areas. Member states' attachment to sovereignty, their national identities and interests, lack of a coherent framework and unanimity voting requirements are traditionally identified as brakes on this fledgling cooperation and the ability of the Union to act visibly and with any speed. The legacy of these constraints contributed to the widely-held perception of a slow and mainly reactive European foreign policy which lagged behind actual global events and developments. Seeking to redress the balance and to construct a new identity for the Community, the 1981 London Report provided it with the task to 'seek increasingly to shape events and not merely to react to them' (London Report, Supplement of the *Bulletin of the European Communities*, No. 3/81: p. 14). The renamed CFSP was finally institutionalized in Article 30 of the 1986 SEA and made into a new 'pillar' by section III of the TEU in Maastricht in 1993 (De Giustino, 1996: 258/9; Duff, 1997: 111–28). It remains a valid characterization to define the CFSP of those times as a 'refinement and limited rationalisation of EC external activities' (Lodge, 1993: 243). This is an area, it has to be remembered, which also comprised trade, monetary, development and aid policies. But the Maastricht Treaty also reflected the EU's response to the end of the Cold War, German unification, the wars in the Gulf and former Yugoslavia and other contemporary world events and the resulting external pressures on the EU.

While the CFSP appears as part of a much firmer framework now, it continues to be characterized as evolutionary, rather than revolutionary. With five objectives and instructions for the use of various policy instruments, its inclusion in the TEU, as a 'second pillar', has to be taken with a grain of salt. This is the case mainly for three reasons: firstly and most generally, the Maastricht Treaty suffered from an amount of inbuilt ambiguity regarding terms and responsibilities, which made it hard to gauge what was feasible in the area of foreign policy and who was behind it. Responsibility and actorship, in other words, were often opaque; what 'foreign policy' is, was not entirely clear from the TEU. Secondly, it has always been persuasive to see the post-Maastricht EU represented by a 'pillar' or 'temple' structure (e.g. Haynes-Renshaw and Wallace, 1997: 13). Related metaphors such as the common European 'house' or 'home' have contributed to propagating and reinforcing an image of solidity, firmness and clear division of power. However, the development and location of the CFSP is one of a number of examples suggesting that such stability and coherence do not exist in reality. In conjunction with interference by varying policy positions among member states and unilateral actions, this points to the downside of an incremental development.

Thirdly, Maastricht-style CFSP was tentative and introduced on the grounds that the EU needed to 'assert its identity on the international scene'. The preamble to the CFSP section stated that the EU should aim to 'ensure the consistency of its external activities as a whole in the context of its external relations'. This aim has, however, always been informed by intergovernmentalism. In practical terms, it remains largely outside the 'central' Community pillar and the associated jurisdiction by the

ECJ. It has not become supranational and was not 'communitarized'. In this respect, the very description as a *Common* Foreign and Security Policy reveals itself as a misnomer; the CFSP does not constitute a 'common' policy, in the same way as the Common Agricultural, Trade or Commercial Policies. The metaphor of 'EPC changing into CFSP like a caterpillar into a butterfly which is colourless and cumbersome and had great difficulty getting off the ground' (Dinan, 1999: 508) in Maastricht amply illustrates some of the basic problems, mainly in the area of national sovereignty.

The 1996 IGC again focused on the CFSP. The resulting Treaty of Amsterdam – after the SEA and TEU, the third major amendment to the Treaties of Rome and Paris – was signed on 2 October 1997. It put the Union on a stronger human rights footing, helped to export its values and aimed to give Europe a stronger voice in world affairs. Security, Economic and Development policies were expressly added to the CFSP preamble in the new Treaty. This gave rise to limited political expectations that the EU would now reduce institutional constraints and become a more assertive global force. A new flexibility clause, new actors and policy areas and tools such as 'constructive abstentions', 'opt-outs', and 'common strategies' have been seen as a step in the right direction (Duff, 1997: 111–35).

In terms of the development of the CFSP, however, the Treaty is still modest, in the eyes of some it is little more than a *trompe-l'oeil*, or crafty illusion (Duff, 1997: 124). Representing a 'lowest-common-denominator' agreement, it largely mirrors what was acceptable to the political ideologies of the leaders of the 'big three', France, Germany and the UK. In foreign policy, divisions among member states over issues such as the position of the Foreign Policy Representative or qualified majority voting (QMV) prevailed during the negotiations. An initial proposal by the Dutch Presidency, aiming at much closer cooperation and a specific flexibility clause in CFSP matters, was later dropped on the initiative of Austria, Ireland, Greece and the UK. However, the security field of the CFSP was extended to the so-called 'Petersberg' humanitarian and peacekeeping tasks. In general, a new liberal intergovernmentalism (Moravcsik, 1993: 31), pervades the new Treaty, revolving around concerns about limitations of a future transfer of more sovereignty. This ensures that the end result is likely to be a mixed blessing. Amsterdam represents an amalgam of little 'communitarization', hesitant institutional and voting reform and the preservation of the post-Maastricht *status quo*. It may include a stronger, co-deciding EP, but leaves a number of issues unresolved. The course of a reform-focused IGC in 2000 may be further evidence of a Union 'obsessed merely with institutional alterations' (Stavridis, 1997: 87–122).

Representation and management of the CFSP

The history of the CFSP, in the Union's own words a largely 'untried ambition', has produced a proliferation of political actors and brought with it the danger of further bureaucratic overload. Apart from two new Commissioners, the Policy Planning and Early Warning Unit, a Foreign Policy Representative, an EP with advisory and budgetary control functions and a powerful Foreign Affairs, Security and Defence Committee, the basic framework in this concert is still delineated by the member states acting collectively in the General Affairs Council (GAC) or the European

Council. They are supported by a spider's web of bodies – the Political Committee, COREPER (the Committee of Permanent Representatives), Working Parties and the General Secretariat – in their initiating, promoting, assisting and implementing functions (Beyers and Dierickx, 1998: 289–317).

This basic framework, the continued relevance of national sovereignty and a gradual interinstitutional shift in the balance of EU power away from the Commission over the last two decades, has meant that the work of the European Council and particularly the management of Council business and representation of the Union through the six-month rotating Presidency has become a more substantial and public task, if not in every case a very effective and visible one. Amsterdam has introduced a small but by no means marginal change in EU external relations: the organizational rota of the Presidencies has moved on from Presidencies arranged in alphabetical order (in the native languages) to a system in which larger member states alternate with smaller ones. This impinges on policy agendas – European as well as domestic ones – and on the image and balance of power in external affairs. But the position of the Presidency itself is subject to constant change in the way in which new and old players interact. New and reformed ways of participation, prioritization and cooperation will all affect the manner in which consensus is reached, agreements are forged and vital interfacing with other EU bodies and institutions and the world is accomplished.

Representation of the EU in external affairs through a collectively managed Presidency, based on the Treaties, was meant to avoid leadership by a single individual, such as in WEU or NATO, and be aimed at distributing responsibilities more evenly. The fact that now just such a figurehead has been appointed Foreign Policy High Representative is a new venture with an ironical twist. Ironical, because the very ex-chairman of NATO has been chosen for the task, and unprecedented, because it implies the addition of a new layer of activity and responsibility in EU foreign policy. It carries the advantage of higher visibility and outward unity, channelling the case for reform and further development and diverting immediate attention away from the member states. There is little doubt that the move has been conceived as a step further on the road to 'speaking with one voice', to making the EU appear more unified, in an effort to draw some conclusions from the tragedies in Albania, Algeria, Bosnia or Rwanda.

However, some critics argue that the new position only continues what the EU has been doing since Maastricht, by merely plugging the credibility–expectations gap and by inventing new actors or tools, in order to be seen to be doing something. This may be an exaggerated perception, in light of the cases where EU foreign policy has been successful, such as South Africa. But the new High Representative still faces a number of teething problems, much as the EU Ombudsman did, when that was a new office some years ago. Mr Solana will have to fit into the above network of players in EU external relations, and this means for the moment that his position is not nearly as clearly defined as one might wish for. Vague delineations, however, bring with them the danger of overlapping portfolios, as the work of the last Commission – and its eventual demise – has illustrated in early 1999. A potential clash of foreign policy agendas, involving interinstitutional quarrels between Council, Presidency, CFSP Representative and Commission, would be the worst-case-scenario in the EU's external position, for it runs counter to the heightened expectations for firmer, faster, more flexible and more determined action on the Union's part.

Bearing in mind the political dangers implied by the old adage about too many cooks spoiling the broth, it is, however, important to emphasize some of the more constructive points of a culture which is decentralized and has allocated foreign policy functions to a variety of bodies. If the danger of institutional confusion is one side of the coin, the other side is represented by the ideas of positive coordination, double-checking and filtering on different levels. Within the CFSP activity triangle formed by the incumbent Presidency, the GAC and COREPER, national foreign ministries work just as much on external affairs as does the little-known group of the 'Friends of the Presidency'. Working in close contact with COREPER, the 'Friends' encompass a number of Ambassadors' Assistants and other delegated functionaries in a counselling role. It is no coincidence that, similar to the Council of Ministers, the structure of this body alters with the political, external or financial subjects under review. Participants are mainly charged with supporting work which includes preparation, scrutiny, networking and interfacing, and a much more detailed assessment and clarification of issues under debate. They often act as a linkage with the Commission which may provide them with papers, proposals and other documents.

The CFSP-related work of these bodies is complemented by the Commission as an associate and with a non-exclusive right of initiative and, one hopes in the interest of the new President Romano Prodi, a less cumbersome distribution of competencies and collision of interests in the future. This has a stronger bearing on external affairs than might be assumed at first glance, especially after one takes into account the Commission's shared right of proposal in CFSP matters and its diplomatic delegations around the globe in more than 123 countries and with 5 international organizations. These EU Missions are responsible for much of the international economic and diplomatic cooperation between the Union and third states. In conjunction with fact-finding operations by the troika and the Commission they form an important part of EU external relations. This is complemented by the diplomatic and consular Representations of both member states (Hayes-Renshaw, Lequesne and Mayor Lopez, 1989: 119–37) and non-member states. There are now more than 170 missions by countries or territories accredited to the EU. Diplomatic cooperation between the Commission and member states, as well as among member states, takes place 'at home' and, in some cases, through embassies in third countries, implemented by national diplomats of the member states. This is often overlooked but forms a vital part of external relations between Brussels and third states, through collective forms of decision-making and informal habits and practices akin to *engrenage*. This term refers to the practice of involving national civil servants with the work of the Commission and is also known as 'bureaucratic interpenetration' or 'enmeshing'. It is related to – but not to be confused with – the *Comitology* practice in the relationship between the Council of Ministers, Committees and the Commission.

The situation for any incumbent Presidency representing the EU in CFSP matters during six months in office is a minefield of demands at home and within the Union. It is also a chance to transfer a particular issue or style on to the EU level. This often functions as a national shopwindow and can be a highly successful and rewarding, but also a time-consuming and demanding, exercise. One of the examples where it can, however, occasionally go wrong, was the attempt, during the 1998 British Presidency, to bring the concepts of an 'ethical foreign policy' and a 'code of conduct for arms sales' to the Union, while at the same time providing the Indonesian military with fighter planes which were subsequently used in East Timor when the territory was preparing for a referendum about autonomy/independence. But a new Presidency also imprints a certain management culture on the Council and brings with it the temptation to make the Presidency into a public event for the country organizing the European Council at the end of the term. This tension goes hand-in-hand with EU internal expectations, particularly towards the smaller member states, and is largely hostage to both internal priorities and external events. Thus, EU enlargement, reform through Agenda 2000 and EMU have been on the priorities list of a number of recent Presidencies. Outside these projects, which demand strong attention because they have been classified as historic chances, the importance attached to external relations and CFSP wavers between occasional statements and a strong focus. National and colonial histories may play a role in the choice of region or activity prioritized and sometimes a country or a region moves in and out of the foci of successive Presidencies on the grounds of global events. EU policy towards Asia (Wiessala, 1999a: 92–112) or Latin America are examples of these 'floating' priorities, particularly since the currency crises of 1997/98. Sometimes prioritization of topics is down to an incumbent who wants to 'impose a particular topic on colleagues, or to ride an individual minister's hobbyhorse' (Hayes-Renshaw and Wallace, 1997: 135, 145). As far as the promotion of further Presidency reform goes, some ideas, such as the appointment of a person responsible for CFSP, and the change to the rotation scheme, have already been put into practice. It remains to be seen whether monetary union and EU enlargement will strengthen other concepts, such as an extension of the troika to a piatnika (the collaboration of *five*, instead of *three* member states within certain policy areas) and the idea of Presidencies led by a team of different countries.

Conclusion and future prospects

The dynamics and reform of the EU's internal development impinges on external relations and foreign policy; it is not possible to conceive of the latter without the former. The EU has moved away from a civil and economically-oriented body and has developed a much stronger identity on the international scene. It interacts on a global scale, with both states and groups of states and international organizations. This has been necessitated by external events and by the export of values and internal priorities and reforms of the Union and their 'externalization'.

In addition to establishing trade and aid frameworks and development and humanitarian policies, the EU has expanded from informal habits of political cooperation to a highly regulated and formalized foreign policy. This part of the Union's activities is, however, still firmly rooted in the area of intergovernmentalism, whereby member states work together without creating an overarching body with binding powers over them. This is only changing very slowly and causes the EU to be reactive, rather then proactive, in its foreign policy. Staying with the misleading but very widespread 'pillar' model, the very considerable strength the Union has developed in its central pillar comprising the European Communities, is far from sufficiently balanced in the deficient 'second' pillar of CFSP. Current attempts at 'communitarization' of more policy areas, such as Schengen or immigration, have left this imbalance mainly intact. It is precisely the Union's strength in pillar 1 that pulls it down in pillar 2. In spite of some remarkable foreign policy successes of the Union, a 'capability–expectations gap', separating its ability to achieve things from expectations, is, with some qualifications, still apparent. Nevertheless, the portrayal of an EU that speaks 'not with one voice, but increasingly like a choir' is gaining more and more currency. More generally, the parallel and opposite models of EU governance represented by intergovernmentalism and supranationalism seem to have become more irreconcilable and have the potential to push the EU in two opposite directions at the same time. It may be time, during and after the 2000 IGC (at the time of writing), to be more 'maximalist', to revisit the 'pillar' structure altogether and to go beyond mere institutional reform.

For the Common Foreign and Security Policy, one of the most important conclusions therefore has to be that a CFSP that deserves the 'C', can only be advanced if member states understand the interrelationship and potential for mutual benefit between their national interests and those of the EU and – more importantly – act upon this understanding. In CFSP matters, the flexibility that has otherwise been recognized by Amsterdam needs, in the short to medium term, to be translated into action and voting procedures. Different perceptions of national sovereignty and identity, while rightly protected by Maastricht and Amsterdam, must go hand in hand with the removal of the obstacles of unanimity, or consensus, which is still the order of the day. In foreign policy, as in many other areas of EU activity explored throughout this book, much depends on the political will demonstrated by the member states and on faster reflexes in the face of challenges and crises. It cannot be denied that important steps have already been taken, not least towards the funding of the CFSP.

Views on the merits of an EU 'speaking with one voice' are changing but need to go further, in order for a more comprehensive externalization of these processes to take place. New Commissioners and a High Representative contain the potential for conflicting interests, but also for a redefinition of the EU's identity, which may, in time, translate into a clearer understanding of its external reflections. This is a step in the right direction in times of a common currency and the prestige that enlargement brings. But whether the trend towards abstentionism will fulfil the potential for a more constructive EU remains, at the very least, doubtful. It seems that at the current time of transition from one millennium to another, the search for the EU's true meaning and its mirror-image in external relations is an ongoing process.

CHAPTER FIVE

The Problems and Prospects of the European Union's Social Dimension

Jack Hampson

The social dimension of the European Union (EU) is still relatively underdeveloped and, indeed, it was claimed in the mid-1990s that 'it remains rudimentary' (Pierson and Leibfried, 1995: 3). In terms of social provision at the level of EU government, this is clearly the case but there has been evident growth in regulatory powers, if not in direct social expenditure. In addition, taking a broad definition of social policy, there is a long history of intervention for social purposes via the Structural Funds and the Common Agricultural Policy (CAP). Nevertheless, despite the formal recognition of a 'social dimension' in the 1990s, it is the lack of development which has been the most evident feature. In terms of study, however, there has been a huge output of academic literature on the social dimension, with many official publications of the European Commission. A wide spectrum of views has been a noticeable feature of this research and many scenarios have been put forward, as either normative statements or predictions. In a short chapter on the current problems and prospects of the EU social dimension, space does not permit the inclusion of extensive historical material, nor much specific analysis of particular areas of social provision; instead, a critical assessment of the various 'scenarios' will be made, with a concluding section exploring the likely future of social policies at EU level. As a structure for the analysis of scenarios, the chapter will analyse the most ambitious, 'maximalist' proposals and then move towards an evaluation of 'minimalist' strategies for a social dimension. Prior to the assessment of these scenarios, however, there will be a preliminary section on the role of the EU. It is necessary to discuss the 'federal' role of the EU.

The EU and federalism

The approach taken in this chapter is that the EU should be viewed within a framework of federalism. Whatever the powers of the EU may be, its existence is sufficient, *for the specific purposes of this chapter*, to regard it as a level of government in a federal structure (it is acknowledged that other contributors would find this an inappropriate description of the EU for their specific purposes). In a different phrase but following a similar approach, the EU can be included in a 'multi-tiered system of governance' (Pierson and Leibfried, 1995). Nevertheless, the history of the EU is clearly different from the development of individual member states, so it is important to be aware of this when making comparisons between the EU and federal countries, such as Germany and the USA. In addition, a federal structure is consistent with various models of welfare state regimes. Although frequently identified as 'conservative' and 'corporatist', Germany has been an early developer of social policy in different periods of history and, in general, it is renowned for its comprehensive range of policies; by contrast, the USA is a classic example of the liberal, residual welfare state regime (Esping-Andersen, 1990). Recently, the UK has become more federalist with devolution of powers to Scotland and Wales, so federal structures can vary as political change takes place. While ideological and political factors may have shaped the nature of social policy in particular countries, much analysis of federalism has taken place on technical, economic and functional grounds, so it is worth examining briefly some of the literature.

In broad terms, the study of 'fiscal federalism' offers some insights into the potential for each level of government in a federal structure. Writing entirely within an American context, Oates has claimed that the highest level should have the 'primary responsibility for macro-economic policies' (Oates, 1972). For several strong economic reasons, this argument has been widely supported and its relevance to the EU is evident; economic and monetary union has now been accepted as essential at the EU level. On the 'fiscal function of distribution', there are some interesting arguments which can be related to the EU. First, as Oates argues for the USA, the capacity for redistribution at local or regional levels of government is limited (Oates, 1972). Thus, if poor areas try to relieve their own poverty by aggressive taxation policies, they will drive away higher income groups and so reduce the resources available. Hence, on technical/economic grounds, responsibility for redistribution needs to be at a higher level of government. Similar arguments apply to countries within the EU, but the extent of the problem does depend on the degree of mobility of labour and capital. In addition, relatively poor EU member states, such as Greece and Portugal (see Chapter 12 in respect of Portugal), will only have limited opportunities for internal redistribution; in the same way as poor local areas, they too will need redistribution from a higher EU level.

Following the same 'fiscal functions' approach (Musgrave and Musgrave, 1976), the third role of the state concerns 'allocation'. Analysis of this function suggests that responsibilities should be linked with the spatial effects of the various goods and services. Some examples are fairly easy to distinguish (i.e. defence at a high level of government and street lighting at a low level). For social services and even social security, the distinctions are less obvious and the choices greater. Much more recently, with the revival of the concept of subsidiarity as a guiding principle for the EU, similar problems have arisen. The definition of subsidiarity is straightforward enough (see Spicker, 1991) but it is difficult to operationalize for social provision. Both the allocation function and subsidiarity require additional principles such as efficiency, equity and autonomy before any firm guidance can be given on the appropriate level of government for responsibility (Kleinman and Piachaud, 1993). In the case of subsidiarity, there is also the extra dimension of deciding horizontally between the private sector and the public sector, as well as choosing the appropriate vertical level (Spicker, 1991).

An early analysis of fiscal federalism in relation to the EU was included in the MacDougall Report of the 1970s (European Commission, 1977). Similar functional and economic analysis was undertaken and the results favoured extensive EU involvement in areas already identified, such as defence and macro-economic management. On the social dimension, the criterion of economies of scale was not considered important, but the Report did recognize the emerging issue of spillovers or externalities, especially in relation to the migration of labour. More recent literature has also emphasized the impact of spillovers and the implications for public intervention. In other respects, the MacDougall Report was more realistic than earlier proposals for harmonization and it did not foresee much scope for direct social provision at the EU level.

Overall, therefore, a review of the technical, functional and economic approaches to federalism does not reveal a strong role for the EU level of government in terms of the social dimension. The allocation of services such as health care, education and housing cannot be justified on economic criteria apart from the influence of spillovers. For social security and wider policies of redistribution, the scope is greater but again it is in the field of spillovers that the most likely intervention is necessary, with the mobility of labour the most important factor; further redistribution in favour of people or geographical areas is more dependent on the degree of political homogeneity and ideological influences.

'Maximalist' proposals

In general, maximalist proposals for a social dimension are associated with an institutional model of welfare at the level of the EU and the advocacy of a 'social democratic' welfare state regime (Esping-Andersen, 1990). Before commenting on such proposals, however, it is important to recognize an even more ambitious perspective. In a strong challenge to the excessive focus on economic and monetary issues, an interest group, the European Foundation on Social Quality, has been formed (Beck *et al.*, 1998). The key concept of 'social quality' is defined as a standard by which EU policies can be assessed; in addition, it is claimed that social quality should be the goal of both economic and social policy (Beck *et al.*, 1998: 3). Although the intention of the group is to link economic and social concerns, it is a challenge to the assumed subordination of social policy to economic policy and so it can be interpreted as clear support for a strategy of market-correction. In assessing this approach, however, it is difficult to see how the concept of social quality can be operationalized and it does not provide as sharp a critique of the economy as, for example, that of Hirsch (1977). More critically, Jones, C. (1999) comments on the 'deep-rooted aspirations' and the 'righteousness of observations' associated with the social quality lobby but she casts doubt on the reality of its propositions.

Similar airs of unreality surround proposals for the creation of a supranational welfare state, in which the EU would be the highest level of a fully federalist structure but, importantly, would be directly involved in social provision. This has been termed an 'institutional model of welfare' equivalent to the federal level of the US Government (Weale, 1994: 7). There is, however, some confusion over the language used in this approach and there are also some fundamental questions to be asked over the nature of federalism. First, there is a danger of equating Weale's institutionalist position (Weale, 1994: 16) with the 'institutional-redistributive' model of Titmuss (1974); the latter has been updated and amended by Esping-Andersen (1990) into the 'social democratic' welfare state regime associated with Scandinavia. As indicated earlier in this chapter, a federalist structure can be consistent with different models of welfare state regimes, so it is important to distinguish structure from regime type. A strong 'maximalist' proposal for a social dimension in the EU would combine the two characteristics, i.e. an acceptance of the highest level of government at the EU level with the implementation of social democratic principles. A 'minimalist' strategy could accept the federalist role for the EU but link this with much less interventionist social policies.

The second problem to be considered is the nature of federalism and the extent to which comparisons can be made between the EU and individual member states. According to Pierson and Leibfried (1995: 7), the EU is part of a multi-tiered system of governance rather than an international agreement. On the other hand, they also claim that: 'The European Union is not, and undoubtedly will not become, a federal welfare state like those of traditional nation-states' (*ibid.*: 433). Going further and adding to the problems of comparisons, it has been argued that there are different types of federalism; whereas the USA corresponds to the familiar 'vertical' structure, the German case is more 'horizontal', with responsibility shared between the centre and constituent units. In this analysis, the EU is clearly a more horizontal type of federalism, thus limiting the scope for 'maximalist' proposals over a social dimension.

Whatever the complexities in the theoretical analysis of federalism, it has not prevented the advocacy of maximalist proposals for the EU. For example, Lipietz (1996) has put forward several policy suggestions which amount in total to an 'alternative Social Europe'; going beyond social democratic ideology, he proposes a combination of Keynesian economic policies with concerns for both equity and ecology. While the optimism of Lipietz cannot be denied, his proposals do appear to be wildly unrealistic (Teague, 1998: 132). Less ambitious but still too optimistic, even the social democratic ideology now seems too much for a maximalist welfare state option. In the face of recent and current economic pressures, the social democratic option has been regarded as no longer feasible (Sykes, 1998: 262). In part, global and regional competition has meant that the economic costs of high levels of social expenditure cannot be maintained. In addition, the requirements of European monetary union have placed restrictions on government spending in most member countries. For some countries such as Sweden, these restrictions have been identified as a main causal factor in the erosion of its welfare state (Gould, 1999). On the other hand, restricted public spending has taken place in Finland irrespective of EU membership (Timonen, 1999). More generally, however, it has been claimed that the pursuit of the Maastricht criteria has had a clear negative impact on the EU social dimension (Teague, 1998).

How far specific elements of a social democratic regime could be extracted for EU intervention is more problematic. Although optimism is shown over the power of political will to implement some generous policies of social provision and to tackle issues such as social exclusion (Cannan *et al.*, 1992; Abrahamson, 1998), the reality is less convincing. Such intervention requires acceptance of the principle of solidarity and of the practice of redistribution; both are very unlikely at the European level and they are rare even at national levels. Within the EU, there is some support for solidarity (European Commission, 1994a) but it is more rhetoric than strong commitment; as Weale points out, the strains of securing redistribution from Berlin to Bangor or from Copenhagen to Calabria are just too much (Weale, 1994: 10). In practical terms, though, the EU has been able to tackle some specific elements of social concern. For example, the three poverty programmes are widely reported as examples of direct intervention by the EU but, in hindsight, the total expenditure involved was small and even here the political will was not sufficient to adopt the fourth programme on social exclusion (Spicker, 1996). Overall, predictions for an EU social dimension based on social democratic ideology are unrealistic on several grounds and proposals would suffer the same fate as recommendations for harmonization in the 1970s.

Intermediate scenarios

Several different scenarios can be classified under this heading. Some are proposals which claim to modify social democratic ideology to the pursuit of a few, limited objectives, while others attempt to combine social concerns with economic requirements; in a more pragmatic way, some scenarios try to tailor social intervention to the likely predictions over political acceptance. In addition, different interpretations of policy processes can be considered within the intermediate framework.

First, there are some scenarios which appear to differ from maximalist proposals but, in reality, are still relatively ambitious. For example, Weale argues in support of a 'progessive liberal model', in which the EU would supplement national welfare states with the provision of a second tier of basic social assistance (Weale, 1994). In reducing the political challenges to national governments, this may be more realistic on political grounds but, as indicated above, the limited attempt towards some degree of vertical redistribution is still a most optimistic scenario. Second, there are commentators who recognize the value of economic criteria in the justification of social policy and they attempt to justify government intervention as 'market-braking' rather than 'market-correcting'. For example, in the debate over the finance of social provision, universalism financed by taxes is contrasted with insurance contributions based on the wages of labour. In resolving this debate, it has been claimed that 'universalistic systems have less distortive effects on markets' and so they can be justified on economic grounds (Vobruba, 1998: 133). Nevertheless, when the same author proceeds to recommend 'generous universalism', the overall strategy is more ambitious than just market-braking (Vobruba 1998: 133).

In a slightly different way from within the EU, the Green Paper (European Commission, 1993a) and the subsequent White Paper (European Commission, 1994a) have both recommended a social dimension which tries to balance social and economic requirements; in addition, the White Paper incorporates minimum standards as a limited objective. The importance of economic criteria in both official publications is evident (Kuper, 1994; Spicker, 1996) but the advocacy of minimum social standards is still relatively ambitious, although it clearly does depend on the levels expected. The rejection of earlier aims such as harmonization is realistic and so is the target of balancing 'convergence with diversity' (European Commission, 1994a: 12). In general, the political pragmatism of the EU can be detected. Since 1994, the objective of minimum standards has been pursued in limited ways consistent with political acceptance, but sometimes this has meant lower standards (Falkner, 1998: 197). As a consequence, however, this kind of intermediate scenario does have more realism than the previous proposals reviewed.

Other interpretations of policy processes place less emphasis on ideology and policy-making; instead they stress the importance of actors and institutions. In broad terms, the focus moves towards the influence of incrementalism. Several interpretations have suggested that the development of social policy owes more to incremental change than grand design. During the period when Jacques Delors was President of the European Commission, it has been argued that the most effective changes took place through the influence of EU institutions. In particular, the strategies of incremental growth adopted by the European Commission (Wendon, 1998) and the increasing significance of decisions made by the European Court of Justice (ECJ) have been highlighted (Pierson and Leibfried, 1995: 11). With the influence of the ECJ, it is important to recognize that social policy development has often occurred more by regulatory powers than actual expenditure (Sykes, 1998: 261–2). Taking all these factors into account, the following prediction seems valid: 'Social policy evolution in the EU is more likely to be the result of mutual adjustment and incremental accommodation than a consequence of central guidance' (Leibfried and Pierson, 1995: 75).

Moving further away from the 'maximalist' end of the spectrum, there are some intermediate scenarios which come closer to supporting minimal change even though they may sound more interventionist. There are several proposals for pragmatic reform which would have the effect of permitting multi-level standards or flexible integration. In order to overcome the problems of trying to force convergence on some absolute minimum standard, one interesting idea is to link the standard with an indicator of economic development; for example, the EU could adopt a directive to maintain social expenditure at an agreed share of GDP (Scharpf, 1997). When examined more closely, this might correspond to existing national practice, so it could simply maintain the *status quo*. Clearly, once again, the precise implications would depend upon the operationalization of the policy. In the current EU of 15 members, ratios of social expenditure to GDP are not far apart, but these figures include both private and public sources of expenditure. A more stringent and ideological approach could create a directive for maintaining the absolute levels of government social expenditure and this would prove much more problematic. Nevertheless, this kind of proposal could prevent further erosion of the welfare state in some member countries where deflationary policies are being followed in pursuit of monetary targets.

An interesting set of proposals for flexible integration comes from the Centre for Economic Policy Research (CEPR) (Centre for Economic Policy Research, 1995) and this can be located towards the minimalist end of the intermediate framework. The proposals include a mix of agreed intervention and voluntary participation. Member states would accept a 'common base' of economic and political intervention by the EU, while remaining schemes would be 'open partnerships' which countries could choose to join. The CEPR proposals place social policies in the latter category, so a variety of optional partnerships might emerge. Clearly, this could lead to clusters of member states around particular interests or even groupings based on political and economic differences. Since January 1999, the launch of the single currency has had just such an effect with a division between the 11 participants and the 4 countries outside. For Teague, fragmentation would lead to chaotic competition and such flexible integration would become the 'nadir for the European social model' (Teague, 1998: 134). On the other hand, the EU in the twenty-first century will soon expand its membership to embrace more widely differing countries, so flexible patterns of integration might be necessary; if not, the impasse of convergence could stultify social development. Given the existing diversity of welfare state regimes, proposals for a variety of optional schemes could prove attractive. As a specific example of potential flexible integration, the development of health care might profit from two optional schemes of integration, one relating to social insurance and the other to national health services.

Overall, the range of intermediate scenarios is considerable. From the approximations to social democracy to the above proposals which permit variety and flexibility, there are many possibilities for predictions. Before giving some conclusions, we will now consider a number of options which will be categorized as 'minimalist'.

'Minimalist' proposals

After more than forty years since the Treaty of Rome, any proposals for 'minimalist' change need to be placed in a relative context. Given the extent of political and economic integration, minimalist proposals are effectively suggesting little development from a changing *status quo*. As argued by many, the *acquis communautaire* is always an important starting point. While backward steps are logically possible, an assumption of this chapter is that such a direction is unrealistic. In terms of the social dimension, this assumption is even more valid since progress towards EU involvement has clearly been limited, and so there are few backward steps to take. As a result, one of the scenarios offered by Kleinman and Piachaud (1993) can be rejected; they considered the option of a 'customs union' as a possibility, in which case there is no need for any social policies at all (Kleinman and Piachaud, 1993: 8). Retrogression to this situation is highly unlikely.

A second scenario of Kleinman and Piachaud is entitled 'economic integration' and although this was written in the context of a post-1992 EU it contains some valuable points of analysis from this chapter's point of view. Following a rigorous economic approach, the authors advance arguments in support of social policy as a facilitator of economic growth; most specifically, European social policy is required in order to promote labour mobility. Admittedly, social policy is still secondary to the economy and so it remains the traditional 'handmaiden' of economic policy (*ibid.*: 9). In broader terms, the EU situation would approximate to that of a liberal or minimal state. In a similar way, Weale (1994) characterizes a 'market liberal' model as the minimal option in his predictions for the social policy of the EU. Unlike the previous analysis, however, a different case is presented for this minimal prediction based on the high costs of making the transition to any kind of European system of welfare state (Weale, 1994: 9). While this case is strong, it does present a negative defence of the minimalist position and it is the positive arguments of Kleinman and Piachaud which are more relevant to other proposals.

The promotion of labour mobility can take several forms and these vary in the extent to which they are 'market-making' or 'market-supporting'. When there are restrictions on the movement of labour, intervention can help to release market forces and it is in this context that many commentators have recognized the contribution made by the ECJ. Legal intervention by the ECJ to eradicate discrimination and to uphold individual rights can be viewed as market-making (Streeck, 1995: 399). Even further intervention by health and safety legislation can be interpreted as action to rectify market failure and similar arguments apply over policies to deal with spillovers. In all these cases, conflict between intervention and market principles is much less evident than for the 'market-correcting' strategies more commonly associated with social policy.

Other proposals for labour mobility which have been defended as acceptable intervention for the market include a variety of supply-side measures. In particular, active labour market policies have been viewed as being superior to regulation through minimum wages (James, 1998) and more generally strategies which promote social investment in human capital have been recommended. In recent years, several countries have adopted approaches to welfare which stress responsibilities as well as rights, so that income maintenance becomes conditional on entry into programmes of training, education and work. The New Deal initiatives in the UK and the minimum income strategies in both France and Portugal conform to these approaches. Although these measures of intervention are not so minimal, they still contribute towards supply-side policies for labour and hence they can be classed as market-supporting.

Placing these suggestions in a broader framework, Streeck (1995: 398) has commented favourably on the 'developing core of minimalist, market-making European social policy', and he has taken this approach further to advocate a social policy regime for the EU which is consistent with his preferred minimalist strategy. Under the general heading of 'neo-voluntarism', Streeck recommends that member states can choose to exit from common standards and, going further, he argues for 'governance by choice'; in this scenario, options instead of uniform standards would be the feature of EU policy (Streeck, 1995: 424–9). Within the parameters of the options, recommendations would replace directives, but these could still be based on perceptions of best practice. In an interesting twist, Streeck also suggests that the principle of subsidiarity, originally adopted in the early 1990s, could be widened to include precedence for the market as an appropriate low level of self-regulation. The overall effects of the Streeck proposals would clearly be greater diffusion, diversity and choice. In relation to business interests, Streeck claims that this kind of 'soft, neo-voluntarist' intervention would be much more acceptable and that market-making is less threatening than state-building (*ibid.*: 431).

Overall, the attractions of market-making or market-supporting policies are evident enough for economic growth and they may be more realistic in terms of the power of market forces. How far economic growth by itself can yield improved living standards for the majority of people is an age-old question and, in addition, the ability of the market to cater for vulnerable sections of society is undoubtedly limited. Nevertheless, predictions for the future of the EU social dimension must be based on reasonable expectations rather than statements of preferences and values. In the conclusion to this chapter, further thoughts are offered on the range of scenarios reviewed and the likelihood of their implementation or development in the near future.

Conclusions and prospects

As indicated above, the prospects of the EU social dimension need to be considered most of all in the light of realistic forecasts. Proposals for maximalist intervention in social affairs are often interesting but generally lacking in relevance to the likely future of the EU. In broad terms, minimalist scenarios have the greatest chance of implementation and those which offer a range of opportunities for member states seem the most realistic. Hence the ideas of Streeck on 'market-making' could have a wide appeal on both social and economic grounds. In a similar spirit of voluntarism, the development of flexible integration might also command sufficient support, depending on the extent of common standards. In consequence, those features of the CEPR proposals which allow optional partnerships should lead to more diversity, diffusion and choice. Since these are exactly the effects predicted by Streeck, the two scenarios share the same characteristics. If some of the 'open partnerships' of the CEPR proposals are popular with member states, they might develop towards common standards in a less threatening way than via EU directives. As a result, flexible patterns of integration could permit more than just minimal change. Nevertheless, this would take place, as Streeck argues, in a softer and more voluntary way.

A further complication in the assessment of the two scenarios above is the likely degree of change in social policies irrespective of the EU social dimension itself. If member states are already moving in similar directions, there could be some convergence in social policies which would facilitate common standards and make the optional partnerships less divisive. Once again, however, there are conflicting views on convergence and equally divergent examples of evidence. In his study of social protection expenditure and labour market policy, Greve (1996) identifies a trend towards convergence; in the case of the former, he presents data revealing a progressive narrowing of differences. Even so, much of this change derives from the development of Southern European countries and beneath the expenditure figures different strategies of social protection persist. Such differences are highlighted by Gough *et al.* (1997) and Daly (1997), both emphasizing the diversity of national experience in social security policies. In broad terms, similarities in the shares of GDP devoted to social protection might help in reaching common standards, while the diverse nature of policies could support the proposals for open or optional partnerships.

Although the source of pressure is different, another kind of convergence can be detected in arguments which stress the impact of economic globalization. When these arguments are analysed in terms of the EU social dimension, however, they tend to reinforce rather than challenge the conclusions given above on the merits of the Streeck and CEPR proposals. For example, Rhodes has commented on the pressures of globalization which threaten generous European welfare states and which favour 'leaner and meaner' levels of social provision (1996: 318). In seeking answers to questions on the future, Rhodes acknowledges the force of the Streeck arguments and market-building initiatives. While debates will continue to rumble over the comparative strengths of economic globalization against the political powers of nation-states, it is evident that market-supporting strategies will ease the tensions and this is even more relevant to the more fragile situation of the EU social dimension.

Looking ahead to a future for the EU with more than 15 member states, the benefits of voluntarism and flexible integration are further enhanced. If the current negotiations succeed, the addition of six more members (Cyprus, Hungary, Poland, Estonia, Slovenia and the Czech Republic) will clearly increase the diversity of the EU. The different social situations and social policies in these countries will extend the range of the EU social dimension and make common standards more difficult to attain. If the five second-wave candidates (Latvia, Lithuania, Slovakia, Romania, Bulgaria) and also Malta are accepted within the EU, these claims are intensified. A European Union of 27 members will need the Streeck principles of diffusion, diversity and choice. Flexible integration with a mix of common standards and optional partnerships comes close to meeting these criteria, especially if the common standards are not set too high and are mostly the result of member state choices. Overall, such a social dimension for the EU will also need to respect the requirements of market-building and market-supporting intervention.

CHAPTER SIX

The Problems and Possible Future Development of a European Identity in the European Union

Geoffrey Edwards

The process of European integration has rarely been smooth. It is, after all, a highly political process, especially as it has moved increasingly into what were traditionally referred to as the areas of 'high politics', of political integration. Indeed, in the aftermath of the problems of ratifying the Maastricht Treaty, there were many doubts about whether the process had outstripped popular support, that the 'permissive consensus' in favour of integration – long presumed by political elites – had dissipated. Maastricht, with its timetable for Economic and Monetary Union (EMU), a common Union citizenship and, for all its qualified tone, the prospect of a common defence policy, appeared to be just too much for a growing number in Denmark, France, Britain and Germany. In the academic literature, the focus moved beyond discussion of the EC/EU's 'democratic deficit' to one of a 'legitimacy deficit' and to problems of establishing a sense of European identity with which to sustain the evolution of the Union. Yet despite the surprise or the alarm this engendered among practitioners and academics, within five years further Treaty reform took place without serious incident. The Treaty of Amsterdam came into force in 1998 and extended European competence into areas such as immigration, asylum and the fight against terrorism, issues that touched on the very basis of the traditional nation-state. And, as significantly, a single currency came into being, on time, on 1 January 1999. Moreover, the decade ended with not only agreement at the Helsinki European Council in December 1999 to seek further institutional reform in the face of further enlargement to 27 member states, but additional agreement to establish a European Rapid Reaction Force. Any uncertainties about popular support for European construction, its acceptance and legitimacy were, it seems, either to be dealt with through further integration or simply outweighed by other considerations.

Tension – perhaps inevitably – continues to surround the integration process. However much the 'logic of integration' has outrun the 'logic of diversity' – to use Hoffmann's phraseology (1995) – to create a European political system (Hix, 1998) or a system of European governance (Kohler Koch, 1999, among others), it has done so in a manner that reinforces complexity, creates ever greater confusion and confirms the distance between government and governed. Despite continued expressions of concern about the possible consequences of this lack of identification of people and process, European governance continues to be opaque, inaccessible and not easily accountable: complexity may be, as the pre-Amsterdam Reflection

Group admitted, 'the price that Europe pays to protect our pluralism' (Reflection Group, 1995: 19). Further enlargement is unlikely to improve matters. But complexity has been bought at a high price in so far as it has been a major factor in inhibiting or undermining understanding and/or support for the integration process, regardless of Amsterdam and perhaps Paris, 2000. As Mark Leonard (1998) has pointed out, opinion polls seem to suggest that the public would like to see the EU tackle big issues such as war and peace, unemployment and crime. The political debate, however, more often degenerates into spats over beef or taxes that affect a minute proportion of the population. This focus on detail rather than the 'big' issues 'disconnects' the people from government. It raises the level of uncertainty and discontent about Europe and the role of national governments. Not surprisingly, voters, especially in European and regional elections, have become increasingly unpredictable in their support for traditional parties, which at the national level are found increasingly wanting.

Identity and context

Lack of popular identification with the construction of Europe has been a constant concern of decision-makers even while they have continued their focus on greater efficiency and effectiveness in the detail of policy-making. It was a point made by Leo Tindemans in the mid-1970s in his report *European Union*:

> No one wants to see a technocratic Europe. European Union must be experienced by the citizen in his daily life. It must make itself felt in education and culture, news and communications ... It must protect the rights of the individual and strengthen democracy through a set of institutions which have legitimacy conferred on them by the will of our peoples. The image of Europe ... must demonstrate to those within and without the solidarity of our peoples and the values of our society. (1976: 12)

It was a theme continued a decade later by the Adonnino committee in their report on *A People's Europe* (1985), a report drawn up in response to a declaration by the European Council that: 'it [is] essential that the Community respond to the expectations of the people of Europe by adopting measures to strengthen and promote its identity and its image both for its citizens and for the rest of the world' (Adonnino, 1985).

Just less than a decade after that, the Reflection Group, set up to prepare for the Amsterdam Intergovernmental Conference (IGC), wrote that one of the key challenges was 'the need to ensure that European construction becomes a venture to which citizens can relate' so that as 'the Union's principle internal challenge is to reconcile itself with its citizens ... enhancing its legitimacy in their eyes will have to be the prime objective of the coming reform' (Reflection Group, 1995: 36). While opposition to the Amsterdam Treaty may have been limited, this was probably not because it was clear, concise and fully comprehensible. The Treaty was as opaque and impenetrable as might have been expected, with 14 Protocols and 40 Declarations also attached to it, a record which added 'nothing to the text's readability' as the then Commission President, Jacques Santer, pointed out (Santer, 1997).

Engaging the public in the integration process has thus been a perennial theme which appears to have grown no easier to tackle. But in the mid-1990s it was regarded as particularly significant because it was both a symptom of, and a further contributory factor to, wider questions relating to the nature and capabilities of the modern nation-state and its governance. The paper produced in September 1994 by the leaders of the CDU/CSU group in the Bundestag summed up the wider tensions very acutely. While better known for its advocacy of a 'core–periphery' approach to integration, the Schäuble and Lamers Report suggested that within the EU there was:

- A growing differentiation of interests, fuelled by differences in the level of socio-economic development which threatens to obscure the basic commonality of interests ...
- A process of profound structural economic change. With its mass unemployment, which it will be impossible to overcome in the short term, this crisis poses a threat to already overstretched social systems and social stability. The economic crisis is one aspect of the general crisis of modern society in the West ...
- An increase in 'regressive nationalism' in (almost) all member countries, which is the product of deep-seated fears and anxieties caused by the internal crisis of modern society and by external threats, such as migration. Fear and anxiety tempt people to seek, if not a solution, then at least a refuge in a return to the nation-state and all things national.
- The highly debilitating effect of the enormous demands placed on national governments and parliaments by the above problems. (CDU/CSU Fraktion, 1994: 2)

Some of these problems were far from new, though in combination they produced an intensity that suggested crisis. Some commentators had already drawn the conclusion that the crisis was a fundamental one of legitimacy (see, for example, Habermas, 1976). Issues such as whether the welfare state remained viable in Western Europe, as well as growing structural unemployment, compounded by the dealignment of traditional class and party voting, created an environment in which anti-party and anti-elite attitudes had become increasingly common (Kaase and Newton, 1995). Moreover, the collapse of communism had removed readily available comparisons and contrasts that had bolstered Western governments. In Germany, the possibility of waves of migration from East to West after the collapse of Soviet domination – and of the USSR itself – magnified the complications of a society having difficulties in dealing with reunification, rising unemployment figures and an already large number of migrant workers. In France, too, the fear of large numbers of migrants crossing from North Africa had clearly begun to benefit the extreme Right. As one sociologist has put it: 'Migration, temporary or permanent, suggests that cultural boundaries and jurisdictional boundaries are not coincident, their disjunction producing racist effusions throughout Western Europe' (Cohen, 1998: 33).

Given such concerns, it is not surprising that a greater degree of attention should be focused on the EU, its effectiveness and legitimacy, its 'vocation' and its identity. Thomas Jansen has pointed to three particular difficulties the EC/EU as a political and democratic system has experienced in creating and expressing any sense of a European identity. He listed them as: the absence of a consensus on Europe's constitution or its *finalité politique*; the absence of a consensus on its geographical dimension; and uncertainties concerning the EU's *raison d'être*, with peace in Western Europe taken for granted and the compelling force of the Cold War now lost (Jansen, 1997: 5). These, together with the uncertainties and challenges posed by globalization, provide a useful basis for much of this chapter's subsequent analysis. Of key importance, however, has been the realization on the part of practitioner and commentator alike that the concept of a European identity is intimately tied up not only with notions of the legitimacy of the European enterprise, but also with concepts of state and statehood and national identity. The irony is that the model for creating a European identity has often been that of European nation-state building, states established very largely in opposition to, and frequently through bloody conflict with, their neighbours.

Ends and means

The absence of a consensus on Europe's ultimate constitution has not always been regarded as problematic. Embarking on a *Journey to an Unknown Destination*, to use the title of Andrew Shonfield's BBC Reith Lectures in 1972, was a theme strongly supported by many practitioners. Shonfield himself (then Director of Chatham House) wrote:

> I do not believe that we can establish in advance of the event the formal power and the institutions which will ensure that we manage Europe's future crises. What we can do is to create a mood and a set of habits which will make it feasible in a crisis situation to engage in joint European action on a scale that we have never approached before. (1973: 96)

But while muddling through from one crisis to the next might be a characteristically British trait (and one is tempted to add, 'and look where it sometimes gets the UK!'), it is hardly one that can long pertain to a new polity of which expectations are somewhat higher. After all, national traits and stereotypes have taken centuries to mature (or fabricate). Behind them has been a relatively homogenous culture defined through language and education, sustained by political tradition and protected by a set of constitutional rules. Creating a mood or even habits in the absence of a reliable set of rules is far from easy, even when considered desirable. And it is, of course, the lack of consensus on quite what is desirable that has frequently defeated the best efforts of committees and their rapporteurs to create a new mood. But the Shonfield approach of pragmatic decision-making was very much the norm. Jean Monnet, for example, while believing that the process of integration would end in a United States of Europe, went on to write in his *Memoirs*:

> but I see no point in trying to imagine today what political form it will take. The words about which people argue – federation or confederation – are inadequate and imprecise. What we are preparing, through the work of the Community, is probably without precedent. The Community itself is founded on institutions, and they need strengthening; but the true political authority which the democracies of Europe will one day establish still has to be conceived and built. (1978: 523)

But it was precisely the Monnet approach that had become such a problem in the aftermath of Maastricht. The 'Monnet method' of a technocratic elite deciding policy with national administrative elites became synonymous with 'integration by stealth'. However unreasonable or irrational the reaction to the Treaty might have appeared to those elites, the public appeared to be waking up to the depth to which integration had proceeded. When faced with the institutional and legal arrangements and procedures of the Maastricht pillar structure – together with its opt-outs and its protocols and declarations – few probably made any further attempts to understand it. But without clear, openly agreed guidelines about the purpose and objectives of the venture and its likely impact on more familiar forms of government, they were suspicious.

It was perhaps the elites' misfortune that the suspicion evoked by Maastricht was symptomatic of a wider discontent with government in much of Western Europe. But it should not have been quite so surprising. After all, the Maastricht Treaty reforms were being introduced only five years after the earlier Treaty revision in the Single European Act. However much the Court of Justice among others declared the Treaties to be a constitutional charter, it was an odd constitution that appeared to be under constant revision, certainly alien to national constitutional practices – even that of the British with its still largely unwritten constitution. Moreover, Maastricht called for a further Intergovernmental Conference (IGC), which resulted in the Amsterdam Treaty. And even before that Treaty had been ratified, there were calls for a further round of negotiations on the institutional reforms necessary to cope with enlargement that Amsterdam had shirked – the prospect not being urgent enough to force decisions. Hence the decision at the Helsinki European Council in December 1999 to establish a further IGC devoted, primarily, to the issue of institutional reform. If, in Brussels and national capitals, there were mutterings about 'IGC fatigue', there was an equally understandable lack of excitement and sense of indifference among the wider public.

National governments and the European 'vocation'

But to many such as Jansen, long involved in the European People's Party and the integration movement, 'It is incumbent on the European Union as a political and democratic organization to ensure that its citizens and peoples not only understand but actually espouse the spirit of the Union if they ultimately are to identify with it' (1997: 1). It is not that the EC/EU's institutions have been dilatory in their attempts to change the situation. The European Parliament's Hahn Report on Radio and Television Broadcasting put it particularly clearly and simply (and was cited by the Commission in 1984 in its own Green Paper, *Television Without Frontiers*):

> European unification will only be achieved if Europeans want it. Europeans will only want it if there is such a thing as a European identity. A European identity will only develop if Europeans are adequately informed. At present, information via the mass media is controlled at national level. (cited by Collins 1994: 95).

The situation was little different a decade or so later. As Piet Dankert, like Jansen similarly long involved in European affairs, though from the left rather than the right, put it: 'the European Union is beyond the immediate scope of the European citizen, as one has to pass via the national level in order to reach it' (Dankert, 1998: 65). And at the national level, governments have not always been able or willing to enlighten their electorates about the direction and purpose of Treaty reform. Even more federally-inclined governments have not always found it politic to explain contemporary 'Europe', preferring to rely on familiar references to war and reconciliation. There is, too, the temptation frequently to take credit as a national government for any policy success, whether they originated domestically or at the European level: after all, governments usually wish to be re-elected. It is equally tempting to blame others for failures, whether the scapegoats are the forces of globalization or, closer to home, European institutions, and especially, of course, the European Commission. One of the most damning criticisms of this tendency is that of Christoph Meyer in his study of the EU's communication deficit, where he concludes that:

> The institutional roles and decision-making procedures are fraught with considerable ambiguity and complexity, while the member States as the final arbiters use public communication to bolster their legitimacy at the expense of the Commission. As a result of these arrangements, public debate has neither found an appropriate forum nor does it feature decision-makers who can be held accountable for their views as well as policy outcomes. What has not been publicly communicated can neither be challenged nor approved in the public space. (Meyer, 1999: 636)

The crisis that led to the Santer Commission's resignation revealed the confusion that can surround decision-making in the EU. For its part, the Committee of Independent Experts concluded that 'it is becoming difficult to find anyone who has the slightest sense of responsibility' (1999, cited by Meyer: 633). Mismanagement in the Commission was complemented by muddle in the European Parliament (EP) and its party groups over whether to dismiss the Commission. There was also a not wholly successful attempt by member governments to eschew any responsibility for what was going on: as some in the media reminded them, governments were responsible for appointing Commissioners (see, for example, the *Financial Times*, 19 March 1999). But it is also the case that some 80 per cent or more of European proposals are agreed at the level of the Committee of Permanent Representatives (COREPER). The degree of impenetrability of the bureaucratic machine is thus considerable. But this does not simply reflect the detailed technical nature of so much of European legislation; it is also symptomatic of the degree to which national governments are prepared to delegate decision-making away from too much public attention. To quote Meyer, again, such practices 'enable national ministers to watch European debates from the sidelines, change their stance in case of criticism, and increase their leeway for giving final outcomes a positive "spin"' (1999: 635) Moreover, as Meyer, following Scharpf and others, also points out, with the extension of qualified majority voting, governments can hide behind majority decision-making in the Council in the face of any adverse domestic criticism.

Whether or not one can conclude with Moravcsik (1993) that this strengthens national governments is more debatable. Moravcsik, with some support from Wincott (1995), concludes that the EU's institutional structure 'strengthens the autonomy of national leaders *vis-à-vis* particularistic social groups within their domestic polity' (Moravcsik, 1993: 507). The emphasis is on the ability of governments within the framework of 'two-level games'. Wincott, for his part, added that:

> A brief analysis of elite debate and public opinion in the UK would show that the terms of the discussion of European integration are hopelessly confused . . . An explanation of this . . . can be constructed around the notion of a long-term tendency of obfuscation of European integration by UK elites with the objective, in part at least, of achieving autonomy from domestic opinion. (Wincott, 1995: 601)

There is, too, an argument that governments have used European legislation to strengthen their position *vis-à-vis* their national parliaments. Very few national parliaments have organized themselves to be able to monitor effectively all that their governments have agreed in Brussels. Given the scale of European legislation, especially during the 1980s with the efforts to complete the Single Market by 1992, that may be understandable. But if some 80 per cent of national economic and social legislation does now derive from European sources, there is significant scope for confusion on the part of the public. The greater sense of powerlessness engendered in some politicians has been compounded in the eyes of the public by bewilderment and doubt, not only over the basic rules governing the EC/EU, but also about whose law it is. That in turn creates an element of doubt about the involvement of the Court of Justice in what appears to be national legislation – a doubt not necessarily redounding either to the benefit of national governments if found to be in breach of EC law, or to the enhancement of the Court and Europe's legal order.

Others, however, notably Mazey and Richardson (1997: 234), have taken the alternative view that, if not altogether prisoners of interest groups, governments are increasingly circumscribed in their actions by national and increasingly transnational interests. The logic of the argument could be, to follow a neo-functionalist approach, a gradual shifting of expectations on the part of interest groups to the European level and with it a shift of loyalties to the decision-making process and thus to further integration. Further interest group involvement develops as the process deepens, giving a greater sense of legitimacy to the venture and thus a deeper sense of identity. But it is an identification on the part of especially economic interests and does not necessarily extend further to non-elites and the public at large (see Jachtenfuchs *et al.*, 1997; Lord, 1998; Edwards, 1998). Moreover, as Mazey and Richardson also point out, policy outcomes in the EU process are often uncertain, and they draw the analogy of garbage-can politics. In addition, they also point to the relevance of US politics (at least in relation to lobbying), quoting Heinz *et al.* (1993) that 'by creating structures to control or adapt to uncertainty, they [interest groups] have contributed to the development of a more complex and rapidly changing policy environment' (cited in Mazey and Richardson, 1997: 231). That conclusion does not lend particular stability to an emerging rather than an established polity.

The complexity of EU decision-making also has an impact on government by creating additional problems of coherence and consistency and, therefore, of transparency. The multitude of interest groups and points of access in the process create their own tensions within governments, sometimes reinforcing existing problems of coordination or creating new ones. Whether on major or more ordinary proposals, the EU tends to work through package deals that place a premium on both the role of heads of government and the unity of their governments. Much of the decision-making that takes place within the EU, however, allows for considerable disaggregation of individual national governments and departments. Different departments have different networks and channels of communication and send different messages through them. Heads of government may as a result find themselves constrained as to what they can then negotiate even if they may have sought to construct their preferences in a more Moravcsikian manner. But in either case, the consistent pursuit of a particular overall goal may not always be the result. Even Helmut Kohl when Chancellor, despite his frequently declared support for a federal Europe, sometimes recognized the need for more nationalistic rhetoric – in lambasting the European Court of Justice, for example, for going beyond its mandate – or was prevented from pursuing more integrationist goals by domestic opinion – as in his need to backtrack on qualified majority voting during the final stages of the Amsterdam IGC because of pressures from the *Länder* governments. National governments for a whole variety of reasons frequently send out mixed signals to their electorates about the EU and the objectives and role of the member state within it.

Globalization and unbundling liberal compromises

The relative incoherence and often a defensiveness on the part of government is reinforced by the closely interrelated nature of domestic, European and global challenges. If the constitutional division of responsibilities was left deliberately vague or complicated under the Treaties, so too were policy outcomes. Technological change and new global challenges, as Schäuble and Lamers pointed out, have helped to create a crisis in modern society. John Gerard Ruggie, when comparing the post-Cold War situation to that after the Second World War, suggested that then there had been a compromise: international economic liberalization whose effects for domestic societies 'were cushioned by the newly acquired domestic economic and social policy roles of governments' (Ruggie, 1995: 508). Now, compromise of what he termed 'embedded liberalism'

> has come around full circle. Once again, governments are groping to find a mutually compatible set of policies for international and domestic stabilisation. However, they are doing so in an institutional context wherein little remains the same except an implicit normative commitment to sustain both, and in an international political environment in which their common enemy is not a clear and present geopolitical threat, but more diffuse fears of the consequences of policy failure (*ibid.*: 525).

For the member states, integration within the EC/EU has been regarded as an essential part of that policy response. But the process of integration has highlighted the dilemma facing the nation-state in terms of both sovereignty and territoriality.

Integration and national control?

The puzzle confronting the European member states has been how to pursue integration – for a variety of economic, political and cultural reasons – with all that it entails in terms of strengthening supranational institutions and decision-making while at the same time retaining the appearance before their electorates of being substantively in control. The puzzle and its implications for a European identity can be illustrated by looking at aspects of the Single European Act (SEA), cultural policy, the Common Foreign and Security Policy (CFSP) and immigration policy. Each policy area has profound implications for the nature of the traditional nation-state and its continuing role and identity.

The SEA sought, *inter alia*, to expedite the completion of the Single Market through the extension of qualified majority voting. For some (Andrew Moravcsik (1998), for example), this was a rational response by national governments to the demands of their own domestic interests. Others, such as Maria Green Cowles (1995), have argued (persuasively) that the SEA was very much more a response determined by European business groups exercising influence over governments.

Certainly, member states throughout the 1980s and into the 1990s had to find new responses to competition from the USA and Japan and the other so-called 'Asian Tigers'. Creating a Single Market base from which European companies could better compete globally was one outcome. But much of that competition was undertaken by multinationals, increasingly able to exploit new communications technology, to move vast sums of capital at speed, etc. The result was that governments faced further difficulties in exercising effective macro-economic management, with fiscal policies blunted by the need to attract inward investment, and with taxation tending to fall more heavily on smaller and medium-sized enterprises and on the less skilled, less mobile sectors of society (Panic, 1998). At the same time as the size and reach of financial markets undermined the role of governments in determining exchange rates, the Single European Market also strengthened the 'logic of integration' towards a single currency. Increasingly, if not ineluctably, the EU was moving (not, of course, exclusively, but still significantly) into issues of economic management, employment and social welfare, the very issues on which governments are elected or defeated at the polls. It was perhaps impossible in such circumstances not to try to seek national triumphs. This was especially so in view of the more extreme 'globalizing gurus' such as Ohmae, who declared that:

> The nation state has become an unnatural, even dysfunctional, unit for organizing human activity and managing economic endeavor in a borderless world. It represents no genuine shared community of economic interests; it defines no meaningful flows of economic activity. (1993: 78)

Exaggerated though such a view might seem to be, globalization with its multiple facets has clearly had a profound impact on the nation-state and integration. Cultural globalization, frequently seen in Europe as synonymous with Americanization, has also been regarded with ambivalence and, during the 1980s, at least in terms of film and television, it turned into a major political issue, which again interacted with the European level. The concern was, as Pragnell has put it, that:

> heavy viewing of programmes from other countries (particularly from the United States with its strong culture or variety of cultures) would over time erode the culture, values and proper pride in their own traditions of the countries of Europe. The fear is also that an undue use of American material would have a similar effect on that common sense of identity in Western Europe as a whole which already exists to a significant extent and which is the aim of European institutions to foster. (Pragnell, 1985: 5, quoted in Khan, 1996)

For the Commission, it was particularly galling since, as its then President, Jacques Delors, told the EP: 'Under the terms of the Treaty we do not have the resources to implement a cultural policy.' Nothing daunted, however, he went on: 'but we are going to tackle it along economic lines. We have to build a powerful European culture industry that will enable us to be in control of both medium and its content, maintaining our standards of civilisation, and encouraging the creative people among us' (Delors quoted by Collins, 1994: 90). With a leading role played by the French, audio-visual policy reached the highest levels of the then European Council. With the strong personal support of President Mitterrand – and against a decidedly reluctant British Prime Minister who viewed the issue more as one of liberalizing a trade in commodities rather than protecting of a national culture – the result was the *Television Without Frontiers* directive, which aimed to sustain (protect) European and especially French (together with minority) cultures by establishing quotas for non-European productions.

If there is a certain irony in the French being obliged to protect their culture through European Council policy, it was not the first time member states had sought to establish an identity distinguishable from that of the USA. In 1973, Dr Kissinger, then US Secretary of State, in what became known as the 'Year of Europe' speech, called for a new Atlantic Charter (Nuttall, 1992: 84–5). In the course of his speech, however, he declared: 'The United States has global interests and responsibilities. Our European allies have regional interests.' This, as Nuttall put it 'hurt the pride not only of the traditional Nation State, but also of the nascent European political persona' (*ibid.*: 86). The result was the 'European Identity Paper' agreed in December 1973 by the European Council's then nine Foreign Ministers, which, while declaring the need to maintain and preserve close ties with the USA, added: 'These ties do not conflict with the determination of the Nine to establish themselves as a distinct and original entity.' Moreover:

> International developments and the growing concentration of power and responsibility in the hands of a very small number of great powers means that Europe must unite and speak increasingly with one voice if it wants to make itself heard and play its proper role in the world. (Nuttall, 1992)

The problem has been, of course, quite how to play such a role and whether and to what extent it entailed 'Europe' remaining simply a 'civilian power' or whether it should acquire the means to use force in pursuit of its agreed policies. Subsequent debates have frequently been loud and public between the 'Atlanticists', led by the British and Dutch intent upon maintaining the primacy of NATO, and the 'Europeanists', led by the French in favour of a European defence and security identity separate from that of the USA. The debate, though, was not always particularly enlightening as to its long-term purpose. Ambiguities grew in the aftermath of the Cold War and the removal of one of the 'great powers': the Maastricht Treaty, for example, declared that the common foreign and security policy (CFSP) 'shall' include all aspects of security 'including the framing of a common defence policy, which might in time lead to a common defence' (Article J.4.1). The prevarication at the behest of the Atlanticists was reinforced by their insistence that Article J.4.4 should also provide for the need to respect the obligations of the North Atlantic Treaty. It was not perhaps surprising that Danish voters among others were a little bewildered as to the Treaty's intentions.

More unfortunately, those who were the object of the EU's CFSP were also confused, not least those in the former republics of Yugoslavia. The disarray of the EU member states and their dependence on the USA to help resolve the war in Bosnia were clear. Yet this resulted in no greater clarity in the Amsterdam Treaty as to the future role of the EU. Nonetheless, the member states did agree that the EU could play a role in the so-called 'Petersberg tasks' drawn up within the framework of the Western European Union (WEU), which included humanitarian assistance, peacekeeping and even peace-making that might involve the use of combat forces. They also agreed, however, that any action could be undertaken by the able and willing, with those either unable or unwilling entitled to abstain – so long as they agreed that the others could go ahead. It does not seem the strongest basis on which to build credibility. Moreover, the conflict in Kosovo saw again Europe's reliance on the USA and NATO. But again, it created a reaction, one that evolved via a British change of heart on the merits of a serious European Security and Defence Identity – as in, for example, the St Malo declaration with the French in December 1998 – to the Helsinki European Council's decisions of December 1999 on establishing a European Rapid Reaction Force and exploring the consequences of dissolving the WEU, not least for those EU member states who have not been WEU members. But even this still leaves considerable confusion about when and how that force can be employed, and quite what role the USA has in the event of any conflict when the Europeans require American intelligence and equipment. The almost simultaneous announcement by the Federal German Government of cuts in its defence budget did not suggest that all member states were committed to any significantly enhanced role. Nonetheless, this stumbling, muddled approach towards a European security and defence policy distinct from NATO illustrates further the changing nature of the EU and, indeed, of the European nation-states.

If the security of Europe is to rest on a new joint effort in terms of military cooperation and integration, its protection from other threats to its stability is also becoming not simply 'Europeanized' but 'Communitarized'.[1] The slow but steady incorporation into the European arena of issue areas such as the fight against international crime, especially terrorism and drug trafficking, and immigration and asylum policies, culminated in the reforms of Amsterdam. Cooperation – albeit behind firmly closed doors – had gradually intensified since the mid-1970s when Justice Ministers instituted a more regular series of meetings to combat terrorism (the so-called TREVI Group) until the Treaty of Maastricht included them and other related groups into the third, intergovernmental pillar, Justice and Home Affairs (JHA – for a history of the development of JHA, see Monar and Morgan, 1994).

However, if there was generally strong public support for combating terrorism and drug trafficking, there was an equally wide sense of unease and dissatisfaction about immigration. What created particular alarm was the inadequacy of EU border controls that might allow, alongside legitimate immigration, huge numbers of illegal immigrants from Central and Eastern Europe and North Africa. This potential influx of 'economic refugees' was linked in the media and public mind to rising unemployment. This was compounded by increasing problems of assimilating immigrants through the usual educational channels and with an intensification of problems in the inner cities. It also coincided with changes in policing methods which appeared to emphasize the involvement of centralized intelligence services rather than the traditional, local forces of law and order (den Boer, 1998). All this, of course, at the same time as the completion of the Single European Market allowed for the free movement of people already in the Union. The growing recognition that free movement within the EU required compensation in the form of a more proactive immigration policy as part of a raft of measures to ensure public security was one of the primary concerns of the pre-Amsterdam Reflection Group. For, as the French Minister for European Affairs put it:

> Major threats loom over our continent, threats to do with illegal immigration and certain types of slave-trading ... from Asia and other Eastern countries. There are other threats, bound up with organized crime, the Mafia and drugs. These are today

> continental, international threats, and, together, we must find answers. But these must be real, not words, incantations or dreams. (Michel Barnier, 14 February 1996)

The significance of this 'communitarization' of 'internal security' issues was not lost on some parties to the negotiations, particularly the UK. Until the Conservative Government's defeat in May 1997, it resisted what it saw as encroachment not on the rights of the individual but on the prerogatives of the nation-state. For the majority of the member states, however, it was a matter less of principle – individual rights were after all to be protected and even enhanced – than of efficiency and effectiveness. On individual rights, the majority were in favour of proclaiming clearly 'such European values as equality between men and women, non-discrimination on grounds of race, religion, sexual orientation, age or disability', and wanted the Treaty to include 'an express condemnation of racism and xenophobia and a procedure for its enforcement'. However, as the Reflection Group's Report went on: 'One of us believes that the rights and responsibilities we have as citizens are a matter for our nation states; reaching beyond that could have the opposite effect to that intended' (Reflection Group, 1995: 22).

Economically, culturally and politically, therefore, the EU and its member states have pursued policies that, if not contradictory, have frequently been ambiguous, confused and confusing. It is perhaps not surprising in such circumstances that it has been difficult to establish a European identity.

Of course, there are those who might question whether such an identity is necessary: whether, in Chris Lord's words, the 'Union will only need a minimal identity limited to the comparatively modest task of regulating relationships between a club of separate national democracies' (Lord, 1998: 109). However, Lord is right to conclude that more than a 'minimalist' identity is necessary in order to ensure the acceptance of the supremacy of Union decisions over national ones in areas where it is competent and to guarantee that the Union is able to resolve conflicts through democratic means, and that it can involve the public in a debate over decisions taken at the European level. Some sense of political identity is necessary, in other words, to ensure both effective and democratic governance within the EU.

The future past

Enlargement is a further massive complication. So far, enlargement has proceeded in slow waves; it now promises to be a flood. And if the institutional structure was stretched, even if with some difficulty and only with significant reforms, from incorporating 6 states to 15, the prospect within a decade or so expanding to over 25 is sometimes daunting. But enlargement itself, of course, has been surrounded by ambiguities. It has been regarded as both an opportunity and a challenge, of vital immediate importance – though not urgent enough to oblige the 1996–97 IGC actually to reach any conclusions on institutional reform. If it has been supported by some, notably the British, as a means of loosening the Union, it has been used by others as a means of deepening the integration process. Despite the superficial attractiveness of a dichotomous relationship between widening and deepening, the majority of governments have determined that enlargement and institutional reform should go hand in hand. And so far they have been successful: each wave of enlargement has been accompanied not only by institutional reform but also by a widening and deepening of the scope of EC/EU policies. However, given the numbers involved in the enlargement to Central and Eastern Europe and the Mediterranean and the varying levels of development, the extent to which past practice offers practical guidance for the future is questionable.

There are, of course, some basic questions that remain unanswered. There have been differences, for example, over who among the countries of Central and Eastern Europe should join and when, with divisions over who might make up any first or second wave of acceding states. If the then Twelve could in 1993 agree to the so-called Copenhagen criteria (i.e. the conditions on which any further enlargement could take place, such as liberalization and democratization and an ability actually to implement the *acquis communautaire*), there were niggling doubts about quite where *Europe* ended. Even beyond the prevarications of the Greeks in pursuit of their own past, there were others too who have not been wholly convinced that Turkey was eligible to join the EU – among Christian Democrat groups in particular – and if so on what conditions. The decision at the Helsinki European Council in December 1999 to accept Turkey as a candidate for future membership (its application having been lodged over a decade earlier) does not exhaust the problems of the geographical limits of Europe – after all the Council of Europe includes Russia (since 1996), as well as Georgia (since April 1999) among its 41 members, Turkey having joined in 1950. Even as a 'mere geographical expression', Europe remains a pretty vague concept.

The ending of the Cold War and the 'velvet revolutions' in Central and Eastern Europe was welcomed, if not with a sense of triumphalism, at least with relief, hope and a profound sense of opportunity. Europe's leaders were strong on the rhetoric of peace and reconciliation, a 'return' of so many to 'Europe' and its values. Yet from the beginning, the EU was determined to protect what it had established with the emphasis on continued stability in Western Europe. The PHARE (Poland and Hungary Economic Assistance and Reconstruction) programme, for example, established in 1990 was no European Marshall Plan (Niemann, 1998); the European Agreements were far from generous in providing a boost to economic liberalization; and, inevitably perhaps, preliminary enlargement negotiations were rapidly reduced to detail. In their Agenda 2000 exercise, for example, the member states seemed intent on maintaining EU expenditure at its existing levels while ringfencing their own receipts *and* beginning the enlargement process (Galloway, 1999). Given the need for changes in key policy areas, not least agriculture and the structural funds, the new member states will be subject to long, varied transitional periods to try to square the circle. As Kohler Koch put it: 'Facing enlargement, institutional reforms are need to preserve the functioning of the Union ... The focus of governments and the European Commission is clearly on output legitimacy: efficiency comes first' (1998). Whether that remains enough to instil legitimacy and create a sense of identity with Europe remains problematic. The welcome to those long divided by the Cold War was not and is not unalloyed; it clearly makes for further complications. Significantly, there has been little change in the 'foundational' rhetoric or 'myth-making' that might characterize the 'input' side of legitimacy that might encompass the challenge posed by enlargement on the output side.

Building on the common heritage of Europe to create a new identity faces, to use Helen Wallace's words, 'the difficulty of dealing simultaneously with the mundane and the metaphysical in the search for legitimacy' (Wallace, 1993: 100). But the metaphysical itself is problematic. European leaders frequently have recourse to genealogy and the foundation of the EU as the means to prevent war ever again breaking out between France and Germany. Lily Gardner Feldman has argued that Franco-German reconciliation was fundamental not simply to the creation of the EU but also to its continuing legitimacy, internally and externally. Internally, she argues: 'the success of peace and reconciliation within the EU has sustained the success and durability of the entire integration project. And it shows how both remain salient values that resonate for European elites and public opinion' (1999: 67). In terms of external legitimacy, she sees the EU as a focus and model for the peaceful resolution of conflict, and quotes Hans van den Broek when one of the Commissioners responsible for external policy, when he said that the EU is: 'a genuine security community in which the very idea of war between any members can be dismissed out of hand. Indeed, I would describe the Community as the greatest confidence-building measure in the history of Europe' (*ibid.*: 68).

In emphasizing the role of reconciliation, Gardner Feldman takes issue with Daniela Obradovic, who has argued that: 'The mythological discourse, so sorely needed for establishing Union policy legitimacy, cannot ... be derived from the Community's foundational ideals: peace, prosperity and supranationality' (1996: 212). Such ideals may not have the same potency for existing member states though they may for the prospective members of Central and Eastern Europe who have somewhat different attitudes towards Germany and Russia and who, with the end of the Cold War, sought to 'rejoin' Europe (Kolankiewicz, 1993). But in Western Europe itself, they may not provide the idealistic rationale for further European construction – and perhaps not even elsewhere in Europe given the tough bargains forced by the Union. But a political generation and more had passed since so many had attended the European Movement's Congress at The Hague in 1948. While Franco-German reconciliation may have been vividly illustrated by Mitterrand and Kohl on the anniversary of the battle at Verdun, German reunification (in part perhaps because of its speed) threatened to reawaken the deep-seated fears derived from past European conflicts.

European integration has not yet reached the stage where such 'slaughters' can now be inscribed as 'family history'. They are too recent and too real to be treated in the way Benedict Anderson has suggested that other more ancient slaughters have been in a national context – as 'reassuring fratricide' that assists in the construct of national genealogies (Anderson, B., 1991: 201). Moreover, even ancient conflicts are not necessarily recalled in order to reinforce the benefits of any present unity. They are more frequently used to point up continued differences. The 'thousand years of British history' about to be 'lost' and to which many Eurosceptics have appealed were, for considerable periods, years of fighting the French; the French, if the hostility created by their ban on British beef in the aftermath of 'mad cow disease' is a sign, are able to raise British passions in a way others cannot (the Germans had maintained a similar ban). But subsuming Europe's historical conflicts is no easy task; there may be a common European heritage, but there is no European 'nation' to appeal to.

Mythologizing the EC/EU's past thus denies current leaders a tool that has been vital in fabricating other, national identities. Creating and sustaining a European identity too distinct from the national has not been a priority. Among the uncertainties created are the ambivalences of member governments, fearful, perhaps, of Eurosceptic claims that integration must be a zero-sum game – that if 'Europe' wins, the member states must lose. In some respects, national leaders over the last decade or so have faced a too uncertain political electorate to forego reliance on national media re-emphasizing national solidarity. But given the sustaining influence of national myths, so heavily dependent on war and the exclusion, usually, of the other European nations that now make up the Union, the lack of priority is becoming counterproductive, a challenge to the efficient working of the Union and its institutions. Perhaps the introduction of the single currency will underscore a common European destiny. EMU and political union are fundamental, radical challenges to the traditional nation-state. There may be little that is new in the political rhetoric that surrounds them, but constant reiteration has been a basic part in building a sense of identity at the national level, not least in periods of particular uncertainty. The problem for Europe, however, is the frequent conflict between cynicism, born in large part out of the past emphasis on the mundane and material, and rhetoric that traces the past without looking to the future. The resulting confusion may well alienate rather than bind.

Note

1. A generalized process that Jan Ole Kiso in *European Voice* (4–10 September 1997) called 'Brusselisation'.

PART III

Problems and Prospects of Selected EU Member States

CHAPTER SEVEN

The Problems and Future of Germany

Joanna McKay

Introduction

The Federal Republic of Germany (FRG), founded in 1949, is ostensibly a very successful state. It is a highly stable democracy, a model federal state, composed of 16 *Länder*, and a good example of consensus politics in action. It has been transformed from a devastated, defeated country at the end of the Second World War into the strongest economy in Europe, and from an enemy into a highly valued friend courted by countries all over the globe. In addition, the events of 1989/90, culminating in German reunification on 3 October 1990, suggested that the FRG was the country the citizens of the other German state, the communist German Democratic Republic (GDR), wanted to belong to too.

But despite post-war Germany's shiny exterior, memories of German history from the first half of the twentieth century are never far below the surface. The past affects German thinking in virtually every policy area, including monetary policy, the welfare state, the electoral system and asylum. And in spite of German politicians' best efforts to convince the wider world otherwise, the country is still equated with the Nazi past, especially in the British media.

Some people would argue that the start of the twenty-first century is the ideal opportunity to draw a line under the past and for Germany to become a 'normal' European state, 55 years after the death of Adolf Hitler, and ten years after German reunification. However, others disagree, arguing that the Nazi period should always be remembered in an effort to prevent its repetition. What is indisputable is that Germany faces many challenges at the turn of the century. Some relate to the question of German identity and the country's place in the international order. Others relate to practical problems that have tarnished the country's image as a model liberal democracy and social market economy, and threaten the consensus on which domestic stability rested for several decades.

For the FRG, the new millennium also coincides with the beginning of a new era in the country's history in other ways. Towards the end of 1999 the Federal Government finally moved from Bonn to Berlin. The re-establishment of Berlin as the capital and seat of government of Germany was a highly controversial move. Bonn had symbolized a peace-loving, cooperative, democratic German state. But Bonn was also very much associated with the old West Germany, and not with reunited Germany with 17 million new citizens from the former GDR. In contrast Berlin was associated with German aggression and expansionism, with dictatorship and the Holocaust. On the other hand, during the post-war period, divided Berlin had been the ultimate symbol of the injustice of the Cold War and of the artificial division of Germany and Europe into hostile blocs. Now reunited, Berlin symbolized both the unity of Germany and the end of the division of Europe. All these arguments surfaced during the unusually passionate parliamentary debate of the proposal to restore Berlin to the position of German capital. The move was approved in June 1991 but only by a narrow margin of just 18 votes[1] since many MPs were fearful of the message the move back to the old imperial capital would send to Germany's neighbours, not to mention the huge cost involved.

In 1999 the parliamentarians finally moved back to the Reichstag, Germany's Parliament in the days of Bismarck and the Kaisers, during the ill-fated Weimar Republic and the Third Reich. The building was restored with a spectacular glass dome from which the citizens could look down on democracy in action. The architect was Britain's Sir Norman Foster, provoking comments regarding the unlikelihood of a German architect ever being allowed to redesign the Houses of Parliament. Observers both at home and abroad wondered what the new 'Berlin Republic' would be like, with many hoping that many aspects of the old 'Bonn Republic', in economic and democratic terms the most successful German state ever, would continue. But the move was bound to bring some changes. Firstly the German capital was now in eastern Germany, forcing politicians from the West to confront the continuing economic problems in the East. Secondly it was located at the very heart of the 'new' Europe, closer to Warsaw than Brussels or Paris, which would have implications for trade and foreign policy. Finally it was hoped that the move of the capital to the East would bring the people of Eastern and Western Germany closer together, for, despite the fact that they were officially reunited in 1990, a genuine sense of 'inner unity' was yet to be achieved.

The move from Bonn to Berlin also came hot on the heels of other major political changes. Firstly the formation of the FRG's first ever Social Democratic–Green coalition government as a result of the federal election on 27 September 1998. Secondly, the FRG entered the European single currency along with ten other European Union (EU) members on 1 January 1999.

This chapter examines the most important issues facing contemporary Germany at the start of the new millennium, including social and cultural concerns, economic challenges, the party political landscape and the international role of Germany. All in all, the dawn of the new millennium is more significant and potentially more exciting for Germany than for any other major European country. It provides the FRG with the opportunity, even the obligation, to ensure that German history in the twenty-first century will not be a rerun of the first half of the previous century.

Political issues

Party politics

The FRG now has a small multi-party system, within which two parties dominate. German elections are fought using a mixed proportional representation system. This helps relatively small parties that would not beat the large broadly based parties if a first-past-the-post system were used, as is the case in British general elections. The system also tends to work against any party gaining an absolute majority. However, according to the constitution or Basic Law, parties have to win a minimum of 5 per cent of the total vote to gain seats in the federal or regional parliaments. This means that very small extremist parties that could threaten democracy and cause disruption in parliaments rarely gain seats.

Until the 1980s the FRG had a three-party system. The two broadly based 'people's parties' dominated: the Social Democratic Party (SPD), a Centre-Left party, and the Christian Democratic Union (CDU), a Centre-Right party. The CDU operates at federal level in alliance with its Bavarian sister party, the Christian Social Union (CSU), a conservative regional party. These parties continue to dominate German politics today, and in spite of the fact that their combined share of the vote has fallen in recent years, every one of the 16 *Länder* is headed by a minister president or governing mayor from these parties. The final component of the three-party system was the relatively small Free Democratic Party (FDP), a typical liberal party. Since neither of the dominant parties gained an overall majority of the vote at federal level[2] they needed the support of a smaller party to form a coalition government. Until 1998 the FDP usually performed this function, although a coalition government between any two of the three main parties was possible due to their agreement on the fundamentals of West German political culture (Pappi, 1984: 11–14). However, the FDP did not constitute a threat to the dominance of the two largest parties; hence the FRG was sometimes said to have not a three but a 'two and a half' party system.

New parties first made an impact in the 1980s, by which time the two main parties had become increasingly indistinguishable and younger voters in particular were tiring of them. The Greens, an ecological, post-materialist party, entered the Federal Parliament in 1983, and later that decade, a Far Right Wing party with a nationalist/racist programme, the *Republikaner*, began to gain support in certain regions.

German reunification brought a new addition to the party landscape in the form of the Party of Democratic Socialism (PDS), a reformed version of the old communist party of the GDR. Due to its eastern origins and vocal support for the rights of eastern Germans, the PDS gained support in the east of the country, polling on average 20–25 per cent, and 40 per cent in its stronghold, East Berlin. Surprisingly the post-communists' vote share is increasing and not decreasing as one might expect as East Germans become more politically mature. This is all the more remarkable in view of the fact that the party is descended from the regime East Germans overwhelmingly rejected in 1989/90. It is largely attributable to the fact that many of them feel disadvantaged and under-represented in the political system which remains dominated by West Germans.

Another development during the 1990s was the rise of a second Far Right party, the German People's Union (DVU). Right Wing extremism often thrives where there is high unemployment, social deprivation and widespread disaffection with the mainstream parties, and this is certainly the case in many areas of eastern Germany which have some of the highest rates of unemployment in the EU. The DVU took advantage of East Germans' disappointment with the political system of the FRG and their lack of experience of multicultural society. The party's best election result was 12.9 per cent in the eastern *Land* of Sachsen-Anhalt in 1998, a result that caused widespread dismay across the country.

The other significant development since reunification was the merger of the West German Greens with civil rights groups and Greens from the East. Consequently they are now officially known as Alliance 90/The Greens (*Bündnis 90/Die Grünen*).

Apart from the two Far Right Wing parties, all of the parties mentioned above are currently represented in the Federal Parliament (Bundestag), which was last elected in September 1998.[3] Since Germany is a federal state composed of 16 *Länder*, each *Land* also has its own government and parliament, responsible for specific policy areas, as defined by the constitution. The number of parties with seats in the *Land* parliaments varies. The FDP and Greens are very weak in the eastern *Länder*, while the PDS is practically non-existent in the West. Though not represented in the Federal Parliament, the two Far Right Wing parties do have seats in certain *Land* parliaments.

The 1998 federal election

The 1998 federal election in Germany was historic for several reasons. Firstly, the incumbent chancellor, Helmut Kohl, the longest serving chancellor in the history of the FRG, and the architect of reunification, was voted out of office by the German people. Previous German chancellors had either resigned or lost their majority due to a change of allegiance by their coalition partner. Secondly, the election produced the first ever Red–Green coalition at federal level, in other words, a government composed of the Social Democratic Party (SPD) and the Greens, led by Gerhard Schröder, a Social Democrat. Like the British Labour Party until 1997, the SPD had been out of government at national level for a long period (16 years), and Schröder modelled himself on Britain's Tony Blair, portraying himself as 'business-friendly' and the embodiment of the 'New Centre' in German politics. This strategy paid off and produced a comfortable majority for the Social Democratic–Green coalition in 1998. However, in the eyes of members of the 'Old Left' within his party, Schröder had abandoned too many traditional social democratic principles to please big business and the middle classes. As a result, the chancellor received criticism not only from opposition parties but also from within the SPD. Unlike the British Prime Minister, he had a coalition partner to contend with, and it was rumoured that Schröder would have preferred a 'Grand Coalition' with the Christian Democrats rather than a Red–Green coalition. The presence of the Greens in the coalition had serious implications for environmental policy and defence, although the party had already given up many of its uncompromisingly 'green' positions. Even so the Greens' plans to increase tax on petrol and to end the use of nuclear energy in the FRG were highly controversial. The first major test of the cohesion of the coalition was on foreign policy, which is examined below.

A year after the great federal election victory for the SPD and the Greens, both parties suffered losses in a series of *Land* elections held in the autumn of 1999, while the CDU made considerable gains. However, at the turn of the century, the CDU became embroiled in a corruption scandal involving illegal donations to the party accepted by the former chancellor, Helmut Kohl, which looked set to seriously damage the image of the most successful party in post-war German politics.

Overall, since its foundation, democracy in the FRG has proved to be very stable, proving those wrong who had believed the Germans were culturally incapable of living within democratic structures. Turnout at elections has been consistently high by Western standards. Although their share of the vote has fallen, the two main political parties, the Social Democrats and Christian Democrats, still poll over 75 per cent of the vote. Reunification has changed the party landscape but not revolutionized it, although noticeable differences in electoral behaviour between eastern and western Germany remain. Ironically such differences are most marked in Berlin, the symbol of reunited Germany which has undergone its own mini-reunification process (McKay, 2000). Recent electoral successes for Far Right Wing parties in some eastern *Länder* caused alarm due to the country's history. However Right Wing extremism does not appear to pose a serious threat to German democracy at federal level, and it is important to note that Right Wing extremist parties are much stronger in France and Austria than in Germany. Nevertheless, the total vote in eastern Germany for parties which are at the very least unconventional, indeed, some would say unconstitutional, suggests that many East Germans are not content with their lot and do not believe the mainstream parties are doing enough to remedy this situation.

The federal system

Contemporary Germany is a federal republic composed of 16 individual states or *Länder*. They vary greatly in terms of geographical and population size, and in terms of wealth. There are ten 'western' or 'old' *Länder* and five 'eastern' or 'new' *Länder*, plus reunited Berlin, a *Land* in its own right. German federalism is more than decentralization. It is a complex system whereby power and responsibility are divided between the central government and the *Länder*, with both levels of authority playing an important role. German-style federalism has several distinctive features. Firstly, it is often described as 'cooperative federalism' based on the principle that the two levels of government should cooperate as far as possible for the good of the country as a whole. Secondly, a sense of solidarity among the *Länder* is necessary to ensure they protect their common interests *vis-à-vis* the central government. The interests of the *Länder* are represented in Germany's Upper House of Parliament, the *Bundesrat*. Finally a complicated system of financial equalization operates with the objective of achieving similar living standards throughout the country. Essentially this is achieved by the government giving funds to all the *Länder* and the relatively rich *Länder* subsidizing the poor *Länder* (Paterson and Southern, 1991: 154–60; Jeffery, 1996: 83–7).

However, cooperative federalism is highly idealistic and assumes that all the actors concerned are willing to cooperate for the common good. In practice things function rather differently. The financial equalization process causes competition for funds, leading to tension between the *Länder*, which in turn undermines their solidarity. The rich resent subsidizing the poorer ones, and the gap between rich and poor has greatly increased with the addition of the *Länder* from the former GDR. In addition, *Land* solidarity has always been undermined by the fact that the *Länder* are ruled by different political parties and coalitions. Since the 1980s the Federal Government has attempted to claw back powers from the *Länder*, a threat that they can only resist through joint efforts. The *Länder* have also seen their powers undermined by the dramatic increase in legislation passed at the European level, where they themselves do not have a voice since foreign policy is the responsibility of the Federal Government.

The problems of federalism are not new problems but they have been exacerbated by reunification. For now the absence of alternatives may preserve the *status quo*. However, one suggestion that is mooted from time to time is to redraw the map of German federalism to reduce the total number of *Länder* and make them more similar in size and resources. On the face of it this appears to be a logical proposal. However, regional identity is strong in the FRG and a recent proposal to merge Berlin with its hinterland, Brandenburg, was defeated in a referendum (McKay, 1996: 485-502). In addition there would be opposition from those fearing job losses as a result of the merger of local bureaucracies, and in the case of mergers between eastern and western *Länder*, many eastern Germans would fear domination by more experienced westerners. Finally the current inter-*Land* competition for funds might merely be replaced by intra-*Land* competition between different areas within each *Land*. For all these reasons the most obvious way to reform German federalism is unlikely to happen in the near future.

Economic issues

For decades Germany was regarded as the economic power house of Europe with a reputation for high quality products, a hard working, skilled labour force, good industrial relations, and a generous welfare 'safety net' providing financial support for those who fell on hard times. These features were characteristics of the so-called 'German Model' which for years was the envy of other European countries. The FRG became the largest contributor to the budget of the EU and the Deutschmark the region's strongest currency. However, from the beginning of the 1990s, the 'German Model' has faced two serious challenges: German reunification and globalization.

When the two German states were 'reunited' in 1990, the government had hoped for a repeat of the celebrated 'economic miracle' of the immediate post-war period, and forecast 'blossoming landscapes' in the former East Germany. Since then some 7,000 billion DM have been pumped into the East by the Federal Government to modernize communications, renovate homes, rebuild city centres and clean up the environment. But nearly a decade later, and in spite of huge public and private investment, many are still waiting for the landscapes to blossom, especially in smaller towns and villages and on Germany's eastern border.

Since the mid-1990s government borrowing has reached unprecedented levels, largely to finance the regeneration of eastern Germany.[4] For some time government indebtedness had threatened the FRG's chances of meeting the Maastricht convergence criteria as a prerequisite for joining the European single currency. Meanwhile domestic growth slumped from the mid-1990s with economists predicting growth of just 1.5 per cent for 1999 (*Economist*, 1999a: 10). This in turn prevented a consumer boom which could have alleviated the most pressing economic concern, namely unemployment (Harding, 1999: 67). While jobless figures are a matter of concern throughout the FRG, the situation in the East is particularly grave. There the average rate of unemployment is double that of the West,[5] with many areas still with jobless figures of around 20 per cent of the workforce. Women have been hit particularly badly, especially those with children. Over 90 per cent worked in the old GDR, helped by readily available, cheap childcare facilities provided by the state. Nowadays childcare is neither a right, nor is it cheap. In addition thousands of East Germans took early retirement in the 1990s, while others are on short-term job creation schemes. The situation has not been helped by the availability of cheaper labour over the border in former communist countries keen to be competitive in the global marketplace. Overall, the absence of work in the East has contributed to social problems, caused disenchantment with the political system of the FRG and hindered the development of 'inner unity' between East and West Germans.

The other development that brought the viability of the 'German Model' into question was the acceleration of the process of globalization, which exposed all advanced Western economies to global competition from the 1980s. Suddenly the 'German Model' was no longer a shining example of sound economic management, but one of rigid structures, outmoded practices and over-regulation. Indeed, it is said that everything that the state can control it does control, and every year thousands of new laws and ordinances relating to business, industry and investment are passed (*Economist*, 1999a: 9). As a consequence, commentators have questioned the extent to which the FRG's celebrated social market economy truly functions according to market principles (Dyson, 1996: 199).

The other major disadvantage for the FRG in the global marketplace is the high cost of German labour, which explains why there is a net outflow of investment in Germany, with German companies preferring to invest in their overseas locations rather than at home (Harding, 1999: 66–7).

Many commentators believe that the German economic structures and practices will have to become more flexible in order to increase the attractiveness of the FRG as an investment location, both for multinationals and German companies. However, economic actors, such as employers' organizations and trade unions, are extremely powerful within Germany's semi-corporatist structures, and may be unwilling to accept reforms that could threaten their influence. They may also be unwilling to give up what has until now been a 'winning formula', in spite of the fact that the world has changed considerably since the 'German Model' was first devised.

The welfare state

The welfare state (*Sozialstaat*) has been an integral part of the FRG's social market economy since the immediate post-war period when social harmony was paramount and unemployment virtually non-existent. But times have changed. The cost of the welfare state in Germany was already an issue in the late 1980s due to increased global competition, but it was the economic and social consequences of reunification, in particular the sudden increase in people dependent on welfare, that brought the problem to a head.

At present Germans work fewer hours per week than most of their European counterparts, and receive relatively high benefits determined by previous income. Consequently non-wage labour costs, including contributions towards unemployment benefit, pensions and health insurance, are comparatively high in Germany, amounting to around 42 per cent of gross wages (*Economist*, 1999a: 9). They are funded equally by the employer and employee, which inevitably deters employers from taking on extra staff. Consequently many people would argue that the only way to resolve Germany's unemployment crisis is by reducing the cost of labour itself, in particular, welfare contributions.

However, huge obstacles must be overcome before reforms can be implemented. Firstly, the welfare state in Germany is sacred. Here again the influence of the past is evident. A generous system was established primarily to prevent a repeat of the widespread poverty experienced during the depression of the late 1920s which was exploited by the Nazis in their quest for power. In addition, people have become accustomed to the generous system and to erode it could be electoral suicide for any political party brave enough to do so.

Perhaps the biggest challenge in the near future will be how to cope with an ageing population – a problem shared by other post-industrial states. At present Germany operates the so-called 'generational contract' whereby those in work support those who are on pensions, believing that they themselves will be supported when they reach retirement age. But people are now living longer and the proportion of the population of working age relative to the proportion that has retired is shrinking fast. It is estimated that by 2030 there will be only one person working for every retired person, compared with 2.5 working for every pensioner in the early 1990s.[6] In addition, the number of people aged 80 and above is set to rise dramatically. This problem is worse in Germany than elsewhere in the Western world because many Germans enter the workforce relatively late, often approaching 30 years of age due to prolonged years of study. Six years at university is quite normal. The other reason is that the ranks of the retired were increased very suddenly during the early 1990s due to the early retirement schemes implemented in eastern Germany. Furthermore, as former citizens of the GDR, the individuals concerned had not paid into the system.

Solutions to Germany's economic malaise

The current German Government inherited a state that was rapidly slipping down the league table of the world's richest nations, with huge debts eating up a quarter of federal tax revenue on interest alone. Consequently it introduced a drastic package of cuts (*Sparpaket*) and a radical shake-up of the tax system. The stated objective was to 'balance the books' in eight years by drastically cutting government borrowing each year and to make the tax system fairer so that the burden of cutbacks was shouldered by as many individuals as possible.[7] However, the whole package brought Chancellor Schröder much criticism especially from Left Wingers who believed he had given up the traditional social democratic principle of wealth redistribution in favour of *die neue Mitte* or the 'New Centre', a German version of the 'Third Way' advocated by his British counterpart, Tony Blair.[8]

Attempts to reform the German welfare state had already been made during the early 1990s. Legislation had been passed to raise the retirement age gradually, a move which would keep people paying into the system longer (Mangen, 1996: 258-60), although this would not help youth unemployment. Some cuts in benefits were also made, and workers now have to contribute to a fund for long-term care in old age.

The professed aim of the Schröder Government was to rebuild the welfare state and not to dismantle it. The first major innovation was the introduction of the ecological tax on petrol and electricity in 1999 to finance cuts in social security contributions. It was hoped that this would lead to a reduction in the costs of labour and therefore safeguard jobs. Meanwhile an 'Alliance for Work' was established which brought together the government, trade unions, and representatives of business and employers to tackle the task of cutting unemployment. In addition pensions would rise in line with inflation not wage increases, and the tradition of non-contributory pensions for millions of public servants was ended.

On the surface, the immediate future for the German economy looks grim since it is currently underperfoming on every major macro-economic indicator. However, there is evidence that the 'underlying micro-economic strength' of the economy is undiminished. Inflation is low, the technological infrastructure is strong, and the so-called 'German Model' has adapted to change in the past (Harding, 1999: 68, 85). In addition, long-term investment in industry and manufacturing give the German economy the capacity to bounce back,[9] and its reputation for quality engineering lives on. Most of all however, the future of the German economy would appear to depend on the continued corporate consensus, the cooperation between governments and both sides of industry which many argue contributed a great deal to the country's post-war economic success. However, the scale of reform required, and the potential for disputes over strategy, pose the greatest threat to that corporate consensus since the establishment of the state itself. The Government is also counting on the population's willingness to 'mach mit' or 'join in' and to make sacrifices for the common economic good and this may prove crucial.

Sociocultural issues

Inner unity

In 1990 German reunification did not produce a new state but an enlarged FRG, since the territory of the old GDR was simply attached to the existing FRG, commonly known as West Germany. The absorption of a former communist state, with a centrally planned socialist economy, into an existing capitalist state was a task for which there were no precedents or models. The process has proved very expensive and painful for many individuals, but the pain has not been shared equally by eastern and western Germans, and this has impeded the development of a sense of 'inner unity' between the two groups.

When the opportunity for reunification arose in 1990, it made material sense for East Germans to believe in the continued existence of a unitary German nation, and West German politicians encouraged such a belief with promises and handouts in the name of the national bond. However, after the initial euphoria over national unity had died down, eastern and western Germans, known colloquially as '*Ossis*' and '*Wessis*', soon discovered that after 40 years apart, they had very little in common beyond their German heritage. Instead of 'two states of one nation', which was how Willy Brandt had described the situation on German soil in the early 1970s, there now appeared to be 'one state of two nations'. Particularly in the early 1990s, to many East Germans, West Germans were condescending and chauvinistic towards the East. Meanwhile, in the eyes of many West Germans, East Germans were backward, lazy and expected charity. Further tension was caused by the fact that easterners had to adapt to the western way of doing things, while life for most westerners went on as before. All these problems gave rise to the phrase '*die Mauer im Kopf*' or 'the wall in the mind'. The implication was that although the Berlin Wall in its concrete form had come down, a psychological wall continued to divide East and West Germans.

While the collapse of the GDR freed East Germans from the bondage of a repressive communist regime, they also lost the positive aspects of life in the GDR. These included free education and healthcare, jobs for life, cheap childcare, and subsidized arts, sports and leisure facilities. Suddenly they had to cope with the competition and hard choices of a capitalist society. Particularly in the job market, their lack of experience, even naïveté, put them at a disadvantage compared with West Germans.

During the 1990s, East Germans manifested their disappointment with reunification and their self-perception as 'second class citizens' in the FRG in various ways. Their resentment encouraged the development of a strong sense of regional identity and solidarity in the eastern *Länder*, demonstrated by a preference for local produce and familiar eastern brands. As mentioned earlier, in elections 20–40 per cent still vote for the only eastern-based political party, the PDS, in spite of the fact that it is descended from the ruling communist party of the GDR. In contrast the other parties remain essentially western in outlook and are dominated numerically by western members. However, many people would argue that due to its communist past and its appeal to a specific East German identity the PDS perpetuates the East–West divide in Germany and works against the full integration of the eastern *Länder* into the FRG.

At the beginning of the new millennium it seems that eastern and western Germans are gradually learning to live with each other, especially as younger generations grow up without the preconceptions of their parents. As is traditional in the old *Länder*, citizens in the new *Länder* increasingly identify first and foremost with their town or *Land* as opposed to basing their identity on being *Ossis* or *Wessis*. However, a decade after reunification there is still a long way to go before 'inner unity' will be achieved. While opinion polls consistently indicate that many problems and concerns are shared by East and West Germans, in particular, unemployment and rising crime, results for federal and *Land* elections continue to show that they have different views as to which political parties are most likely to solve them.[10]

Immigration and citizenship

East–West tension is not the only threat to social harmony in contemporary Germany. The FRG is now a multicultural country, in spite of successive governments' reluctance to acknowledge this fact via changes in the German citizenship law. Many large cities in western Germany have high non-German populations, the majority descendants of the 'guest workers' (*Gastarbeiter*) who came in the 1960s to provide a temporary labour force during the country's economic boom years. In addition, millions of 'ethnic Germans' (*Aussiedler*) have migrated to the FRG from Eastern Europe and the former Soviet Union.[11]

In the early 1990s a new migration issue reached the top of the political agenda, namely asylum. The flood of asylum seekers into the FRG (and a new wave of ethnic Germans) was triggered by the opening of formerly closed borders with Eastern Europe and the war in former Yugoslavia. Germany received far more asylum applications than other West European countries due to its close proximity to Europe's trouble spots, its liberal asylum law, and its high standard of living. In 1992, at the start of the war in Bosnia, Germany accepted 80 per cent of those seeking asylum in the EU.[12] The numbers arriving caused widespread public concern and an increase in acts of racist violence, particularly in eastern Germany where people were unused to foreigners as a result of the GDR's policy of strictly limited immigration and segregated accommodation for immigrants. Eventually the Government of the day capitulated and tightened up the rules governing asylum claims. However, this merely detracted from the main questions regarding the FRG's position as a *de facto* country of immigration.

The whole issue of immigration is linked with the notion of German nationhood and citizenship. The German Citizenship Law dates back to 1913 and is based on the principle of *ius sanguinis*. Thus to be a German citizen it is necessary to be German by descent or blood and it follows that it is not possible to become German by residency or birth. This is out of step with the Western norm whereby citizenship is based on place of birth and/or residence. Today 7.3 million residents of the FRG (8.9 per cent of the population)[13] are officially foreigners without German citizenship, 1.63 million of whom were born there. Furthermore the majority are ineligible to vote in elections because the constitution or Basic Law states that only the German 'people' (*das Volk*) can vote. This legal situation has encouraged the native German population to regard foreigners as undesirable and temporary, and discouraged efforts at mutual understanding and integration. In contrast, ethnic Germans, who may have lived all their lives in the former Soviet Union but can claim German ancestry, may migrate to the FRG and automatically acquire full citizenship rights, including the right to vote.

For decades, governments of all political persuasions refused to accept the permanence of Germany's immigrant communities, fearing that such a move would lose them votes among the indigenous population. However, in 1999 the first Social Democrat–Green Federal Government revised Germany's anachronistic citizenship law. A Bill was passed granting German citizenship to children born in Germany of non-German parents[14] and came into force at the beginning of the year 2000. Until their 23rd birthday they could hold dual citizenship, at which point they would have to choose which citizenship to keep. In addition, longstanding foreign residents could apply for naturalization after just eight years' residency, provided they fulfilled specific conditions,[15] but in this case dual citizenship would not be permitted. While this change still fell short of a full revision of the 1913 Citizenship Law and did little for those who had already grown up in Germany,[16] it was radical enough to provoke a backlash from the country's conservative parties, the CDU and CSU, who collected 5 million signatures against the new Law. The whole episode demonstrated just how entrenched attitudes towards immigration, citizenship and ethnicity are in contemporary Germany. Evidently it is unlikely that German law will come into line with the European norm for some time to come, especially if the conservative parties increase their power in Germany's upper house of parliament or take over the federal government.

Foreign policy

At the start of the twenty-first century the FRG is a state in search of an appropriate international role. Prior to reunification, it was often labelled an 'economic giant and political dwarf' because its economic strength was not matched by diplomatic or military influence. There was no chance of independent action in foreign policy or defence, and Britain, France and the USA retained occupation forces in West Germany until shortly after reunification, albeit more to protect the country from the Eastern Bloc rather than to contain it. German military power was constrained via her membership of NATO, in which she was a second class member, subject to severe restrictions on troops and weaponry. In addition West Germany was securely integrated into the EU from its foundation as the European Coal and Steel Community, a benevolent method of keeping tabs on the new German state. Meanwhile politicians in Bonn nurtured a close relationship with the old enemy, France.

All these constraints were accepted by West German politicians who were keen to prove that Germany had changed following the defeat of the Nazis. Although the German national interest was a taboo term, membership of multinational bodies also brought the country advantages in the form of trade partners, military protection and legitimacy. As a consequence of the FRG's involvement in European and international organizations, politicians accepted multilateral solutions to international problems and the post-war generation developed a strong sense of identity as Europeans. Other countries' sensitivity regarding the use of German troops combined with a healthy bank balance allowed West German politicians to engage in 'cheque book diplomacy', paying others to fight their battles for them. It also encouraged a pacifist mentality among young West Germans which was demonstrated by mass opposition to the deployment of nuclear weapons during the 1980s and the establishment of the most successful Green party in Europe.

Upon reunification the FRG was finally granted full sovereignty by the Western Allies and the Soviet Union. This led to the question of whether or not the FRG was now a 'normal' state that ought to assume 'normal' international responsibilities. However, suspicion of German motives continued amid fears that the incorporation of the former GDR into the FRG was merely the next stage in Germany's quest for domination throughout Europe.

Reunited Germany has already faced various foreign policy challenges that have revealed a high level of uncertainty regarding Germany's international role and a tendency to appear over-assertive, especially at the European level. The first crisis was the Gulf war of 1991 during which Germany was widely regarded to have contributed too little towards the war effort. This was partly due to a constitutional prohibition on the use of German troops outside the NATO area which has since been lifted. In spite of this, Germans still seem reluctant to become involved in military action. The Kosovo war of 1999 was a major test for the inexperienced Red–Green Coalition Government led by Gerhard Schröder. Germany's position was complicated by the participation of the Greens in the governing coalition. Pacifist Green members could have forced the resignation of the pragmatic Green Foreign Minister, Joschka Fischer, a key figure holding the governing coalition together, but they failed to do so. Furthermore the participation of German troops in the NATO force was bound to be a sensitive issue due to the country's involvement in Serbia during the Nazi period. Had the war deepened with the use of ground troops, things may have ended differently.

Although the German Government emerged more or less unscathed from the Kosovo war, the episode highlighted many problems for the current and future German governments in the field of foreign policy. Today's politicians face difficulties pleasing NATO allies and Russia simultaneously, overcoming differences in public opinion between East and West Germans, and resolving potential conflicts with and within the Greens.

European integration and the single currency

Ever since its establishment in the early 1950s, the FRG's membership of the EU has been taken for granted. Together with France the two countries have formed the 'motor' of European integration, devising and endorsing bold schemes to advance the European project. However, at times it appeared to outsiders that the Germans were aiming to impose their own vision of Europe on other countries, and, worse still, a Europe in which Germany would dominate.

The most ambitious European project to date was Economic and Monetary Union (EMU), a central feature of which was a single European currency. This proved problematic for Germany in two ways. Firstly, the country struggled to meet the Maastricht Convergence criteria, drawn up to ensure that only EU members with economies deemed sufficiently healthy and performing similarly would be eligible to join EMU. But the criteria were drafted before the true cost of German reunification was known; indeed, the original Delors Plan for EMU was drawn up before there was any indication of the collapse of communism in Eastern Europe at all. But a single currency without the strongest European currency, the Deutschmark, was unthinkable, and through unpopular measures such as severe austerity measures, including previously unthinkable cuts in social security spending, the German Government just managed to meet the convergence criteria in time, and took the country into EMU at its birth on 1 January 1999.

The second problem concerning the single currency has been the fact that for the first time, public opinion was at odds with elite opinion on European policy. For the citizens of the FRG, the Deutschmark was a symbol of the country's post-war economic success. Pride in the economy and the stability of the currency provided a substitute for nationalism in a country where nationalism had been abused and discredited, and helped legitimize the state which was initially an artificial creation and not a nation-state. The significance of currency stability is all the more poignant in view of the disastrous results of inflation and instability during the late 1920s. The economic crisis was a main factor in the fall of the Weimar Republic and the rise of the Nazis. Consequently many Germans remain paranoid about currency weakness, and fear that the strong Deutschmark has been replaced by the weaker euro. This is perhaps ironic since many other Europeans (mistakenly) regard the euro as merely the Deutschmark in disguise, encouraged by the fact that the new European Central Bank is located in Frankfurt. German public opinion regarding the single currency was consistently sceptical, particularly in eastern Germany where anti-Europeanism is somewhat stronger. Since there is no constitutional facility for a national referendum on the euro a large proportion of Germans used the 1999 European Parliament elections to demonstrate their new-found Euro-scepticism. Only 45.2 per cent of voters cast their votes, the lowest ever turnout for a nationwide election in the FRG.

The future of the Franco-German relationship

Throughout the post-war period the Franco-German relationship lay at the heart of Bonn's European policy and together the two countries provided the 'motor' for European integration. During the 1990s the two old rivals even joined forces to form the 'Eurocorps', potentially the foundation for a fully-fledged European army. However, the golden age of that relationship, cemented by personal friendships between Helmut Schmidt and Giscard d'Estaing, and later Helmut Kohl and François Mitterrand, is now over. Within the French political elite there are fears that Germany will no longer need her old partner, France, now that the centre of Europe has shifted further eastwards and Germany is reunited and fully sovereign. While meetings between the leaders of the two countries continue, the personal rapport has gone. Furthermore, unlike Chancellor Schröder, the current socialist Prime Minister of France, Lionel Jospin, represents the 'Old Left'. However, French fears that Germany will turn its back on its old ally are somewhat premature, partly due to the existence of entrenched networks between the two countries. In short, close relations with France will continue, but not to the exclusion of all other relationships.

At present the future of Germany's European policy is uncertain. As the largest EU member with the highest population, a major role seems inevitable. What is clear is that German European policy will in the future be far more eastern orientated. Indeed the German Government has been a keen advocate of eastern enlargement of the EU since the early 1990s, not least because unrest in Eastern Europe would literally be on Germany's doorstep. Therefore the FRG has good reason to hope for economic success and political stability for her eastern neighbours. However, the initial expansion of the EU will give Poles, Czechs and Hungarians the right to move to other member states to work, and the FRG must expect an influx of outsiders whom it was previously able to exclude. Relationships with these countries will also have to be balanced by the relationship with Russia. The future of this relationship is much harder to predict due to uncertainty regarding Russia's political stability.

The FRG's economic difficulties have had implications for foreign policy. In 1999 Chancellor Schröder demanded a reduction in German contributions to the EU budget, suggesting that the days when his country was willing to sacrifice its national interests for the broader European interest were over. Also the defence budget was drastically cut, provoking an attack from Washington.

Overall there is little evidence at this stage that the foreign policy objectives of the 'Berlin Republic' will differ widely from those of its predecessor, the Bonn Republic.

However, future German leaders may adopt a more assertive style in foreign policy, indeed, many people would argue that it is high time for this. For the first time, Germany and most other major European countries are led by politicians too young to remember the Second World War. Memories of wartime devastation had acted as a psychological constraint, encouraging politicians to regard military conflict as a last resort to be avoided at all costs, a belief particularly strongly felt by Helmut Kohl. Some fear that the absence of this constraint may encourage German leaders to be more reckless. So far, however, it seems that the post-war Germans are a pacifist generation, even more reluctant to take up arms than their European neighbours. Besides, in spite of diminishing first hand experience of war, other countries, or rather their media, are unlikely to allow the reminders of past German aggression to disappear.

Conclusion and future prospects

The beginning of the twenty-first century presents the FRG with many challenges and several problems. It could even be argued that it faces more challenges than any other country in Western Europe. Firstly, politicians and bureaucrats will have to get used to new lives and different perspectives on their own country and on Europe from Berlin. Secondly, somewhat belatedly, people will have to come to terms with the heterogeneity of contemporary Germany. The first steps have been taken to acknowledge the fact that German society is multicultural, but changing the law will not change attitudes overnight. In addition, expressions of hope that the move to Berlin will accelerate the process of East–West reconciliation among Germans suggests that a decade after reunification this has not yet been achieved. Finally, everyone in the FRG will have to get used to 'tightening their belts' to safeguard the economy for future generations. Economic actors face particular challenges and will need to exercise both innovation and courage if the country is to move with the times. In terms of foreign policy, reunited Germany has yet to define an appropriate international role for a country of its size and significance. However, the politicians charged with this task will no doubt be wary of Germany's past attempts to define the role of Germany in the wider world.

These challenges are not merely practical but also psychological. The FRG's need to come to terms with internal diversity and to find its place in the new world order are part of the same question, namely what it means to be German at the beginning of the twenty-first century. What does seem clear is that after 50 years on probation in Bonn, the politicians of the FRG have proved that German democracy is in safe hands and is mature enough to return to Berlin without cause for concern among Germany's European partners and neighbours. This does not necessarily mean that Germany will not dominate Europe. But if it does, this may be more by accident than design. The new millennium marks a turning point in the history of the FRG, but it also provides the chance, even the obligation, to ensure that Germany's history in the twentieth century is not repeated.

Notes

1. The vote was taken in the Federal Parliament on 20 June 1991, 338 MPs voted for the move to Berlin and 320 against, with one abstention and one invalid ballot paper (Presse-und Informationsamt der Bundesregierung).

2. With the exception of the CDU in 1957.
3. Analysis of various aspects the 1998 federal election can be found in a special issue of *German Politics* devoted to the subject: *German Politics*, 8 (2) (1999).
4. The federal deficit (as a percentage of GDP) stood at −2.1 in 1998, compared with an EU average of −1.5 (Government Centre for Strategic Studies in 1999). The level of federal indebtedness tripled during the period 1996–99 to reach 1.5 trillion Deutschmarks, according to the Bundesministerium der Finanzen.
5. German unemployment, October 1999: 9.9 per cent. West: 8.2 per cent; East 16.9 per cent (Bundesanstalt für Arbeit).
6. *Financial Times*, 9 April 1996, p. 17.
7. Bundesministerium der Finanzen.
8. In June 1999 Blair and Schröder published a joint paper entitled 'The Way Forward for Europe's Social Democracy' based on the principles of Blair's 'New Labour'.
9. 'Corsets on an expanding economy', *Guardian*, 10 June 1999.
10. For results of the 1998 federal election for East and West Germany, see Gibowski, 1999: 11.
11. Around 2 million ethnic Germans have entered the FRG since 1990, the majority from the former Soviet Union, plus sizeable numbers from Poland and Rumania. In 1995 alone, 217,898 ethnic Germans were accepted but since 1998 numbers have fallen below 100,000 per annum. The figure for the period January–September 1999 is 64,512 (Bundesinnenministerium).
12. *Economist*, 1999a: 16.
13. End 1998. 28.8 per cent of foreigners in Germany were Turkish (Bundesministerium des Innern).
14. Providing at least one parent had legally resided in the FRG for at least eight years.
15. These include sufficient knowledge of German, no criminal convictions, no unconstitutional behaviour, and the payment of a fee.
16. An exception was made for foreign children born in Germany who were under 10 years old. Until the end of the year 2000 their parents could apply for dual citizenship, subject to certain conditions, in particular, the parents' own residential status (Bundesministerium des Innern).

CHAPTER EIGHT

The Problems and Future of France

Robert Harmsen

Apart from a brief period of World-Cup-induced euphoria, the French media have tended, in recent years, to describe the prevailing mood in the country as one of malaise or morosity (see Ardagh, 1999: 715–36). Many commentators have linked this feeling of disquiet to the 'end of French exceptionalism'. Under the combined pressures of globalization and European integration, it is often argued that many distinctive characteristics of French civilization are being lost. Some would go so far as to say that French national identity itself may be imperilled.

These dire predictions must be placed in context. France is certainly not alone in facing the challenges of globalization and European integration. The current sense of malaise is also not unique. It is, indeed, difficult to think of any time during the post-war period when some form of exhaustively diagnosed *mal français* did not animate political and intellectual debate in the country. Yet the current debates do reflect an underlying social reality. The last two decades of the twentieth century have seen significant transformations as regards both French domestic politics and France's place in the world. This chapter explores those changes.

The first sections of this chapter look at domestic political developments, highlighting the gradual redefinition of the model of political power established under the Fifth Republic. Next, France's position in the European Union (EU) is examined, as well as French responses to globalization. The past two decades of the twentieth century are shown to have thrown up major new challenges to traditional French political and economic models in terms of both the domestic scene and the wider outlook. The external and internal dimensions of change are brought together in the conclusion, which further highlights the problems which continue to face the French state.

Remodelling the Fifth Republic

The Constitution of the French Fifth Republic, as adopted in 1958, was an ambiguous document. Key questions concerning the distribution of power between the President and the Prime Minister were not clearly settled. Despite this textual ambiguity, a clearly defined model of political power rapidly emerged. De Gaulle's tenure as President unequivocally established a practice of presidential dominance as the norm under the new Constitution. Breaking with the shifting coalition politics of the Fourth Republic, the early years of the regime also saw the emergence of a disciplined Gaullist majority in Parliament. The twin pillars of the 'Fifth Republic model' were thus put in place: strong presidential rule supported by a cohesive parliamentary majority.

This presidentialist and majoritarian model of the exercise of power defined the regime from the end of the Algerian War in 1962 through to the 1980s. The accession of socialist François Mitterrand to the presidency in 1981 seemed to provide decisive confirmation of the Fifth Republic model. Mitterrand, once one of the regime's harshest critics, governed in a manner which did not at first depart much from the style defined by de Gaulle. Yet it was also during the course of Mitterrand's two seven-year presidential terms (1981–95) that the practice of power under the Fifth Republic started, in often unanticipated ways, to be redefined.

A recent major study of the Fifth Republic has spoken of the regime's 'death' in the last two decades of the twentieth century. Donegani and Sadoun (1998), in pronouncing the regime's demise, are not commenting on the stability of the constitutional arrangement itself. The Fifth Republic, in over four decades of existence, has acquired a deeply entrenched legitimacy. Nevertheless, the nature of the regime has changed significantly during the course of those four decades. The initial, 'heroic' exercise of political power, defined by the direct relationship between the President and the French people, has been replaced by a more complex and more diffuse political system.

Both pillars of the Fifth Republic model have, over the last two decades of the twentieth century, suffered some erosion. The practice of presidential dominance has been attenuated, both by changes in the policy environment and by the growing frequency of cohabitation. The party system has undergone a partial fragmentation, with the emergence of new political forces and the use of proportional representation qualifying its once strongly majoritarian logic. This, in turn, may be linked to potentially deeper problems, pointing to a declining level of public confidence in political elites.

The attenuation of presidential dominance

The attenuation of the presidential role has, in part, been the product of a more general redefinition of the role of the state in contemporary France. The public policy environment within which the French President operates has undergone substantial changes (Wright and Elgie, 1996). Governmental action has been increasingly hemmed in by both external and domestic constraints. As discussed elsewhere in this chapter, globalization and Europeanization have reduced the capacity for action of the traditionally interventionist French state. A significant diffusion of power has also taken place within the French political system. Although France remains a comparatively centralized state, the process of territorial decentralization initiated by the 1982 Defferre laws has nonetheless created new sets of political actors and policy processes. There has further been a marked 'juridicization' of the political process in France. This juridicization most obviously refers to the central role which has been assumed by the Constitutional Council in the French policy-making process. The Council has developed a sophisticated body of jurisprudence, placing limits on governmental action relating to both the constitutional text and broader principles of law. Beyond the Council's growing importance, there has also been a more general development of various forms of regulatory and judicial control on governmental action. Most prominently, investigating magistrates (*juges d'instruction*) have adopted an increasingly assertive attitude, resulting in a number of highly publicized corruption cases. One commentator (Minc, 1998) has gone so far as to speak of a 'second French Revolution', critically highlighting the growing subordination of politics to law. Yet, whatever one may think of changing institutional balances in France, it is undeniable that changes are taking place. There has been a marked affirmation of what are tellingly termed the '*contrepouvoirs*'- the counterweights to strong executive authority. As a result, the ability of a President to shape the national political agenda has been attenuated. While a President may still use the resources of his office to put forward his own policy priorities, he will have to negotiate through an increasingly complex institutional environment in order to realize those goals.

The most direct redefinition of the presidential role has to do with recurring periods of 'cohabitation'. Cohabitation refers to a situation in which the President is faced with a hostile majority in Parliament and must, in consequence, appoint a Prime Minister from amongst his political opponents. In such a scenario, a fundamental redistribution of powers takes place between the President and the Prime Minister. This redistribution has been classically described by Maurice Duverger (1987: 9–37) as producing a 'duo' in foreign policy and a 'duel' in domestic policy. The President and the Prime Minister share responsibility for the conduct of foreign affairs, with considerable emphasis publicly placed on the need for France to speak with one voice abroad. By way of contrast, in domestic matters power largely passes from the President to the Prime Minister and the Government. In most areas of domestic policy, the President can cajole and criticize, but cannot alter government policies to which he is opposed. The President is, in effect, reduced to the role of an opposition leader. An institutionalized logic of conflict and competition may thus be seen to underlie the practice of cohabitation. Politics is defined by both competing policy options and conflicting institutional legitimacies.

There have been three periods of cohabitation to date, each with its own distinctive characteristics. France's first experience of cohabitation (1986–88) was a comparatively conflictual one. As both President Mitterrand and Prime Minister Chirac were prospective candidates for the 1988 presidential elections, their relationship was dominated by the search for strategic advantage in the upcoming electoral contest. In the event, Mitterrand's ability to play successfully on two distinct registers, appearing as both a guardian of national unity and the leader of the left, trumped Chirac's rather more partisan approach. The second period of cohabitation (1993–95) was a distinctly more consensual affair. Prime Minister Edouard Balladur's conciliatory style of governance, coupled with the Right's overwhelming victory in the 1993 legislative elections and President Mitterrand's failing health, served to minimize conflict.

The most recent period of cohabitation opened in 1997. The victory of the Left in parliamentary elections forced President Chirac to appoint socialist Lionel Jospin as Prime Minister. This period differs in two significant respects from its predecessors. First, the 1997 legislative elections marked the first time in the history of the Fifth Republic that a President's decision to dissolve Parliament prematurely resulted in an opposition victory. The two previous periods of cohabitation had resulted from legislative elections which occurred at the end of the normal five-year parliamentary term. In this sense, President Chirac has suffered a more direct electoral rebuke than President Mitterrand. Second, the present period of cohabitation has the potential to last much longer than its two predecessors. Both previous periods of cohabitation started two years before the next regularly scheduled presidential election and could be expected to end with that election. The present period of cohabitation, on the other hand, began only two years into President Chirac's seven-year term. Cohabitation, on this occasion, must consequently be understood more as a 'normal' mode of governance and less as merely a prelude to an impending presidential contest.

Indeed, one may speak more generally of a 'normalization' of cohabitation. There has been a marked shift in perceptions about the 'proper' functioning of the Fifth Republic Constitution. The possible failure of a President to secure a supportive parliamentary majority was, for many years, regarded as the Achilles' heel of the regime. It was felt by many commentators that such a non-coincidence of presidential and parliamentary majorities could, potentially, provoke a serious if not fatal constitutional crisis. By the early 1980s, perceptions had evolved. In the run-up to the 1986 legislative election, prevailing wisdom seemed to regard cohabitation as a regrettable, but manageable deviation from the Fifth Republic norm (debates summarized in Le Gall, 1997: 107–25). More recently, prevailing understandings have again been transformed. Although there are ongoing discussions of constitutional reforms intended to reduce the likelihood of cohabitation occurring, the practice now seems widely regarded as one of several possible and 'normal' modes of governance under the Constitution of the Fifth Republic (Keeler and Schain, 1996a). The implications of this change should be underlined. If cohabitation is normalized, then presidential dominance can no longer be the norm. Presidential dominance, once the model of governance under the Fifth Republic, has become only one of several possible configurations of power.

What clearly emerges is that presidential dominance under the Fifth Republic has been attenuated. With a supportive parliamentary majority, a President continues to possess a substantial latitude for action. Tellingly, however, the French electorate has chosen to deprive successive Presidents of such a majority on three occasions within the space of eleven years. Moreover, the President faces an increasingly restrictive policy environment even when he or she is able to secure a supportive parliamentary majority. Thus, while a French President may still wield considerable power under the right circumstances, the days of largely unfettered presidential dominance would appear to belong to the past.

A fragmenting party system and the 'cycle of rejection'

The last two decades of the twentieth century saw a fraying of the once strongly majoritarian and bipolar logic which structured the French party system under the Fifth Republic. This partial fragmentation must be understood relative to the historical development of the party system after the 1958 regime change. Although General de Gaulle always sought to place himself 'above parties', one of the major innovations of the early years of the Fifth Republic was the emergence of an electorally successful Gaullist party. Gaullism gave rise to the first 'voter-directed' or 'catch-all' party in France (Charlot, 1971). The Gaullist movement became a broadly based, pragmatic conservative party capable of winning over 30 per cent of the vote (46 per cent in 1968) and secure parliamentary majorities. It thus put paid to the chronic governmental instability which had plagued the Fourth Republic. Equally, this reorganization of the Right called forth a corresponding set of developments on the Left. After a number of false starts in the 1960s, François Mitterrand's accession to the leadership of the Socialist Party (PS) in 1971 marked a turning point. After a long erosion of its core support, Mitterrand was able to rebuild French socialism as a significant political force. Throughout the 1970s the party polled around 20 per cent of the vote. This placed the socialists on an equal footing with the communists on the Left, as well as placing the Left as a whole on an equal footing with the long dominant Right.

This bipolarizing movement reached its high point with the 1978 legislative elections. The party system, at this time, was commonly labelled a 'bipolar quadrille'. The system was characterized by a perfectly balanced bipolarism, with coalitions of the Left and Right each enjoying the support of almost exactly half the French electorate. The system further formed a 'quadrille' in that each of the two broad coalitions was itself evenly divided between two parties. The socialist and communist parties on the Left, like the Gaullists and the Giscardians on the Right, existed in finely balanced, often sharply competitive, relationships with one another. Each of the four parties represented between a quarter and a fifth of French voters.

The 'bipolar quadrille' unravelled in the early 1980s. François Mitterrand's presidential victory in 1981 saw the PS emerge as the clearly dominant force on the Left. In the legislative elections which immediately followed Mitterrand's presidential victory, the socialists took 38 per cent of the vote and were able to secure a majority of parliamentary seats on their own. Two other significant developments occurred at this time. Mirroring the socialists' rise, the Communist Party entered into a period of rapid decline. Having consistently polled around 20 per cent of the vote throughout the first two decades of the Fifth Republic, the communists' vote plummeted in the 1980s. The party has won around 10 per cent of the vote in legislative elections since 1986, while turning in much poorer performances in presidential contests. On the other hand, the extreme Right National Front erupted on to the scene at about the same time. The Front's first breakthroughs came in municipal elections and parliamentary by-elections in 1983. This was followed by national success in the 1984 European Parliament elections, as the Front won 10 per cent of the vote. The Front's support in national electoral contests has since usually remained at the 10–12 per cent level. It reached a peak of 15 per cent both with party leader Jean-Marie Le Pen's score in the first round of the 1995 presidential election and in the first round of the 1997 legislative election.

The combined impact of these two developments changed the configuration of the party system. From the early 1980s until quite recently, it was useful to think of the French party system in terms of a division between 'presidential' and 'anti-establishment' parties (Cole, 1998: 152–86). Three mainstream parties occupied the centre ground and could reasonably aspire to placing one of their number in the presidency: the PS; the Neo-Gaullist Rally for the Republic (RPR); and the Liberal/Christian Democratic Union for French Democracy (UDF). These three mainstream parties were flanked by two smaller 'extreme' parties: the Communist Party (PCF) and the National Front. The Greens have also intermittently made their presence felt in the French political arena, with recent results indicating that they have perhaps finally managed to secure a more permanent place for themselves.

Roughly this configuration of presidential and anti-establishment parties may be seen in the results of the 1997 legislative election (see Table 8.1).

Table 8.1 The French legislative elections of 25 May and 1 June 1997

Party/grouping	% of first round vote	Members elected (577)
Far Left	2.5	0
Communist Party	9.1	38
PS	23.5	241
Radical socialists	1.5	12
Other Left	2.8	21
Ecologists	6.8	7
Other (unclassified)	1.4	1
RPR	15.7	134
UDF	14.2	108
Other Right	6.6	14
National Front	14.9	1
Other Extreme Right	0.1	0

Source: French Ministry of the Interior.

Even this rather complicated picture, however, no longer provides an adequate portrayal of the French party system. The mainstream Right's 1997 electoral defeat was followed by a series of schisms and, as yet, incomplete realignments. The free market Liberal Democracy group led by Alain Madelin split from the main UDF to form an independent party. In a similar vein, the prominent anti-Maastricht campaigner and former Interior Minister Charles Pasqua broke ranks with President Chirac's Neo-Gaullist RPR. Together with UDF dissident Philippe de Villiers, Pasqua has formed a new, resolutely pro-sovereignty party under the banner of the Rally for France (the initials RPF deliberately harking back to the Fourth Republic Gaullist movement). Recent events on the Extreme Right have further seen a major and perhaps fatal division within the National Front. One of the party's principal strategists, Bruno Migret, acrimoniously split with Le Pen and set up his own rival party. The picture of the French party system at the time of writing is thus one of confusion. This confusion may, however, be partially explained with reference to longer-term electoral trends.

Since the 1980s, French politics have been marked by what Jean-Luc Parodi (1997: 295–300) has described as an 'electoral accordion'. Different types of elections are conducted using different types of electoral system, creating varying logics of party competition. Broadly there is a division between 'first order' elections conducted by two-ballot majority systems and certain 'second order' elections conducted by forms of proportional representation (PR). This has produced an accordion-like effect, with the French party system alternatively appearing to be either bipolar or multipolar depending on the type of election. The decisive second ballots of presidential and parliamentary elections largely continue to be structured by a classic bipolar logic. Here, a traditional Left/Right cleavage remains of central importance, although somewhat disturbed in recent years by the presence of the National Front. PR elections, such as those for regional assemblies and the European Parliament, offer a very different picture. Votes of this type have provided new and marginal political parties with an opportunity to gain an electoral foothold. PR elections, particularly those for the European Parliament, have also been used by dissidents from mainstream political parties as a means of challenging established party leaderships. The picture of the post-1997 French party system sketched above represents a point at which the pendulum has swung markedly in the direction of fragmentation, accelerated by the June 1999 European Parliament election. A degree of restructuring can be anticipated in the run-up to legislative and presidential elections due in 2002. Indeed, the outcome of those elections will, at least in part, ride on the extent to which President Chirac is able to use the resources of his office to impose order on the deeply divided mainstream Right.

The turbulence in the French party system also relates to that which has commonly been termed the 'cycle of rejection' (Keeler and Schain, 1996b). This term refers to the comparative inability of French governments to win re-election. Since 1981, power has changed hands between the Right and the Left on five occasions. This contrasts sharply with the lengthy periods of Conservative rule in Britain and Christian Democratic-led government in Germany over the same period. In the case of France, no 'decisive' election since 1981 (either presidential or legislative) has resulted in a clear victory for the incumbent government. The socialists, having won both the Presidency and a comfortable parliamentary majority in 1981, lost the 1986 legislative elections to the Right. President Mitterrand won re-election in 1988, but did so by beating incumbent Prime Minister Jacques Chirac. In the immediate aftermath of the presidential election, fresh legislative elections allowed the socialists to return to power with a 'relative majority'. Five years later, however, they were handed a crushing defeat by the Right in the 1993 legislative elections. The Right was further able to win the Presidency in 1995, but this too must be nuanced. Chirac, implausibly but effectively, styled himself as something of an anti-establishment figure during his 1995 presidential campaign. In keeping with the anti-incumbent trend, the presidential bid of sitting Prime Minister Edouard Balladur failed. Finally, the Right lost to an enlarged left coalition, the *gauche plurielle*, in the 1997 legislative elections. After an uninterrupted 23-year period of rule by the Right (1958–81), the Fifth Republic has unmistakably acquired the habit of alternation.

A number of explanations may be put forward for this high rate of governmental turnover. Partly, governments of all political stripes have been touched by a growing climate of scandal. Prominent politicians on both the Left and the Right have been implicated in party financing irregularities, as well as instances of personal corruption. One of the more prominent financial scandals was the so-called 'Urba Affair' in the early 1990s. This scandal centred on the existence of a 'dummy' consulting firm established to siphon 'commissions' from public sector contracts into PS coffers. On the right, perhaps the most significant scandal to date has involved the discovery of substantial irregularities in the running of the Paris city hall. These improprieties have significantly involved the misuse of municipal resources to finance RPR party activities. Ongoing investigations concern not only the current neo-Gaullist Mayor of Paris (Jean Tiberi), but also President Chirac. Chirac served as the capital's mayor from 1977 to 1995 and largely established the *systeme-RPR* which has now been called into question. Other scandals, such as the long-running 'tainted blood' affair (involving a delay in screening blood supplies for AIDS until an appropriate French technology had been developed) have similarly sapped public confidence in the political class. Cumulatively, there has been a growing public concern over the existence of a comparatively clientelist pattern of politics. There is a sense that the extensive personal networks of influence established by leading politicians have assumed an unduly central place in French political life, at the expense of more open structures of democratic participation (Elgey and Colombani, 1999: 7–22).

More than allegations of corruption, however, it is probably the failure of successive governments to deliver on economic policy promises that is at the root of the 'cycle of rejection'. As Vivien Schmidt (1999) argues, the French political elite has experienced particular difficulties in finding a discourse which adequately reflects the changed realities of national policy-making in an increasingly globalized economy. French politicians of both the Left and the Right have remained wedded to a *volontariste* economic discourse. 'Voluntarism', in this sense, refers to a belief in the ability of government to effect major economic change. Yet, in ways described in the following sections, that ability has been sharply curtailed in recent years. Both global and European trends have limited the French government's margin of manoeuvre. There consequently appears to be a mismatch between a traditional statist discourse and a changed economic reality. Nowhere is this gap more dramatically illustrated than with reference to the issue of unemployment. Chronically high levels of unemployment have – literally and figuratively – defeated successive French governments.

The strong majoritarian logic which had earlier marked the Fifth Republic has been attenuated, but not displaced, by a tendency towards fragmentation. Nevertheless, more than the partial fragmentation of the party system, it is the 'cycle of rejection' which should give cause for concern. The main parties of the Left and the Right have, in alternation, consistently been able to win viable parliamentary majorities. Yet, a pattern of rapid governmental turnover and persistent public disenchantment with governing elites cannot be ignored. Over the long run, one must question whether the accumulation of governmental 'failures' will begin to erode the legitimacy of the political system itself. In particular, it appears imperative that political discourse change in ways which better reflect the changed realities associated with both European integration and globalization.

France and European integration

France was a founding member of the European Communities and, historically, has been one of the driving forces behind European integration. Perhaps more than any other single country, France has set the rhythm for the integration process. More often than not, France has assumed a leading role in initiatives for the further development of European integration. At the same time, French reticence has also frequently played a key role in stopping or slowing down the integration process. The saga of the European Defence Community in the early 1950s, born of a French plan and ultimately killed by the French National Assembly, speaks volumes of this historically central and ambiguous role.

Nevertheless, France no longer occupies quite as central a position within the process of European integration as it once did. The 'fit' between French and European institutions may no longer be taken as a given. Successive enlargements of the EU have, inevitably, diluted French influence in the decision-making process. France, like the EU's other member states, has been required to engage in a complex and ongoing process of institutional learning.

European integration has also become more of a flash-point in domestic politics. The 1992 referendum on the Maastricht Treaty opened a Pandora's box. A sovereignty/integration cleavage has emerged as a secondary line of division in French politics, causing substantial turbulence within the party system. This turbulence must not, however, be allowed to mask the deeper realities of French politics. If sometimes volatile, French public opinion remains in the main sympathetic to the process of European integration.

A changing position

France's position relative to the European integration project has changed significantly in the past decade. Unquestionably, France, together with Germany, remains one of the 'motors' of European integration. The concerted efforts of the Franco-German axis are still a necessary, if by no means sufficient, condition for the forward movement of European integration. The conclusion of the Maastricht Treaty in 1991 was very much the product of a shared Franco-German commitment to the realization of an ambitious politico-economic project in the aftermath of German unification. Evidently, differences persist between the two countries. This has most importantly been the case as regards Economic and Monetary Union. Here, French preferences for a European 'economic government' run directly contradictory to Germany's unshakeable commitment to maintaining the independence of the European Central Bank (Dyson, 1999). Nevertheless, the habits of consultation and conciliation are now deeply entrenched on both sides of the Rhine. The two countries are likely to continue working tightly in tandem within the EU.

More generally, however, French European policy has appeared increasingly reactive in recent years (Guyomarch, Machin and Ritchie, 1998: 14). French governments have become less inclined to pursue broad European objectives. Rather than trying to set the agenda, France has largely contented itself with responding to such initiatives as they have come from the European Commission or other member states. This was noticeably the case during the negotiation of the 1997 Amsterdam Treaty, in which the French Government appeared uncharacteristically reluctant to assume a leading role (Menon, 1996).

Changing French perceptions of European integration underlie this change of position. France was for a long time an 'exporter' of institutions and policies to the European level. Key aspects of the institutional architecture of the European Communities, particularly the forms of its legal order, derived from French models. Equally, the development of substantive policies, not least the Common Agricultural Policy, clearly served French national interests. From the latter part of the 1980s onwards, however, there has been a growing awareness that this 'natural symbiosis' of French and European interests and practices no longer exists. In significant respects, France has become an 'importer' of policies and institutions. The country has had to bear the burden of significant institutional adaptations and policy changes to comply with European norms.

Both the economic and the political models ascendant at the European level pose fundamental challenges to long-established French institutions and practices (Muller, 1992; Ladrech, 1994). The market liberalization ethos which has driven forward the process of economic integration runs contrary to the strongly interventionist (*dirigiste*) traditions of the French state. Similarly, the emerging EU political system does not fit well with the French Republican tradition. The federalist aspirations of many 'pro-Europeans' clash with deeply entrenched notions of national sovereignty. The day-to-day functioning of EU policy-making, necessarily predicated on a culture of negotiated compromise, does not sit well with the French policy style of 'heroic' decision-making. The network-based nature of EU structures cuts across the more hierarchical organizational patterns typical of the French civil service (Lequesne, 1993, 1996). Overall, there emerges a perhaps surprising 'clash of cultures' between the French polity and its developing European counterpart. Reflecting these differences, French participation in the integration project has been marked by a growing reticence. Whereas Europe could once largely be conceived as a platform for French national interests, it now appears more as an arena within which those interests may be pursued.

Europe as a political issue

French public opinion was long quiescent as regards the European issue. An elite-driven process of further integration appeared to rest on an unproblematic tacit consensus. The Single European Act, notably, generated little public debate. This quiet consensus was, however, upset by the 1992 referendum on the Maastricht Treaty. President Mitterrand did not have to call a referendum in order to ratify the Treaty on European Union. He did so as a strategic political choice. In part, the referendum was intended as a strong display of public support for EU in the aftermath of the first (negative) Danish referendum on Maastricht. Public opinion polls at the time of Mitterrand's decision showed a clear 'yes' vote (around 70 per cent) in prospect. The referendum was also motivated by domestic political objectives. Mitterrand hoped that the poll would exacerbate divisions among his Right-Wing opponents in the run-up to the 1993 legislative elections.

The referendum produced a very different result to the one initially anticipated. The Treaty was approved by only a wafer-thin majority of French voters: 51 per cent voting 'yes' against 49 per cent voting 'no'. Polling data revealed the existence of clearly demarcated cleavages between Yes and No voters (Criddle, 1993; Guyomarch, Machin and Ritchie, 1998: 97–102). Pro-Maastricht voters were disproportionately drawn from the urban, better educated, and more prosperous segments of the electorate. Conversely, the anti-Maastricht electorate was disproportionately rural, less well off, and had a lower level of formal education. Supporters of the Treaty also tended to take more liberal positions on a range of social issues, while 'no' votes were correspondingly more conservative. The portrait could thus (all too easily) be drawn of 'two Frances': the one attuned to the changing realities of European integration and globalization; the other increasingly marginalized in the face of those same developments.

The referendum also sharpened divisions within the mainstream political parties over the European question. Prominent politicians of both the Left (Jean-Pierre

Chevènement) and the Right (Philippe Seguin, Charles Pasqua) campaigned against the Maastricht Treaty. For the most part, they did so in the name of a 'Jacobin' conception of the nation-state. From this perspective, neither the existence of genuine political democracy nor the preservation of meaningful social solidarity is conceivable outside the framework of the nation-state (Seguin, 1992).

Echoing these divisions, the aftermath of the referendum saw further turbulence in the French party system. As Alain Guyomarch (1995: 120) notes, the 'multi-faceted' nature of the European issue, encompassing both instrumental and symbolic dimensions, gives it a particularly strong disruptive capacity. This disruption has been unequally felt on the Right and the Left.

In the case of the Left, the European issue has not had a particularly destabilizing impact. The Communist Party campaigned against the Maastricht Treaty, repeating its traditional criticisms of a 'Capitalists' Europe'. More recently, however, the party has moved towards a more 'Euroconstructive' position under the leadership of Robert Hue. Jean-Pierre Chevènement's small Citizens' Movement (MDC) splintered from the main PS, largely over the European issue. The MDC, nevertheless, remains part of the governing *gauche plurielle* coalition. The PS itself appears relatively united behind Lionel Jospin's moderately pro-European stance.

The picture has been rather different on the Right. With some individual exceptions (notably Philippe de Villiers), the UDF has consistently maintained a pro-European (and occasionally even federalist) line. In contrast, the Gaullist RPR has been hit hard by divisions over Europe. In the Maastricht referendum, two Gaullist voters out of three voted against the Treaty. In doing so, they broke ranks with Jacques Chirac, who had publicly announced his support for the Treaty (albeit with a self-avowed lack of enthusiasm). Since then, the European issue has continued to bedevil the Gaullists. As noted in the previous section, it has, at the time of writing, apparently led to a definitive split in the party. The pro-sovereignty forces have rallied around Charles Pasqua to form a new political party.

The turbulence created by the European issue should not, however, be allowed to obscure the continued, underlying support of a majority of the French electorate for the broad lines of the integration project (Duhamel, 1999: 59–87). The years immediately after the highly charged Maastricht referendum did see a decline of support for the EU in France. Eurobarometer surveys, which showed a decline in support across the member states at this time, pointed to a particularly sharp fall in the French case (Cameron, D.R., 1996: 345–63). Recent years have, however, seen this tendency reversed. For example, the 1998 annual IPSOS/French Foreign Ministry poll on European issues (IPSOS, 1998) showed that over 71 per cent of those surveyed regarded European integration as a 'good thing' (up 8 per cent from the previous year). This figure is indicative of a broad consensus which continues to prevail on European issues. The centre of gravity in French politics is moderately pro-integrationist. It is telling that serious contenders for the Presidency in France have, in recent years, always carefully established their pro-European credentials. While the Maastricht referendum represented a serious expression of popular discontent, it is not an entirely accurate reflection of underlying attitudes as regards the integration process. France will continue to be a highly engaged, if perhaps increasingly volatile, partner in the unfolding of that process.

France, Europe and globalization

Globalization has generated considerable political and intellectual debate in France. In cruder formulations, globalization is often equated with 'Americanization', implying the triumph of homogenizing 'Anglo-Saxon' values over the distinctive characteristics of French culture (see Ardagh, 1999: 711–14). More serious discussions have centred on the economic implications of globalization, focusing on the changing balance of power between states and markets. Critics of globalization decry the hegemony of neo-liberal economic theory. The growing loss of state control over markets is seen as the product of a '*pensée zero*' or a '*pensée unique*'- a 'zero level' or 'stifling orthodoxy' of thought which abandons the creative use of public power for collective ends (Todd, 1998). Such analyses have, as their logical implication, the need for a reassertion of political power ('voluntarism' in the literal sense). This line of argument, more often than not, is further linked to calls for a return to a more protectionist economic policy.

On the other hand, globalization also has its advocates in France (Minc, 1997). In these more positive assessments, globalization is usually linked to a modernization discourse. External pressures are seen as a means of pressing a domestic reform agenda, forcing a beneficial acceleration of market liberalization measures. If globalization inevitably presents challenges to France, its advocates see the country as well placed to derive substantial rewards from this changed situation.

The divisions outlined above are, evidently, not unique to France. Nevertheless, in comparison with other major West European democracies, France has experienced the effects of globalization with a particular intensity (Schmidt, 1999). International market liberalization was bound to have a particularly disruptive effect in the French case, given the historically central role played by the state in the nation's economic life. The traditional *dirigiste* state has faced downsizing and retooling in the face of a rapidly changing European and international environment. Both the foundations of French economic policy and the structure of French capital have undergone dramatic transformations since the 1980s. Notwithstanding such changes, *dirigiste* reflexes are not dead. Some echoes remain at the national level. More strikingly, French governments have demonstrated a keen interest in 'exporting' key elements of the *dirigiste* model to the European level. It is in this light that one must understand France's consistent, if somewhat problematic, advocacy of a 'European social model' (see below).

Rolling back the *dirigiste* state

The meaning of *dirigisme* may most simply be conveyed with reference to the root of the word. The verb '*diriger*' would usually be translated as 'to direct'. The *dirigiste* state is one which, correspondingly, assumes a directive role as regards the national economy. This directive role found expression in the existence of a highly developed regulatory framework. It also provided the justification for a comparatively large public sector, significantly expanded by the wave of nationalizations which followed the Liberation. The defining characteristic of *dirigisme*, however, lies in the expectation that the state will set clearly defined priorities for national economic development. The state will, in other words, set the tone and indicate the direction of economic activity. It is assumed, by implication, that market forces will follow this political lead. This belief in the primacy of political decision-making underpinned the French practice of indicative planning, whereby a state agency established non-binding sectoral growth targets and development priorities. A similar philosophy also informed the so-called 'national champions' strategy. This strategy entailed the selective state backing of promising industrial concerns in key economic sectors so as to ensure a strong French presence in those sectors.

Needless to say, *dirigisme* is an ideal type. The French state could not escape the constraints imposed by both the domestic and the international environments. Although relatively weak and ideologically divided trade unions could usually be ignored, major business interests were generally consulted and co-opted in areas of concern (Hayward, 1986). Nonetheless, the importance of the model itself should not be diminished. *Dirigisme* created a climate of popular and elite expectations that the state should assume a leading role in economic affairs.

The last two decades of the twentieth century saw a substantial retrenchment of this *dirigiste* model. The turning point in French economic policy can be dated to the reversal of policy by the Socialist Government in 1982–83. The socialists, elected in 1981, had unsuccessfully attempted a Keynesian reflation of the national economy. After this failure, President Mitterrand was faced with a decisive choice. The French Government had either to adopt a policy of severe budgetary austerity or it would have to withdraw (temporarily) from the European Monetary System (EMS). Following heated debate within the Government, the President ultimately opted to maintain France in the EMS. From this moment onwards, French economic policy was progressively reshaped by a process of liberalization which undermined the core tenets of the *dirigiste* model. This liberalization has been pursued, in varying degrees, by governments of both the Left and the Right. It has led to a substantial reduction in the state's capacity for economic intervention, coupled with a concomitant legitimation of the market.

The move away from a *dirigiste* model may be illustrated with reference to the traditional instruments of state economic intervention. There has, since the mid-1980s, been a substantial (if still, by some standards, incomplete) deregulation of the French economy. For example, price controls have largely been abolished and employment laws have been made considerably more flexible. There have further been major privatizations. The French Government has now largely ceded ownership of the banking sector, while also wholly or partially privatizing major state-controlled industrial groups. Beyond domestic deregulation and privatization, French governments have had to deal with the increasingly vigorous implementation of competition policy by the European Commission. Cumulatively, these changes have deprived the state of significant levers of economic control.

In parallel to the reduction of the state's capacity for intervention, the structure of French capital has been transformed. Once largely dependent on medium- and long-term borrowing, French industry has increasingly been able to resort to the stock market and other forms of equity financing. Already in the years prior to the 'little bang' on the Paris Bourse, the balance between banking and non-banking sources of business finance had been reversed (Schmidt, 1996b: 112). French capital, following trends in other industrialized countries, has also undergone a notable internationalization in the past two decades. Comparing the periods 1973–80 and 1981–92, Szarka (1998: 154) notes that foreign direct investment in France increased almost fivefold, while French investments abroad increased by almost tenfold. From the *dirigiste* perspective, the French economy has become markedly less amenable to traditional forms of control.

The policies pursued by successive French Governments since the mid-1980s have had the effect of reducing the state's capacity for intervention in the economy. At the same time, the French economy has been transformed in ways which would make a return to the previous situation impossible, even if there were to be a political desire to renew with older statist practices. Elements of the old *dirigiste* model remain. French governments still tend to assume a central role in the restructuring of troubled industries, subject to the vigilant surveillance of the European Commission. One should also not ignore the exceptional homogeneity of the French elite. Key decision-makers in both the public and the private sectors remain, in large measure, the products of the same elite educational establishments (Schmidt, 1996b: 285–346). Nonetheless, the traditional *dirigiste* model has been substantially superseded by a more market-based alternative. French economic policy, once defined by the expectation that the state would assume a directive role, is now largely reactive to the lead given by market forces.

A European social model?

In the case of all EU member states, the relationship between the effects of European integration and globalization is necessarily a complex and multidimensional one. European integration acts, in varying contexts, both as a conduit for broader international developments and as a buffer against them (Schmidt, 1999). In the previous section, European integration was identified as a factor contributing to the rolling back of the traditional *dirigiste* state in France. The economically liberal thrust of the integration project has amplified the effects of globalization. Yet, on balance, European integration still tends to be viewed in France as a means of cushioning the impact of globalization. One 1998 poll, for example, found that 73 per cent of those surveyed regarded European integration as a means of protection against the effects of globalization (IPSOS, 1998).

This view, moreover, finds a strong echo in governmental policy. As core aspects of the *dirigiste* model have become decreasingly sustainable within the domestic context, successive governments have appeared increasingly anxious to 'export' those features to the European level. France has consistently advocated the development of a European-level industrial policy, seeking by strategic public support to ensure a European presence in key high-tech sectors. In a similar vein, France has also been concerned to develop a European-level notion of 'public service'. French governments have argued that a better balance must be struck between the promotion of competition and the need for the universal provision of services of general public interest. In both cases, the French position is tellingly one which reasserts the existence of a distinctive public interest against a belief in the primacy of the market. It is equally revealing that these efforts have met with, at best, modest success.

Beyond specific policy initiatives, French governments have further shown a general interest in developing the social dimension of European integration (Duhamel, 1999: 113–39). President Mitterrand spoke frequently of the need to build a 'social Europe'. More recently, Prime Minister Lionel Jospin has stressed that he accepts a market economy, but not a 'market society'. This catchphrase encapsulates the desire of the French Socialist Government to distance itself from British New Labour's 'Third Way'. Jospin has been at pains to emphasize the distinctively 'humanist' values of his party's social democratic project, in contrast to the more market-driven orientation of a Blairite 'social liberalism' (Jospin, 1999). Yet, though French political leaders have offered strong support for a 'European social model', the content of that model remains somewhat problematic. Emphasizing the need to protect a more caring European form of capitalism against a less compassionate (Anglo-)American variant, the image which often emerges is that of a 'social market economy'. Paradoxically, this places France in the position of defending a 'Rhineland model' of capitalism which does not correspond to its own national traditions (Albert, 1991). France's traditionally more statist model of political economy does not, in particular, provide for the extensive, institutionalized consultations with the 'social partners' (business and labour) which are usually seen to be one of the defining traits of the 'Rhineland model'. Thus, even if a distinctive European social model does take shape (see Chapter 5), it appears likely that this model will itself entail a continued need for France to adapt its existing institutions and policies to a changing external environment.

Conclusion and future prospects

French politics and society have undergone major transformations in the past two decades. The role of the state has been fundamentally redefined. Domestically, there has been a significant diffusion of power, marking a shift away from traditionally centralized and hierarchical power structures. Externally, both globalization and European integration have necessitated a thoroughgoing reassessment of traditional conceptions of sovereignty. At the same time, there has been a basic rebalancing of the relationship between the state and the market. These changes have, unsurprisingly, been accompanied by a growing sense of disquiet in French public opinion.

This disquiet may partly be seen as the belated price of the modernization which took place during the first two decades of the Fifth Republic. The 'Gaullist modernization' of France's economy and society (Hewlett, 1998: 119–45) placed little store in the development of participatory structures. The Fifth Republic aggravated the chronic weakness of the *corps intermediaires* – the representative mediators such as political parties and interest groups – which has longed marked French political life. In consequence, change still tends to be imposed from the centre. There are few formalized structures which would allow the adaptations necessitated by globalization and European integration to be managed through processes of negotiated reform. Periodic explosions, such as the paralysing wave of strikes in December 1995 directed against the Juppe Government's budget cuts, are thus likely to remain a feature of French life.

Beyond this democratic deficit, France further appears to be suffering from a discursive deficit. There seems, in the French case, to be a singular difficulty in devising a political discourse which may serve to legitimate changing power structures. As it stands, there is an exceptionally wide gulf between rhetoric and reality. While the role of the state has been fundamentally redefined in the past two decades, neither political discourse nor public expectations have kept pace. This gap will have to be closed if the French political system is not to suffer a longer term delegitimation.

Such threats should not, however, be overestimated. Perhaps the most striking feature of the past two decades is how successfully the French state has coped with a dramatically changed environment. Feelings of disquiet should not be allowed to mask the basic health of both the polity and (unemployment apart) the economy. France continues to be a comparatively successful modern industrialized democracy. Despite alarmist predictions to the contrary, France also remains France.

CHAPTER NINE

Britain – Still Not a 'Team Player'?

Peter J. Anderson

Introduction

This chapter will focus predominantly on five policy areas which the author feels are of particular regional and national importance and interest for the Britain of the present and of the future. These are the domestic economic and social policy dimensions, the domestic politics dimension, defence policy, Britain and Europe, and, much more briefly, the ethical dimension of British foreign policy. Other policy areas and concerns will be woven into the discussion in each of these sections, but only to the extent that they are relevant to them.

The domestic economic and social dimensions

With the exception of Northern Ireland, whose future remains uncertain at the time of writing, the UK, under the Central Government of the Labour Party led by Tony Blair, and the devolved administrations of Scotland, Northern Ireland and Wales, appears as a highly stable society with a successful economy and a welfare state that, if not without its problems, still functions with a broad degree of public acceptance. Its overall mortality rates, while not as good as some other European societies, are still good on the global average (*Economist*, 1999b: 147) and unemployment, a key factor often related to health and mortality, has been going down noticeably under the Labour Government. There are keenly directed programmes to try and improve education standards and access nationally, to improve the quality of various categories of care and treatment within the National Health Service and to reduce the incidence of poverty. However, even while pointing to its achievements, the Government is careful to admit that there are still crucial problems that remain unsolved:

> Our unemployment is lower than much of the European continent. Our labour markets are more flexible, and we are growing some of the industries of the next century, such as biotechnology, design and software development . . . Our productivity in manufacturing remains poor by comparison with France. The quality of our products is not as good as it should be, and we can learn a lot from Germany on this. (Hoon, 1999)

Every British government that wishes to be seen as innovative has its key economic themes. For the Blair Government, the themes seem to have been the acknowledgement of the alleged successes of the Thatcher Government's reshaping of the British economy and industrial relations within it, the commitment to sound finances as a basis for everything else, an enthusiastic promotion of new technologies within the industrial sector, and a commitment to the Third Way, in which goals such as the eradication of unemployment problems will be pursued via means which it believes take the best from market capitalism and social democratic economics, without adopting the serious failings of each (see Hutton, 1995 or *Economist*, 1998: 47). On the surface, the Blair Government's record on these aims seems to have been successful in many respects as it passes the halfway stage of his administration. The state finances seem impressively secure, unemployment continues to decline and new technology-based industries continue to be established within the UK, particularly in and around 'greenfield sites' such as Cambridge (at the expense of the old industrial cities, where redundant land often requires expensive clearing before reuse – see Elliott, 1999: 3).

However, as is often the case in politics and economics, things are not necessarily all that they seem. The British economy is afflicted by a variety of serious weaknesses, the effects of which, in a number of cases, as yet are not satisfactorily quantifiable. One of the key problems is what some see as a strength, namely the heavy reliance on globalization to help solve some of the traditional weaknesses of the national economy. Most obvious among the latter are short-termism in industrial investment thinking and a reluctance to invest adequately in domestic enterprises. Such problems automatically make foreign industrial investments welcome, and Britain has been a successful attracter of Far Eastern, in particular Japanese, overseas investment, most particularly in its electronics and motor industries. The share ownership patterns of British industry, together with an Anglo-Saxon complementary fondness for solving downturns in company fortunes by shedding jobs rather than reducing shareholders' returns, have made it additionally desirable that Britain should attract from elsewhere investment that would help pick up some of the consequences. While globalizing patterns of industrial investment have helped rescue the British economy from what otherwise would have been a sorry fate, the very global mindset of the investing companies means that many of them are just as likely to relocate elsewhere should economic conditions within the world economy change in favour of such a move. Their lack of national loyalties, in other words, makes them a potentially unstable leg upon which to rest overheavily the future of a developed economy. Equally, British multinationals, like the retailer Marks and Spencer, have shown themselves to be ruthless cutters of domestic manufacturing contracts in favour of overseas contracts when the economic going has started to get rough – again with the interests of shareholders predominantly in mind.

A key part of the above-mentioned domestic investment problem is what might be termed a very British disease, namely the overpreoccupation with home ownership. The Thatcher Government made a particular point of promoting home ownership through such devices as council house sales. There have been a number of significant negative economic consequences of this, as several leading industrialists pointed out to the UK Government during autumn 1999. First, huge amounts of money that could be invested productively in British industry are lodged non-productively in bricks and mortar, thereby severely handicapping the potential of the British economy. Second, the huge discrepancy between house prices in different parts of the country, most particularly between prices in London and the South-East and the many less glamorous regions in the old industrial North of the country, make labour mobility out of the question for many of Britain's citizens, further holding the economy back. Third, periodic booms in the house prices of the more prosperous areas, most particularly the South-East, can lead to distortions of interest rates and other consequences which damage the trading position of many British exporters considerably. No government as yet, the Blair administration included, has dared to address these problems in any credible way and they remain a serious liability for the British economy in the twenty-first century.

Finally, while the Blair Government has paid tribute to the Thatcher years for shaking up and modernizing the British economy, it is not at all clear how many of the companies that were driven into bankruptcy by the Thatcher Government's policies could actually have recovered, grown and prospered under different economic policies, saving enormously on unemployment benefit costs, the cost of dealing with health problems frequently associated with sustained unemployment and the incalculable misery that undoubtedly followed for many as a result of Thatcherism. One of the questions to be raised about the current British economy is whether it has anything like the right balance between long-term industries with staying power, like the 'metal bashing' industries of the West Midlands, and more short-term industries, such as semi-conductor manufacturing, which can evaporate almost overnight as nationally based producers (Fujitsu being a good example in a UK context), leaving sudden and unexpected local economic and social problems. Indeed, at the time of writing, serious questions existed concerning the future of UK motor manufacturing and its associated industries, threatening a further reduction in the proportion of 'long-stay' industry within the British economy. It is notable that during the first half of 2000 non-Eurosceptic economists (see, for example, Hutton, 2000) and several motor manufacturers laid the blame for this firmly at the door of the high pound and the damage that it had done to British competitiveness globally, which they believed to be in part a consequence of Britain's failure to adopt the euro.

Another serious question mark that must be placed beside British economic performance relates to the marked decline in unemployment. The decline in unemployment masks the poorly paid nature of much of the new employment that has been provided in recent years, most particularly in the service sector, and 'the invisible people' – those who are unemployed in any reasonable sense of the term but who are ineligible to claim for benefits under current regulations. It is notable also that the gap between rich and poor in Britain is now one of the largest within the developed world. Some parts of the UK – parts of Glasgow, Liverpool, Salford, Barnsley, Newcastle and Cornwall, for example – are among the most socially deprived in Europe, with some serious drugs problems and drugs-related crime.

Given the interconnectedness of economic and social conditions in any society, this last point leads the discussion neatly into Britain's overall position socially at the beginning of the new century. The Blair Government has laid down some bold aims, including a commitment, for example, to eradicate poverty within 20 years. But to many, there seems a long way to go before such goals start to look in any way credible. It was perhaps recognition of the difficulty of persuading people otherwise, that led him to spark a new debate on the North–South divide in December 1999, stressing the positive effects of his Government's New Deal, together with those of its implementation of the minimum wage, the Working Families Tax Credit, winter allowances for pensioners, rises in child benefits and its general economic policies, which he claimed were significantly reducing unemployment (Smith, 1999).

However, while the Government has won praise for such policies from such Centre-Left opinion-formers as the *Guardian*, the same paper pointed out in a leader only a few days before Blair's December debate that: 'As we have noted before, Labour has honoured the first half of its welfare mantra ("work for those who can"), but still has a considerable way to go to achieve the second half ("security for those who can't")' (*Guardian*, 1999a, p. 23). It emphasized the widening gap between the better off and the poor with regard to both death and illness rates. In short, while, as was pointed out at the beginning of this section, there is much that initially looks impressive about Britain at the beginning of the twenty-first century, both economically and socially, there are also serious problems that are as yet unsolved. Bearing in mind the scale of social problems in particular that Labour inherited from the Conservatives, it would perhaps be unfair to judge them on their record on dealing with these until well into their second administration, provided that they win the next election as currently expected. However, it is also apparent that some problems, such as the national overfixation with home ownership, are not being tackled by the Government at all and their consequences, therefore, will continue.

The domestic political dimension

Domestically, as pointed out above, Britain looks likely to remain in the control of the Labour Party at the next general election, which will be held very early in the twenty-first century. The two main opposition parties present no credible challenge to the present government on the basis of all of the existing opinion polls data, and this is likely to remain the case until the current Conservative leader, William Hague, is replaced. The Conservatives have moved too far to the Right for the majority of the British electorate, despite the fact that Britain has remained a predominantly 'conservative' country in its instincts. However this very conservatism restricts the range of policy options that is open to the Labour leadership if it wishes to remain in power. The difficulties that it faces with regard to any early move towards the European Union's (EU's) new single currency have been demonstrated already. It also has to play down the implications of even the limited social and wealth redistribution programmes that it has implemented so far if it wishes to retain the support of many of its wealthier supporters. It has to be careful too with regard to taxation, and this constraint restricts both the extent to which it can meet its social welfare obligations and the extent to which it can put real flesh on the bones of all of its talk about making the European contribution to NATO more substantial and more credible.

Britain remains predominantly a stable country politically, in so far as significant public disturbances of a political nature are very rare. (However, this should not be taken as meaning that Britain is a state without any significant threats to democracy within it, as will be seen below.) How likely it is to remain a unified one is less certain, given the extension of differing degrees of devolution to Scotland, Northern Ireland and Wales during the Blair Labour Government's first administration. The direction in which Scotland and Northern Ireland will go in during the next few years, if their devolved assemblies are felt to work by their peoples, and by so doing generate a new sense of confidence in their independent identities, is uncertain. The Welsh

Assembly is less likely to generate such confidence, given its less comprehensive range of powers and its unimpressive start as a devolved decision-making body, although it has since been showing some real signs of striking out a distinctive pathway of its own. The situation in Northern Ireland remained stalemated at the time of writing, with devolved power-sharing having been granted and then withdrawn as a result of the continuing disagreements over paramilitary weapons decommissioning.

The first threat to UK democracy that has been identified within recent years takes the form of the loose nature of the British constitution and the opportunity which this offers for 'strong leaders' with large majorities, such as Tony Blair or the Conservative leader of the 1980s, Margaret Thatcher, to run the country in a 'presidential' style at the expense of the more parliamentary form of democracy favoured by several past leaders, and which for many has been the essence of 'the British model'. Blair's favouring of bilateral dealings with his ministers at the expense of frequent Cabinet meetings means that it is psychologically more difficult for ministers to voice effectively any real doubts about government policies than it would be should they have a greater opportunity for expressing their views together in Cabinet. Of concern also to those most defensive of House of Commons traditions, such as the veteran Labour Left-Winger Tony Benn, has been the effective downgrading of the House of Commons by the Prime Minister, who has been criticized for allowing a number of key announcements to be made to the press before they were made to Parliament itself. Another symptom of this apparent downgrading has been the reduction in the number of occasions on which the Prime Minister can formally be questioned within the Commons.

The second significant threat to democracy in the UK comes from the difficulties facing electors who would wish to try and influence the many EU decisions that now affect directly or indirectly Britain's citizens. The first problem in this regard lies in the ability of the Council of Ministers, upon which the British Government sits, to make key decisions with little public scrutiny. By the time those decisions reach the European Parliament, the cumbersome procedures of the latter make it less than easy for such decisions to be blocked or amended, although this is technically possible now for many EU policy areas, and does indeed happen to an as yet limited extent. On top of this, however, is the fact that the European Parliament has not been effective in selling itself to the British electorate (Anderson and Weymouth, 1999: 155–7), while, equally, much of the British media has taken little interest in it and has therefore made little effort to make the UK public aware of its importance. Few people in Britain know about or understand the Parliament, thus reducing further their ability to exercise their democratic rights in protection or furtherance of their own interests as they are determined within the EU. Finally, the volume of EU legislation is now so huge that it is not possible for UK parliamentary committees to keep up with all of it and to try and influence it most effectively in the direction of Britain's interests, and the interests of the nation's electors.

A third and major threat to democracy within the UK is globalization. The globalized economy is creating enormously powerful dominant players, like Bill Gates of Microsoft, and Rupert Murdoch of News International, who, even as foreign nationals, are able to get access to the British Prime Minister and to influence his thinking in a way that is simply not possible for ordinary UK citizens. Murdoch, for example, has played a significant role in helping to keep Britain out of the European Monetary Union (EMU) by encouraging his big-circulation newspapers to act as propaganda sheets against it, thereby affecting citizens' ability to obtain the fully informed view on such issues that is necessary for a properly functioning democracy. The World Trade Organisation (WTO), also, is a body which is seen by many of its critics as pursuing globalization and the elimination of trade barriers in the interests of global corporations, and often at the expense of ordinary citizens. It is argued, for example, that WTO policies threaten to undermine the ability of democratically elected governments, such as that of Britain, to respond adequately to their electorate's concerns concerning genetically modified organisms. In addition, the massive, rapid shifts of industrial investment or finance capital that are possible in a globalized world economy can undermine very quickly an elected government's ability to deliver on its pledges to its people, as the Major Government discovered in 1992, when it was forced to make a quick and inglorious exit from the European Monetary System (EMS).

These were three of the most immediately visible threats to democracy in Britain, and in Britain within the EU, at the time of writing, and there seemed little likelihood of credible solutions to any of them being implemented by the Government within the foreseeable future.

Defence policy

Strange though it might seem to make such a remark, British defence policy is not all about defence. Part of its purpose in recent years has been, for example, to help create an image of a strong and determined government unafraid of firm action, to enhance the image of the Prime Minister of the day as an internationally respected statesman/woman in the hope that this will increase faith in their judgement domestically, to strengthen the case for Britain retaining its seat on the UN Security Council, and (since December 1998) to improve Britain's standing and bargaining power within the EU given its problematic lack of immediate participation in the EMU.

This fact creates a problem, in so far as these purposes, which are often not explicitly stated, can conflict with those that are. The intention here is to concentrate mainly on stated purposes and to evaluate the extent to which policy has made it possible for those aims to be achieved. However, in passing, it should be noted that other implicit purposes will be brought into the discussion where relevant.

The Labour Government that has taken Britain from the old century into the new set about a major reassessment of defence policy at the beginning of its period of office. While the declared thinking that came out of that review has been changed in some respects since, most of it remains in place as policy. What it is intended to do here is to look at the outcome of the review through two contrasting perspectives and then draw some conclusions as to its significance for Britain's role in Europe and the world at the beginning of the twenty-first century. The first perspective, which for purely short-hand reasons will be referred to as a mainstream, centrist, defence analysis perspective, is that of Colin McInnes. The second, more radical perspective, is that of David Edgerton.

The review

On 28 May 1997, the new Labour Government formally launched the strategic defence review that its manifesto had promised. It did so in the context of a defence policy inherited from the Conservatives which had seen the defence budget as a percentage of GDP shrink to its lowest level during the twentieth century and the armed forces reduced to a number that was smaller than any previously sanctioned since the 1930s (McInnes, 1998: 825). Yet, under the Conservatives, great emphasis had continued to be placed on Britain's world role and global responsibilities, including its coveted permanent seat on the UN Security Council.

The review was not finally published until July 1998. It claimed to be foreign-policy-driven and McInnes identifies several key themes within the foreign policy baseline. First, there is a higher emphasis than in previous Conservative policy on new risks, such as those deriving from terrorism, the scarcity of particular resources and drug, ethnic and population pressures (McInnes, 1998: 833). Second, while the risk of a major European war against NATO is downplayed, there is a clear commitment to a continuing active British role in promoting international security, which would include British military deployments when necessary (McInnes, 1998: 834). McInnes states that:

> The Labour party and government are internationalist by inclination: they believe they can be a 'force for good in the world' and that Britain has special responsibilities, not least as a permanent member of the Security Council. The Labour government is also internationalist for pragmatic reasons, notably the large number of overseas British investments and trading interests ... as George Robertson states ... 'We must be prepared to go to the crisis, rather than have the crisis come to us.' (McInnes, 1998: 834)

Third, the traditional emphasis on the importance of keeping the USA politically and militarily engaged in Europe is upheld, as is, fourth, the importance of NATO as opposed to any possible competitor or replacement European defence structure. (However, this was later to be modified during 1998/99, as will be seen (McInnes, 1998: 834–5).)

In the eyes of many military analysts, Labour inherited an overstretched military and yet proceeded, in time-honoured fashion (see, for example, Darby, 1973; Frankel, 1975; Northedge, 1974), to cut the defence budget substantially without cutting back on commitments. They attempted to accommodate this by reorganizing and re-tasking their forces in a manner which they hoped would enable them to achieve their defence mission objectives more effectively at a lower cost (McInnes, 1998: 841). This reorganization produced little in the way of real cuts in existing force levels, concentrating mainly on trying to tailor forces and equipment more to the mission roles now deemed to be most appropriate. The three existing small aircraft carriers, for example, are now to be replaced by two larger ones. The Trident nuclear deterrent is to be retained on the grounds of status and the dangers inherent in a world of nuclear weapons proliferation, despite past Labour Party controversy over its moral legitimacy, and the number of planned warheads reduced from 300 to less than 200. This is to be balanced by a commitment to the importance of accelerating global nuclear disarmament negotiations (McInnes, 1998: 838–42).

Overall, McInnes argues that the review introduced a number of major changes in defence policy. These include: a shift away from NATO defence towards strategic mobility and power projection, the development of defence diplomacy as a core tool in the promotion of international stability and crisis prevention, and the priority given to new perceived security risks (McInnes, 1998: 844).

He argues that, via a policy that minimizes cuts and maximizes emphasis on more effective organization of existing resources, New Labour has attempted to devise a force structure capable of meeting the requirements of its defence missions (McInnes, 1998: 845).

Edgerton, on the other hand, and arguing from a radically different perspective, is deeply concerned about Labour having become gripped by what he sees as a new 'moral imperialist' fantasy. He argues that:

> Defence policy highlights the continued centrality of the Atlanticist, rather than the European dimension, as well as the continued importance of the military at the heart of the British state. A deep commitment to the maintenance of strong armed services, a strong defence industry, and an increase in British abilities to intervene around the world characterize New Labour's defence policy. (Edgerton, 1998: 123)

Unlike McInnes, Edgerton sees scant evidence for the review being led by any coherent foreign policy or convincingly-argued rationale and concludes that one of its main functions is to enable Britain to continue being the USA's 'little helper'. He comments on observations made by John Keegan, defence editor of the *Daily Telegraph*:

> Crucially ... he [John Keegan] suggests that the planned aircraft carriers ... will continue to allow Britain, in the eyes of the service chiefs, to provide a complete air, sea, and land force, though on a small scale, to assist US operations. He claims that the composition, rather than the size of British forces, is what allows Britain to be the USA's principal partner. It is little wonder that the service chiefs are happy, as are – to judge by the business pages – the arms suppliers. (Edgerton, 1998: 124–5)

He goes on to accuse the Blair Government of trying to reinvent Britain as a global contender, effectively following in the footsteps of Margaret Thatcher (Edgerton, 1998: 125).

He also argues that the rationale offered for Britain's global defence role, as contained both in the *Strategic Defence Review* and in the speeches of the then Defence Secretary, is 'half-baked' and in some respects 'risible'. Even the economic arguments offered are, in Edgerton's view, 'weak and partial' (1998: 126). He approves of the opinion of William Wallace, whom he quotes: 'Rejection of closer European defence cooperation, at the outset of the review, left the special relationship with the Americans defining the political context' (Edgerton, 1998: 127).

Overall, he sees the review as a wasted opportunity to rethink British defence strategy in the widest sense, most particularly with regard to its longstanding Atlanticist orientation and the burden which, he argues, is placed upon the economy by high levels of defence spending. Instead of making an effort to genuinely re-evaluate Britain's defence policy priorities and commitments, Labour remains deeply committed to the old Atlanticist policy, in his view. He believes that the *Strategic Defence Review* has 'provided a cover and a means of incorporating potentially dissident factions into a new moral imperialism' (Edgerton, 1998: 129).

So, having looked at these two perspectives on the review, what overall conclusions can be drawn concerning their accuracy and the current and projected nature of British defence policy? First, it has to be noted that, since the above articles were published, British policy on its defence relationship with Europe and the USA has changed significantly. This came most notably to public notice in December 1998, when Prime Minister Blair and President Chirac of France launched the European Defence Initiative, whereby it was proposed that a European defence capability should be developed to be used in crisis management operations in which the Alliance as a whole is not involved. This was endorsed unanimously at NATO's fiftieth anniversary summit during the following year (Foreign and Commonwealth Office, 1999a)

In a Joint Declaration issued at the end of a subsequent Anglo-Italian summit of July 1999, the new British commitment to an EU defence dimension was re-emphasized. The British and Italian Governments stated that:

> Among the clear lessons of Kosovo are the continued importance of a strong and effective NATO and the pressing need for improved European military capabilities, both for a more effective European role in NATO and to ensure the EU has the capacity for autonomous action in the field of the Petersberg tasks (humanitarian and rescue tasks, peacekeeping and crisis management including peacemaking) backed by credible military forces. (Foreign and Commonwealth Office, 1999b)

Publicly available documentation shows clearly that the British Government was in full agreement with the NATO Cologne summit's view that 'a more effective role for the European Union in conflict prevention and crisis management would contribute to the vitality of a renewed alliance'. (Foreign and Commonwealth Office, 1999a). As the chapter on NATO shows (see below – Chapter 14), the commitment to an EU military dimension was further solidified at the December 1999 Helsinki summit with full British agreement. All of this was a radical turn-round from the situation during, for example, February 1998, when Foreign Secretary Cook had stated unreservedly on British television that defence policy was the concern of NATO alone and not of the EU.

The explanation for the change in policy is unsurprising. As the EMU rapidly progressed from being a probability to an actuality, there seems to have been a realization that Britain was once more travelling out towards the margins of EU influence. Some way of halting this process had to be found, and a shift in the British position on the Common Foreign and Security Policy seemed the most practical means available. Britain's strong professional military is not hampered by the continuing historical overhang from the Second World War that still imposes limits on the ways in which Italian and German armed forces can be used, and therefore it represents a major, vital ingredient for a common defence policy. A move to embrace the idea of a defence role for the Europeans would therefore constitute some real compensation for Britain's non-membership of the EMU, until it was able to join. As the chapter on NATO will show, however, another reason for Britain's change of policy was the Kosovo conflict of 1999, with its demonstration both of US reluctance to contribute ground troops to a conflict in which US core interests were not at stake, and of Britain and Europe's inability to compensate for this without a strong European military identity.

What has happened, therefore, is that the Blair Government has retained the Atlanticist focus within its defence policy (given most particularly its belief in the need to retain the American nuclear guarantee to Europe so long as Russia remains a nuclear great power), while amending it in such a way that a European defence focus also becomes possible, providing it remains complementary to the American linkage. This accommodation of previously conflicting interests was justified by Blair in his November 1999 speech at the Lord Mayor's Banquet, when he insisted Britain did not face a choice between the EU and the USA: 'It is a false choice. The fact is that we are listened to more closely in Washington if we are leading in Europe. And we have more weight in Europe if we are listened to in Washington' (Blair, 1999a).

As far as the question of Britain's continued *relatively high level of defence spending* is concerned, then, provided humanitarian peacekeeping and peacemaking are accepted as key policy goals for a declaredly 'internationalist' Labour Government, Edgerton's criticisms seem to be unjustified in the light of the overstretch of British forces clearly evidenced once the Kosovo peacekeeping mission had been added to that already in place within Bosnia.

The only truly contentious element within the review, therefore, seems to be *the nuclear deterrent*. For those who find the potential for inflicting mass destruction which such weapons possess unacceptable on moral grounds in any circumstances or context, then the decision to retain them is clearly a mistake. For those who believe that, in a world where nuclear weapons are now in the hands of periodically unstable states, such as Pakistan and, for that matter, Russia, it might be more morally justifiable to retain them for their deterrent value than to scrap them unilaterally, then clearly they are a continuing wise investment. Even if the second view is accepted, however, the fly in the ointment is the fact that the British deterrent is under *shared*, not national, control. The Trident submarines are an American design, supplied to the British for building in their own yards. While the nuclear warheads are made in the UK, the Trident missiles themselves are manufactured in, and serviced in, the USA. The missiles are targeted via US strategic facilities in Nebraska. In short, there are no credible circumstances in which they could be fired without American permission.

All of this of course raises considerable questions as to why the British are spending scarce defence resources on them if they are not wholly under their control. The answer goes back to the time of the Cold War. In short, whatever past British governments have said about the 'independence' of the deterrent for domestic political consumption, they have long found a strategic value in its effective integration (since the late 1950s) with the US nuclear military. Given that other nuclear powers are perfectly aware of this integration, they must take into account that any nuclear attack on Britain or its forces abroad may well be regarded by American governments as equivalent, or at least nearly equivalent, to an attack on US forces. This will occur most particularly in circumstances where there are strong personal ties between British and US leaders, as in the case of Macmillan and Kennedy, of Thatcher and Reagan or of Blair and Clinton, for example. The lack of independence of the British deterrent is not a problem from this point of view. It is in fact an asset, which strengthens Britain's security, and therefore justifies the money spent on it.

Finally, with regard to *defence diplomacy and the identification of new risks to Britain's security, such as terrorism and drugs*, the first of these two concerns hardly seems a contentious one. Its core focus on crisis prevention is one that aims both to prevent bloodshed and to reduce the likelihood of the costs of major military campaigns being incurred. The second, equally, would seem to be little more or less than a recognition of threats that need to be taken seriously and dealt with appropriately if the fabric of British society and stability is to be protected. Whether the right emphasis relatively is being put on each of these areas is something that will only become fully apparent as the policy is implemented, as will the appropriateness or otherwise of the methods of implementation.

So, at the moment, it seems hard to justify most of Edgerton's complaints concerning the *Strategic Defence Review*, although allowance must be made for the fact that he could hardly foresee the somewhat dramatic turn-round on British attitudes towards the Common Foreign and Security Policy that occurred after the completion of his article. The question of the nuclear deterrent, however, is a different matter altogether, given the unique nature of the weaponry and its capacity for the instant destruction of large numbers of people. Ultimately, given the real primary reasons for its retention by the Government, whether its continued deployment is justifiable or a gross mistake depends essentially on which corner of the debate on the morality of nuclear deterrence individuals sit in.

An appropriate point on which to end this section would seem to be to consider *the overall reasoning behind Britain's defence posture under Labour*. Edgerton identified and criticized a number of arguments within the review which supported Labour's defence posture and which he felt to be insubstantial. His criticism in some respects is justified in terms of the arguments themselves, one or two of which might be described as 'traditionally fatuous'. However, to some extent he is missing the point concerning the discourse of political documents. It is no secret that, in cases where the subject matter is particularly sensitive, as are key elements of defence policy *vis-à-vis*, for example, the remnants of the traditional Left of the Labour Party, policy documents contain 'overground' and 'underground' dimensions. The former are the surface justifications intended to make a policy as palatable as possible for as many people as possible, and are not necessarily to be taken at face value, although some of them can be. Edgerton refers to some examples of these in his discussion. The underground dimensions, unsurprisingly, are the real, unmentioned reasons for a policy that are not stated in public documentation, either for reasons of security or for reasons of domestic political sensitivity. When current policy is analysed, therefore, as many as possible of the latter must be identified and some of the former discarded, where available evidence would seem to justify this.

There is not the available space to do a comprehensive job in the above respect here, but what will be done is to identify and explain briefly some of the key reasoning underlying the review and subsequent amendments to it. In short, defence policy is rather more foreign-policy-driven than Edgerton allows. A key foreign policy aim, inherited from the previous Conservative administration, but entirely in line with Labour's policy of internationalism and of trying to 'punch with as much weight as possible', is that of maintaining Britain's seat on the UN Security Council at a time when there are both increasingly loud claims from states such as Germany and Italy that Britain and France's seats should be replaced by a single EU seat and growing demands from inside Japan that it should have a permanent seat at the UN's 'top table'. The defence policy response to this aim takes the form of the preparedness to provide appropriate forces for key humanitarian, peacekeeping or peace-making operations such as Kosovo under NATO or UN, and now EU, auspices, as a means of maintaining Britain's claim to retain a seat at the UN's 'top table'.

A second key foreign policy aim, that of keeping the Americans in Europe militarily, and firmly committed to NATO, is explicitly stated in the publicly available policy documentation. What is not explicitly stated is one of the key reasons which traditionally has underlain this British attitude. In short, the British military has in the past regarded many of its European counterparts to be second rate in terms of their effectiveness when compared to American forces.

In addition, there is the perception that, in a world in which only the USA has a level of nuclear weaponry capable of unreservedly deterring the continuing nuclear might of Russia, should the latter switch back to a threatening posture again at any stage, it would seem exceedingly foolish to create or allow the development of a situation in which America's nuclear shield was withdrawn from NATO. The defence policy response to the perceived need to avoid such a situation is to maintain the posture in which Edgerton rightly refers to Britain as being 'America's little helper'. This is Britain's contribution to the informal 'purchase price' of a continuing substantial American military involvement in Europe. The review, for example, clearly does set out to maintain a mix of forces and equipment that will enable Britain to intervene in a small but complementary fashion to American operations around the world, where justifications for such action can be provided for domestic consumption.

At the same time, the Blair Government has realized, since coming to office, that the end of the Cold War, and such politically damaging failures as the US Somalian involvement during the early 1990s, have created a situation in which American military involvement in European security issues is more situationally-determined than guaranteed. Most particularly, it has realized that even where the USA does decide to intervene, it will be extremely reluctant to provide ground troops while active hostilities are continuing. This has forced the British Government finally to move to a position where it has agreed to the building up of a credible European defence dimension, complementary to NATO, but capable of acting on the ground within specifically defined circumstances when the USA is unwilling to. This is despite its previously mentioned continuing private reservations about some of its European military partners. It has realized that its declared humanitarian and peacekeeping objectives might not be realizable in future European crises should such preparations not be made.

An additional foreign-policy-led reason for this change of policy has already been mentioned concerning the EMU.

Britain and Europe

British policy towards European integration traditionally has suffered from a two-way pull. On the one hand, since the 1950s Britain's economic interests increasingly have been perceived as being crucially dependent on Western European markets by key sections of the political and economic elites. This was one of the determining reasons which persuaded British policy-makers, both Conservative and Labour, to begin trying to enter the then EEC during the 1960s. Even the 'arch-nationalist' Prime Minister Margaret Thatcher believed firmly in the virtues of the European

Single Market and strongly promoted the need for its completion during her period of office. There were also worries, particularly during the Macmillan Government of the early 1960s, that if Britain did not join the European integration process, it could rapidly find itself demoted on the world stage politically if the European Communities began to develop a strong political dimension.

On the other hand, there was also a strong transatlantic pull. The USA most fundamentally was the ultimate guarantor of Britain's security during the Cold War, given that only it could match the Soviet Union in all departments militarily, most particularly with regard to nuclear weapons. Strong linguistic and cultural ties between the two states together, intermittently, with close links between the British and American ruling elites also served to make the American connection an attractive one. As the European Communities became the European Community, and then the European Union, the increasing economic and political significance of the partially supranational structures that have emerged at the heart of the new organization has meant that British governments necessarily have to start taking the political dimension of the EC/EU increasingly seriously. This has complicated the old way of doing things, in which Britain integrated with the USA in significant respects militarily, most notably in the fields of nuclear deterrence and electronic intelligence, while simultaneously integrating economically with the EC/EU, short of EMU, while trying as far as possible to avoid political integration within the developing European institutional structures. As the EU's integrative efforts have spread into the core fields of EMU and defence, then the Blair Government has been faced with a dilemma that originally worried the Conservative Prime Minister, Macmillan, in the early 1960s. In short, if Britain chooses to remain outside major new integrative efforts, which necessarily carry with them significant political implications, then it will find itself increasingly marginalized within Europe and less likely to be listened to by the USA. Indeed, 'The three leading figures in the cabinet – Blair, Brown and Cook – all recognize that Britain increases its global status and influence by being a serious, influential EU player' (Hughes, K. and Smith, 1998: 95). However, even in his speech at the launch of the Britain in Europe campaign on 14 October 1999, the Prime Minister would not go beyond the position that, 'In principle, if the single currency succeeds and it is in Britain's economic interest, we should join. In practice, the economic conditions must be met. Meanwhile we prepare so we can decide' (Blair, 1999b).

The major problems that have held the Blair Government back in this respect have been significantly press-generated. The strongly anti-EMU attitude of the Eurosceptic press in Britain, most particularly that of the Murdoch papers, *The Times* and the *Sun*, has been a powerful brake on the Labour Government's progress towards membership of the EMU. This is for the simple reason that the premier goal of the Blair administration is to secure a second term of office in order to be able to carry through aspects of its policy aspirations that are not immediately feasible. It believes that the *Sun* in particular can be crucial in helping to swing elections one way or the other, and that there is little point in provoking its hostility prior to an election by making an early move on EMU which it remains in strong disagreement with. It is for this reason that, while conducting a campaign to try and convert at least some of the Eurosceptic press to the view that EMU membership might actually benefit Britain more than damage it, the Government has clung to the formula that

Britain will only sign up to the EMU when the conditions economically are right (Anderson and Weymouth, 1999).

It was shown in the previous section how the Govenment used a shift in British defence policy to try and counter the negative effects of this position in terms of loss of influence. This helped avoid Britain's complete relegation to the margins of EU decision-making and has won particular support from the French Government. However, it has not been able to prevent a loss of bargaining leverage with the 'Big Two', as is perhaps illustrated by the concessions that the British were forced to make to France during the beef row of autumn 1999.

On the surface, it might have been hoped that the apparent political compatibility between the Centre-Left Labour Government and the Centre and Centre-Left governments that predominated within the EU at the time Labour came to power, would in itself create a greater closeness between Britain and its partners than had existed for some time, and help to bridge some of the 'influence gap' while Britain remained outside the EMU. However, in 1998 Hughes and Smith noted perceptively that:

> Despite pressure for change in the various manifestations of the continental social market model, there remain many differences between this model as a whole and the Anglo-Saxon economic approach. This has naturally led to caution over how Blair's attempt to marry the two models – the so called 'third way' – differs from the economic policies and social inequalities associated with Thatcherism. (Hughes and Smith, 1998: 94–5)

The decision to defer entry into the EMU and not to hold a referendum until after the next election provides the Government with campaigning time to try and change the attitudes of a predominantly hostile British press and public. In his November 1999 Guildhall speech, for example, the Prime Minister addressed directly the arguments of the Eurosceptics concerning the alleged loss of sovereignty that would be involved in joining the EMU. He stated that:

> If you read parts of the British media, it is absolutely saturated with the notion that wherever Britain cooperates with others, not only in Europe but elsewhere, it is somehow yielding up its national sovereignty. This argument is powerful ... But it is wrong. It defines national sovereignty as standing alone and then confuses it with national strength. And it grossly underestimates the impact of globalization on the power of an individual nation state ... By working together they [states] can effectively tackle problems they were powerless to address on their own. By working together, they can collectively reclaim the sovereignty they lost to globalization, while still reaping its benefits. (Blair, 1999a)

However, the length of the delay in joining the EMU will be crucial for British influence within the EU. While it is unlikely that the virulently anti-EMU Conservative Party will regain power at the next election, in which case British membership of EMU and influence within the EU could probably be ruled out for the entire lifetime of the next Parliament and beyond, it is still possible that a stubborn British public and press opinion could cause continuing delays, or even a Government defeat in a referendum on EMU membership. This could be a serious problem given that, as Hughes and Smith note,

> Timing is critical. Joining three years late, in 2002, would not be particularly damaging economically: but ... Britain's political influence will continue to fall for so long as it does not participate in this key policy. As policy discussions, bargains and coalitions

> develop around EMU, these will impact on other areas as deals are done. Delay in joining until 2004/5 would leave Britain increasingly marginalized in the EU ... (Hughes and Smith, 1998: 99)

Already, by November 1999, it was being noted that: 'The foreign office is worried that Britain is being excluded from key European meetings because it is outside the euro zone' (MacAskill, 1999: 12).

As far as EU enlargement is concerned, Britain's failure to make major progress in the East in terms of trade, together with its geographical distance from Central and Eastern Europe, has left it without the interests and concerns that are a part of German or Austrian policy, for example. Hughes and Smith see another opportunity here for Britain to try and compensate for its continuing position as an EMU outsider. They see a potential British role in keeping the EU's commitment to enlargement alive in the face of serious questions about its timing and in developing 'a genuine strategic approach to the new, post-1989 Europe' (Hughes and Smith, 1998: 100). However, the actuality has not matched the potential in so far as the British Government has little in the way of a positive conceptualization of what the Europe of the twenty-first century should look like politically. If anything, it is too far hamstrung by the perceived need not to be seen domestically to be 'selling out' Britain's interests to 'Brussels' for it to be able to do very much in the way of developing and selling imaginative new visions of the Europe of the future.

Overall, therefore, the Britain at the beginning of a new century does not look tremendously different from the Britain of past decades in terms of its degree of connection to and influence within the EU. The Labour Government's 1998 Presidency was marred by an early gaffe on the part of Blair in virtually ignoring EU opinion in favour of the traditional US policy preference when problems with Iraq arose once more at the beginning of the year. This was to some extent compensated for by a subsequent shift towards a European dimension in defence policy later on during 1998, but this was not able completely to repair the damage, and it certainly did not compensate for the loss of influence which Britain suffered as a result of the decision to remain out of the EMU until the economic conditions were deemed to be right. This could be seen in Britain's failure to make any significant inroads into the 'heart of Europe', most particularly the continuing Franco-German EU duumvirate, although some progress was made in the defence field. Blair's hopes of persuading his Centre and Centre-Left colleagues in Europe of the virtues of his 'Third Way' as a means of cementing closer EU linkages did not fall on particularly receptive ears on the whole and his attempts to try and persuade the British voters and press to be more friendly to the EU continued to be undermined by the determined opposition of the Eurosceptic press to such overtures, and by disputes with other Union members over the kinds of issues mentioned above. He did not help himself, with regard to the press, by attempting to portray 45 largely routine EU 'achievements' as a significant success story for his Government at the halfway stage of the 1998 British Presidency.

Britain's prospects of increasing its influence within Europe, therefore, hinge on two key things. First, it is crucial that either the Labour Party, or the Labour Party in partnership with the Liberal Democrats, is returned to power at the next general election (in practice current opinion poll data suggests that the former is the most likely outcome, given the continuing problems and poor ratings of the Conservatives nationally). A Conservative election victory clearly would be a major setback for Britain's EU relationship, given that the party is in the hands of committed Eurosceptics who are opposed to both EMU entry within the foreseeable future and anything resembling an EU defence dimension. Second, as Hughes and Smith point out above, it is crucial that the British Government manages to join the EMU without too much further delay. Every year, while Britain remains outside, new coalitions and formal and informal procedures are developing among those states already within the EMU which will shape and limit the parameters within which the UK will be able to try and influence policy-making when, or if, it finally joins the EMU. Just as Britain suffered from being outside the European Community during the crucial years in which the Common Agricultural Policy was being shaped and implemented, and then had to live with a policy that had been designed according to the needs of others and which it found great difficulty in trying to change, similar problems will confront it with the EMU. Furthermore, given that the European defence dimension is the only area where Britain seems to be willing or able to play a leading role, and given that the expansion of the defence dimension is always going to be limited greatly by the time-honoured reluctance of European governments to foot the bill for all that this requires, Britain will be condemned to remain on the second level of the EU power structure along with Italy for as long as it is on the outside of the single currency union. Should it remain aloof for too long, then there may well be no remaining routes open to the top level of EU decision-making when or if it finally signs up.

Ethics and foreign policy

Right from the start of its period of office, the new Labour Government attempted to put human rights to the forefront in its presentation of the *distinctiveness* of its approach to foreign policy. Unfortunately there is not the space available here to do adequate justice to the policy, so some overall comments only will be made. The Government has stated that it 'seeks to apply consistent standards – as enshrined in the international instruments – to all countries where human rights violations occur' (Foreign and Commonwealth Office, undated); and that:

> Our foreign policy must have an ethical dimension and must support the demands of other people's for the democratic rights on which we insist for ourselves. The Labour Government will put human rights at the heart of our foreign policy and will publish an annual report on our work in promoting human rights abroad. (Wheeler and Dunne, 1998: 851)

Overall, it is clear that the Government's record of achievement so far in the implementation of its ethical dimension of foreign policy has been a chequered one, with critics feeling that some states are being treated more leniently than others on non-human rights grounds that conflict with what Wheeler and Dunne term the requirements of 'good international citizenship' (Wheeler and Dunne, 1998: 868). On the other hand, the difficulty of the task which the Government has set itself has to be acknowledged, given that, for example, the cancellation of an arms contract on human rights grounds can lead to shrinkage of the domestic arms industry and potentially damaging electoral fall-out within the adversely affected areas. It could be argued that a government committed to human rights that loses power partially through over-zealous pursuit of its objectives is a government that lacks the wisdom to see that it could perhaps have achieved more by attempting to achieve those objectives at a more measured rate of progress, over the course of two administrations, for example. A more gradual, 'softly softly' approach could lead to less domestic opposition and a greater chance of significant long-term success. In this respect, it is perhaps too early yet to judge the success or failure of the Labour Government's attempts to implement its ethical foreign policy dimension. If it achieves a second term of office, and turns out at the end of it to have brought about a truly significant change in the framework within which British foreign policy is shaped through a measured and gradualist approach, then it can legitimately claim a considerable success.

Conclusion

This chapter has aimed deliberately at drawing most of its relevant conclusions within its individual sections. What can be said overall is that much of the foregoing has demonstrated just what a conservative country Britain still is. Some of its most deep-seated economic problems are so interwoven into the national culture that it is difficult for governments to unpick them, and this is true also of Britain's crucial attitude towards the EU. In both of these cases, the consequences of such conservatism are that Britain's power and influence are less than they should be. This in turn affects the chances of other goals being realized – Britain would be able to advance the ethical dimension of its foreign policy more effectively if it was a leading, rather than a secondary, member of the EU, for example. Very simply, the words of its leaders would carry more political clout on the world stage. Equally, a leading role within the EU would boost its influence in Washington to a degree where it would not need to be so dependent on the fortuitous occasions when American and British leaders with close personal relations hold power simultaneously. Finally, domestically, the continuing consequences of such ingrained, economically damaging national traits as the overfixation on house ownership are that not only is the British economy held back, but wider social goals, such as improving the National Health Service, are in part frustrated owing to the economic knock-on effects. Equally, the investment consequences of such traits contribute to a degree of reliance on globalization that could leave the British economy more vulnerable and exposed within the future than other developed economies that retain a higher proportion of large nationally-based producers, such as France. In short, the British economy may look initially impressive, but it is a model that ought to be contemplated with considerable caution.

Thus, while possessed of many enviable traits, not least a seemingly enduring political stability and an adaptability to changing circumstances domestically, as evidenced by the smooth transition to devolution on mainland Britain, the UK enters the twenty-first century as a state whose potential continues to exceed significantly its achievements in key areas of policy.

CHAPTER TEN

New Wine in Old Bottles? The Problems and Future of the New Italian Republic

Peter J. Anderson (with Simona Talani)

Introduction

Italy is a comparatively young state. It was brought into being between 1859 and 1870 by the Italian Wars of Unification. Prior to that, the peninsular had not been united under a native political authority since the fall of the Roman Empire in the West in the fifth century. It presents those coming fresh to an examination of its problems and prospects with a web of complexities and paradoxes that in some respects find their most immediate comparison not in Europe, but in Asia, with Japan (see, for example, *Economist*, 1990). Italy is one of Europe's four largest economies, is a member of the G7/8 council of leading economic powers, has a population that is roughly similar to that of Britain and France and is a key member of the European Union (EU). Were it not for the economic drag factor of the less prosperous South, it would most probably be considerably stronger economically than Britain. Yet, like Japan, its political influence internationally has for many years been much smaller than its economic potential and its population size suggest that it should be.

It is possible here to discuss in any detail only a few of the current crucial issues and dimensions of this unique country, which obviously and inevitably does scant justice to so complex a society. Given Italy's actual and potential economic and political *regional* importance, its most *externally* relevant policy dimensions will be given greater priority than predominantly domestic ones, such as those relating to social policy and issues, where coverage will be indicative rather than overly detailed. Furthermore, the fact that some issues, such as the importance of regional politics and the role of such political forces as Umberto Bossi's Northern League, are largely left out of the discussion *is not a judgement that they are unimportant*, but simply a consequence of limited space and the necessary prioritization outlined above. The discussion begins with a selection of key domestic political issues.

The domestic political and social dimensions

The political dimension

Italy has undergone major changes since 1992, when the old political order collapsed in a welter of scandal. After the March 1994 elections, for example, 452 of the 650 parliamentary deputies and 213 of the 315 senators were elected for the first time

(US Department of State, 1998). In the wake of a drastic loss of support for the socialists and the dissolution of the conservative Christian Democratic Party – the great traditional 'war-horses' of Italian multi-party politics – a trend towards two large coalition groupings of the Centre Left and Centre Right emerged from 1995 onwards. At the 1996 national elections, the parties of the Centre Left joined together in the Olive Tree Alliance, while those of the Centre Right formed the Freedom Pole. In the summary words of one traditionally closely interested external observer, 'This emerging bi-polarity represents a major break from the fragmented, multi-party political landscape of the post-war era' (US Department of State, 1998). The extent to which this 'major break' has or has not helped Italy achieve any greater *stability* in its governance is, along with other issues to be discussed shortly, an important question. But many Italians, never mind foreign observers, argue, with only minimal frivolity, that to try and analyse this and other questions of current Italian politics is an exercise of inbuilt futility, given that, despite the above changes and the reduced dependence on proportional representation (see below), by the time this book is printed, there will have been at least one change of government. Some analysts are known to have stopped counting once Italy reached its fiftieth post-Second World War government. Nevertheless, what one can talk about without too much danger of instant obsolescence are some of the broadly defining, key characteristics of current Italian political society and their consequences for the way in which the country works – or does not work – internally and externally. It is within such a context that the issue of the impact of the 'major break' will be returned to later.

The first major 'port of call' in the analysis of Italy's domestic political arena to be conducted here is corruption, which has been one of the great, nationally and internationally weakening problems of the modern Italian state both prior to and since the 1992 political upheaval. This has been blamed frequently on the pre-1992 guaranteed dominance of an established political elite that was a consequence of the post-Second World War Western concern with preventing the rise of additional dictators and frustrating the attempts of the communists to achieve power. With regard to this latter consideration, the British and Americans meddled actively in Italian politics during the early post-war years. Their efforts, it has been argued, were so successful in helping guarantee the dominance of a non-communist elite that they removed key natural competitive party political checks and balances that would otherwise have helped prevent a lapse into complacency and a descent into corruption so that a situation existed whereby corrupt people were free from challenge owing to the elite's apparently unshakeable grip on power. Indeed, it was only after the fear of communism lost its hold with the collapse of the Soviet Union that the dominance of the old elite disintegrated. Even then, and despite a succession of corruption investigations and trials during the 1990s, it was not until the period of office of the apparently completely untainted Romano Prodi that it began to seem truly possible that the problem of corruption in national politics might at least be seriously reducible, even if it could not be completely eliminated.

The corruption problem within Italy as a whole has been a factor which has reduced significantly its external influence, both within the EU and within wider world councils (see, for example, Jones, 1999b: 9). EU governments frequently have been understandably wary in engaging in key dealings with Italian politicians as a result of corruption, and it has affected the degree to which they have been prepared to involve Italy in core policy discussions. Southern corruption has been a factor also which has helped hold back Italy's economic power and overall prosperity. The known influence of the Mafia and the Camorra has been a big disincentive for foreign investors who otherwise might have seen the South as an attractive location for a variety of forms of low-cost industrial activity.

Political corruption and the slowness and frequent ineffectiveness of the policy-making system nationally (see below) have been strong factors, however, in helping create a high level of popular enthusiasm for European integration during the recent past. For many, it has seemed that the transference of some key powers to Brussels might actually make Italy a better governed state, given the problems created by these major domestic difficulties (see, for example, *Economist*, 1990). However, as will be noted later in the chapter, some are arguing that this belief now has fewer adherents than was the case during the late 1980s and early 1990s.

The scandals of the 'old world', the world which collapsed in 1992, linger on. The 'new order' of Italian politics promised a bright and corruption-free future, and was initially symbolized by Forza Italia, the Right Wing vehicle on which media mogul Silvio Berlusconi swept to power. However, it soon became apparent that the new had some of the strangely familiar trappings of the old. Silvio's brother Paolo made the headlines after corruption allegations and then Silvio himself followed. During recent years he has been convicted three times for crimes committed during his business career, and he has more trials yet to come (*Economist*, 1999c: 39). Despite this depressing picture of Italy's political elite, the people at the heart of the scandals have, in a number of cases, made remarkable comebacks. Berlusconi's party, for example, performed successfully in the June 1999 European Parliament elections and during September 1999 opinion polls had both himself and his party in the lead nationally (*Economist*, 1999c: 39).

Should Berlusconi or others caught up in corruption scandals be returned to power, of course, there are likely to be negative consequences for Italy's position internationally. Its external influence will remain much lower than it should be. EU governments will be cautious about what they tell to, and the deals that they make with, a state whose political class appears to be so obviously compromised. Domestically, there is always the danger that high levels of elite corruption, and the disillusion among many on the Left that it creates, could lead to a significant future resurgence of terrorist extremism.

On the other hand, however, there are more promising signs visible on the domestic political horizon. The fact that a former Italian Prime Minister, Romano Prodi, should be chosen as an ideal 'Mr Clean' to head the European Commission, *as the spearhead of an anti-corruption ticket*, is symbolic of the influence that potentially awaits Italy should Prodi's example begin to seep back into and become embedded within the domestic political culture as he proceeds on his clean-up crusade.

Furthermore, it is not inconceivable that Prodi will return to the Prime Minister's job after his reign as Commission President. At the time of writing, the governing coalition of the Centre Left, led by former Communist Massimo D'Alema, was looking politically weak. If that weakness continues into the next election and D'Alema does badly, some see this as being likely to leave Prodi with the chance to seize the Centre-Left ground on his return from his Commission job and make a renewed bid for the premiership (*Economist*, 1999d: 34). Should he also make a notable success of the Commission Presidency, then that would give him the chance of acquiring a degree of status within Italian society (where Eurocentrism is still a prominent, although diminished, theme) that would allow him (should he become Prime Minister again) to introduce a level of reformist, anti-corruption changes within the Italian polity that has not previously been possible. His chances of achieving all of this should not, perhaps, be underestimated. He succeeded in remaining in office for two and a half years, outlasting all but one of his post-1945 predecessors on the ever-revolving roundabout of Italian government (Levi, 1999: 10). He also, as will be seen later, succeeded in bulldozing Italy into the European Monetary Union (EMU) despite strong opposition from some sectors of, for example, the German and Dutch elites. The one possible slur on his reputation, a set of corruption allegations that were made against him in late 1999 in Italy, was dismissed in detail and with apparent ease. Provided that nothing further comes of this, his reputation should remain intact.

Another key problem with a significantly weakening impact politically on Italy both domestically and internationally has been the electoral system. Proportional representation, in its past and (in the eyes of critics like Prodi) present forms within Italy, has not served the country well in terms of effective government. In short, in the past decisions have often been slow to emerge from the top and when they have appeared they have often been pitched at the level of the lowest common denominator in order to achieve the necessary underlying consensus to keep the fragile alliance of the day in power.

A highly problematic consequence of this 'slow reaction' politics has been, as mentioned above, that Italy has frequently fallen foul of EU institutions as a result of its dilatory pace in implementing new European Community/Union legislation. A further problem complicating this situation has been that the difficulty of maintaining broad coalition agreement across a range of issues has led to frequent breakdowns of the consensus necessary for effective governance and a consequent staggeringly high incidence of changes of government. This has been a further brake on progress in the passage and implementation of new legislation required as a result of EU decisions and has been an additional cause of Italy's surprisingly frequent appearances before the European Court of Justice. Such difficulties have greatly damaged Italy's credibility as a key player within the EU and have reduced its influence correspondingly.

A further consequence of these domestic political problems has been that they have created a situation in which it is difficult for Italian governments to give sufficient attention to foreign policy towards the wider world, thus further reducing Italy's influence beyond its borders.

After the reforms promoted by Mattarella were approved in August 1993, the role of proportional representation was scaled down to a level where 25 per cent of the seats in the Chamber of Deputies are now elected proportionally, while 75 per cent are determined by a first-past-the-post system (Parker, 1996: 46). However, this new system seems to have produced a lot less change than some observers had hoped. The Berlusconi Government that came to power in the wake of the new reforms, proclaiming itself to be a breath of fresh air and a break from the past, lasted less than a year, falling in January 1995 when one member of his coalition ceased to support it. The Government in power, at the time of writing, that of D'Alema, depends on around ten different parties to stay in power (Blitz, 1999: 3). In April 1999 a referendum was held on the question of whether or not to abolish proportional representation altogether. Those presenting the case for abolition argued that a key factor in post-Second World War governmental instability has been the large number of small parties that proportional representation has allowed to be elected. It was argued that it was these small parties that brought down the governments that won the 1994 and 1996 general elections, for example (Blitz, 1999: 3). Others have argued that there are factors other than proportional representation that have allowed small parties to remain important to political outcomes since the Mattarella reforms (Hine, 1996: 324–5)

Ultimately, the abolitionists failed and Italy remains subject to a system that, in the specifically Italian context, helps make it extremely difficult for Rome governments to make a consistent and significant mark on the European and international stages. It also complicates attempts to secure the governmental and economic stability that is required for successful membership of the EMU.

The effects of the continuing role of unstable coalition politics are exacerbated by what some in Italy see as a crisis in leadership. For example, just taking one day from the ongoing domestic political debate, that of 7 January 2000, one finds even Prime Minister D'Alema curiously agreeing with his Treasury Minister's, Amato's, comments about the weaknesses in Italian political leadership at that time, an interesting admission given his position as *primus inter pares* (Agenzia Giornalistica Italia, 2000a). At the same time, the leader of the PDCI, Cossutta, was adding his agreement, saying that Amato was right to point to the lack of giants among Italy's current politicians – to the absence of a De Gasperi, a Togliatti, or a Di Vittorio. For Cossutta the only route to political stability would be a resolve to focus not on individuals, but on an alliance motivated by a common democratic and social inspiration (Agenzia Giornalistica Italia, 2000b). However, the dim prospects of such a common focus had already been foreseen by the research department of the Banca Commerciale Italiana in the preceding November, when it commented wryly on the desire of the Democrats within the governing alliance to get their revenge for former Prime Minister Prodi's ousting (by an alliance between Cossiga, the UDR leader and former President, and the then current Prime Minister, D'Alema). It argued that their aim was to get rid of Cossiga and reduce the influence of D'Alema in favour of their own, a strategy that would leave the latter as a lame duck leader. (Banca Commerciale Italiana, 1999) Even current EU Commission President Prodi – the previous Prime Minister – had by this time become involved publicly in the verbal fisticuffs between alliance groupings. It hardly needs emphasizing that such public in-fighting, itself a testimony to the absence of a strong leadership, is hardly a launching pad for a strong regional and international role for the Italian state.

Finally, as far as the book's core themes are concerned, there are several potential threats to Italian democracy that can be identified in the context of the present and the foreseeable future. The above mentioned problems of corruption, the electoral system, and the lack of strong leadership and consequent public in-fighting are obvious candidates in this respect. If left undealt with, these problems collectively have the capacity to weaken seriously the electorate's commitment to the preservation of the democratic system should it come under severe pressure from undemocratic forces within the future. However, they would only become a serious threat should the EU fail in its perceived role as an organization to which governmental functions can be passed up from areas where the domestic polity simply is not working, thereby leaving the door open for undemocratic solutions to be offered for Italy's political problems.

Another potential threat arises from an apparently diminished interest in politics since the end of the Cold War. If this trend accelerates over the next few years, then it could also effectively undermine democracy by leaving politicians to get on with the running of the country without taking into account the interests of an increasing number of the politically disinterested, reducing thereby the extent to which Italian democracy could claim to be truly representative.

There are, of course, also, the problems which globalization can potentially cause. More Italian companies, including those with some of the country's most famous names, are being taken over by foreign multinationals so that proportionately more decisions affecting the Italian economy are being taken outside it. If this trend continues, it will affect the extent to which Italian governments are able to deliver on the pre-election spending commitments made to the electorate, which in turn will affect their degree of democratic economic responsiveness.

These various factors offer a range of threats to Italian democracy, the most severe of which are not immediately visible and pressing, but future changes in the political environment inside and around Italy could easily make them so. Factors such as globalization offer a more gradual and insidious threat, not necessarily to the existence of the Italian democratic process, but to its quality. Given that the latter is, as this section has noted, already lacking in a number of key respects, this is not good news for the Italian electorate.

The social dimension

Necessarily, space limitations, and the prioritization criterion outlined at the beginning, mean that there is only limited scope for the discussion of social issues here. This section, therefore, will be indicative rather than detailed in its analysis.

Many of Italy's social problems are well known. Those relating to the significant discrepancies between North and South in economic terms, together with the related problem of the attractiveness of crime for some Southern youngsters as a means of filling the consequent career gap, and the cries, which the cost of supporting the *mezzogiorno* has generated among Northern separatists, that the economically burdensome, budget-draining South should be cast adrift, are familiar to anyone who takes a reasonably close interest in the country. However, as Schioppa Kostoris notes, it would be simplistic to assume that the North–South split is the whole story of Italy's divisions. He states that: 'Italy is a heterogeneous, fragmented country, and it is much more divided than the conventional concept of economic dualism would imply, although admittedly the regional schism is probably the most painful' (Schioppa Kostoris, 1996: 289).

Equally, the substantial changes that have occurred in people's voting preferences away from the traditional big parties of the Cold War era have been well signposted within recent literature (see, for example, Gundle and Parker, 1996), as have the debates over Italy's immigration policies (see, for example, Severgnini, 1998). Less widely appreciated perhaps, are the declining influence of the Roman Catholic Church over Italian society as a whole, the massive socioeconomic nightmare resulting from the erection of large numbers of shoddily and dangerously constructed buildings during Italy's post-war 'economic miracle', the growing problems of a rapidly ageing society, and the not yet fully socially quantifiable effects of membership of the EU's EMU. All of these could have substantial consequences in the medium term, with the former, for example, gradually removing, for better or for worse, some of the current limitations on Italian defence policy and eroding also the frameworks within which existing societal mores and behavioural limits are shaped. As there is only room here to discuss one of these issues in any detail, the ageing crisis is the one that will be chosen, given its huge potential economic costs and its overall implications for Italian society. However, some brief comments will be made on the social impact of the EMU also. The 'ageing problem' can be summarized briefly. Currently, the ratio of employed taxpayers to non-employed pensioners is around 3:1 in the developed states. 'By 2030, absent reform, this ratio will fall to 1.5:1, and in some countries, such as Germany and Italy, it will drop all the way down to 1:1 or even lower' (Peterson, 1999: 44). Indeed, Italy is projected to reach a position by 2003 in which around 19 per cent of its population are of pensionable age. Unless existing fertility rate trends go into reverse, the populations of Italy and Western Europe as a whole are projected to shrink by about 50 per cent by the end of the next century (Peterson, 1999: 43–5) These trends, resulting from such factors as increased affluence, mass contraception and legalized abortion, threaten Italy and other states with a situation in which there will not be enough people left in productive work to pay for either the substantial increases in health care costs that will result, or the unfunded liabilities for pensions. The result will be probably that Italy will find it of crucial importance that it should attract more young immigrant workers from overseas to solve the problems of labour shortages. Given the less attractive dimensions of observed human nature, this situation may well lead to increased problems of civil order within Italy as a result of probable backlashes from racist elements within Italian society.

Even with such compensatory immigration, however, it is still probable that the costs of looking after such a dramatically expanded older population will remain a major budgetary headache for Italy and other developed states. Another consequence of mass immigration could be that, as new immigrant groups become absorbed into Italian society, and begin to participate actively in the Italian political system, the internal and external policies of Italian governments will begin to change in response to their influence (see, for example, Peterson, 1999: 43–6). The direction of that change will depend, of course, on the composition, shared interests and concerns and political effectiveness of the new waves of immigration.

Lastly, and very briefly, it is necessary to comment on the broad impact of EMU on Italian society. Talani[1] observes that, as far as the position of the trade unions is concerned, the path to EMU, as defined by the Maastricht Treaty and by the agreement on the Stability Pact, directly and substantially affects their powers and prerogatives within their traditional policy realms. In particular, the statutory European Central Bank goal of a low and stable inflation rate will have undeniable consequences for the limits within which they will be able to conduct wage negotiations. Moreover, the implementation of monetary policy by the European Central Bank, through the decisions over the level of European interest rates, is sure to affect investment decisions and, consequently, the level of unemployment. Finally, the rigid limitations on the conduct of national fiscal policy imposed by the Maastricht Treaty for the transition to EMU and by the Stability Pact for its aftermath, are already deeply modifying the terms of the debate over the survival of the welfare state in all of its present forms.

The domestic economy

During his time as Prime Minister, Romano Prodi's greatest achievement in economic policy was to succeed in taking Italy into the EMU against what, at the beginning of his period of office, seemed almost impossible odds. Why this was the case will be explained shortly. First, it is necessary to look at some of the fundamentals of the Italian economy.

As mentioned earlier, Italy is one of Europe's four biggest economies and has some notable economic success stories in the prosperous North. One of the explanations that traditionally has been offered for this is the phenomenon of clustering. Even though many Italian companies are much smaller than their German or French counterparts, the habit of complimentary enterprises clustering together and supplying locally each other's needs has meant that they have been able to enjoy many of the advantages of larger companies without suffering from the big company rigidities that can hamper the rapidity and flexibility of responses to changes in customer demand (*Economist*, 1990a). For example, Italy's machine tool industry is the fourth largest in the world with sales of $3.45 billion in 1997. Individual companies generally are small, and tend to be located around the manufacturers who rely on their machines to produce their goods, 'like mushrooms amid the roots of big trees' (*Economist*, 1999e: 57). While new technology, such as video-telephones, has reduced some of the traditional advantages of clustering, it still remains important.

Many Northern manufacturers are symbolic of Italy's ability to hold on to key market sectors through an emphasis on design and quality. This has enabled it to continue to be highly successful at the top end of the market in its production of goods such as tiles, cashmere clothing, spectacles, gold jewellery and leather (*Economist*, 1999e: 58). It also remains a major player in the automotive, food and aerospace industries, among others. However, to return to the book's core themes, it should be noted that the increasing impingement of globalization on the Italian economy may start to take away some of its current competitive advantages. This is particularly true with regard to the flexibility of the clustering mode of production referred to above. Should multinational takeovers and buyouts start to impinge heavily on this kind of activity, the economy could suffer as a result of the relatively inflexible structures of many big corporations and some of Italy's competitive advantage be lost as a result. It should also be noted that the current level of globalization of the world economy meant that manufacturing in Italy was hit heavily by the 1998/99 financial crisis in Asia, Russia and South America, and recovered only slowly (Banca Commerciale Italiana, 1999).

Another explanation for the success of the high-performing sectors of the Italian economy is 'that it is the logical result of a collective propensity to ignore general principles and dominant ideas and to circumvent laws, affirmative actions, and economic policy rules' (Schioppa Kostoris, 1996: 291). Furthermore, while the banking sector still has its problems, it does possess the major asset of the Italian people's enthusiasm for saving, which is one of the highest in the world (Merlini, 1993: 237–8).

However, the country retains also many of the economic weaknesses that have long held it back from realizing the full extent of its enormous economic potential. In the eyes of business-oriented critics, Italian state pensions remain far too high, its public sector is still horribly inefficient and its government debt is mountainous (*Economist*, 1999f: 97). There is also still the enormous North–South regional disparity within the economy which was mentioned above in the section on Italy's social dimension. The question arises, therefore, of how Prodi managed the apparent conjuring trick of squeezing Italy into the strict economic straitjacket of the euro zone.

One part of the answer to this question, is that, while there are still significant sectoral and regional weaknesses within the Italian economy, the above-mentioned strengths of areas such as the prosperous North are so great that they offset the problems of the rest of Italy, including those generated by inefficiencies within the public sector (Schioppa Kostoris, 1996: 291).

The second part of the equation is filled in by Jones, who argues that Prodi did it by meeting enough of the requirements of the EMU economic convergence criteria to get within shooting distance of admission, and then filling the rest of the gap through sheer diplomatic and political skill. In short, he achieved key elements of the economic aims of his strategy by such means as substantial spending cuts and tax increases worth $65 billion (Jones, T., 1999: 9). However, many critics have argued that he acted as something of an illusionist with other economic measures, which appeared to be designed to provide more of an appearance of helping Italy to meet the convergence criteria rather than being possessed of any real substance (Anderson and Weymouth, 1999). In addition, he was only able to get part of some of what he believed to be the most crucial reforms through, such as those relating to pensions. Some privatizations, such as that of Telecom Italia, have been argued to have been rushed through too quickly (Jones, T., 1999: 9).

Nevertheless, the crucial result of his efforts was that Italy emerged within sight of the convergence targets. Diplomacy then took over. His diplomatic campaign for euro membership has been described as 'incredibly good: clever, threatening, charming in turns' (Jones, T., 1999: 9). When it looked as though European Commission economists and the EU's statistical office would not be prepared to accept his arithmetic, he forgot the meaning of subtlety. 'They brought all the influence they had to bear, and more,' says a former Commission official. 'It could have gone badly wrong for Prodi, but he got away with it' (Jones, T., 1999: 9).

Seven months after entering the euro zone, questions were being raised as to whether Italy had taken the lira into the euro at too high an exchange rate and the economy seemed to be dangerously near to recession (*Economist*, 1999f: 97–8). More fundamental questions remained as well, however, as to whether, from an economic point of view, the country had entered the EMU too early, thus imposing strains on an economy still in need of many crucial reforms. As early as February 1999, for example, the Commission was warning the Italian government that it would have to introduce further tax increases or spending cuts if Italy were to stay within the rules of the Growth and Stability Pact (*European Voice*, 1999a: 2). That necessity could make it difficult for Italy to remain within the euro zone should there be a substantial downturn in the global economy which impacted on key employment sectors. Unemployment in Italy at the time of writing was among the worst in the EU, hovering around 12 per cent (*European Voice*, 1999b: 23).

However, Talani contends that, for Italian business at least, and initial teething problems aside, the EMU itself has been seen as highly attractive because the introduction of a single currency for all European countries eliminated *tout court* the problems linked to the overvaluation of the lira and thus, also, the need for its devaluation. Moreover, the Maastricht definition of the EMU solved, once and for all, the problem of Italian monetary policy, that is, the problem of Italian interest rates and prices and of their differentials relative to those of European competitors. Indeed, the EMU has eliminated national monetary policies altogether and substituted them with a common European monetary policy enforced by a European Central Bank committed to low and stable prices. Lastly, the likelihood of lax fiscal policies was greatly reduced by the implementation of the Maastricht fiscal criteria and by their extension to the post-unification period, as guaranteed by the Stability Pact.[2]

Talani believes that all of this has extremely important consequences also in terms of power relations with the other national interest groups, particularly the trade unions. Indeed, it institutionalized the shift of the decision-making process from the national to the European level for a set of politically extremely sensitive macroeconomic policies. Far more importantly, it institutionalized the aims towards which they have to be geared: low interest rates, low prices, low public deficits and debts. These aims, while possibly having some uncertain, if not negative, consequences on employment and the labour market,[3] correspond perfectly to the preferences of Italian, and, importantly, European entrepreneurs.

Finally, to return briefly once more to the book's core themes, the impact of globalization on the EMU decision also needs to be considered when any questions about its correctness are asked. In short, the Italian and the British Exchange Rate Mechanism (ERM) crises during the early 1990s had demonstrated clearly to the Italian Government precisely how vulnerable even the currencies of large European states within the ERM now were in the face of globalized and liberalized currency markets, unless they were able to shelter under the more substantially protective barrier of an EMU.

Whatever Italy's future fate within the EMU, free marketeers are convinced that its overall membership of the EU has been of enormous benefit to the Italian economy. Merlini, for example, notes that:

> public economic policies and corporate strategies have been profoundly affected by Community participation, in bringing about free market and competitive approaches in a 'milieu' previously often prone towards protectionist practices ... [it] forced the Italian productive system to jump into the cold pool of competition. (Merlini, 1993: 234)

The memoirs of Guido Carli, former governor of the Bank of Italy, reinforce this view (see Aliboni and Greco, 1996: 47). What will be interesting to see over the next several years is whether the free marketeers remain so influential if the combined effects of the Single Market and the EMU ultimately prove to have significantly higher social costs than have so far been anticipated.

In conclusion to this section, it is clear that while it has been argued by some that Prodi saw joining the euro as much more strategically valuable than economically beneficial (Jones, T., 1999: 9), his decision to go for EMU membership provided a drive for economic reform that had simply not been present across previous administrations. While, as has been pointed out already, the results appear to have fallen short of what the EU Commission had hoped for, they nevertheless were impressive when compared to the sluggish rate of reform that had characterized the situation previously. As will be seen in the section on foreign and defence policy below, such reforms and the achievement of EMU membership, when combined with the reduction in corruption that characterized the Prodi period of office, and the ability of his immediate successor to hold Italy to a firm NATO line during the bombing of Kosovo, despite strong domestic opposition, all combined to give the country some firm ground on which to try and build a higher political profile both within the EU and within the wider Atlantic area. However, the D'Alema Government's weakness at the time of writing was putting a brake on the chances of this being achieved. Whether future governments will be able to make more effective use of the opportunities now available to them remains to be seen.

Italian foreign and defence policy

Italy's international profile was, for many years after the Second World War, relatively low as a result of: the time which it took to shake off the taint of having been ruled by an aggressive fascist regime; the various internal distractions from the world outside Italy that were occasioned by the unstable domestic political system and the need to focus on the key project of economic reconstruction and development; the lack of popular enthusiasm for a proactive international role after the disasters of the Mussolini era; Western distrust of Italy bred by obvious political corruption within government; and the convenient fact that the overlap of NATO/US strategic interests with those of key circles within the Italian political parties that were dominant during the Cold War meant that much of Italy's security concerns could be protected and subsumed within an organization far larger than the country itself. The fact that, for many years, the socialist–communist opposition strongly objected to the Western Alliance did not affect greatly any of this, given that the two groups did not achieve enough electoral success to threaten effectively the policy preferences of the governing elite.

The above-mentioned East–West split within the Italian foreign policy debate was complemented by a debate between advocates of Mediterranean and European priorities, the body of thought associated with the first of these frequently being referred to as *terzomondismo*. Key circles within Italian society have seen a role for their state in which it acts as a bridge between Europe and the developing countries, most specifically those in the Middle Eastern and Mediterranean areas. Mediation between East and West, North and South, between the Israelis and the Palestinians has been seen as a core concern of *terzomondismo* (Merlini, 1993: 232). Ultimately, overwhelming perceived economic interests meant that the Europeanists became the most dominant faction from the late 1970s onwards, although the Mediterranean perspective still remains important. Jones, for example, notes that Prodi 'sees Italy as the power the Mediterranean needs: influential in the troubled Balkans and Maghreb regions and making overtures to Tehran before anyone else thought of the idea' (Jones, T., 1999: 9).

Where Italian foreign policy thinking goes in the next few years is governed obviously not just by events and processes within the European region and the wider global political/economic/security/environmental framework, but also by the unpredictable vagaries of domestic politics as they are constituted under the present electoral arrangements. It is necessary, therefore, to be extremely cautious about trying to make any predictions in this regard. Writing in 1996, Aliboni and Greco characterized contemporary Italian thinking about the direction in which their country's foreign policy should be channelled:

> Current Italian foreign policy debate is focused on several specific issues, notably the future of the European Union, the enlargement of NATO and, to a lesser extent, the Mediterranean and the so-called 'eastern question', by which is meant the issues pending with Slovenia and Croatia. But it also, and pre-eminently, concerns broad foreign policy directions. This debate, generally speaking, is crystallising around a contrast between internationalism and/or universalism emanating from the post-war experience, and a range of diverse political tendencies towards re-nationalising foreign policy or adopting more stringent and assertive forms of nationalism. (Aliboni and Greco, 1996: 44)

What is of course missing from this picture is the Italian concern with preventing unacceptably high levels of German dominance within the EU and the East, into which the Union shortly will start to enlarge. Within the wider debates, there are advocates of pro-Americanism in, for example, the context of defence, most particularly as a result of what are felt to be condescending attitudes towards Italy in foreign and defence policy matters amongst, to differing degrees, British, French and German elite circles. There is also a strong recognition of the fact that the USA has been a powerful stabilizing force within post-Second World War Europe and an anxiety to ensure that that influence is not withdrawn. But there also are pro-Europeanists where military matters are concerned, wishing to see a stronger European defence dimension with Italian participation. Theirs has been a particularly prominent tendency on a number of occasions in recent years. During its EC Presidency in 1990, for example, Italy put forward a proposal on 18 September in which it said it was high time to 'extend the competencies of the Union to all aspects of security without limitations' (Sjovaag, 1998: 28). This was an idea too far ahead of its time to meet with the necessary agreement. But Italian governments periodically have continued their efforts to bolster the European arm of the transatlantic defence relationship. Italy was part of a coalition during the 1996 EU Intergovernmental Conference, for example, which argued that it was necessary to establish a closer EU–WEU (Western European Union) relationship in order to strengthen European defence capabilities and enable the European pillar within NATO to enjoy more autonomy (Gourlay and Remacle, 1998: 64–5). In May 1999, Taylor noted that Italy was 'keen to give the EU the potential to launch offensive campaigns like the current NATO attacks on Serbian forces' (Taylor, 1999c: 7). However, Italian ambitions were frustrated by the fact that only France agreed with it.

As far as Eastern Europe and the former Yugoslavia are concerned, Italy's most significant involvement recently has been very much under the wider auspices of NATO. While not enormous, Italy's clearly visible military contribution to NATO peacekeeping forces, most recently in Kosovo, and its agreement to its territory being used as a launch pad for the bombing of Kosovo and Serbia, have been high-profile signs that it is becoming more aware of past accusations that it was a free-rider on NATO's back during the Cold War (Aliboni and Greco, 1996: 45), and that it needs to make more of an effort to be a credible contributor to European security and peacekeeping if it is to acquire more influence in the post-Cold War world. The Italian embassy in Washington, for example, was keen to let Americans know that Italy had provided 6000 troops for KFOR (the Kosovo implementation force) in Kosovo in addition to its other deployments within the region (Italian Embassy in Washington, accessed 2000).

On the matter of EU membership, while Italy remains a strongly pro-EU member, it is being argued within Italian society that the commitment has visibly declined amongst some sections of the political elite, and there were definite signs of Euroscepticism during the brief period of the Berlusconi Government during the mid-1990s. This may become significant again, given that, at the time of writing, Berlusconi is doing well in the polls, despite the various past corruption scandals still tarnishing his reputation. (There is an interesting discussion of three possible ways forward for Italy in its relations with the EU which Cesare Merlini produced in 1993, which still remains relevant. While there is not space to consider it here, readers might find it useful to consult it for themselves. See Merlini, 1993: 241–4.)

As far as Italian Mediterranean policy is concerned, this perhaps reached its most ambitious heights in the early 1990s, when, with Spain, Italy established the Conference on Security and Cooperation in the Mediterranean. This encompassed the entire Middle East as well as the Mediterranean itself. The intention was to follow the example of the then CSCE (Conference on Security and Cooperation in Europe). However, this grand design has not been greatly successful so far, not least, it has been argued, because of its immense scope and the complexity of the security problems and interests which it attempts to encompass. It has lacked also a clear common policy from the European states included within it (Pinar Tank, 1998: 180). Nevertheless, as noted already, while subordinate to the priority goal of making a success of EU membership, the Mediterranean dimension of Italian foreign policy thinking is still important in the minds of some key players, as has been demonstrated by past Italian initiatives towards Iran, and Prodi's pledge, when Prime Minister, to grant asylum to persecuted peoples, including those of Turkey and Iraq (Jones, T., 1999: 9).

To focus in now on the two main concepts around which the Italian foreign policy debate was seen as crystallizing in the above quotation, from Aliboni and Greco (1996) *internationalism* sees Italy's post-Second World War foreign policy of acting in harness with its treaty partners in NATO and the EU as having been a successful policy which has served the state well at a much smaller cost than would have been involved had Italy been in a position where it had no alternative but to fend more for itself. *Nationalism*, on the other hand, sees the Cold War in particular as a period in which Italian governments surrendered the handling of key national interests to international alliances to an unacceptable degree and, within the greater flexibility of the post-Cold War world, would favour Italy reclaiming direct control of some of its key foreign policy interests.

Internationalism tends to be popular on the Centre Left, while the renationalization of foreign policy characterizes many on the Centre Right, although it should not be forgotten that these tendencies are not exclusive and that there are, for example, some nationalists amongst the Left (Aliboni and Greco, 1996: 44). However, having noted this, the evidence so far available suggests that political parties do not always follow the foreign policy directions that the above preferences might lead analysts to expect. Renationalizers who expected the Centre Right coalition underpinning the 1994–95 Berlusconi Government to follow their line were largely disappointed. For some analysts, the Berlusconi administration did not pursue any foreign policy that could be called strategically consistent. Under the successor Dini Government, on the other hand, it has been argued that Italian foreign policy followed a combination of both trends (Aliboni and Greco, 1996: 45).

Overall, Aliboni and Greco conclude that the disagreement between different schools of thought might be less important than it at first appears. While criticizing loudly the preferences of the internationalists, 'so far the neonationalists have failed to indicate a convincing alternative course of action on any of the concrete foreign policy issues facing Italy' (1996: 50–1). This should not be too surprising, for the simple reason, as noted earlier, that while Italy is one of Europe's big powers economically, its various domestic political weaknesses, unsolved economic problems and difficulty in establishing a consistent presence on the European and global stage owing to its proverbial merry-go-round of governments, all undermine any basis for a significant renationalization of foreign policy. Another weakness lies in the military/defence field. While Italy's credit with its Western partners has gone up because of its policy concerning Kosovo, it still has problems as a credible military partner. As *The Economist* notes, 'It has a large but out-of-date army, a still strong reluctance (often encouraged by the Vatican) to use military force, and a lingering if not always deserved reputation for backsliding earned at the end of the second world war' (*Economist*, 1999g: 53). While the skill of the elite among its air force pilots is much admired professionally, its army is still dominated by conscripts and is seen as being of limited effectiveness because of the lack of professional dedication that this is seen as implying. Although Italy has seen Britain as a useful partner in military matters in recent years (see, for example, Foreign and Commonwealth Office, 1999b), even though it has been disappointed in its original hope that an Italian–British axis within the EU might be possible as a counterweight to the Franco-German duumvirate, its influence within such arrangements is limited by the above-listed types of (what to British and other key Western military personnel are) weaknesses.

At the level of declared policy, the Italian defence minister at the time of writing had pledged to move to a more effective, smaller professional army within five or six years. His chances of being able to achieve this, however, are apparently limited by opposition from some within the Catholic Church who are worried that abolition of the draft will lead to the loss of those young males who traditionally have opted for 'civilian service', and have formed a bedrock of its charitable activities in this capacity. He also has to overcome domestic opposition to the raising of defence spending from its currently very low level of less than 1 per cent of GDP *and* to deal with the implications of any increase for Italy's continuous battle with its budget deficit, especially given its new obligations under the EMU (*Economist*, 1999g: 53).

Consequently, until Italy can deal with all of its problems in an effective manner, its influence is going to remain much smaller than one might expect it to be simply by looking at its territorial size and its relative GDP. This was perhaps most recently demonstrated during the May 1998 summit to launch the euro, when the Italian Prime Minister was forced to look on while the crucial wheeling and dealing over jobs at the European Central Bank took place between Germany, France and the British Presidency (Jones, T., 1999: 9). Nevertheless, the very fact that Italy was able to bamboozle its way into the EMU, despite stiff opposition from key political circles within both Germany and Holland, for example, illustrates the fact that the country has rather more weight than is at first realized. It seems generally accepted that its influence within the EU noticeably increased during Prodi's premiership. As pointed out earlier, if Prodi makes a success of his Commission Presidency, then, should he return to Italian politics and become Prime Minister again, his personal prestige would be a useful tool to help further increase Italian influence. In addition, that same prestige may rub off domestically and give him the authority to introduce the key changes, such as further economic and electoral reforms, that should help significantly in improving Italy's political and economic stability and external political credibility. Should it enable him also to push through the reforms necessary to produce a leaner, meaner, entirely professional army, then Italy, at long last, would be in a position to start exercising some of the major influence within the EU and beyond that so far has generally eluded it. Under Prodi, it is clear that such influence would be exercised within an internationalist rather than a nationalist context.

All of the immediately above seems quite feasible, and is the most compelling of the various future possibilities as far as this author can judge. However, Italy always retains a full deck of cards up its sleeve where the business of trying to predict political futures is concerned and all of the informed speculation advanced here may yet be rendered completely irrelevant by the future passage of events.

Conclusion

What can be seen, overall, is that Italy is very much a society in transition. Its political reforms under the 'New Republic' remain incomplete and have not yet succeeded in removing the problem of the merry-go-round of short-term, frequently weak governments and their attendant problems. Equally, while the Prodi period in government in particular led to a reduction in political corruption, it is too early to tell whether this will be a long-lasting phenomenon, and there is still some considerable way to go before the problem can be regarded as having been dealt with adequately. For these, and the other reasons described in this chapter, Italy, despite its economic weight and its position as one of the EU's Big Four, continues to exercise far less influence in global and regional politics than one might expect. However, this position did begin to change under Prodi, and, as has been noted above, may undergo a yet more radical transformation should he be able to return to power after his period as Commission President. Complicating his efforts and those of his successors, however, will be the potential time bomb of Italy's ageing crisis, and the huge budgetary and other problems that this threatens for the Italian state within the twenty-first century. In addition, economic globalization is something of a two-edged sword. Just as it has helped Ducati to sell (around the world) within hours its entire production of a new hand-built motorcycle via the sales and marketing opportunities now offered on the internet, it is capable also of damaging severely Italian export markets (as in the earlier mentioned 1998 crisis) or undermining the competitive position of Italian industry. While Italy left the 1990s in a far more promising position than that in which it entered the decade, there are still a number of serious uncertainties about its future.

Notes

Thanks are due to Umberto Morelli for reading and commenting on this chapter.

1. All written comments kindly provided by Simona Talani are acknowledged within the relevant section of the text.
2. See Fossa, 1996. See also Villari 1992, pp.xiii, xiv.
3. See Confindustria, 1992.

CHAPTER ELEVEN

The Problems and Future of Spain

Neil Hughes

Globalization is radically transforming the economic and political life of European nations. Nowhere is this more true than in Spain, a country which has undergone a series of profound structural changes in the last 20 years. Democratization, membership of the European Community (EC), NATO and Economic and Monetary Union (EMU) have all contributed to Spain's transition from relative isolation to global engagement. This chapter will analyse the impact that adaptation to the changing global environment has had on a number of aspects of the Spanish economic and political landscape.

The first aspect examined will be the economy which, it will be argued, has been revolutionized by the competitive challenges unleashed by the forces of globalization. The main stimulus for the transformation of the 'historically inward-looking, import substituting foreign investment hostile' (Lipsey, 1997: 79) Spanish economy has been membership of the EC/EU. The removal of barriers to trade and investment has represented a considerable challenge to successive governments in Spain. Stripped of recourse to protectionist policies, Spain has sought to increase competitiveness by restructuring industry, reducing factor costs and providing business with a stable macro-economic environment.

The second major theme of this chapter is the effect that adjustment to globalization has had on Spanish politics. It will be argued that governments, regardless of their ideological affiliations, have abandoned socially progressive policy commitments in favour of measures to facilitate integration into the global economy. This has been the catalyst for conflict within Spain as trade unions and social movements have sought to extract a political price for what they consider acts of government 'hypocrisy'. The two areas where the emergence of this important democratic deficit will be outlined are employment and foreign aid policy. Also, the impact of globalization on the state's relations with regional authorities will be discussed. The haemorrhaging of power to supranational institutions has led to a decline of broad identification with the state in Spain. This is creating tension between the centre and the periphery characterized by increasing demands for a downward transfer of power to the regions. The two other issues to be addressed in this section are the relationship between globalization and the corruption scandals that have blighted Spanish politics during the 1990s and the extent to which policy-making autonomy has been impinged on by the emergence of transnational governance agreements. In the case of the latter, preliminary findings would suggest that, in the Spanish case, such agreements have had less bearing on policy-making autonomy than integration into the EU.

Economic trends

Characterized until the 1980s by insularity and high levels of protection, today Spain is fully integrated into the global economy. In terms of investment, for example, Spanish involvement in this important area of global economic activity has grown rapidly in recent years. In 1998 Spanish foreign portfolio investment increased 63 per cent, reaching some pta 16.9 billion (*El Pais*, August 15, 1999). Foreign investment activity in the Spanish stock market also experienced a dramatic rise in 1998 with shares worth pta 19.6 billion changing hands compared to 1997's figure of pta 10.2 billion (*El Pais*, 22 August 1999). One of the major destinations for both Spanish portfolio and foreign direct investment (FDI) is Latin America, where Spain was the second largest investor after the USA in 1997. Major Spanish electricity, telecommunications and banking companies have all identified Latin America as a target for their globalization strategies. Privatization has provided many of these companies with an opportunity to enter key markets in Argentina, Brazil, Chile, Colombia, Mexico, Peru and Venezuela.

The impact of globalization can clearly be seen in the context of Spain's economic relations with its Iberian neighbour, Portugal. According to *El Pais*, '12 or 13 years ago a Spanish or Portuguese businessman on a half full flight between Madrid and Lisbon was a rare sight' (*El Pais*, 13 June 1999). At that time the value of trade between the two nations was less than pta 200 thousand million. By 1998 this figure had increased tenfold, reaching some pta 2.07 billion. Spanish investment in Portugal peaked in 1996 when pta 380 thousand million was invested mainly in the form of acquisitions. This compared favourably to the pta 39 thousand million invested in 1990. Spanish companies are increasingly visible in Portugal in sectors as diverse as food distribution, construction, real estate and tourism, where the Melia Group is the market leader. Trade and investment traffic has not been just one way. Portuguese firms have also increased their FDI and export penetration of Spanish markets. For instance, between 1990 and 1998 Portuguese FDI in the Spanish economy increased from pta 4 thousand million to pta 39 thousand million. The value of exports also rose from pta 338 thousand million to pta 552 thousand million pta during the same period (*El Pais*, 13 June 1999).

Government policy

Since the early 1980s two political parties have enjoyed power in Spain. Between 1982 and 1996 the Centre-Left Partido Socialista Obrero Español (PSOE) successfully steered Spain towards the consolidation of democracy and membership of the EC. Since 1996 the Centre-Right Partido Popular (PP) has reinforced Spain's position at the heart of Europe. Having successfully fulfilled the convergence criteria agreed by the now European Union (EU) member states at Maastricht, the PP was able to sign Spain up for the European single currency in the spring of 1998 (the EMU). The economic policies of both of these governments have largely been determined by the transformations that have taken place in the global economy. The removal of trade and investment restrictions has meant that both parties, despite their ideological differences, have adopted broadly similar policies in their attempt to attract and retain capital. Such policies include: integration with Europe, measures to boost the competitiveness of Spanish industry and tight control of monetary policy.

Europe

Barry Gills sees globalization as a phenomenon that involves two structural cross-currents:

> Firstly, there is the tendency for increasing integration among the core zones, both in terms of transnationalisation of capital, and political and strategic policy coordination. Secondly, there is the countervailing trend toward regionalisation of trade and investment, with the concomitant potential for currency zones to emerge accompanying regionalisation of the world economy. (Gills, 1994: 189)

In the Spanish case, adjustment to globalization has largely been conditioned by the second of these cross-currents, regionalization. According to Murphy, 'EC membership has driven Spain's conversion to a modern capitalist economy through the practical need to compete in a single market and in the wider global economy' (Murphy, 1998: 167).

Spain's experience mirrors that of other medium-sized powers such as Canada and Mexico whose response to globalization has also been to consolidate their position within regional trading and investment blocs. Membership of the North American Free Trade Agreement (NAFTA) and the EC/EU has shaped the policy options available to decision-makers in all three of these countries. The two aspects of EU membership that have had most impact on economic and social policy-making in Spain have been the removal of barriers to trade and investment and movement towards the EMU.

In the 1980s Spanish industry was characterized by its domestic focus, dependency on foreign sources of both energy and technology and weak export performance. Industrial activity was concentrated in labour-intensive sectors plagued by low levels of demand, including iron and steel, shipbuilding, consumer durables, textiles, leather and footwear. Despite the partial liberalization of the economy precipitated by membership of multilateral bodies and the signing of a preferential trade agreement with the EEC in 1970, protectionism continued to be an integral part of Spanish industrial policy. Membership of the EC/EU effectively brought an end to Spanish economic introspection. Tariff barriers on imports from EC/EU member states started to be dismantled in March 1996 with a 10 per cent cut in import duties, and by the end of 1991 import duties were down by 90 per cent (Alonso Zaldivar and Castells, 1992: 81). The opening up of the domestic market had a profound impact on the Spanish trade balance. Already subject to deficits due to dependency on energy imports, the trade balance suffered an immediate setback as European imports flooded into the country. Thus between 1986 and 1992 the trade deficit rose to 6 per cent of GDP per year. Two sectors, in particular, witnessed large increases in imports, cars and consumer durables. Both of these sectors had enjoyed high levels of protection prior to EC/EU membership. For example between 1986 and 1996 cars as a percentage of total imports rose from 7.8 per cent to 14.5 per cent and consumer durables from 7.6 per cent to 13 per cent (Hernando Moreno, 1997: 155).

The removal of investment controls led to a massive increase in foreign direct and portfolio investment in the Spanish economy. According to Salmon, 'This represented a significant transfer of control over the economy to foreign owned (especially European) multinational companies and a reorganisation of trade such that an increasing proportion occurred within multinational company networks' (Salmon, 1995: 21). Between 1985 and 1990 pta 7000 billion of net foreign investment flooded into Spain (Salmon, 1995: 18). This was ten times greater than the total for the previous five years. Both the manufacturing and service sectors of the Spanish economy proved attractive to foreign investors. In the case of manufacturing, investment was concentrated in high demand sectors, such as technology, food and drink, and food distribution. Within the service sector, banking and insurance were major recipients of foreign investment. By 1989 there were almost 22,000 companies with some foreign capital located in Spain. In 10,000 companies participation was equal to or greater than 50 per cent (Salmon, 1995: 20). Geographically, over 80 per cent of foreign investment activity was concentrated in Madrid and Barcelona.

Competitiveness

According to Porter (1990) competitiveness is affected by six major determinants: factor conditions; demand conditions; related and supporting industries; firm strategy, structure and rivalry; the role of government; and the role of chance. Two of these determinants have been at the heart of the policies designed to boost competitiveness implemented by both the socialists and the PP: firm strategy, structure and rivalry, and factor conditions. Restructuring of the public sector has been achieved by a programme of rationalization, organizational concentration and privatization. The main areas of concern in terms of factor conditions have been labour market rigidity, poor infrastructure and inadequate education and training provision.[1]

The first step the PSOE Government took towards improving the competitiveness of Spanish industry was the introduction of a wide-ranging restructuring programme designed to reduce costs and boost productivity. In July 1983, following intense negotiations with employers and trade unions, the Government published its strategy in the *Libro blanco sobre la reconversion industrial.* The sectors earmarked included ones which had already undergone some restructuring following the economic crises of the 1970s, namely consumer goods, textiles, iron and steel, shipbuilding and new sectors such as fertilizers. Areas hardest hit by closures and job losses, such as the Cornisa Cantabrica (Asturias, Cantabria and the Basque Country), were designated *Zonas de Urgente Reindustrializacion* (ZUR). In order to attract new investment, firms willing to relocate their activities to the ZUR were offered generous subsidies and tax inducements.

The PSOE also introduced a policy of organizational consolidation involving whole industries. The objective of the policy was to create powerful nationally based industries capable of competing with the major players in European and global markets. Sectors affected included electricity supply, telecommunications, petrol distribution and gas. In the electricity sector for example, ENDESA prepared for greater competition by diversifying both horizontally and vertically. This involved a series of mergers, asset swaps and the purchase of shares in private sector companies such as Viesgo, Fecsa, Sevillana, Saltos del Nansa. ENDESA also adopted a global strategy. Attention focused on Portugal and, in particular, Latin America, where it has taken advantage of the privatization of electricity companies. In Chile for example, ENDESA took a 32 per cent share in the national utility Enersis, which was privatized by General Pinochet in the 1980s (Delano, 1999).

Privatization

In an attempt to expand the market economy in Spain many of the public sector firms involved in restructuring have been sold off. The PSOE's privatization programme acted as a major stimulant for inward investment by some of Europe's largest multinationals including Volkswagen (1986, SEAT) GEC Alsthom (1989, MTM) and Fiat Iveco (1990, ENASA). In order to retain political control over strategic sectors, the state kept a 51 per cent interest (golden share) in a number of partially privatized companies including REPSOL (oil), Telefónica (telecommunications), Tabacalera (Tobacco), Argentaria (financial services) and ENDESA (electricity). Additional measures were introduced to boost private participation in the public sector, including structural changes to the status of state-owned enterprises enabling them to enter into partnership with private sector firms and the introduction of compulsory competitive tendering in areas such as health, education and refuse collection. Under the Partido Popular, the pace of privatization intensified. At least 20 firms have been either totally or partially sold off since the PP came to power in 1996 and many more privatizations are in the pipeline. According to Murphy, the twin goals of PP privatization policy have been to increase the shareholding base and generate funds to help meet the Maastricht national debt criteria (Murphy, 1998: 168). Many of the companies involved are both substantial exporters and outward investors. Iberia, for example, which was to be privatized by the end of 1999, owned 10 per cent of Aeorolineas Argentinas and 1.3 per cent of Royal Air Maroc. Privatization under the PP is also giving a boost to European cross-border corporate integration. The imminent purchase of the state-owned military aircraft manufacturer CASA by one of Europe's leading aerospace companies[2] is a further step towards the formation of a European aerospace industry large enough to compete with US giants Lockheed Martin and Boeing. Privatization fever, at the end of 1999, surrounded state-owned insurance companies such as Musini, Inisas, Credito y Caucion, S.A. and CESCE.

Labour market deregulation

Labour market rigidity was identified by the PSOE as a major structural source of competitive disadvantage. It was the Government's conviction that job security and high employment costs constituted an unnecessary burden on business and an obstacle to job creation. This thesis, which enjoys wide political consensus in Spain, has also underpinned the PP Government's labour policy since coming to power in 1996. Through a series of measures both Governments have sought to make the labour market more flexible by removing controls on the hiring, dismissal and deployment of employees, improving the skills base of Spanish workers and encouraging wage restraints.

Three major labour reform packages have been introduced, two under the socialists (1984 and 1994) and one under the PP (1997). The most important aspect of the 1984 reforms was the introduction of temporary contracts. Until then, legislation dating from the Francoist period (*ordenanzas laborales*) had effectively blocked employers from taking on workers on a temporary basis. The introduction of short-term contracts had a considerable impact on employment practices in Spain. By 1995, for instance, 32 per cent of the Spanish workforce was employed on temporary contracts, up from 16 per cent in 1987 (Martinez Lucio, 1998: 450). These figures almost certainly underestimate the level of real deregulation in the Spanish labour market. According to Martinez Lucio, employers have sidestepped restrictions on temporary employment by switching employees between work experience, job training and work sharing contracts (Martinez Lucio, 1998: 450).

In the early 1990s, the Government entered into negotiations with employers and unions on the introduction of further labour market deregulation. Although the Government failed to secure the trade unions' agreement, a new package of measures was introduced in 1994. These affected all aspects of the labour market. In terms of hiring practice, the *Reforma del Mercado Laboral* contained provision for the extension of part-time and temporary contracts and the reintroduction of apprenticeships. Under the new scheme, 16- to 25-year-olds are hired on contracts lasting up to three years on salaries below the minimum wage. The Government also sought to liberalize the recruitment process by ending the monopoly held by the Spanish employment agency, INEM, over job placement.

New contractual arrangements have also been introduced by the PP. One of the main objectives of the PP reforms has been to make redundancy cheaper and less bureaucratic. Spanish workers have historically enjoyed substantial payments, particularly in cases where employers are unable to justify dismissal. Under the *Estatuto de Trabajadores* workers made redundant in such circumstances were entitled to compensation of up to 45 days' wages per year of service up to a maximum of 42 months' pay. At the time this represented the highest statutory rate within the EU. According to Martinez Lucio this led to the belief that,

> the high cost of shedding labour on permanent contracts was . . . a further deterrent to employment adjustment in firms. For this reason 'labour market reform' making it easier and cheaper for companies to dismiss workers has become the panacea for unemployment and low labour market involvement. (Martinez Lucio, 1998: 451)

Under the new contractual arrangements, introduced by the PP in May 1997, compensation is limited to 20 days per year with a 12-month maximum. Administrative obstacles to redundancy have also been removed: no permission is required for dismissals of less than ten workers over a three-month period, or for 10 per cent of the workforce in companies of more than 100 employees up to a maximum of 30 dismissals.

Monetary policy

Both the socialists and the PP have sought to boost competitiveness by adopting an orthodox monetary policy. On coming to power, the Socialist Government established a reduction in the level of inflation as a key objective. Controlling prices was considered imperative if Spain was to provide the stable macro-economic environment necessary for domestic and foreign businesses to plan ahead with confidence. Tight control over government spending, high interest rates and wage restraints all contributed to reducing inflation from 16.5 per cent in 1980 to 8.2 per cent in 1985. Wage restraint was achieved through bipartite (*Acuerdo Nacional sobre el Empleo*, 1982) and tripartite (*Acuerdo Económico y Social,* 1985–60) collective agreements. As a result wage rises throughout the first socialist mandate remained below the level of inflation. In 1986, for example, while inflation was at 8.3 per cent wage increases were set at 8.1 per cent. A breakdown in collective wage bargaining in 1988 meant that thereafter the PSOE had to rely on reductions in social spending to meet strict money supply limits. For example, unemployment benefit was targeted in an effort to cut public spending. This led to a reduction in the size and duration of benefit entitlement, greater emphasis on controlling fraud, penalties for refusing job offers and the introduction of training courses (Cooper, 1995: 124)

According to a number of analysts (Ariztegui, 1993; Cooper, 1995; Heywood, 1995; Salmon 1995) Spanish monetary policy since the late 1980s has been dictated by the demands of the EMU. The convergence process began when Spain joined the Exchange Rate Mechanism (ERM) of the European Monetary System (EMS) in June 1989. Since signing the Maastricht Treaty in December 1992 Spanish monetary policy has been determined by the strict convergence criteria for countries wishing to sign up for full EMU. These include: inflation not to exceed by more than 1.5 per cent the average rate of the three lowest-inflation EU countries; long-term nominal interest rates no higher than 2 per cent above the average of the three lowest rates in the EU; the currency to remain within the narrow band of the ERM for at least two years without devaluation; a budget deficit below 3 per cent of GDP; public debt below 60 per cent of GDP. Following introduction of the euro, responsibility for the broad tenets of monetary policy such as setting targets for European money supply has been transferred to the European Central Bank (ECB). The ability of medium sized European nations such as Spain to have any impact on the ECB's decision making processes is seriously compromised by voting arrangements based on member states' population and GDP (Heywood, 1995: 240).

Attempts to accommodate the Maastricht convergence criteria translated into broadly similar policy responses from both Governments. The PSOE outlined its strategy for meeting the EMU criteria in 1992. The plan which included renewed measures to deregulate the labour market and liberalize the public sector was premised on a growth rate of 1 per cent above the European average. This proved overly optimistic given the recession in the US economy, persistently high interest rates in Germany and the ERM crisis in September 1992 (Heywood, 1995: 230–40). The turmoil in the foreign exchanges forced the Government to devalue the peseta three times between 1992 and 1993 and contributed to a 3.5 per cent deterioration in the budget deficit. This seriously compromised the PSOE's targets and forced the Government to revise its convergence timetable on the basis of more realistic growth figures. The EMU convergence criteria have also dominated monetary policy under the PP. Differences between PP and PSOE monetary policy have been marginal as the PP has sought to retain strict control over spending, accelerate privatization and foster further deregulation of the labour market. The PP has been the beneficiary of a favourable international economic environment which has meant that growth rates have exceeded expectations. The combination of budgetary austerity and favourable economic climate meant that Spain was successful in its attempt to meet the convergence criteria and thus enter the third phase of EMU. Although trumpeted by the PP as a major economic achievement, EMU has been attained at a considerable cost to national sovereignty over future economic and social policy. By supporting centralization of control for European money supply and interest rate targets in the hands of the European Central Bank, Spanish governments have effectively surrendered their capacity to redistribute wealth via either lower taxes for the poor or increased social benefits (Murphy, 1998: 176).

Political change

The globalization process has also had a profound impact on the Spanish polity. Four of the most important consequences of globalization for the Spanish political system will be discussed here, namely the erosion of democracy, tension between the centre and the periphery, political corruption, the loss of policy-making autonomy.

As Peter Anderson points out in Chapter 1, to be democratic, after elections, governments must not deviate significantly from the spirit and the letter of the promises which they have made during their election campaign, or introduce radically new policies which affect the fundamental interests of electors, without first securing a mandate to do so via the conduct of a referendum or another general election. In Spain, this basic democratic principle has been undermined by governments of the Left (PSOE) and the Right (PP) who have been prepared to sacrifice election pledges on the altar of greater European integration. In both cases the willingness to abandon policy commitments has brought governments into conflict with important groups within Spanish civil society.

Criticism of the PSOE centred on the marked divergence between the promises made to the electorate during the 1982 election campaign and economic policy practice once in power. During the campaign the PSOE promised to create 800,000 jobs and increase social spending. In fact unemployment increased from 9 per cent in 1979 to 22 per cent in 1985 and public spending remained tightly controlled (Salmon, 1995: 12). Lack of unity among Spanish trade unions, however, meant that industrial unrest remained low during the first socialist mandate. The *Union General de Trabajadores* (UGT), due to its historic links with the PSOE, largely accepted the Government's assertion that a period of painful adjustment was a necessary prelude to Spain's joining the EC/EU. The *Comisiones Obreras* (CC.OO) and some smaller trade unions, however, attacked the PSOE's abandonment of socially progressive policy commitments. Following the socialists' second election victory disillusionment with government policy led to a rapprochement between the two main unions, thereby creating the basis for concerted industrial action. Conflict centred on the Government's refusal to contemplate higher wages (Spain was enjoying an economic boom precipitated by EC/EU membership) and failure to implement the commitments it had made during collective negotiations. The PSOE was portrayed by unions as having jettisoned socialist principles in favour of a neo-liberal discourse which emphasized the free working of markets and deregulation of the labour force. Tension culminated in a hugely successful one-day strike on 14 December 1988, which was supported by an overwhelming majority of the workforce. The strike effectively broke the 100-year link between the UGT and the PSOE and sealed the fate of wage restraint in Spain. As a result, subsequent wage rises were generally above the level of inflation. Between 1990 and 1992, for example, wages increased 20 per cent (Malo de Molina, 1993: 1164). Tensions between Government and unions plagued the next eight years of socialist rule. Under the PSOE, Spain suffered one of the highest rates of strike action in Europe. Total working days lost in 1993, for example, at 250 per 1000 employees, were higher than any other EU country, except Greece (Martinez Lucio, 1998: 448).

Foreign aid policy

Election promises have also been forgotten by the PP as it has struggled to fulfil the Maastricht criteria for EMU. This too has led to social tension between the Government and civil society. In the area of foreign aid policy for example, the Government has failed to honour promises to increase aid as a percentage of GDP, invoking the demands of the convergence criteria as justification. One of the main obstacles to winning power facing the PP during the 1996 election campaign was the legitimacy deficit conferred on it by its neo-Francoist heritage. Aid provided the PP with an opportunity to both alter public perceptions as to its suitability as a party of government and criticize the PSOE's record over an important aspect of foreign policy. Under the PSOE, the issue of foreign aid had become highly politicized. This was due to two factors, popular solidarity with the victims of the Rwandan and Bosnian crises and the emergence of a powerful social movement, the *Plataforma 0.7*, capable of mobilizing popular support for an increase in the quantity and quality of Spanish aid. The Rwandan and Bosnian crises took place at a time when the domestic political scene was being rocked by a series of financial and political scandals reaching the highest levels of government. The juxtaposition of personal greed and corruption with immense human suffering had a powerful impact on public opinion, leading to widespread support for the *0.7*'s demands (Hughes, 1998: 179). A number of measures were included within the PP's election manifesto demonstrating the party's progressive credentials in this area. The most important commitments included an increase in aid spending to 0.35 per cent of GDP by the end of its first year in power and the promise to bring in legislation to regulate the disparate elements of Spanish aid policy. Since coming to power, the PP has been conspicuous by its failure to meet the commitment on aid made to the Spanish electorate in the run up to the 1996 elections. During the PP's first year in government, for example, aid at 0.22 per cent of GDP was at its lowest for six years. Although the level of aid has since increased, reaching 0.26 per cent of GDP in 1998, it is still some way from the 0.35 per cent promised at the elections. In a meeting between representatives of the *0.7* and the Government, the Minister for International Cooperation, Fernando Villalonga, stated that due to the demands of the convergence criteria, the Government was unable to honour its commitments made during the election campaign (*El Pais*, 4 October 1996). In response, the *0.7* organized a number of demonstrations ensuring that the issue of aid remained firmly in the public consciousness. In December 1996, for example, a march of several thousand *0.7* sympathizers took place through the centre of Madrid. According to

ABC, marchers expressed their dissatisfaction with the Government by denouncing 'the hypocrisy of the large political parties which support our demands when in opposition and forget about them when in power' (*ABC*, 15 December 1996).

Regional tension

Conflict between the centre and the periphery has been a staple of Spanish politics throughout the twentieth century. The clearest example of this is the ongoing war between the Basque separatists, ETA, and the Spanish state. Despite recent optimism, the abandonment by ETA, at the end of November 1999, of a 14-month ceasefire has plunged the future of Spanish/Basque relations into a new period of uncertainty. In recent years both the number of issues and number of regions involved in disputes with the Spanish state has multiplied. This mirrors the experience of other countries with powerful regional constituencies, including Italy and Canada. According to some commentators, centre/periphery tensions reflect the fact that the emergence of macro-regional structures of governance has been accompanied by a powerful decentralizing dynamic. As sovereign nation-states have suffered what Yoshikazu Sakamoto describes as 'the powerlessness of the powerful – a contradiction which indicates the erosion of the authority, competence, credibility and legitimacy of the sovereign states in the age of internationalization' (Sakamoto, 1995: 131), substate authorities have sought to increase their autonomy *vis-à-vis* the centre. According to Rosenau, this represents a dialectical process in which increased globalization contains the seeds of localization that, in turn, reshapes the globalizing dynamic (Rosenau, 1995: 51).

Highly symbolic of the tensions between the centre and the regions in Spain is the current dispute (at the time of writing) over national sports teams. A number of autonomous communities have declared an interest in establishing representative sports teams, including the Basque Country, Catalonia, Andalusia and the Balearic Islands. In the case of Catalonia, regional legislation was passed in August 1999 enabling the formation of such teams to begin. This provoked a furious response from the Government. According to Mariano Rajoy, Minister for Education and Culture, this could lead to a situation in which 'Spain will be competing with part of Spain'. The Government has threatened Catalonia with an appeal before the Constitutional Court if it continues with its plans. A more substantial source of tension between the centre and the periphery in Spain has been the level of autonomous community spending. While the Government retains control over macro-economic policy, the division of spending powers between the state and autonomous communities has remained unclear. This has led to a number of problems, for instance the duplication of spending in areas such as education and health and accusations that autonomous communities are exploiting such anomalies for political ends. A good example of this is pensions policy. In November 1998 the Andalusian Regional Government decided to fund increases in basic pensions above the rate of inflation. This caused an immediate outcry from the PP. In an appeal before the Constitutional Court, the Government claimed that Andalusia had no power to unilaterally raise pensions, as this would lead to inequalities across Spain and break the state's monopoly over pensions policy. The Court's decision to uphold Andalusia's action led regional governments in the Balearic Islands, Canary Islands and Catalonia to adopt similar measures. In August 1999, for example, the Catalan Regional Government (*Generalitat*) announced its decision to make an 'extraordinary payment' of 8000 pesetas to 60,000 Catalan pensioners. The payment was justified on the grounds that inflation between 1995 and 1998 was higher in Catalonia than in the rest of Spain, leading to a loss in purchasing power. According to Jordi Pujol, the President of the Generalitat: 'The welfare state in Catalunya has to be *our* welfare state: we must ensure that things such as this [the inflation differential] do not prejudice our citizens' (*El Pais*, 25 August 1999). The Government's response has been typically robust. According to Spain's Deputy Prime Minister, Rodrigo Rato, the Catalans' actions represent the 'gravest and worst' attack that the Spanish social security system has faced in the last 20 years (*El Pais*, 25 August 1999).

Corruption

Politics in a number of European states including Italy, the UK, Belgium, Spain, France and Germany has been tarnished in recent years by corruption scandals. In the Spanish case, three broad categories of scandal have emerged during the 1990s: illegal funding of political parties, state-sponsored anti-terrorist activities and influence trafficking.

As in other countries where there are statutory limits on party financing, Spanish political parties have sought to boost funds through illegal sources of income. In early 1991, for example, the newspaper *El Mundo* reported for the first time that the PSOE had been using ficticious consultancies in the Barcelona-based Filesa group to channel funds into party coffers (*Guardian*, 4 December 1999). The second, more serious set of allegations surround state complicity in the so-called 'dirty war' against Basque nationalists. Between 1983 and 1987 the anti-terrorist group *Grupo Antiterrorista de Liberacion* (GAL) carried out a number of attacks against suspected ETA terrorists. During his investigation of these events the Judge Baltasar Garzón uncovered a web of involvement in the GAL affair reaching the highest echelons of the Spanish state. According to Jose Amodia,

> the reaction of many of the offenders – in some instances those at the very top of party and government – has been not only to reject the accusations, as was to be expected, but to be unwilling to accept political responsibility for the misdemeanours and sleaze, and on occasion to interfere with police investigations and with the judicial process. (Amodia, 1998: 30)

Despite this, in August 1998 two former socialist ministers, Jose Barrionuevo and Rafael Vera, were jailed for 13 years for their role in the GAL affair.

One area of political corruption that seems to have left neither the PSOE nor the PP untainted is influence trafficking. According to Jaime Pastor Verdú, there is a close link between this category of corruption and globalization. He states: 'Powers, visible or invisible, national or transnational, act behind and above government and parliament in the context of globalisation of the economy, finance and mass media' (Pastor Verdú, 1998: 252). A number of scandals have come to light in recent years in which public officials have accepted bribes from private companies in exchange for influence. The latest case concerns the Italian Euro MP and former Prime Minister, Silvio Berlusconi, who is alleged to have made illegal payments to Spanish political parties between 1990 and 1993 to facilitate the setting up of a new independent television channel, Tele 5 (*El Pais*, 1 December 1999).

The former Prime Minister Felipe Gonzalez has also intimated at the link between the removal of barriers to trade and investment and the emergence of a powerful media and finance based oligarchy:

> A finance and media based oligarchy is being formed in Spain with the aim of appropriating power and endangering equal opportunities and even respect for the rules of the democratic game including the acceptance of electoral results. (*El Pais*, 17 November 1999)

Gonzalez's remarks stem from a claim made in February 1998 in an interview in the magazine *Tiempo* by Luis Maria Anson, the former editor of the conservative newspaper *ABC*. According to Anson the the PSOE's 1996 election defeat was engineered by a powerful group made up of important figures within the Spanish media and banking that conspired to undermine the PSOE and pave the way for a PP victory.

Autonomy

One aspect of international relations that has most occupied theorists in recent years is the emergence of transnational governance agreements. Such agreements, it is argued, have impinged on the ability of nation-states to exercise autonomous control over policy-making. Transnational governance agreements can be identified at both the regional and the global level. As has already been demonstrated, integration into the EU has meant that the Spanish state has ceded control over policy-making in a number of domains, in particular, macro-economic policy and industrial policy. Agreements at the global level, otherwise known as 'transnational governance regimes', are defined by Young as: '[s]ocial institutions that consist of agreed upon principles, norms, rules, decision-making procedures, and programs that govern the interactions of actors in specific issue areas' (Young, 1997: 6).

Transnational government regimes are brokered by international organizations and exist in a number of policy areas. In economics, for example, institutions such as the G-8, World Bank, International Monetary Fund (IMF) and increasingly the World Trade Organization (WTO) have shaped the rules that govern global trade and finance. These organizations are also responsible for monitoring states' compliance with the established regime norms. Regimes have also emerged in other areas of international relations including the environment and development aid. In the case of aid, the institution responsible for harmonizing the aid polices of donor nations is the Organization for Economic Cooperation and Development's (OECD) Development Assistance Committee (DAC).

Evidence from an analysis of the impact of the transnational aid regime on the Spanish policy-making process suggests that governance regimes have had less bearing on policy-making autonomy than integration into the EU. In its discussion of Spanish compliance with DAC aid regime norms in the areas of partnership building, economic well-being, and human development, the Spanish non-governmental organization Intermón identified a number of areas in which Spain has failed to honour its international commitments. In terms of attempts to build partnerships, for example, Spain is accused of maintaining a top-down approach and imposing models and priorities on recipient nations. In the case of measures to promote human development, Spain is still far from meeting international targets for spending on basic health care and education. Finally plans to use Spanish aid to promote gender equality are described by Intermón as 'non-existent' (Intermón, 1998: 41–53).

Future prospects and conclusions

Ten years ago only 50 Spanish companies had overseas subsidiaries. Today the figure is more than 250. According to the Industry Minister Josep Pique: 'the spectacular growth in investment means that the Spanish economy has become a modern economy with behaviour patterns similar to those of developed countries. The domestic market is no longer enough' (*El Pais*, 15 February 1998). The number of companies establishing overseas operations is set to increase with Spain's small and medium-sized firms (PYMEs) likely to be at the forefront of any future developments. Hitherto domestically focused, this sector of the Spanish economy is already taking advantage of low labour costs and expanding overseas markets. The high cost of labour within the euro zone, however, means that future PYME investment is likely to be concentrated in regions such as Latin America, the former Soviet Bloc, China and North Africa.

The search for competitiveness will continue to dominate the policy agenda of Spanish governments. A number of competitive disadvantages will need to be addressed if Spain is to continue to adapt to the demands of the global economy. These include, deficiencies in infrastructure, telecommunications and information technology, lingering protectionism, the rising cost of labour and an inadequate skills base (Murphy 1998: 170–5). A likely focus of future Spanish government action is education policy. A number of issues will need to be urgently addressed if Spanish workers are to be equipped with the skills necessary to succeed in the global marketplace. In terms of higher education, for example, poor staff–student ratios, a high drop-out rate and the lack of emphasis on vocational training are just three of the issues in need of government attention.

In relation to the domestic economy, the prognosis at the end of the twentieth century and the start of the twenty-first is positive. Growth, currently at 3.6 per cent per annum, is forecast to remain above the euro zone average at least until 2002 (*El Diario Vasco*, 30 November 1999). One of the main reasons for this is a boom in consumer spending fuelled by low interest rates and a decline in the unemployment rate to 15.45 per cent. High levels of foreign and domestic investment particularly in the construction sector are also contributing to an expanding economy. On the downside, there are fears that the consumer spending boom could lead to an increase in inflation (currently at 2.5 per cent). Inflationary pressures could also stem from the drop in the value of the euro, which by the end of 1999 had fallen to around $1. The other main worry for the Spanish government is the worsening trade balance. Spanish exports fell during 1999 due to the recession in the Far East and Latin American markets. Although exports are set to rise in 2000, the trade balance is likely to remain in deficit due to high demand for imports fuelled by the consumer boom (*La Vanguardia*, 30 November 1999).

As this chapter demonstrates, several times since the transition to democracy, popular discontent with government policy has erupted into social protest. Measures to liberalize the labour market, privatization and monetary orthodoxy have all led to conflict and disillusionment with democracy in Spain. In the 1980s and early 1990s the main focus for discontent was labour relations. As the 1990s have progressed, however, other societal groups, such as the *Plataforma 0.7*, have emerged as sources of opposition to unpopular government policies. In the future, challenges to the government are likely to come from a loose network of activist groups including students, anarchists, environmentalists, anti-Nazis, gays and lesbians, and squatters (*okupas*) prepared to participate in direct action. As in other major European states such as the UK and France, this network is increasingly focusing its attention on globalization itself. Spanish groups, for instance, participated in the internationally coordinated 'Carnival against Global Capitalism' timed to coincide with the G-7 Summit in Cologne on 18 June 1999.

At the start of the new millennium, perhaps the source of greatest tension within Spain is the pressure from autonomous communities for further devolution. The reaction to such demands will be a major test for Spain's democratic institutions. Will the state accede to the regions or will it risk inflaming nationalism by seeking to centralize power? At present the configuration of the Spanish Parliament means that the government has no option but to look favourably on the demands of Catalan and Basque nationalist parties, on whose parliamentary support it depends. If, however, either the PP or the PSOE is able to win an absolute majority at future elections, tensions could be stretched to breaking as the centre seeks to reassert its authority over regional governments.

Notes

1. See Rigby, 1998 for a discussion of education and training reforms. See Boix, 1998 and Bandrés, 1993 for a discussion of investment in infrastructure.
2. British Aerospace, Aeroaspatiale and Daimler Chrysler Aerospace have all expressed an interest in acquiring CASA.

CHAPTER TWELVE

The Problems and Prospects of Portugal

Jack Hampson

The case of Portugal is an interesting example of the 'New Europe in Transition'. When placed in a historical context, Portugal has been relatively late in embracing Europe and only joined the European Union (EU) in 1986. In examining these historical changes, conflicting pressures of Atlanticism against European integration feature as partial explanation of the late arrival of Portugal on the main European scene. In addition, when viewed in political, economic and social terms, Portugal is still a transitional society. After many years of authoritarian rule, Portugal still has the characteristics of a young democracy and there are a number of political and institutional problems which will affect its future. The Portuguese economy experienced late and partial industrialization; while modernization has been evident in recent years, there are structural problems which restrict economic progress. On the other hand, macro-economic developments in the 1990s have been most impressive in relation to the requirements of the EU. According to many social indicators, Portugal is the least developed of all the current members of the EU; during the 1980s and 1990s, Portugal tried to establish basic elements of social provision and attempted to catch up with the welfare states of more advanced societies (see Chapter 5). In all these aspects of Portuguese society, a mixture of modernity and tradition is noticeable and so Portugal is very much in a state of transition. This chapter will analyse the current problems and the likely future of Portugal by developing the above introductory comments in the same sequence; some relevant historical background will precede the analysis of political, institutional, economic and social dimensions. Concluding thoughts on the likely future of Portugal will complete the survey.

Historical background: Atlanticism versus Europe

Although Portugal has been categorized in modern times as a 'developing European country', it is important to remember the rich history of the fifteenth and sixteenth centuries; in the 'age of discoveries', Portugal was a leading nation and eventually established a significant empire to the extent that Portuguese is now one of the most widely-spoken languages of the world. Nostalgia for this period of history is still very evident today and it is captured in Portuguese popular outward-looking attitudes towards the sea. This maritime tradition has become important in Portugal as the ideology of Atlanticism (Jacquemin and Wright, 1993: 394) and as such it has conflicted with other views favouring more inward-looking attitudes towards European integration. In reviewing the historical background to the debate over

Atlanticism and Europe, the 1960s is particularly important and so the debates of this period will be considered in more detail here.

Prior to the 1960s, Portugal was generally isolated from mainstream developments in Europe due to its long period of authoritarian rule. Specifically, a dictatorship emerged in the early 1930s under the personal control of Salazar, who created the 'New State' (*Estado Novo*) in 1933. Until the 1960s, Salazar maintained a strong dictatorial regime and he pursued backward-looking policies. Salazar was a devout Catholic and he perceived his mission as the restoration of social order; this required a conservative strategy in both economic and social affairs. The New State was in favour of economic retardation instead of industrial development (Porto, 1984: 85) and Salazar followed the principle of subsidiarity in restricting the role of the state over social intervention. In foreign affairs, Portugal tried to maintain neutrality in Europe while maintaining a strategy of exploitation towards the Portuguese colonies. With extensive state control, political opposition was stifled and opponents often exiled or imprisoned. In this period, the Salazar regime clearly supported Atlanticism rather than European integration.

Pressures for changes in the Salazar regime emerged during the 1960s and the process of orientation towards Europe began in 1960 with a decision to join the new European Free Trade Association (EFTA). At the same time, other factors were starting to create new difficulties for the dictatorship. A huge increase in migration to other European countries, such as France and Germany, brought other links through remittances and visits. The development of tourism, especially in the Algarve, was a key feature of the 1960s and this again placed challenges on the backward situation within Portugal. Most importantly of all, emerging problems with Portuguese Africa led to military campaigns in defence of the colonies. Ultimately, this provoked opposition within the armed forces which eventually led to the collapse of the regime in the revolution of 1974.

During the 1960s, those who wished to maintain the regime were associated with the preservation of the African colonies; originally known as the 'Africans' (*Africanos*), they soon became the 'Atlantics' or '*Atlantistas*' (Barreto, 1994: 1053). By contrast, opponents of Atlanticism were known as the modernizers, liberals or Europeans in such a way that these labels could be attached to all those who opposed the authoritarian regime. Hence, the debate was an integral element of the conflicts in Portugal during the 1960s.

After the peaceful revolution of April 1974, the balance between Atlanticism and Europe gradually shifted strongly in favour of the latter. Europe now became a symbol of parliamentary democracy and even a programme for election campaigns (Barreto, 1994: 1055). In the first free election for over 50 years, held in April 1975, all political parties, except the communists and the Extreme Left, gave wholehearted support to European integration. Thus the results of the 1975 election show that 83 per cent of the votes went to parties supporting Europe (Gallagher, 1983).

Although political life for the rest of 1975 was dominated by a series of conflicts and Portugal was perceived by outsiders as highly unstable, eventually democracy was more firmly established in 1976 and a new forward-looking Constitution was prepared. In the general election of April 1976, the Socialist Party (*Partido Socialista* – PS) gained the most votes and formed a minority government led by Mario Soares, who was strongly in favour of European integration. In 1977, a formal application to join the EU was made, again with the support of all political parties except the Communists and the Extreme Left. The business sector and one of the two main groups of trade unions (*Uniao Geral dos Trabalhadores* – UGT) were in agreement over membership of the EEC. With such a consensus towards Europe at an early stage of the new Portuguese democracy, the triumph of Europe over Atlanticism seemed evident.

Since the 1970s, there are grounds, however, for claiming that the debate is not entirely closed even though opposition to Europe is significantly less than in other European countries such as the UK. First, during the mid-1980s, a reversal of the trend towards Europe can be located in a new political party founded by Ramalho Eanes who was President of Portugal from 1976 to 1985. Eanes was a former army officer whose position as President meant that he had been above the political intrigue and instability of the first ten years since the revolution. Despite consensus over Europe, Portugal had experienced fifteen different governments during these years. In the general election of 1985, Eanes led a new party called the Renewal Party (*Partido Renovador Democratico* – PRD) and won 18 per cent of the votes. The PRD campaigned on nationalist lines and Eanes himself followed the Atlanticist position. The reversal of the European trend, however, soon turned out to be short-lived as the PRD fell back to 5 per cent of the votes in the 1987 general election and then less than 1 per cent in 1991, after which the party collapsed (Gallagher, 1988; Jornal de Noticias, 1991).

The rise and fall of the PRD needs to be placed in a wider political context in order to appreciate the changing debates concerning Europe and its alternatives. In the 1985 general election the largest proportion of votes at almost 30 per cent was secured by the Social Democratic Party (*Partido Social Democrata* – PSD) under the new leadership of Anibal Cavaco e Silva. The PSD formed a minority government with conditional support from the PRD (Gallagher, 1986). Within two years, Cavaco and the PSD had established a strong enough position to gain 50 per cent of the vote in the next general election of July 1987 (Gallagher, 1988). The PRD lost its role in power and the PSD went on to become the party of government until 1995. Portugal's democracy entered a new stable phase with Cavaco as Prime Minister for the same period and there was similar stability at the presidential level with Mario Soares holding office from 1986 to 1996. By the early 1990s, Portugal had also been a member of the EU since 1986 and so it did seem as though the debate over Atlanticism and Europe was history. According to David Corkill, 'Portugal has taken its place as a natural member of the European Community. Atlanticism no longer competes as an alternative scenario' (Corkill, 1993: 116).

In the mid-1990s, however, a resurgence of ideas associated with Atlanticism emerged in Portuguese politics. After the 1974 revolution, there was a political party known as the Centre Social Democrats (*Centro Democratico Social* – CDS). This party was led by Freitas do Amarel for 20 years and it had an image of being the 'party of the rich' (Corkill, 1996: 406). From 1975 to 1985 the CDS regularly gained between 8 per cent and 10 per cent of the overall vote. By 1987, however, the CDS vote was reduced to 4 per cent and it secured only 4.4 per cent in 1991. The CDS was the most conservative and nationalist of the Portuguese parties but it still gave consistent support to membership of the EU (Barreto, 1994: 1062). In 1995, the lack of popularity of the CDS led not only to a change of leadership but also to a new name; a young Manuel Monteiro gave a fresh dynamic to the party, which was optimistically called the Popular Party (*Partido Popular* – PP). Monteiro moved the PP firmly to the Right, espousing more conservative values, a stronger sense of nationalism and a clear anti-European stance. The PP brought back Portugal's 'Atlantic vocation' (Corkill, 1996: 406) and it even dared to associate itself with Salazarism. With a more youthful and more distinctive new identity, the PP managed to double its share of the vote in the 1995 general election to just over 9 per cent (O Publico, 1995). Since then, Monteiro has continued to promote the PP and the party did secure 10.3 per cent of votes in the European elections of June 1999. While it is unlikely that there will be any significant resurgence of Atlanticism and anti-European views in Portugal, there has been some change in the political spectrum and the PP offers an opportunity for such views to be expressed.

Political and institutional dimensions

Any assessment of current problems and the likely future of Portugal must involve an analysis of Portugal's political and institutional dimensions in addition to those related to Atlanticism versus Europe, discussed above. As already mentioned, Portugal experienced authoritarian rule from the late 1920s to 1974 and so democratic institutions have only been developed in recent decades. Indeed, it is still valid to claim that Portugal has a young democracy. Antonio Barreto extends this claim to argue that Portugal has a 'very young and defective democratic culture' (Barreto, 1994: 1067). With the inexperience of youth combined with the legacy of dictatorship, various political and institutional problems remain.

First, it is possible to take an incremental view of political change and so challenge the idea of a 'radical break' after the 1974 revolution. Despite new democratic institutions, the administration of policies in Portugal has frequently been criticized for centralization, excessive bureaucracy, a lack of accountability and a display of attitudes that are more reminiscent of the previous period. For example, on the question of attitudes towards social policies, Boaventura de Sousa Santos has claimed that:

> [T]he public welfare administration has not yet fully internalized the conception of public welfare as a matter of right, and in some respects goes on conceiving it as a matter of state benevolence, as was the case during the fascist regime. Indeed, the revolution of April 25 left the administration relatively untouched and even if there were changes they took place at the level of personnel not at the level of structures. (Santos, 1991: 34)

On the issues of centralization and bureaucracy, many criticisms have been made which cast doubt on the efficiency and flexibility of public administration. For example, the education system is renowned for its over-centralization and bureaucratic administration (Lima and Afonso, 1995; OECD, 1995). More generally, similar problems have been recognized in the making of state policy and its implementation (Barreto, 1994; Pereirinha, 1997, Corkill, 1999a). Even within the Government, it is common to point to the 'impenetrable bureaucratic processes', as admitted by the Secretary of State for European Affairs (Costa, 1997). Relatively minor decisions are regularly referred to central authorities in Lisbon and the results eagerly awaited in the daily official publication, the *Diario da Republica*. When decentralization has been tried in recent years, it has either led to different problems of regional inequities (Hampson, 1997a) or it has been perceived as a 'shedding of responsibility ... by central government' (Pereirinha, 1997: 216). In the 1998 referendum on regionalization, government proposals for regional authorities (originally envisaged in the 1976 Constitution) were rejected decisively (Corkill, 1999b), so Portugal is not following trends in other European countries.

In addition, further problems associated with the administration of the Portuguese state need to be considered. For example, there are significant differences between policies and outcomes. A popular term in Portugal is 'reality' (*realidade*) and this is used to explain that laws and policies do not always work on the ground. Santos gives various reasons for the gaps between rights and reality; he includes toleration of the violation of laws, selective application, lack of monitoring and inadequate budgets (Santos, 1990: 214–15). Illustrations of these problems include illegal housing and employment, inequalities in service delivery among different areas of Portugal and widespread use of the private sector instead of an unpopular state. In these situations when the state cannot deliver, other mechanisms come into play; in Portugal, the importance of 'connections' (*cunha*) is broadly recognized for access to particular favours from people working in public sector institutions. This is a limited version of 'clientilism' which seems a prominent characteristic of Southern European societies (Ferrera, 1996).

Another aspect of the political system in Portugal is the relatively young local government. Under the new Portuguese Constitution of 1976, local authorities were established within a democratic framework and so local democracy is a very recent achievement. The most important bodies are the municipalities (*municipios*) and these are relatively large in European terms with an average of more than 32,000 inhabitants (Pereira, 1991). At a higher level, administrative regions were envisaged in the 1976 Constitution but these have never been implemented. Within the municipalities, the local executive board is important (*Camara Municipal*) and its head is a powerful Mayor (*O Presidente*). In terms of local powers, the municipalities have relative autonomy within restricted areas of responsibility; this means that the local *Presidente* can spend money with discretionary power, but in practice the main objects of expenditure are housing, transport and environmental services. Separate hierarchies exist with centralized responsibility for the administration of health care, social security and education, so important social services lie outside the scope of local government. While functions are not limited by the *ultra vires* doctrine, local authorities are clearly restricted in what they can do and there are typical problems in collaborating with other institutions such as the National Health Service (Pereira, 1991: 143). In addition, the use of discretionary powers gives further opportunities for allocation of resources by 'connections' (*cunha*). Overall, the scale of local government in Portugal is very small when compared to other countries; in 1990, the share of total government expenditure, excluding social security, was 10 per cent as against 61 per cent in Germany, 50 per cent in Sweden and 22 per cent in France (OECD, 1993: 30). Even compared with a centralized state such as France, the very limited powers of Portuguese local government are evident.

A number of additional features of Portugal's young democracy are less easy to evaluate. Probably as a consequence of the absence of democratic institutions for so long, the processes of democracy are generally taken seriously at all levels. Elections and voting are generally popular within organizations at lower levels and political meetings are also well-supported. The right to speak is fully accepted to the extent that 'interventions' are restricted and speeches take considerable time. In a similar way at national level, important decisions are frequently referred to commissions of inquiry rather than being taken quickly by government ministers. A good example concerns social security policies in which long-term factors are significant. In 1996, a Commission on Social Security was created to produce a White Paper. When the Commission reported in December 1997, the White Paper was a huge document based on extensive research (*Comissão do Livro Branco da Segurança Social*, 1998). Several minority reports were included and the issues were then debated on television. Overall, the case is a classic example of rational planning, except for the lack of subsequent implementation. The mixed conclusions on these aspects are that democracy is now more established but it has taken a very long time.

In recent years, however, there are some signs of maturity in the sense that Portugal may be following the pattern of political developments elsewhere. A new kind of stability in Portuguese politics has become evident since the general election of 1995. Prior to this year, a stable democracy had been provided by the PSD with Cavaco as Prime Minister for ten years. In the 1995 campaign, it was noticeable that the PS was less strident in its opposition to the PSD and it adopted a more 'modern' approach which minimized policy differences and maximized the attractiveness of a 'new governing team' (Corkill, 1996: 403). In the pursuit of this strategy by the PS and also in the defence offered by the PSD, party machines played an important role. The success of the PS and perhaps its new strategy can be seen in the results; the PS secured almost 44 per cent of the votes (compared with 29 per cent in 1991) and formed a new government under Prime Minister Antonio Guterres (O Publico, 1995). Another significant conclusion from the 1995 results is that the two main parties polled 78 per cent of the votes and so the claim can be made that Portugal now has a bipolar party system (Corkill, 1996: 408). Since both major parties pursue largely similar policies a new version of political stability has emerged. With recent evidence suggesting no substantial changes, this stability is important, especially for Portugal's future in the EU.

Dimensions of political economy

The development of the Portuguese economy will now be examined, both in terms of structural aspects and also in relation to macro-economic variables. Since the management of the economy is very much a political issue, especially with recent requirements of the EU, all these questions are considered as dimensions of political economy. Within this framework, some assessment of current problems and some predictions of the future direction of the Portuguese economy will feature.

Portugal has generally been recognized as a late developing economy. In 1960, the sectoral shares for employment were 43 per cent primary, 29 per cent secondary and 28 per cent tertiary (Bravo, 1989). Since the 1960s, Portugal has experienced both late and limited industrialization; the peak share of employment for the secondary, mostly manufacturing, sector was 37 per cent in 1982 and this fell to 32 per cent by 1995. Although late, a predictable and consistent decline in primary employment has occurred – 26 per cent in 1982 and 11 per cent by 1995. In line with these changes, the tertiary sector increased from 37 per cent in 1982 to 56 per cent in 1995 (Barreto, 1996). As a partial explanation of late development, the policies of the Salazar dictatorship favoured economic retardation rather than growth, at least until the 1960s. In addition, after the 1974 revolution, Portugal was attempting to develop in political and social terms as well as making changes to the economy; conflicts in policy objectives are evident in this period and it is important to remember that the external context was unfavourable with crisis and recession in the international economy.

While the 1974 revolution was clearly very popular within Portugal, it was not well-timed in relation to international economic events. During the remainder of the decade and also the first half of the 1980s, economic instability had both domestic and external causes. Inflation regularly exceeded 20 per cent and peaked at 29 per cent in 1984; unemployment was also high relative to previous experience, rising in the late 1970s to peak figures of almost 11 per cent between 1983 and 1985 (Bravo, 1989). At the same time after 1974, structural changes were made on political grounds; as part of a socialist strategy, a programme of nationalization was implemented quickly during 1975 and 1976. Major industries, banking and transport companies were taken over by the state so that the public sector became very large (Corkill, 1993). In consequence, public expenditure was high and there was a rapid increase in the public debt. According to Corkill, this occurred because 'political priorities took precedence over strictly economic considerations during the 1970s' (Corkill, 1993: 40). He is critical of the lack of attention devoted to efficiency and modernization. As late as 1986 when Portugal joined the EU, the economy was in 'dire need of reconversion and restructuring' (Corkill, 1993: 52). Not only did industrialization come late to Portugal but opportunities for economic development were further delayed by conflicts with political objectives.

In retrospect, therefore, it is only since the mid-1980s that the Portuguese economy has been subject to a double strategy of both modernization and the pursuit of macro-economic stability. In terms of structural change, a new strategy of privatization was implemented by the PSD administration under Cavaco and this has been continued by the PS government since 1995. Starting in 1989, many companies have been sold to private ownership in banking, insurance, newspapers, construction materials and other industries; recent privatizations have included telecommunications and electricity (OECD, 1998a: 93; Corkill, 1999a: 60–4). Modernization became a hallmark of the Cavaco years and again this has been followed by the PS. Until the early 1990s, these developments took place against an improving economic performance as a whole. Thus economic growth averaged 4.6 per cent from 1986 to 1990, unemployment fell from 8.4 per cent in 1986 to 4.1 per cent in 1991 and the rate of inflation , though more problematic, did remain within a band of 9–13 per cent over this period (Banco de Portugal, 1994).

In April 1992, the Portuguese currency (escudo) entered the Exchange Rate Mechanism of the European Monetary System and macro-economic policies now placed high priority on the requirements for meeting Maastricht Treaty criteria. Although the economy was moving into recession, restrictive budgets were implemented in 1992 and 1993 (OECD, 1993). Apart from attempting to maintain a stable exchange rate, macro-economic policies were designed to tackle the persistent problem of inflation and large government deficits; in addition, it was recognized that interest rates in Portugal were too high (Banco de Portugal, 1993). From 1992 to 1995, the Cavaco Government continued with this economic strategy and a review of the indicators does suggest clear progress; by 1995, the rate of inflation was 4.1 per cent, the government deficit was 5.7 per cent of GDP, the public debt ratio to GDP was 66 per cent and long-term interest rates were down to a range of 9–10 per cent (OECD, 1996; Banco de Portugal, 1998). Other macro-economic indicators for 1995 were reasonably favourable as the economy had been recovering from the earlier recession of 1992–93. With a new government taking office in October 1995, the economic prospects for Portugal in the EU seemed promising.

With no disagreements over macro-economic strategy between the two major political parties, the PS Government under the leadership of Antonio Guterres aimed at further convergence. The same priorities for policies remained and progress continued. By January 1998, it was possible to claim that 'Portugal is well-placed to meet the Maastricht criteria' and 'the scale of progress made over this period (the past decade) is an illustration of Portugal's ability to adjust' (OECD, 1998a). Figures for 1998 show the success; the inflation rate was now 2.4 per cent, the government deficit was 2.3 per cent, the public debt ratio had been reduced to 57 per cent and long-term interest rates were down to 4 per cent (Banco de Portugal, 1999). In comparison with other EU members, Portugal was in a relatively strong position and the more advanced countries may have been surprised when 'it qualified for monetary union with apparent ease' (Roberts, 1998). On 1 January 1999, Portugal joined the third phase of European Monetary Union, having satisfied the conditions alongside ten other members. Again, this has been achieved without failure on other macro-economic indicators; economic growth in 1997 and 1998 averaged 3.9 per cent while the rate of unemployment was falling to within the range of 5–7 per cent (Banco de Portugal, 1999).

In recent years, the Portuguese government has frequently restated its conviction to meet all the necessary conditions for membership of the European Monetary Union. Indeed, it is 'more than just conviction, it is a certainty that I, as Minister of Finances, and a Portuguese, have engraved' (Franco, 1997: 51). The Minister of Finances has revealed not only strong rhetoric but also evident commitment and optimism regarding Portugal's economic integration in Europe. In terms of the requirements of monetary union, the results so far support his claims; how far his optimism is justified on other aspects of the Portuguese economy is more difficult to judge. In his Report on 1996/97, Antonio de Sousa Franco argued that Portugal should not be placed in a special 'Southern European or Mediterranean' grouping of countries; instead, he claimed that Portugal should be linked with Austria, Finland and Ireland, whose performances have been similar (Franco, 1997: 51). In the assessment of such an ambitious claim, it is important now to take a broader view of the Portuguese economy.

Beyond the main macro-economic indicators, structural dimensions need to be reconsidered. Portugal has always been very much an 'open economy' dependent on trading relationships; its shares of exports and imports in national income are higher than all other Southern European countries, as well as countries such as Germany, France and the UK. By destination, the EU now forms a larger proportion of Portuguese trade than previously, with figures of 80 per cent exports and 74 per cent imports for 1995 (Corkill, 1999a: 102–4). Within this, the trade with Spain has more than doubled since 1986 and there have been extensive links with capital investment. Much of this, however, has been inward investment by Spanish firms and there is a growing sense of apprehension over Portugal's place in a new Iberian economic community (Corkill, 1999a: 106–14). In attempting to evaluate these and other structural factors, it is necessary to look behind the trade figures and also to examine briefly labour and capital markets in Portugal.

The structure of the Portuguese economy in terms of production and employment does cause concern. Although there has been a clear decline in the primary sector and a rise in the service sector, the content of manufacturing has remained very much the same from the 1960s to the 1990s and it has been described as a 'rigid economic structure' (Marques-Mendes, 1993: 10). Indeed, there has been a reinforcement of the traditional specializations, with an increased reliance on industries such as textiles, footwear, clothing, cork, wood products and ceramics (Corkill, 1993: 66). In 1989, the two industrial sectors of textiles and forestry contributed 45 per cent of Portugal's total exports (Martins and Guimarães, 1993: 71).While modernization has taken place within ceramics, traditional methods of production have continued in other industries and some of these, such as textiles, are making the kinds of products which are vulnerable to competition from newly-industrializing countries. Overall, it has been claimed that Portugal's comparative advantages still depend upon low technology, resource-intensive and labour-intensive sectors (Lopes, 1996: 294). While exports of such products as paper pulp, cork and marble may continue to be successful, the low productivity and relatively cheap labour might not be so advantageous in the future (Corkill, 1999a).

The characteristics of the Portuguese labour market are mixed and they have changed in recent decades. The rigidities of the 1970s and 1980s have been tackled by governments since those times and the labour market is now 'highly flexible' (OECD, 1995a: 12). Also, real wage flexibility is a prominent feature (Corkill, 1999a: 180). Apart from various labour legislation reforms, greater use of fixed-term contracts has been made so that they constituted 15 per cent of employment in 1997 (Banco de Portugal, 1998: 22). Labour force participation has been high in recent decades, especially among women; by the end of 1998, for example, the female participation rate was 63 per cent (Banco de Portugal, 1999) and this can be compared with significantly lower rates in other Southern European countries (Gough, 1996: 14). On the other hand, some features of the labour market are more traditional; for example, as late as the 1990s, over 50 per cent of young people were employed by their family members (Gough, 1996: 15). In addition, child labour in Portugal is notorious (Williams, S., 1992), there are many illegal immigrant workers (Corkill, 1999a) and independent workers form some 25 per cent of total employment (Banco de Portugal, 1999). The payment of wages in arrears is widespread and there are huge problems concerning the debts of firms for the payment of social security contributions (Hampson, 1997b: 169).

In general, capitalism in Portugal is more fragmented and under-developed than in other European countries (Corkill, 1993) and a capital market has only emerged since the 1970s. There are few large companies and the economy is dominated by small firms; in agriculture and industry, the vast majority of firms employ fewer than 20 workers (Corkill, 1993). The geographical interior of the country is most under-developed as there is a concentration of industrial activity in the coastal littoral.

Foreign investment is predominant in a wide range of manufacturing industries and also highly significant in the financial sector where large increases followed entry to the EU in 1986 (Lopes, 1996: 296). All in all, taking account of both capital and labour markets, the situation in Portugal can only be evaluated as partially successful at this stage; when the structural problems of production are also recognized, an overview of the Portuguese economy is much less favourable in micro-economic terms. This has to be set against recent macro-economic successes. Hopefully, the economy as a whole is stronger than the sum of its constituent parts.

Social dimensions

While there have been evident signs of change in Portuguese society in recent decades, many social indicators still place Portugal as one of the least developed countries in the EU. In terms of living standards, Portugal's per capita GDP is frequently reported as similar to that of Greece, the lowest two EU member states (Eurostat, 1991; OECD, 1998a). In all studies of poverty, Portugal has the highest rate in the EU; for example, in 1989, the proportion of households with less than 50 per cent average national expenditure was 26.5 per cent compared with its closest counterparts, Italy at 22 per cent and Greece at 20.8 per cent (Abrahamson and Hansen, 1996). Other sources confirm these poverty indicators (Ramprakash, 1994; Pereirinha, 1997). In other respects, such as educational attainment, infant mortality and housing conditions, comparative data generally reveal the least successful indicators for Portugal; on the other hand, however, measurements over time suggest that Portugal has gradually been catching up from its weak position in the 1960s (OECD, 1993; Barreto, 1996; Carreira, 1996).

In broader terms, it has been claimed that Portugal has changed from a closed, dual society in the 1960s to an open, plural society in the 1990s (Barreto, 1995). As already noted, Portugal is now more open politically and economically; socially, however, there was a noticeable duality in the 1960s between a more advanced urban sector and a more backward rural sector in the interior (Barreto, 1995: 842). While these spatial divisions are certainly less pronounced today, there are still some persistent regional inequalities which give grounds for concern. For example, recent figures show that not only has Portugal the highest rate of relative poverty but the disparities within the country are huge and widening; from 1983 to 1993, incomes in Lisbon rose from 81 per cent of the EU average to 96 per cent while in the rural interior of the Alentejo, incomes fell from 48 per cent to 42 per cent of the EU average (O Publico, 1996). In the distribution of doctors, only 3 districts (Coimbra, Lisbon and Porto) were superior to the average in 1993, leaving all other 15 districts significantly inferior (Giraldes, 1995). In both examples, evidence of a dual society continues into the 1990s.

In other aspects of Portuguese society, mixed patterns of dualism exist. Given the high figures for poverty, many people are still traditionally poor; low income is the major cause of poverty and this is often associated with retirement (Bruto da Costa, 1998). For some, until recently, very poor housing conditions have been the most important factors, but for others, there have been a range of multidimensional factors. In the 1990s, the elimination of almost all shanty dwellings (*barracas*) and improvements in social services helped reduce the problem of traditional poverty.

At the same time, however, in line with other countries, awareness of social exclusion has increased and drawn attention to new elements of deprivation. Two examples can illustrate the changes: first, homelessness has become a new problem in the major cities (Bruto da Costa, 1998) and second, the absence of skills relevant to employment is continuing with the current generation of young people (Pereirinha, 1997).

As an explanatory factor in the study of social problems, the lack of development of social policy is often emphasized and it is important to realize that Portugal has only been establishing basic elements of social provision since the 1970s during which time other more advanced European countries have been engaged in reform. In 1979, a 'Basic Law' was passed to establish a National Health Service but private insurance schemes have continued to be available for some 25 per cent of the population. The mixed system of public and private health care is typical of Southern Europe (Ferrera, 1996). Expenditure on both public and private health care provision has increased steadily to a high figure of 8.2 per cent of GDP in 1996 (OECD, 1998a). In the case of social security, the Basic Law was passed in 1984 but the system has remained fragmented with only slow progress towards increased coverage (Hampson, 1997a); nevertheless, an important innovation has recently been made in this area with the introduction of a guaranteed minimum income in 1997. In the field of education, the Basic Law was delayed until 1986. Since then an incremental approach has resulted in a phased extension of schooling to nine years; this was only completed in 1996. In education and also in health care, there are continuing concerns over efficiency and outcomes; moreover, higher rates of expenditure have not led to commensurate increases in achievement (OECD, 1995a; OECD, 1998a).

In other areas of social provision, the timescale is similar so that Portugal can be viewed as a good example of the 'Latin Rim' model, with features of a 'rudimentary welfare state' and a 'catching up' process (Leibfried, 1993). The extent and nature of the development of social provision is, however, more debatable. While a few commentators claim that Portugal has reached the level of expenditure of mainstream welfare states and followed the 'conservative' or 'Catholic' family of Continental Europe (Castles, 1995; Esping-Andersen, 1996; Katrougalos, 1996), the majority of studies place Portugal in a Southern European grouping (Ferrera, 1996; Gough, 1996; Rhodes, 1997; Pereirinha, 1997; Trifiletti, 1999). In the 'reality' of Portugal, social change, however, is far more complicated than it first appears. Whereas the scale of expenditure on social provision is now approaching the same ratios of GDP as in other European countries, the nature of social provision is different. As Ferrera claims for Southern Europe in general, there is a distinctive welfare mix (Ferrera, 1996) and specifically for Portugal at least, there is a relatively weak welfare state (Pereirinha, 1997; Santos, 1991).

Within the welfare mix, there are both traditions and recent changes which reduce the dependency of Portugal on state-provided social provision. Under the Salazar dictatorship, private and charitable social provision was promoted in line with the Catholic principle of subsidiarity. As a result, a fairly strong welfare society did develop. Despite the political changes after the 1974 revolution, social provision continued to fill a variety of gaps in the welfare state; more recently non-profit, private sector institutions have again been supported by government (Dias and

Fernandes, 1993). Throughout education, housing, social work and health care, such organizations (*Instituicoes Particulares de Solidariedade Social* – IPSS) provide a range of services. Some of these are the traditional agencies of the Catholic Church (*Misericórdias*) but others are secular institutions and associations of mutual support. The strengths of the welfare society in Portugal have been widely acknowledged (Santos, 1991; Pereirinha, 1997; Rodrigues and Monteiro, 1998).

In terms of the future of social provision in Portugal, there are some grounds for optimism, despite the current limitations of the welfare state. In relation to social policy developments at the level of the EU, expectations in Portugal are not as high as elsewhere and the limited nature of the Portuguese welfare state is a good match for current EU social policy. In both Portugal and the European Union, a relatively strong welfare society may be a realistic feature for the future. Despite the pressures of meeting the economic criteria of monetary union, Portugal has managed to increase social expenditure in the 1990s; admittedly, the increases have been made from lower levels but this seems an easier task than attempting to maintain high social expenditure as in countries such as Germany, France and Sweden. In assessing problems further ahead, demographic factors do cause concern in Portugal, especially for social security, but on a comparative basis, the timescale is not quite as urgent; the social security system is 'still relatively young' (OECD, 1996: 63) and forecasts suggest that Portugal will face severe problems later than most other EU countries (European Commission, 1995a: 42).

Conclusions and future prospects

In view of the historical background of Portugal and its relatively late development, the current situation does, in general, exceed earlier expectations. Portugal's young democracy has now matured and political stability has been achieved since the mid-1980s; in particular, there is a strong consensus on support for the EU. During the 1990s, this support has demonstrated itself through Portugal's macro-economic performance which was geared towards meeting the requirements of monetary union. In social provision, a process of catching-up has been evident, especially in ratios of social expenditure. Both currently and in the future, the mix of social provision in Portugal may be more in line with developments at the EU level than in other member states. Overall, Portugal has moved a long way from the closed society of authoritarian rule in the 1960s when Atlanticism was able to compete with Europe. The claim that 'Portugal has its head in Europe and its feet in the Third World' now seems very dated (cited in Corkill, 1993: xiii). Instead, the ambitious claim that Portugal should be a country which might best be compared to Austria, Finland and Ireland has already been quoted (Franco, 1997).

As far as present and future prospects are concerned, there is widespread agreement that the Portuguese state has difficulties in implementing policies and delivering services; too much centralization stifles initiative and bureaucratic traditions persist. There are even doubts over the capacity of state administration to resolve these problems in the future. In the economic sphere, continued dependence on traditional products indicates vulnerability in the industrial structure while low levels of productivity indicate problems in both labour supply and the education system. Within the social dimension, there are persistent concerns. As Corkill claims, 'the standard of living still has much ground to make up' (Corkill, 1999a: 242). High rates of poverty cause particular concern, and weaknesses in the welfare state are apparent. Overall, critics can still categorize Portugal as 'peripheral to Europe' (Barreto, 1995) and indeed 'semi-peripheral' in a wider analytical framework (Santos, 1991). Less stringent analysis locates Portugal in a Southern European setting but even here there is a tendency to view such countries as 'poor relations' of more advanced European families.

The validity of these varied concerns is not easy to test. Portugal is clearly a society in transition within a changing Europe. With an expansion of membership in the EU, a country such as Portugal will no longer be located at the foot of a well-established hierarchy. Lower living standards in the new member states in Central and Eastern Europe will also certainly mean a diversion of funds away from Southern Europe (Corkill, 1999a: 222). In the new EU of more than 20 members, Portugal will face new challenges and it will indeed be fortunate if the progress of recent years continues well into the twenty-first century.

CHAPTER THIRTEEN

Denmark's Responses to Global Challenges

Alastair H. Thomas and Frands S. Pedersen

This chapter considers Denmark's responses to the global challenges of:

1. The competitive pressures of global market forces. These no longer permit economists to plan and manage their national economies on the assumption that they have a substantial measure of control over how their economy would respond. This has called into question the substantial welfare provision that made Denmark a pioneer in the development of the 'Nordic model' of society, economy and welfare.
2. Concern about the effects of high levels of production and consumption on the environment, which elsewhere gave rise in the 1970s to the vigorous growth of 'green' political movements.
3. Technological development. For about the first 60 years of the twentieth century the Danish economy relied heavily on its agricultural sector, together with production of agricultural machinery, furniture, electronics and other manufactures to high standards of design and production. Subsequently agriculture has become highly capital-intensive, and employment has shifted into a rapidly expanding tertiary service sector. The challenge faced by the Danish economy is to remain highly adaptive and innovative, as other economies become increasingly competitive and sophisticated technologically.
4. The need for small states to form regional groupings, the better to pursue and safeguard their economic, environmental, political and security interests. Denmark has done so by becoming increasingly active in the Baltic, West European and all-European arenas, and somewhat less active in the Nordic arena. This has included encouraging economic and political development in the three Baltic states and Poland.

A highly successful small open economy with generous social provision

Denmark's successful small open economy has shown itself well able to hold its own in the large and competitive global economy. The country is the richest in the European Union (EU) after Luxembourg, measured in GNP per head.[1] Measures of per capita GNP are notoriously limited as indicators of quality of life, whereas the weighted index of social progress (WISP)[2] developed by Richard Estes (1988) gives a far broader measure; recalculated over time, it also shows trends of improvement or deterioration. In 1995 Denmark was ranked first of 160 countries, with Norway second, and Sweden third equal with Austria. Denmark was similarly placed at the top of the table in 1990 and has been in the top three countries over the quarter-century 1970–95. For comparison, the UK was in 15th equal place in 1995, five places lower than in 1990, and the USA was 27th, nine places lower than in 1995. In the 1995 study Denmark scores 98.4 out of 100, compared to averages for North America of 79, Europe of 82, and Australia-New Zealand of 84.

Generous social provision contributes to Estes' (1998) conclusion that Denmark leads Europe in social development. Social security expenditure is about one-third of GDP,[3] almost half[4] of this going as pensions to the elderly, disabled and widows/widowers. Estes particularly admires the fine-meshed social security net in Denmark. If a Dane has an accident or becomes an invalid, he or she immediately has a social system for support. As well as high per capita GDP, other features characteristic of Denmark include a low average inflation rate, a slow rate of population increase, low infant mortality, a smaller than average proportion of age-dependent children, and a high average life expectation and therefore high proportion of elderly people.

Denmark refutes the monetarist case that asserts that generous spending on social security makes an economy inefficient and unenterprising. Indeed, the converse seems true. Analysis by Albæk and Sørensen (1998) of worker flows and job flows in Danish manufacturing concludes that replacement hiring is strongly pro-cyclical:

> that separations from continuing jobs increase in good times indicates that the cyclical behaviour of separations from existing jobs is dominated by workers finding better jobs in booms rather than plants purging bad matches in recessions, i.e. the dynamics of job separations is dominated by a pro-cyclical quit rate . . . Workers move from unattractive plants to jobs yielding higher rents in cyclical upturns . . .

a model of employee-initiated separations which implies individual confidence in the economy and its supportive social security infrastructure. Moreover, Estes demonstrates that Denmark has retained its leadership in social development over the quarter-century 1970–95. This continues a trend started at the end of the nineteenth century and taken a major stage further by K.K. Steinke's social reform package of 1933 (Andersen, 1982). Despite support for the populist, anti-tax and anti-state Progress Party for about a decade from 1973, there is broad acceptance of the high levels of tax required to sustain generous spending on social security.

Table 13.1 Attitudes to public expenditure in Denmark, 1990: Responses to the statement: 'The public sector spends too much, enough, or too little money on . . . ' (percentages)

Variable	*Enough or too little money*	*Too much money*	*Do not know*
Medical and health care	95	3	2
Basic pension	93	1	6
Day care centres	81	7	12
Social assistance	57	25	19
Public administration	29	62	9

N = 1008. *Source*: Valgundersøgelsen (1990).

Commitment to universalist policies has been the philosophy underlying Danish welfare provision, at least since the 1930s. Popular support for these values remains high, as is illustrated in the attitudes to public expenditure summarized in Table 13.1.

There is a distinct difference between the proportion of the population supporting universal policies, compared to the proportion supporting means-tested policies, in line with Korpi's (1980: 305) argument that policies covering a large share of the population are likely to enjoy broad support. The issues of fraud and misuse have been raised, but the Danes questioned were notably less likely to agree that this is a problem than were Norwegians or Swedes (Table 13.2). Further analysis by Nordlund showed that increased or unaltered spending was endorsed by a large proportion of all social groups (see Nordlund, 1997).

Table 13.2 Attitudes to misuse of welfare policies (percentages)

Proposition	*Country*	*Agree partly or fully*	*Do not know*	*Neither agree nor disagree*	*N*
'Many of those using health services are not all that ill'	Denmark	39	17	17	2021
	Norway	59	4	—	1768
	Sweden	60	—	—	1501
'Many of those receiving unemployment benefits could get a job if they only wanted to'	Denmark	57	7	10	2021
	Norway	65	3	—	1769
	Sweden	70	—	—	1504
'Many of those receiving social assistance are not entitled to it'	Denmark	49	16	14	2021
	Norway	66	7	—	1764

Danish source: *Medborgerundersøgelsen* (1990). 'Disagree' responses are omitted.

Thus Danes have maintained support for their well-developed welfare society. Whether they or the other Nordic countries can continue to support the proportion of GDP that they spend on welfare is much debated. They are conscious of the increased pressures of the more open markets of the 1990s, and have adapted their strategies of economic management accordingly. Denmark joined the European Common Market in 1973 and took on its rather higher levels of unemployment than the country was previously used to.[5] The ensuing 25 years brought adaptations, but the core welfare principles were retained. In 1992–93 Finland suffered its most severe recession of the twentieth century, and Sweden was also hard-hit, Norway much less so. Denmark weathered these financial headwinds with least disruption.

Economic and trade policy

Health, education, social welfare and the environment are areas where expenditure, and to a degree also its organization, is protected by popular sentiment. To meet public expectations of extensive public welfare provision, and a high level of public service in general, the Danish Government has adjusted its economic strategy to the demands of greater European and global integration. Denmark has had to adapt to its international environment, and has done so with relative success. Economic stability and growth was facilitated in the 1990s by the continuation of a policy of monetary stability based on linking the Danish currency (the *krone*) first to the German mark and then to the common European currency, the euro. (Although eligible on the economic criteria to join the euro at its inception on 1 January 1999, Denmark, with Sweden and Britain, decided not to do so.)

As a small high-income country with an open economy, Denmark has actively supported the liberalization of trade through multilateral agreements within the framework of GATT/WTO and within the EC/EU. Such agreements offer the best protection for small countries that are vulnerable to trade restrictions imposed by large importers of goods and services. Denmark's foreign trade is relatively large compared to most other EU member states, accounting for 25–30 per cent of GDP, compared with an EU average of 21–23 per cent (Bjørn and Brixen, 1998: 17). The importance of trade to industry and agriculture is far greater, however. In these two commodity-producing sectors, trade as a proportion of production value increased from 25 per cent in 1950 to 50 per cent in 1996. This shows increased dependency on trade and greater competition in the 'home' market. More significantly, the composition of exports has changed: in 1961 agricultural trade accounted for 55 per cent and in 1994 for 24 per cent of total exports. This fall was compensated primarily by a rise in the export of industrial products, especially pharmaceuticals, machinery and furniture and an increase in the export of services.

Another measure of Denmark's reliance on free trade is its exposure to foreign competition. According to 1995 OECD figures (OECD, 1995b), Denmark's degree of openness (the ratio of exports plus imports to production) was 51 per cent compared to 32 per cent for the UK and 16 per cent for the USA. More important, perhaps, the degree of exposure to foreign competition at home and abroad is as high as 78 per cent compared to 52 per cent for the UK and 26 per cent for the USA.[6] The high degree of exposure to competition has increased the competitiveness of many companies, but it has also led to greater specialization of production in order to avoid direct competition on price (Maskell, 1998: 30–2). The globalization process is one of the main reasons for this. The localized capabilities and competencies that used to give a country or region an advantage in international trade are being acquired by other, in particular low cost, countries at ever increasing speed.

Like other small, high-cost countries, Denmark has sought to adjust to this development by increasing its investment in education and research in the hope of staying ahead of competition from low-income countries. While attempting to attract high-technology sectors, such as the pharmaceutical industry, by targeting its R&D budget, Danish decision-makers face the difficulty of assessing the usefulness of such a strategy, considering the risks involved. Few companies or capital-owners are willing to face the risks and bear the costs of development. Other limitations include too few workers with the appropriate skills, a market too small to take advantage of derived benefits in related industries, as well as the absence of domestic suppliers of advanced components. Despite these difficulties, Denmark, like the other Nordic countries, has maintained a high level of wealth.

Exporting companies from small, high-cost, countries

The question remains: what is it that enables exporting companies from small, high-cost countries like Denmark to succeed in the globalized market? Nelson and Wright (1992: 41) have suggested that their success is due to their ability constantly to make improvements at all stages from finance through supply and production to marketing and distribution. Such improvements are highly knowledge-dependent and can be achieved more easily in some countries than in others. The complex combination of factors such as market recognition and knowledge, the relationship between supplier and producer, the qualifications of employees, the existence of traditions and routines, and a complex legal framework, is of crucial importance. These factors are complemented by the ability of companies to acquire and use knowledge, including that obtained through exchange with other companies. In a small country such information is more easily available, but the exchange depends on the willingness to exchange. Trust between the parties becomes an important factor influencing competitiveness (Maskell, 1998: 42). In Denmark a favourable combination of factors of production, organization and knowledge does exist and has helped Danish companies to remain competitive in the global market.

Trends in Denmark's trade policy

In recent years Danish exports have comfortably exceeded imports: in 1990 to 1996 exports as a percentage of imports were successively 111, 111, 117, 121, 117, 111, and 113. There has been a significant fall in the share of exports to the UK, and an increase in trade with the EU's low income members, Greece, Portugal, Ireland and Spain. Denmark's exports have been increasingly directed towards non-EU-countries, the share going to third countries having increased from 30 per cent in 1961 to 40 per cent in 1994. From the Danish case Bjørn and Brixen (1998) argue that the trade-related aspects of globalization involve nothing new, qualitatively or even quantitatively. The sometimes painful sectoral adjustments necessary to succeed in the international marketplace are no greater in relative terms than those brought about by previous trade liberalizations. The Danish response to the challenge of globalization has been effective in tackling the problems that arose in the last quarter of the twentieth century.

Environmentalist concerns

Environmentalist concerns arise out of both consumerism and social democracy in a country with an economy based originally on agriculture rather than 'smokestack' industries and now with a rapidly developing service sector. These concerns have never supported a 'Green' vote big enough to gain even a single seat in the proportionately elected Parliament (*Folketing*), not least because they have been taken up across the central core of the political spectrum and have been sharpened by the Red–Green perspectives of the Socialist People's Party (SPP). They were reinforced by the 1973 oil crisis (which reminded Danes of the need for energy conservation in a country with minimal natural energy sources) and were heightened by the Chernobyl disaster, which re-emphasized the risks of nuclear power.

During much of 1982–93, Poul Schlüter's Conservative-led minority coalition cabinet was able to remain in office with additional parliamentary support for its economic policies, but faced over 100 defeats from a Centre-Left coalition of Radical Liberals, Social Democrats and the SPP. Some of these were defence concerns, reiterating the Danish reservation on NATO nuclear arms policy and the long-standing ban on nuclear weapons in Danish territorial waters, while others raised issues of environmental policy within the EC: pollution of food, land, water, air and the workplace environment.

Environmental concerns often impose additional costs on producers, whether commercial, industrial or agricultural, but they can also open up opportunities and confer important trading and social benefits. This is well illustrated by the advantage gained by Danish bacon producers, who expected to gain a significant edge in the British market in 2000 (worth £250 million in 1999, about a quarter of the bacon sold in Britain). In response to domestic consumer demand, Danish producers began in 1997 to phase out feeding antibiotics as growth-promoters to their pigs, after researchers showed that humans could be affected by eating meat from pigs routinely fed antibiotics. According to Anna Birgitte Lundholt, managing director of Danske Slagterier (the association of Danish Slaughterhouses), consumer demand made it worth the considerable difficulties of doing so. Public alarm was based on warnings from bacteriologists, seriously concerned about the evolution of antibiotic-resistant bacteria, and from immunologists who were encountering patients with allergic reactions to antibiotics. Swedish farmers faced similar consumer pressures, and made the mistake of stopping antibiotics before husbandry systems had been improved, so bacteria multiplied to take advantage. In Denmark the better-prepared phasing-out programme did not require increased use of veterinary antibiotics. The use of antibiotic growth promoters in the Danish pig industry dropped from 107 tonnes in 1997 to 49 tonnes in 1998 and was banned completely from 31 December 1999. Danish bacon sales were expected to benefit accordingly, and British supermarkets were in a quandary: if some foods were labelled antibiotic-free, consumers might infer that food not specifically labelled as such was full of antibiotic residues (Brown and Meikle, 1999: 8).

Pollution of water supplies by agricultural nitrates has been reduced by 50 per cent from the mid-1980s to 2000 by three successive action plans based on regulations adjusted to the production conditions of each farm (Daugbjerg, 1998a). Another important component of Danish environment policy has been the comprehensive waste management policy that includes innovative taxes designed to promote reuse and recycling. The relatively small-scale and consensual (Elder, Thomas and Arter, 1988) Danish policy-making style, of which these are instances, confers a competitive advantage on the Danish economy.

Although Denmark has a distinguished record of nuclear research (dating from the work of the theoretical physicist Niels Bohr, Nobel Prize winner in 1922, and continued by his son Aage Bohr, awarded the same prize in 1975), the country has never built a nuclear power station, and has insisted that no NATO nuclear weapons be based on Danish territory (including the Faeroe Islands but in practice excluding Greenland). The debate in Sweden leading to the nuclear power referendum in 1980 was closely followed in Denmark, not least because the nuclear power station at Barsebäck in Swedish Skåne is just across the Sound from Copenhagen. The referendum offered three choices and was inconclusive, but successive Swedish governments have signified an eventual intention to run down the Swedish nuclear power plants. A consortium of Danish and Swedish electricity producers[7] was formed in November 1998 in a direct attempt to strengthen their positions in the liberalized electricity market, but the Copenhagen mayor, Jens Kramer Mikkelsen (Social Democrat), and his colleage responsible for environmental policy, Bo Asmus

Kjeldgaard (SPP), insisted on the condition that Barsebäck must be run down within a year (Nielsen, 1998). Thus Danes have used regional market forces to urge Sweden towards this long-held Danish environmental objective.

Denmark and Sweden face a dilemma, however. Their dislike of nuclear power makes it harder for them to comply with internationally agreed targets for CO_2-emissions. Gro Harlem Brundtland, the Norwegian Ex-Prime Minister[8] who chaired the World Commission on Environment and Development, was fully supported by all the Nordic countries in their Report's recommendation to reduce emissions country by country. Consequent interest in renewable energy sources has led Danish firms to make substantial advances in harnessing wind power, and now wind farms are a frequent feature of the Danish landscape and an important contribution to Danish energy production. Important earnings also derive from the export of surplus wind-generated electricity to Sweden and Germany and the sale of wind turbines.

Major developments of infrastructure have been undertaken in the final decade of the twentieth century. A 'fixed link' of bridge and tunnel opened in 1998 and replaced the ferry westwards from Zealand, carrying road and rail traffic across the Great Belt to the island of Funen. An even longer fixed link crossing the Sound (Øresund) between Malmö in Sweden and Copenhagen started taking traffic in 2000. This further develops the existing cross-national urban region with its excellent air, land and sea transport links and improves its ability to compete vigorously in Europe. The Øresund link alone is expected to create an annual regional capital growth of 20 billion Danish kroner (roughly £2 billion). Assuming that this effect is divided evenly between Denmark and Sweden, its benefit to the Danish economy would equal about a quarter of the positive effect of the EEC internal market predicted by the Cecchini Report. A further link southwards to Fehmern in Germany is under consideration. It and the Øresund link bring Denmark, and the Nordic countries generally, into 'association with the inter-European transport structure, which can prevent or combat marginalization, at the same time as the expansion of the transport infrastructure will contribute to ... economic growth and competitiveness' (Lyck and Berg, 1997: 10). This challenge has already begun to be met by the location of growth industries in the new Ørestad city which is developing around Copenhagen's Kastrup airport, some in close association with relevant university departments.

Domestic political adaptation to new international relationships: the *Folketing* Europe Committee

In 1960 the Danish Parliament established a Market Relations Committee (*Markedsudvalg*), initially to monitor the EFTA accession negotiations. This has increased considerably in power, especially since the time of Danish EC membership in 1973. It was important in developing parliamentary involvement in and control over EC policy. The Committee was renamed the Europe Committee in 1994 in recognition of the greater scope of the EU.

Among the Parliaments of EU member states, the Europe Committee is unique. Its members

> assert a detailed prior parliamentary control over Danish Ministers in the Council of Ministers in Brussels. Ministers must submit to the [Committee] the negotiating brief that they intend to take to Brussels on *all* issues. The [Committee] meets regularly, every Friday, even out of normal parliamentary sessions, to examine the agendas of Council meetings scheduled for the forthcoming week. (Fitzmaurice, 1996: 240)

It can be convened at short notice, to allow Ministers to 'test' compromise proposals that emerge during Council proceedings. Its members are senior politicians, able to commit their parties. Provided there is not a majority against the proposed position, the Minister may proceed. It differs totally from most other 'European' committees in other national parliaments. Concerned exclusively with safeguarding Danish national interests and maintaining national parliamentary control, it has none of the information or missionary pro-European functions often associated with European Affairs committees elsewhere. A Minister can nearly always obtain an adequate margin for manoeuvre from the Committee, and the system has several advantages. It guarantees Ministers against surprise defeats in the *Folketing* (otherwise a real possibility for the minority governments which are usual in Denmark), and it ensures that agreements made will 'stick'.

The Committee thus provides the necessary framework for the inevitable compromises on EU policy and is a vital link between policy-makers and the members of Parliament whose support they require, and who are thought to be in touch with public opinion. It also tends to emphasize the primacy of the *Folketing*, and leaves little room for active synergy between the *Folketing* and the European Parliament. It thus expresses the parliamentary sovereignty which Danes are as reluctant as the British to relinquish. This high degree of parliamentary control is an interesting paradox in an increasingly integrated world in which it is assumed that the nation-state has lost its power. The Committee also contributes to foreseeing and diminishing the problems which might arise in the implementation of policy, and helps to place Denmark among the EU member states with the best record of implementing EU policies. This adaptation of Danish political institutions to the changing needs of EU membership has been largely uncontroversial. However, this cannot be said about the proposals leading to the Single European Act (SEA), the Maastricht Treaty and the Amsterdam Treaty (discussed below).

Immigration, asylum and the EU

The linked issues of refugees, asylum and immigration have become controversial across Europe, and have not bypassed Denmark. Denmark was without ethnic conflict simply because it was ethnicly homogeneous: the Jewish community was well-integrated and the German-speaking minority near the southern border was small. Since the late 1960s immigration by foreign workers, initially from Turkey, Pakistan and Yugoslavia, has increased social diversity. From the mid-1980s an even more diverse range of refugees joined them, many from the Middle East. Foreign nationals from 'third countries'[9] increased from 40,000 in 1975 to 80,000 in 1988 and to almost 160,000 in 1996. By the 1990s, although foreigners were still less than 4 per cent of the population, in some places they comprised a visible community and began to assert political demands, e.g. for a Muslim burial ground in Copenhagen. The immigration issue became increasingly salient. One reason was that in 1984 the populist Progress Party switched its focus from 'excessive tax burdens' to 'the threat from immigrants'. In her careful analysis Togeby (1998: 1137–54) finds, however, that even while the number of refugees living in Denmark increased rapidly from autumn 1984, ethnocentrism and xenophobia did not increase, although stereotypes of foreigners changed under media influence. With the imprisonment of the Progress Party's founder for tax fraud, its support fell from 15.9 per cent in 1973 to 3.6 per cent in 1984, whereupon it played the chauvinism card. This took it up to 9 per cent in 1988, after which it again declined. In 1995 it split: the Danish People's Party which was then formed has been much more tightly organized, and more insistent and effective in spreading its chauvinist message, gaining 7.4 per cent of the parliamentary vote in 1998. In 1999 it gained 5.8 per cent of the vote and one of the 16 Danish seats in the European Parliament. Togeby concludes that the changing support for the Progress Party disproves the hypothesis of increased ethnocentrism in Denmark from the mid-1980s. Contrary to expectations, the level of ethnocentrism has not increased, but rather has decreased a little from the 1960s to the 1990s. What has increased is the salience of the immigration issue. During the 1980s the immigration issue moved up the political agenda, but this did not change the more fundamental attitudes and values of the population. The Danish People's Party campaigned actively to attract Social Democrat voters on immigration and social issues, and provoked a vigorous counter-campaign.

Globalization and Denmark as an international actor

The greater saliency acquired by EU matters is one of the main changes to influence Danish politics. Probably the most important element in Denmark's external relations, the EU constitutes an essential, and increasingly important, part of Denmark's foreign policy. Due-Nielsen and Petersen (1995: 41) identify this as one of the changes in the configuration of Danish foreign policy that occurred between the mid-1970s and the mid-1990s. The EU's involvement in the formation of Danish foreign policy has increased, while the importance of Nordic consultations has decreased. The role of NATO as the foundation for Danish security and territorial integrity has been consolidated, as have the roles of universal UN-related institutions in the areas of security, economic welfare and value promotion. These four arenas, suggested by Due-Nielsen and Petersen, are complemented by the addition of the Baltic Sea Region, an arena which has taken on greater significance with the decline of the Nordic context and the transformation of the East–West relationship. The configuration of Danish foreign policy can thus be illustrated in Table 13.3.[10] The changes in the different areas and in their salience are discussed thereafter.

Denmark and the EU

The importance of the EU in Danish politics is as evident as in other member states. However, the public attitude towards further integration is sceptical if not hostile, in line with attitudes found in other reluctant member states such as the UK and Sweden. The different integration philosophies which kept the UK and the Scandinavian countries out of the Communities at the outset, and which have made the UK and Denmark minimalist members, are still of great relevance for understanding the relations between the Nordic countries and the EC (Laursen, 1993: 115–41).

Table 13.3 The configuration of Danish foreign policy in about 1995

	Arenas					
Values	*Nordic*	*Baltic*	*(West) European*	*All-European*	*Atlantic*	*Universal*
Foreign policy cooperation	(X)*	(X)*	X	(X)	(X)	(X)
Security	—	(X)*	?*	(X)	X	(X)
Economic welfare	—	(X)*	X	—	—	(X)
Value promotion	—	(X)*	(X)*	X*	—	X
Identity	X	—	?*	—	—	—

Notes: X: primary role. (X): secondary role. —: insignificant role. ?: contested role. *: change from about 1975.
Source: Due-Nielsen and Petersen (1995: 41) with the Baltic column added.

Ever since entering the EC in 1973, Denmark has been 'the odd man out' (Thomsen, 1993), or perhaps more precisely has belonged to the 'awkward squad' (Marshall, 1994) in the EC/EU. A high turnout (90 per cent) in the 1972 referendum on membership, with a 63 per cent majority in favour of joining, gave the decision a high degree of legitimacy. But in the following years the opposition gained strength, and by the time of the first direct elections to the European Parliament in 1979, a People's Movement Against the EEC gained no less than 4 of the 15 Danish seats. In subsequent European Parliament elections, the Movement (together with the June Movement more recently) has gained an equivalent share of the vote, attracting discontented Social Democratic voters in particular (Worre, 1993).

The Danish political elites remain reluctant to agree to further political integration. This is due to the difficulties in finding, as Lindström (1993) argues, the appropriate forum for the exercise of economic, cultural and political autonomy, now that the nation-state no longer offers an intact arena for this. Thus, the motivation for Denmark's engagement is pragmatic: while some oppose all aspects of the EU, in general the Danes have been more positive towards economic integration than towards political integration. The politicians were acutely aware of this trait of the Danish electorate, during the debate before the 1986 referendum on the SEA. The battle to define the referendum issue led Poul Schlüter, then the Prime Minister, to announce that 'the political union is stone-dead' (Siune and Svensson, 1993). Having convinced the electorate that the SEA was primarily of economic significance, the Government went on to receive 56 per cent support among the 75 per cent of the electorate who took part in the 1986 referendum.

On the other hand, reluctance to surrender sovereignty appears to have been a major factor in the first Maastricht referendum in 1992. This time, the creation of an EU was the issue in name as well as in deed. Although the Maastricht Treaty was supported in parliament by all the parties except the Progress Party on the right and the Socialist People's Party (SPP) on the Left, to the surprise of leading politicians and political scientists alike, the voters rejected the Treaty, with 50.7 per cent of the participating 83.1 per cent of the electorate voting against. As few as 46,847 votes separated the Yes and No alternatives, throwing the EC/EU into the unknown (Siune and Svensson 1993: 102; Siune *et al.*, 1994). After a rescue operation in the form of the Edinburgh Agreement, the Treaty was put before the Danish electorate once again in 1993 and approved. The concessions given in Edinburgh included all four main exemptions asked for in the National Compromise, the agreement between the Government and the opposition parties, including the highly EU-sceptical SPP. Interviews before and after the 1992 referendum revealed that the population was mostly concerned about the loss of sovereignty. If we break down the opposition by issue areas, we find that least support is found for common citizenship (13 per cent), a United States of Europe (19 per cent), common defence and foreign policy (30 per cent and 38 per cent) and a single currency (34 per cent).

The opt-outs remain an important component in the Danish EU debate. It seems widely accepted that they can only be ended by further referendum(s). By 1999 the SPP were divided in their strategy on European integration, and the Social Democrats still include an active group of Euro-sceptics, so Prime Minister Poul Nyrup Rasmussen and the SD party leadership have to constantly assess the balance between pro- and anti-EU views, not least because past experience shows that the electorate are less pro-EU than their parliamentary representatives.

The largest opposition party, the Liberals (Venstre), wanted the four opt-outs ended as soon as possible, but '[did] not want to risk Denmark being excluded from all further European collaboration' by a 'No' vote. In its view there is great advantage for Denmark to have a common refugee and asylum policy built on community rules and not on a need for unanimous inter-state collaboration. Even the leader of the most pro-European party, the Centre Democrats, opposed a Conservative proposal for linked referendums on the four opt-outs. Linking would be too risky, and the opt-outs should not be put to the vote before there was a genuine chance of winning (i.e. opting in). Liberal leader Anders Fogh Rasmussen pressed for a referendum on Economic and Monetary Union (EMU), particularly during the initial euphoria when the euro was launched in January 1999. However, when the euro stood at a 15 per cent discount to the krone and the pound, the prospect of a winnable referendum receded. By September 1999 the expectation was for a campaign to start following the autumn 2000 SD party conference (Seidelin, Lauritsen and Borregaard, 1999), so there was surprise when, on 9 March 2000, the Prime Minister called the referendum for 28 September.

Denmark and NATO

In the post-war period, Denmark has engaged wholeheartedly in international cooperation. As a founding member of NATO in 1949, Denmark believed that a multilateral structure supported by the might of the USA would provide the best security guarantees. However, the renewed frost in the relationship between the superpowers during the early 1980s saw domestic opposition to NATO membership increase. NATO's strategy was seen by many, mainly on the Left of the political spectrum, to put European security at risk.

The Conservative-led Coalition Government was forced to pursue a policy of pragmatic disengagement from the (nuclear) strategy of NATO. The so-called 'alternative majority', consisting of the Social Democratic Party, the SPP and the Radical Liberals, passed repeated reservations to NATO decisions, which the Foreign Minister was obliged to report to his NATO colleagues. The position of the

Radical Liberals was particularly interesting: they supported opposition motions on foreign and defence policy, while at the same time giving regular parliamentary support to the Government's other policies. The thaw in East–West relations in the late-1980s removed the need for such reservations: 'loud disagreement' with the alliance between 1982 and 1988 was followed by 'cautious involvement' (Faurby, 1995).

The arrival of Gorbachev as the leader of the USSR in 1985, and the ensuing fall of the Berlin Wall, signalled the return to consensual foreign and defence policy-making at home, and to greater activism abroad. The constraints of the bipolar system had gone and new opportunities arose, where before there had been hostility. Russia, the Baltic Republics and the rest of Eastern Europe suddenly offered opportunities for economic, diplomatic and cultural interaction.

Denmark was among the very first to take advantage of these effectively new arenas in which to pursue foreign policy objectives. At the same time, however, came the risk that old historical conflicts would revive. As a result of this process, the established post-war pattern of security arrangements in the Nordic region came under pressure, including the so-called Nordic balance (A.O. Brundtland, 1966), as did the set of economic cooperation arrangements dating from 1973. Similarly, the competition between the global, Atlantic, European and Nordic foreign policy orientations that dominated the immediate post-war period acquired new salience in this period of flux in the international system (Strøm, 1992).

A central parameter for Denmark's engagement in all of these arenas has been the relationship with Germany. Constituting the southern side of the 'power triangle' enclosing the Nordic countries (Jervell, 1991), the relationship with Germany has had a defining impact on Denmark's choice of defence and economic cooperation strategies. Danish–German history is reflected in the debate about a more integrated Europe. Opponents of a closer Union have played on the fear of German dominance, whereas proponents of the EU have argued that a binding-in of Germany would be the best way to guarantee Danish security, and that even without the EU, Denmark depends heavily on the well-being of the German economy.[11] To some extent, suspicion of Germany as the old foe has been replaced by distrust of the EU.

Meanwhile, Russian withdrawal from Central and Eastern Europe has significantly reduced the threat to Denmark. In fact, Ola Tunander (1993: 213-30) claims that the 'European worry is no longer a Soviet or Russian military offensive, but the danger of millions of refugees fleeing a Russian civil war'. Developments in the wider European security system in the late 1980s and early 1990s brought about significant changes in the security environment of the Nordic countries. The Cold War gave the Nordic region an unprecedented period of peace, and yet politicians and populations alike were vividly aware of the risk of being caught between two adversaries in a war of total destruction.[12] Attempts were made to establish a new European security order (Buzan *et al.*, 1990; Due-Nielsen and Petersen, 1995). In place of bipolarity, a new and less predictable multipolar order came into being, and with it a revival of ethnic and regional conflicts which had previously been subdued by the interests of the alliances in the bipolar structure. The management through international institutions of these potential conflicts became, and continues to be, a central foreign policy objective for the Danish Government.

Denmark and the universal dimension: UN peacekeeping and development aid

The Danish Government welcomed the new possibilities for multilateral action within the context of the United Nations (UN). Europe and the Baltic Sea Area had both been relieved from (most of) the threat. Denmark was among the first to take advantage of the new opportunities to support the Baltic states in their bid for independence. One means to this end was international recognition. The Danish Government believed that involvement in UN peacekeeping operations would contribute to make independence irreversible (interview with Dan Nielsen, Ambassador, Ministry of Foreign Affairs, August 1997). After training with Danish army units, a joint Baltic–Nordic peacekeeping force was deployed as part of the UN's mandate in Bosnia.

Participation in peacekeeping operations also contributes to the fulfilment of Denmark's foreign policy objectives more generally, including the promotion of human rights and democracy, as well as the enhancement of Denmark's status internationally. The latter has been achieved, most spectacularly, through a new and more active approach in which peace enforcement plays a significant part. In the past Denmark, together with the other Nordic countries, has been fully committed to the traditional approach to peacekeeping operations, requiring the consent of the warring parties and emphasizing the principles of impartiality and the use of force only in self-defence. But as the UN has entered areas of conflict where no or limited consent exists, a new approach to peacekeeping has been adopted. As a result the Danish International Brigade (DIB) was established in 1994. It became fully operational to serve as part of NATO's rapid reaction force in March 1997 (Jakobsen, 1998). The DIB allows 1500 troops to be on peace missions at any one time, with the possibility of adding more for limited periods. These troops are better trained and in a higher degree of readiness than previous Danish peacekeeping forces.

The DIB enables Denmark to honour its obligations to provide an effective conventional war-fighting force for NATO and gives it a capacity to provide personnel for the full spectrum of UN operations, including peace enforcement. The latter is crucial for the Danish ambition to maintain its high UN profile as participation in high-intensity peace support operations has become a major generator of 'power, pride, and prestige' in the post-Cold War era (Jakobsen, 1998: 14).

In addition to its support for the military components, Denmark attributes great importance to the growing civilian components in UN peacekeeping, including civil–military cooperation to limit civilian suffering and cooperation with the nongovernmental organizations involved (Jakobsen, 1998). The inclusion of a humanitarian element is considered of great importance in maintaining domestic public support for Danish participation in peacekeeping operations.

Another area of international relations in which globalization has had a significant impact is on development aid. The free flows of international capital tend to result in increasingly uneven global development. Denmark has made the commitment to a comparatively very high level of development aid to other developing countries and the states in Eastern Europe, including the former Soviet Union, while retaining access to the capital needed to develop its own economy. As a percentage of GNP, Denmark gave 0.88 per cent in 1986/87 and increased this to 0.97 per cent in 1997, the latter figure being the highest of all the 21 countries of the Development Assistance Committee (DAC) of the OECD. Put another way, overseas development aid in 1996/97 amounted to US$342 per Dane, compared to US$30 per head from the USA and US$55 per head from the UK, and the DAC average of US$66. Although intended to help reduce the gap between rich and poor, a small country such as Denmark can only make a limited contribution, and in fact the differences continue to widen.

All-European security cooperation

True to tradition, Denmark together with the other Nordic countries was active in the creation of structures to maintain peace and stability in post-Cold War Europe. All the Nordic countries have supported the CSCE/OSCE process from an early stage. They have also provided relatively large contingents for UN peacekeeping and humanitarian operations, for example in former Yugoslavia. Sweden and Finland thus intended to maintain their neutrality, whereas Denmark, Iceland and Norway were reluctant to see the role of NATO weakened, for example by proposals to develop a foreign policy and defence dimension to the EU. This dilemma was resolved when the Western European Union (WEU) was declared to be NATO's European arm, in addition to its previously declared status as the EU's defence arm. Continued US commitment to the defence of Europe was considered the best guarantee of Nordic security.

Although the fall of the Soviet regime eliminated the threat from a superpower neighbour, new security issues arose. In the Leningrad and Kaliningrad areas the redeployment of forces withdrawn from eastern Germany and other East European countries, as well as greater reliance on sea-based nuclear weapons and on conventional weapon systems as a result of successful arms reduction talks, are two of the factors giving cause for new concern to the Nordic countries in what is otherwise a less threatening situation. Unlike her Nordic sisters, Denmark has almost exclusively benefited from the new order. For example, forces previously stationed in Eastern Europe (including East Germany and Poland) are now further away in Kaliningrad and St Petersburg, while the Russian missiles and fleet based on the Kola Peninsula are of much greater concern to Finland, Norway and even Sweden than they are to Denmark.

Nordic cooperation

The Nordic arena has had some importance in 'low politics' sectors. Some of the most significant and tangible results of Nordic policy coordination have been the creation of a common labour market and a passport union in 1954, adoption of a Treaty on cultural cooperation in 1971, and the 1973 Treaty covering transport and communication. Other areas of cooperation include environmental cooperation covered by a 1976 Convention and a 1989 long-term action programme, and educational cooperation following an action plan adopted in 1988. The Nordic countries have also coordinated their industrial and regional development policies, setting up a Nordic Investment Bank in 1975, followed by a Nordic Development Fund and a Nordic Fund for Technology. Furthermore, they have actively helped other countries, in particular the member states of the South African Development Coordination Conference and the Baltic states.

However, the momentum of European integration from the mid-1980s onwards, exemplified by the SEA and the Maastricht Treaty, put future Nordic cooperation in question. Work programmes for Nordic cooperation with the EU were approved in 1988 and 1992, and Finland's and Sweden's EU membership from 1995 gave new impetus to the Nordic reform process. In order to strengthen Nordic cooperation within as well as outside the EU, the Prime Ministers were given a more prominent role. Efficiency was also increased by prioritizing policy sectors, placing education and cultural policy once again at the core of Nordic cooperation. With their contribution to Nordic identity, these are also the areas in which Nordic cooperation within the EU is most likely to occur. In addition, the Nordic countries work together on issues such as the environment, openness in administration, and cooperation with third countries including the Baltic states.

Denmark and the Baltic connection

Together with Germany, in 1992 Denmark took the initiative to establish the Council of Baltic Sea States (CBSS). Its main objectives were to provide an international forum for the Baltic states to gain international recognition and in which to discuss issues of concern between the Baltic states, the Nordic countries, representatives of the EU, and with the Russian Federation (Joenniemi and Stålvant, 1995).

Economic aspects have been lagging behind and have primarily been dealt with in other institutional contexts, such as the EU and the European Bank for Reconstruction and Development (EBRD). Private investors have identified potential benefits of contributing to the development of the East-Baltic Sea area, but in doing so many have also experienced the risks of the volatile Russian economy. Issues such as environmental protection and educational and cultural cooperation were given priority within the CBSS. In addition, the CBSS offered an excellent framework for influencing, if not directly promoting, politically significant values. One such example is the involvement of the EU in the CBSS, which was met with approval as this helped legitimize the process. Later, on the initiative of the Finnish Government, a Northern Dimension was added to the EU's priorities. This focuses attention on the EU's relations with its neighbours, the Republics of the former Soviet Union, some of them high on the list of candidates for EU membership. Denmark has supported all these initiatives, as they contribute to the overall goal of establishing and maintaining a more secure and stable political environment.

Conclusions and future prospects

Denmark has responded to the challenges of globalization with a combination of adaptation and innovation. The internationalization and globalization processes described in this book's first chapter have reduced national economic control and, consequently, posed challenges to the high welfare standards expected by the population. Globalization has also increased environmental concerns, while offering new opportunities to enhance Denmark's international status.

Denmark's economy is performing well and has had to adjust less than many other European countries. An already high dependency on foreign trade has increased further, continuing a post-war trend. But uncharacteristically among EU member states, the greatest growth has occurred in Denmark's trade with non-EU members. In addition, Danish manufacturers have adjusted to the greater competition at home and abroad, and the reduced significance of localized capabilities, by increasing specialization and the input of knowledge into all parts of the production chain. Investment in new technology is a crucial part of this strategy. Supported by a closely regulated and well-functioning labour market, these adjustments have maintained Denmark's status as a highly prosperous country.

In environmental policy, the greater interdependence and common destiny of the countries in Northern Europe have accentuated old concerns. Impelled by public concern, both Danish and Swedish policy communities have supported a managed reduction in agricultural and industrial pollutants. Nevertheless, Danish concerns regarding Sweden's nuclear power plants remain. Recycling methods have also been improved and waste management through taxation introduced, while worries about traces of antibiotics in food have resulted in a ban on these in animal feed. The latter effectively gives Danish exporters an advantage over their competitors in crucial export markets.

International cooperation remains the favoured method to fulfil national foreign policy goals. But globalization has brought changes in the salience attributed to each arena. For economic policy and development, the political and economic elites regard the EU as the all-important arena, which will continue to provide Denmark with the necessary market protection and scope for international influence. The EU may also help resolve specific issues, such as the flows of refugees. The UN also helps establish the institutional framework for, among other things, the global liberalization of trade and the management of international conflicts and their humanitarian consequences. Due to changes in the international political climate, the UN now offers Denmark an additional arena in which to enhance its status through participation in international activities such as peacekeeping operations.

In addition to these activities, Denmark is increasing its involvement in Baltic Sea cooperation, which is seen to support a whole range of objectives including value promotion. The Nordic arena, on the other hand, only appears to support the decreasingly distinct Nordic identity, which Danes may yet replace with a European identity at some point in the future.

Notes

1. Norway is richer still (in purchasing power standards: *Nordic Statistical Yearbook*, 1997: 175), and Iceland has also been just ahead of Denmark (except in 1993 and 1994), but neither are in the EU and both economies rely heavily on the primary sectors, Norway's on oil and Iceland's on fishing. By contrast, Denmark's economy is more diversified, with very efficient agriculture, technologically advanced manufacturing and a large service sector.
2. The WISP is a composite of ten sub-indices, statistically weighted by the ability of the sub-indices to explain social progress over time. The world average for each sub-index was set statistically at 10 (Estes, 1988). The sub-indices cover education (4 variables); health status (8 variables); women (*sic*) status (6); defense effort (1); economics (5

variables: per capita GDP, real growth of GDP, inflation, unemployment and external public debt); 6 demographic variables; geography (3 variables: per cent arable land, and average annual disaster deaths and injuries); social chaos (4 variables, all negative: violations of political rights and civil liberties; proportions of internally/externally displaced persons; and persons killed in armed conflicts); cultural diversity (3 variables); and welfare effort (5 variables, covering old age, invalidity and death; sickness and maternity; work injury; unemployment; and family allowance). Estes (1997: 1–19).

3. 29.8 per cent in 1990, 32.8 per cent in 1993, 34.2 per cent in 1994, and 33.7 per cent in 1995; thus the increasing trend peaked in 1994. These figures compare with Sweden's 34.6 per cent in 1990, 40.3 per cent in 1993 and 37.8 per cent in 1994, the highest of the Nordic countries.
4. 48.2 per cent in 1995.
5. Over the decade 1967-76 unemployment was somewhat higher in Denmark than the low levels in other Nordic countries, but in 1975 it leapt to an average of 10.8 per cent, and in 1976 was 9.2 per cent.
6. Exposure = (exports/production) + (1 − exports/production) × (imports/(production − exports + imports) × 100).
7. The Copenhagen electricity utility Københavns Belysningsvæsen and the suppliers in South Zealand (SEAS) and North-West Zealand, Nordvestsjællands Energiforsyning (NVE), formed a joint marketing organization with Sydkraft, their counterpart in southern Sweden, with each owning a quarter share. Earlier in 1998 the North Zealand utility NESA allied with the Swedish electricity company Vattenfall.
8. She led Labour cabinets in Feb.–Oct. 1981, 1986–89 and 1990–96, chaired the UN Commission on Environmental Protection, and gave her name to its 1987 Report, 'Our Common Future'.
9. i.e. neither Nordic nor from the EU or North America.
10. Wæver (1994) has proposed an alternative, triangular pattern of organization: in this triangle, NATO represents military ability, the EU produces the economic-political order, and the CSCE/OSCE produces the wider legitimization and norm formulation.
11. In recent recessionary periods, the Danish Government has had a difficult choice between its Nordic and its German interests. On macro-economic issues, however, the Danes have adjusted to German policy decisions rather than, for example, to Swedish devaluations. The entry of Sweden and Finland to the EU may help to alleviate the Danish balancing act between Scandinavia and Germany.
12. That the risk was not all imagined became clear when in 1986 the US President identified 16 choke points worldwide, of which two are in the North, the Kola Peninsula exit for the Russian fleet and the Kattegat entrance to the Baltic (Kennedy-Minnott, 1992). For Denmark, of course, the Kattegat is right on its doorstep.

PART IV

The Challenge of the New Europe

CHAPTER FOURTEEN

NATO and the OSCE: Key Problems and Prospects

Peter J. Anderson

The purpose of this chapter is to examine a key part of the peace and security architecture that has shaped the content and context of Western, Eastern and Central European politics during and after the Cold War. The ever-present budgetary and spatial limitations of this project mean that the focus inevitably has to be on the North Atlantic Treaty Organization (NATO), given that it remains the key arbiter on the question of whether or not potentially devastating military force will be used outside of the remaining core Russian sphere of influence on the continent of Europe. However, it is of course recognized that the above-mentioned architecture includes such organizations as the United Nations (UN), the European Union (EU) and the Organization for Security and Cooperation in Europe (OSCE). Given that the first two are examined in chapters of their own, only the last of these organizations will be covered in its own section here. While the constraints of the project mean that it will be given relatively minor coverage, it is hoped that the most crucial of its contributions to European peace and security, and the factors which limit the impact of these, will be conveyed in a manner that makes up for its necessary brevity via a full reflection of their importance. Material on the EU which is additional to that discussed in earlier chapters will also be analysed where relevant within the discussion.

The analysis inevitably begins with an overview of NATO's role during the post-Cold War period. It will then focus in on some rather more detailed questions currently facing the Alliance.

NATO: the post-Cold War evolution of role and the lessons of the recent past

Since the end of the Cold War the previous relative certainties in the relationship between the USA and its NATO allies have been called into question. The collapse of the Soviet Union began a period of prolonged soul-searching as to precisely what the Alliance's role should be after the fall of its principal opponent, Soviet communism. This period of questioning was tied into obviously related processes of re-thinking about questions of European defence and security within the USA, the EU and the UN. One chain of events that followed from this was mainly limited in its scope but highly symbolic in its nature, and that was the incremental improvement in military-security relations with the former Soviet Union. This, started modestly with the North Atlantic Cooperation Council in 1991, then began in earnest with the launching of the Partnership for Peace in 1994. In the words of NATO:

> The Partnership for Peace [PfP] is the principal mechanism for forging practical security links between the Alliance and its Partners and for enhancing interoperability between Partners and NATO. Through detailed programmes that reflect individual Partners' capacities and interests, Allies and Partners work towards transparency in national defence planning and budgeting: democratic control of defence forces: preparedness for civil disasters and other emergencies: and the development of the ability to work together, including in NATO-led PfP operations. The Alliance is committed to increasing the role the Partners play in PfP decision-making and planning, and making PfP more operational. NATO has undertaken to consult with any active participant in the Partnership if that Partner perceives a direct threat to its territorial integrity, political independence, or security. (NATO, 1999a)

Included within the overall post-Cold War arrangements have been special partnership agreements with Ukraine and Russia. In 1997 the Euro-Atlantic Partnership Council was established, which brought together Eastern and Central European states, together with Central Asian and neutral states. In its statement on its new Strategic Concept in April 1999, NATO said that:

> The Euro-Atlantic Partnership Council (EAPC) will remain the overarching framework for all aspects of NATO's cooperation with its Partners. It offers an expanded political dimension for both consultation and cooperation. EAPC consultations build increased transparency and confidence among its members on security issues, contribute to conflict prevention and crisis management, and develop practical cooperation activities, including in civil emergency planning, and scientific and environmental affairs. (NATO, 1999a)

However, Western aims in all of this have been seen as less than benevolent by a number of analysts. Jonathan Steele, for example, notes that after the collapse of the USSR, one of Washington's main goals was 'to weaken Russia strategically to prevent any chance of a revival of the Soviet Union, but without provoking resistance and turning the country into an enemy again' (Steele, 1999).

Part of this process involved the enlargement of NATO into Eastern Europe, and in Steele's view and that of others, the partnership arrangements with Moscow were intended to contain and reduce Russian anger at this. They did indeed help facilitate the most truly mould-breaking event in all of the above, which in itself formally underlined the shift in the balance of power and spheres of influence within Europe that has occurred since the end of the Cold War, namely the formal joining of the NATO alliance by three of the former Warsaw Pact states, Poland, Hungary and the Czech Republic, in 1999, with Russia's reluctant acceptance of this new reality. When linked with the EU's accelerating plans for enlargement into the East during the same year, the scale of Russia's loss of influence to the USA and Western Europe during the 1990s can be seen in its startling enormity.

That loss left a crucial vacuum in the Balkans, into which first (and unsuccessfully) the EU tried to step, followed, with UN consent, by NATO. The context in which they did so was one in which the several processes of re-thinking mentioned above (within the EU, the US, NATO and the UN) all interlinked in the first major post-Cold War challenge in Europe – the various disputes and wars that started to erupt as the disintegration of the former Yugoslavia began in earnest. The crises that followed from this began to reveal how far US thinking about European problems can diverge from that of the Europeans themselves in the post-Cold War world.

After the Presidency of George Bush, a number of the European NATO allies became increasingly worried as the main initial thrust of President Clinton's first administration seemed to be a diplomatic/economic reorientation towards the New Pacific. The Americans clearly believed that their trading future lay predominantly in that zone, and that Japan and China, together with the new tiger economies, would lead the way for Asia to step comfortably above Europe in the global hierarchy of international trade during the twenty-first century. Some Europeans began to worry that America's post-Cold War military cutbacks within 'the old continent' were the precursor to a re-focusing of American security concerns predominantly on the New Pacific in line with the apparent primary economic preoccupations of the President. Indeed, for some, the long delay before the Clinton administration decided to intervene significantly to help bring to an end the barbarism that characterized the Bosnian conflict was evidence of this fact. They could point, for example, to Haftendorn's comment with regard to the situation in the former Yugoslavia that:

> Only after the war in Bosnia and Croatia had run out of steam, did Washington take the initiative. It forced the warring parties at Dayton to accept a peace agreement, and it convinced its NATO allies to join with the US in providing an intervention force to complement this agreement. (Haftendorn, 1997: 9)

She does lay part of the blame for the Clinton administration's delay in giving a lead on some of the EU states' initial position that Yugoslavia was predominantly a European responsibility, despite the fact that the EU was not yet ready to handle such problems. However, even when the USA finally accepted the need to intervene militarily in the Yugoslavian mire, it did so only on the clear understanding that such an intervention would not involve American ground troops until a peace agreement was in place. The Clinton administration's position on this, of course, was determined not just by a partial reconfiguration of the relative importance of American interests geographically, but also by domestic US opinion. While there were loud voices within Congress and particularly relevant ethnic groups within the electorate in favour of an effective American response to the situation in Bosnia, it should not be forgotten that there are large swathes of the US electorate who are little interested in foreign affairs as a whole, let alone those concerning far-away Europe. Given the experience of the Vietnam War in the 1960s and the 1970s, and the later débâcle in Somalia in the early 1990s, the last thing thereafter that the two Clinton administrations wanted was to have television pictures of US bodybags coming home from a war which many of the public would not deem as being important enough to justify the loss of American lives. Only wars in Europe or elsewhere in which core US interests clearly could be seen to be at stake could now merit the involvement of US forces in ground operations prior to the conclusion of hostilities. This post-Somalia doctrine was reinforced by the crisis over Kosovo during 1998–99.

The Kosovan situation was revealing of the problems and prospects of NATO in a number of respects. First, and most obviously, as implied above, the US refusal to commit ground troops prior to the cessation of active hostilities during the Kosovo campaign, as in the Bosnian war that preceded it, reinforced graphically the USA's post-Somalia doctrine: namely that US forces will only engage in ground operations in Europe, or indeed, anywhere, prior to the conclusion of hostilities in contexts where core goals of US policy are judged to be severely threatened. This can weaken NATO's chances of achieving success within military campaigns considerably, given, as will be seen below, the European's unwillingness to fill all of the gap via higher levels of defence spending and/or more efficient procurement and deployment of military assets, during the recent past. This situation may improve noticeably over the next few years as a result of post-Kosovo declarations by the European powers of their intention to improve their capabilities and effectiveness within the context of both NATO and the EU. However, it also might not, given the past record of European states in defence spending, avoidance of duplication and burden-sharing. Second, the Alliance's involvement in the Kosovan war demonstrated some of the likely factors which would circumscribe the effectiveness of even a well-resourced future European defence force, operating, as current plans suggest, as a European defence 'identity' within the overall context of NATO or as an EU force. The problems which several European states had with the idea of a combat ground force in the Kosovan context illustrate that increasing Europe's role and capabilities (in addition to their existing access to US capabilities when needed) within NATO or in an EU context would not in itself guarantee that the alliance in future would be able to deploy effective ground forces in situations where the USA refused to. Equally, the strong domestic opposition within Greece and Italy in particular to the bombing of civil targets such as power stations, television stations and non-military industrial plants, as opposed to clearly military targets, illustrates that there can be serious problems in trying to get agreement within the alliance even on military strategies that do not include ground troops. Third, the very fact that the alliance now has 19 members, and includes a variety of non-complementary concerns, sensitivities, imperatives and 'bottom lines' deriving from differences in geographical locations and proximities, cultures, ethnic linkages and commercial interests, means not only that it can be difficult to get agreement about what to do concerning specific challenges, but that should agreement ultimately be achieved, it can be just as difficult trying to hold it together in a solid alliance front over even a short period of time once a conflict breaks out. It has been revealed since the end of the Kosovan campaign that the Americans among others had doubts that NATO could have kept its united front intact had the war gone on for very much longer (BBC, 'Nato's war: the untold story', *Newsnight*, 1999). Andrew Marshall noted in June 1999 that, 'The key European allies – Britain, France, Italy and Germany – have been sharply divided over the war' (Marshall, 1999: 4). Britain, he observed, had been strongly supportive of the idea of a ground war, with France sharing the same preference, but to a lesser extent; whereas Italy and Germany were not particularly keen even on the air war, and were definitely opposed to a ground invasion. As far as the position of the most crucial NATO members was concerned, 'America has stayed in the middle, refusing London's pressure for ground operations and blocking moves from Berlin and Rome for a bombing pause' (Marshall, 1999: 4).

Fourth, and worryingly, the conflict revealed graphically the existing inadequacies of the European majority within the alliance with regard to readily deployable hardware. Nearly all of the airstrikes were carried out by the Americans, for example, and the Europeans were heavily reliant on them also for intelligence and airlift capabilities. While there have been declarations of intent to do something about this discrepancy since the end of the conflict (see, for example, NATO, 1999a), there can be little doubt that, as in the past, the Europeans will not be prepared to damage electorally significant domestic programmes by redirecting the necessary resources into their military budgets.

The campaign illustrated also the limitations of air power as an effective military tool when used in isolation. It has become clear since the end of the conflict that very few Serb military vehicles, for example, were hit within Kosovo despite the massive amount of bombs and missiles that were used. It seems that it was only when the West turned instead to attacking the civilian infrastructure of Serbia itself that Milosevic began to fear that the result would be so severe that the population might turn against him in sufficient numbers to secure his overthrow. It is possible also that he assumed wrongly that a ground invasion was increasingly imminent,[1] and that this further weakened his resolve. He was most certainly unnerved by the Russian decision to back the peace proposals that finally heralded the end of hostilities.

Overall, Kosovo was something of a shock to the system for several of the leading European NATO governments. For example, British Prime Minister Blair found that his much-vaunted links with the USA were not strong enough to change the President's commitment to no ground troops prior to an agreement, and that he also came under considerable fire from isolationist politicians (the Right Wing nationalist Pat Buchanan referred to him as 'the mouse that roared') and from some within the American military who are alleged to have observed that Blair 'would have fought to the last American'. All of the leading European NATO governments found that the ludicrously small proportion of their overall forces that were readily deployable in Kosovo meant that whether individual governments wanted to complement the air war with a ground campaign or not, the possibility was not realistically on the table without the Americans agreeing to participate. Furthermore, their dependence on American air power also emphasized that it was difficult for them to act at all in such a context without the USA at least agreeing to engage in an air war. This demonstrated to them graphically that their current weakness meant that they remained almost as unequal partners of the USA in the post-Cold War world as they had been during the Cold War. The new NATO Secretary General, Lord Robertson, stated when taking office that:

> the Kosovo campaign has . . . taught us that to remain effective in future, NATO's Allies must make efforts to improve their co-operation and their contributions. They can only be sure to be able to defend their interests if they acquire the right capabilities: interdependence means accepting responsibilities not relying on the overwhelming might of a single Ally. (NATO, 1999b)

It was partially as a reaction to this kind of sentiment that the move towards a European defence identity gathered pace during 1999, with (since the second half of 1998) the added element of strongly positive British participation (see, for example, Foreign and Commonwealth Office, 1999b). By the end of the year the drive to expand the capacity of European states to act more effectively had resulted in the solidification of the commitment to produce an EU military identity at the December Helsinki summit. In going along with all of this, the Blair Government, as is pointed out in the chapter specifically on Britain, had a concern that was additional to the security issues involved. In short, its helping with the development of a European defence identity gave it an opportunity to make a compensatory contribution to the ongoing process of European integration that it believed would make up for its continued self-exclusion from the European Monetary Union (EMU). The British Government had by this time concluded that such a move would not compromise very greatly its relationship with the USA. It no doubt privately reassured itself also with the thought that it was unlikely that such an 'identity' would get out of hand and be allowed to irritate the Americans so much that they went home and left the Europeans to fend for themselves. For one thing, as is pointed out above, the European NATO members would not be prepared to spend enough to make any lunge for full military independence of the USA feasible. The continued adherence of states like France and Germany to relatively expensive social market ideals that do not 'hamper' the Americans to the same degree would help to guarantee this. For another, the unpredictability of Russian politics, together with the fact that Russia remains a formidable nuclear power that is still deploying new nuclear weapons, means that all of the European alliance members have a continuing interest in remaining under the American nuclear umbrella in case of the proverbial 'rainy day'.

This is not to say that the EDSI is an idea that has not produced any tensions with the USA. In late 1999, there were reports of clear concerns among some parts of the Washington elite about a possible European move away from US leadership while, simultaneously, various Pentagon officials and Right-Wing presidential hopefuls were denouncing the Europeans for the inadequacy of their military capabilities and budgets during the Kosovan campaign. However, the clear line of the Blair Government that the European defence identity is meant to complement NATO and the American role within it and not replace it, together with clear earlier policy statements to the same effect made by the leaders of Italy, France and Germany (see, for example, *NATO Review*, 1999) and the reassurances of the EU High Representative for Foreign and Security Policy, Javier Solana, following the Helsinki summit, are together likely to ease the fears of US policy-makers when the intent is seen to match the practice. Speaking in December 1999, for example, Solana stated very clearly what he believes the EU's defence identity does and does not involve. In short:

> The decision at Helsinki has been misrepresented in some quarters as the first step in the development of a European army . . . And yet, we could not have been clearer about our objectives.
>
> Most importantly, we have made clear that ESDP is not about collective defence. NATO will remain the foundation of the collective defence of its members . . . Nor does ESDP attempt to undermine the right of Member States to retain their own specific security and defence policy . . . So much for what ESDP is not.
>
> What Helsinki has done is to set in train a process which will enable us to assume full responsibility across the whole range of conflict prevention and crisis management tasks . . . What are the tools we need to achieve this? Firstly at Helsinki we have committed ourselves to being able to deploy a corps level military operation within 60 days, and to sustain it for at least a year . . . Secondly, we have endorsed the establishment of new permanent political and military bodies within the Council to ensure both adequate political accountability, and rapid and effective decision-making procedures for the day-to-day management of operations . . . Thirdly, we have taken steps to ensure that appropriate measures are put in place for the consultation and cooperation with non-EU allies, and with NATO.
>
> Helsinki . . . makes clear that the Union has as its objective the capacity to conduct EU-led military operations in response to international crises, but only where NATO as

> a whole is not engaged. This will remain a guiding principle. (European Union, 1999a)

The Helsinki agreement itself stated that:

> More effective European military capabilities will be developed on the basis of the existing national, bi-national and multinational capabilities, which will be assembled for EU-led crisis management operations carried out with or without recourse to NATO assets and capabilities. (European Union, 1999b)

At the same time, it emphasized that those member states that are in NATO would remain full members of the alliance and that: 'NATO remains the foundation of the collective defence of its members, and will continue to have an important role in crisis management (European Union, 1999b). The EU's military role would be restricted to the tasks first set out in the Petersberg Declaration of 19 June 1992. These encompass humanitarian and rescue tasks, peacekeeping tasks and crisis management military operations, including peace-making.

Three things seem clear from all of the above. First, while the USA remains committed to NATO, as evidenced by its continuing military presence in Kosovo and Bosnia, and by the huge airborne and naval resources that it deployed during the 1999 military capaign against Milosevic, the level of its involvement in any given crisis currently is limited strictly by the 'post-Somalia doctrine'. Second, that something rather more substantial than previous attempts to create a significant European Defence and Security Identity (EDSI) is likely to emerge from the current efforts to push the idea of a European defence identity forwards, and that it might give the Europeans the capacity to act alone where the USA is not willing to participate in ground operations or any military operations at all. However, 'might' is the crucial word, bearing in mind the potential constraints on effective European military action that were outlined in the earlier discussion of the lessons that emerged from the Kosovo conflict, together with the previously mentioned reservations concerning how much money the Europeans are actually prepared to spend on the European defence identity. Third, some of those same constraints, together with long-term uncertainties about nuclear-armed Russia, are likely to ensure that the non-neutral EU states retain their commitment to NATO and a continuing major American involvement in European security, with or without the development of an effective EU military dimension.

What was of equally great concern for the future of transatlantic relations within the alliance around the same period was an American proposal to develop and deploy a national missile defence system. A British broadsheet leader of the time noted that: 'France and Germany see it as a step towards an American unilateralism which could fatally undermine NATO's founding concept of common defence. Britain, trying as always to act as what Mr. Blair calls a "bridge" between Europe and the US has been less strident but is privately equally worried' (*Guardian*, 1999b: 23). How this particular problem will pan out was not clear at the time of writing, especially given the complication of forthcoming US presidential elections, so a detailed analysis of this particular issue will be reserved for the next edition of this text.

Having introduced some of the major issues that have confronted NATO over the post-Cold War period, the intention now is to focus in on some of the key questions that face the alliance currently.

NATO: collective security versus collective defence?

Leaving aside the question of the EU defence identity for the moment (given that the EU has stated explicitly that this can only have a distinct military role in situations where NATO as a whole has chosen not to act), one of the key debates within the alliance which is still ongoing is over the kind of missions in which it should engage. The primary missions which NATO currently is capable of undertaking can be broadly divided into those concerned with collective security and those concerned with collective defence. The latter takes the form of the traditional Article 5 commitment to treat and respond to an attack on any alliance member within the geographical Treaty area as if it were an attack on all. Where the former is concerned,

> practical action in support of collective security today usually consists of a multilateral intervention, undertaken with the implicit or explicit consensus of the major powers, directed against international aggression or internal conflict or disorder. This intervention can take many forms, including mediation and conciliation, economic sanctions, preventive or coercive force deployments, peacekeeping, crisis management and peace enforcement. (Yost, 1998: 137)

Such interventions are frequently justified on the grounds

> that all states have an obligation to respect the principles of the UN Charter and other agreements. In recent years, as suggested above, states undertaking such actions and interventions have usually sought political legitimization by referring to a consensus of the major powers – with UN Security Council (UNSC) authorization – or to a broad regional consensus, as with the OSCE. (Yost, 1998: 137–8)

Yost worries that the new alliance focus on collective security may damage its still important collective defence posture. He believes that it might erode the latter in three ways. First, the politically controversial nature of the problems which collective security operations can throw up could undermine the cohesion necessary for the ultimately more crucial objective of collective defence. Second, at a time when NATO's collective defence resources have already shrunk considerably, the demands of collective security operations could further reduce these. Third, 'collective inaction' in collective security situations where member states conclude that their national interests are not sufficiently affected by a particular situation could undermine the credibility of collective defence pledges.

On the other hand, if properly managed, an active collective security posture might actually complement the collective defence posture. It could prevent the alliance from atrophying at a time when there is no immediately visible unifying external threat (Yost, 1998: 146–7).

'Moreover, an intervention justified with reference to collective security responsibilities may serve national and Alliance security by upholding general principles such as the inadmissibility of aggression and by enhancing the credibility of the Alliance's declared will to undertake collective action' (Yost, 1998: 147).

In its 1999 Strategic Concept NATO seemed to allay all of Yost's fears, although, as will be seen shortly, whether it will live up to its promises will have to be seen. The Concept stated that, 'NATO forces must maintain the ability to provide for collective defence while conducting effective non-Article 5 crisis response operations' (NATO, 1999a).

There is, of course, the question of where a threat may come from to necessitate a continuing NATO collective defence stance. Is it possible that analysts like Yost are arguing for the need to prepare for the possibility of a future vicious attack by what, figuratively speaking, is a mere corpse in a European context? While Boris Yeltsin caused some unease during December 1999 by reminding the USA that he still had nuclear weapons at his disposal in response to American criticism of the Chechen campaign, the general assumption in NATO military-political circles during most of the 1990s was that the post-Soviet chaos in Russia would make any renewed military threat from the East unlikely for the immediately foreseeable future. However, as Chris Williams' chapter demonstrates, Russian politics at the moment is anything but predictable, and it is always possible that a future President may choose to emphasize a hard-line image by returning to a hostile stance towards the West. It is arguably for that kind of 'rainy day' that NATO needs to maintain an easily activateable collective defence capability, if only to protect European states against blackmail or bullying. Once dismantled through neglect or conscious removal, such a capability cannot be quickly rebuilt. Equally, it could be argued that should it be allowed to disappear, then the American military link to Europe would be likely to disappear with it. In such circumstances, there is always the danger of a gradual return to traditional power politics within the region and the conflicts of the past.

It would be unwise to assume that, with the end of the Cold War, the peace of the present has now become unconnected to the complex interlinkage of institutions and mechanisms of which NATO's collective defence provision traditionally has been a key part. There is no hard evidence to establish that this is the case. Given the appalling record of events in the former Yugoslavia or, for that matter, within the territorial area of the former Soviet Union, there is certainly no evidence to suggest that the brutal and aggressive side of human nature has been removed from European politics. It is often argued that the Chechen wars and the situation in the former Yugoslavia simply demonstrate that war in a European context has been transformed into an exclusively civil affair and that inter-state wars are a thing of the past. Therefore, NATO's collective defence posture is outdated and should be dismantled as a costly and potentially provocative waste of resources that could be better used elsewhere. But what frequently is forgotten is the strong possibility that one of the key reasons why inter-state wars have ceased to be an option in most of Europe is NATO's collective defence posture as a central plank of a complex economic and military peace and security architecture involving the EU, the USA, the UN and the OSCE. To start dismantling the architecture is to step unjustifiably into the unknown in search of what may well turn out to be fool's gold. The argument of the British Conservative leader, William Hague, that democracies do not go to war with each other, forgets conveniently the historical fact that, without the economic and military security architecture currently in place, including crucially NATO and the EU, key democracies in Europe in the past failed to survive serious shocks and traumas, particularly economic ones (Anderson, P.J. and Weymouth, 1999: 204–17).

With prudent caution, NATO's new Strategic Concept stated that:

> Notwithstanding positive developments in the strategic environment and the fact that large-scale conventional aggression against the Alliance is highly unlikely, the possibility of such a threat emerging over the longer term exists. (NATO, 1999a)

In short, while, potentially, collective security operations can be justified credibly on the grounds outlined within this section, and also, as in the case of Kosovo, on humanitarian grounds in some instances, NATO's commitment to the idea of collective security should not be allowed to damage or undermine its collective defence posture in any way. As the arguments above demonstrate, the potential importance of the latter for the security and well-being of the people of Europe is too great for this to be tolerable.

NATO and the 'out of area' debate

The above discussion leads naturally into a focus on the wider collective security debate. In early 1999, former West German Chancellor Helmut Schmidt – seeing a future world characterized by such threats to peace as nuclear weapons proliferation, terrorism, extreme nationalism and religious and ethnic rivalry, and progressively restructured by the continuing emergence of China as a global power, followed by India, and possibly Brazil and the EU, and in which Japan and Russia will remain of global importance, despite their current weakness (Schmidt, H., 1999: 21) – posed the question of to what extent NATO should become involved in 'out of area' operations. After considering the implications of the alliance's various involvements in the former Yugoslavia, he observed that:

> The American government seems to regard these events as setting a precedent for future cases of intervention in other areas, without necessarily requiring a UN Security Council resolution. But not all allies agree that the North Atlantic Treaty does provide for actions beyond the territory of the NATO member states without specific UN backing. (Schmidt, H., 1999: 23)

Indeed, throughout the period of the Cold War, Article 6 of the North Atlantic Treaty was generally interpreted as ruling out military interventions, other than those in defence of the territory and armed forces of alliance members within the boundaries of the NATO area.

He concludes that a protocol of the North Atlantic Treaty ratified by all members will be required if the USA or anyone else wishes to broaden the alliance's remit to include the joint defence of their interests in 'out of area' territories through the use of military force. He notes with concern that:

> There has been little public debate so far on future 'out of area' duties. NATO's new Combined Joint Task Force (CJTF) concept, an important aspect of its redesigned military structure, foresees possible 'out of area' deployments for peace support missions. The Alliance's lack of clarity on this issue, however, makes it very difficult for the media, the parliaments and public opinion of the allied nations to have an informed discussion on the matter. (Schmidt, H., 1999: 23)

He concludes that any extension of the alliance's geographical and substantive scope will have to ensure that 'such changes are accurately defined' (Schmidt, H., 1999: 23).

NATO's new Strategic Concept did not offer the full clarification that he was looking for with regard to non-Article 5 operations, stating merely that:

> NATO recalls its offer, made in Brussels in 1994, to support on a case-by-case basis in accordance with its own procedures, peacekeeping and other operations under the authority of the UN Security Council or the responsibility of the OSCE, including by

> making available Alliance resources and expertise. In this context NATO recalls its subsequent decisions with respect to crisis response operations in the Balkans. Taking into account the necessity for Alliance solidarity and cohesion, participation in any such operation or mission will remain subject to decisions of member states in accordance with national constitutions. (NATO, 1999a)

However, as can be seen from the above, the Concept did place such operations firmly under the authorizing umbrellas of either the UN or the OSCE. Nevertheless, for many critics the force of this provision was somewhat devalued by the fact that this had already been done in 1994, and yet the alliance had just conducted a major military campaign against Serbia without a UN Security Council resolution to back it up.

The American view that NATO should have a significant out of area capability has been evident for some time. In 1997, for example, Michael O'Hanlon warned that,

> if Americans die in large and disproportionate numbers in a distant war that Europeans should have participated in, NATO could come under intense scrutiny in the US Congress and by the public. Such an event would be deeply regrettable. (O'Hanlon, 1997: 13)

He argues that the European NATO states should enhance their military capabilities to enable them to intervene in areas such as the Persian Gulf and in 'unforseeable scenarios elsewhere outside Europe' (O'Hanlon, 1997: 12).

There is a clear suggestion at times within O'Hanlon's article that the European pillar of NATO should be prepared to act as what, in effect, would be a strategic satellite of the USA in global defence of Western interests.

However, on the other side of the coin, just as some within the USA are fretful about the Europeans' reluctance to commit NATO to becoming the Americans' 'little helper' on the global stage, some within Europe are concerned about what they see as Washington's unreliability with regard to out of area operations within Europe.

> They worry ... about signs of US hesitation to uphold NATO's new collective-security functions, such as the obvious divisions within the US administration and Congress in 1996-97 about staying the course in Bosnia. (Yost, 1998: 155)

The reality is that both sources of concern could cause future problems for the alliance. American willingness to become involved militarily in European problems at any one time, apart from being crucially limited in its extent by the previously mentioned Vietnam/Somalia syndromes, is also a function of such factors as the relative balance of isolationists and interventionists within Congress, the strength or weakness of a President's domestic position and the proximity to or distance from the next presidential or Congressional elections. The USA's involvement cannot be guaranteed, which is an obvious practical problem for the Europeans unless, for example, they carry out fully the ambitious plans which were approved at the December 1999 EU summit in Helsinki and begin to equip and organize themselves more substantially and more effectively, and its absence could lead to serious intra-alliance squabbles and even paralysis in the event of future Bosnia- or Kosovo-type problems, should they arise. Furthermore, to reiterate a point made in an earlier section, as Yost warns with regard to the latter possibility, 'collective inaction [concerning non-Article 5 problems] despite vague declarations of commitment could undermine the credibility of the ultimately more important Article 5 collective-defence pledges' (Yost, 1998: 147).

Equally, American dissatisfaction with European 'free riding' on the USA's back is never far beneath the surface of Congressional politics. Even if European NATO members (with the regular exception of Britain) do not favour the idea of being prepared to engage in 'out of (European) area' global operations as America's partner, they would perhaps be wise to put their money where their mouth was at Helsinki, and in earlier statements on the NATO ESDI, and build up the European pillar's military capability. They could at least argue that they were prepared to make a truly substantial contribution towards the protection of their own continent's security. That would reduce the danger of recurrences of the kind of American complaints that followed the very limited contribution of the European members of NATO to the Kosovo campaign. More particularly, it would lessen the chances of such complaints blowing up into a concerted call for further reductions in America's military contribution to the alliance. It might also keep in check US demands that NATO Europe should help it out elsewhere as part-recompense for America's lead role as 'Western protector'.

As pointed out already, however, few analysts seem convinced that with or without their new European defence identity, the Europeans will be willing to spend the necessary resources to provide a genuinely substantial contribution to Europe's defence and security, never mind any true equivalence to or substantive independence from the USA in European military matters. If such analysts are proved to be correct, that will leave crucial problems on NATO's agenda for the future, including, as has been suggested above, at least partially avoidable uncertainties and potential disputes relating to the 'out of area' question, a situation which all may yet have cause to regret.

NATO and the European peace and security architecture

As far as NATO's relationship to Europe's wider strategic architecture is concerned, the Strategic Concept document stated that:

> The United Nations (UN), the Organisation for Security and Cooperation in Europe (OSCE), the European Union (EU), and the Western European Union (WEU) have made distinctive contributions to Euro-Atlantic security and stability. Mutually reinforcing organizations have become a central feature of the security environment. The United Nations Security Council has the primary responsibility for the maintenance of international peace and security and, as such, plays a crucial role in contributing to security and stability in the Euro-Atlantic area.
>
> The OSCE, as a regional arrangement, is the most inclusive security organization in Europe, which also includes Canada and the United States, and plays an essential role in promoting peace and stability, enhancing cooperative security, and advancing democracy and human rights in Europe. The OSCE is particularly active in the fields of preventive diplomacy, conflict prevention, crisis management, and post-conflict rehabilitation. NATO and the OSCE have developed close practical cooperation, especially with regard to the international effort to bring peace to the former Yugoslavia. (NATO, 1999a)

However, the Kosovo intervention demonstrated that, whatever its protestations, NATO is prepared to act without formal UN Security Council authorization where it believes that circumstances justify this. One might also wonder whether all of the above really provides, or even can be expected to provide, the ground for a detailed enough clarification of the separate 'job descriptions' of all of the elements of the new European security architecture, together with their most appropriate and compatible modes of cooperation and mutually complementary action. Commenting on this problem of organizational role definition prior to the new Strategic Concept, Johnson observed in 1995 that to the question 'Which is responsible for what? The short answer is that no one knows' (Johnson, 1995: 5).

Although the situation seems to have improved since that time, NATO's answer to his question still does not appear entirely convincing. While David Travers' chapter shows that the UN's role in Europe seems to be something of a 'moveable feast' where NATO is concerned, one might observe also that, in practical as opposed to theoretical terms, the definition of the role in and relevance to European security crises of the OSCE at any one time is dependent on such variables as which political tendency is in power in Washington and how much it wishes to see the USA constrained by organizations beyond its borders, and what the attitude of the Russian government is, given that the OSCE is a body which can be immobilized by Russian vetoes as much as anyone else's.

In addition, the EU's Common Foreign and Security Policy s subject to continuing development and shaping, a process that in itself could change substantially the relationship between the EU and NATO beyond that envisaged within the Strategic Concept.

In short, one might conclude that while the individual components of the European security architecture each have crucial parts to play in enhancing the stability and security of Europe, as is demonstrated within the chapters by Georg Wiessala, David Travers and Karen Henderson for example, the precise relationship of all of these to NATO remains rather more dynamic than many within the organizations concerned might desire. To a degree this is inevitable if it is believed that 'flexibility' is one of the key essences of organizational success and survival, but those who would wish for the UN to have a greater legitimating role within Europe, or for the OSCE to play a greater role in trying to prevent conflict than has been allowed so far, could argue that some parts of the relationship with NATO are at present too flexible and operate at the expense of their wishes where it suits the preferences of the USA or other NATO states.

NATO and the future

All of this leads finally into the question of to what extent the new NATO is likely to be able to survive into the future, taking the April 1999 Strategic Concept as its launching board for attempting this. The first important thing to realize in this regard is that the agreement that underlies that Concept is based on a compromise between American perspectives and several key European points of view (see, for example, Cornish, 1997: Chapter 3, on key preceding negotiations) that could be destabilized by future changes of government in France, the USA, Britain and Germany in particular. Another set of problems could arise with regard to the EDSI. An awful lot hangs on the success of new initiatives, such as the appointment of former NATO Secretary General Solana as the EU's High Representative for Foreign and Security Policy. Georg Wiessala's chapter discusses some of the potential obstacles to success that may dampen Mr Solana's effectiveness. These in turn may cause problems in the EU–NATO relationship if his desire to see a strong degree of complementarity between the security and defence aims of the two institutions is blunted. As previously mentioned within this chapter, there is also the question of whether the European states will be prepared to supply the levels of armed forces and modernized and appropriate equipment that will be necessary to make the identity a meaningful reality. Reorganizing existing equipment availability and force levels is only one part of the picture in this regard. The European defence identity could also run into serious difficulties if its future development is handled clumsily or insensitively, leading either to American feelings that the Europeans no longer need them anymore, and therefore Washington might as well begin a substantial scaledown of its European presence, or to feelings that the move towards the EDSI is turning into a snub for the USA and that the President should therefore reduce American military involvement in Europe, if only to teach the ungrateful allies a lesson.

There is also the obvious fact that the loss of the unifying factor of an enemy with terrifying levels of nuclear weapons permanently pointed at Western capitals on continuous alert makes it correspondingly difficult to cement the alliance together with anything like the same degree of cohesion that prevailed during the Cold War, Strategic Concept or no new Strategic Concept. Cornish, however, believes that something 'passably effective' can be done to hold the transatlantic edifice together (Cornish, 1997: 30). In short,

> If the transatlantic security institution is to survive and remain useful, the member states of NATO must at some point decide that the relationship is prima facie worth the effort and that it can be used to address evolving security challenges ... Without the coherence and shared purpose imposed by an external threat, all that remains as the basis for the transatlantic security partnership is a general vote of confidence of this sort: NATO has become an 'alliance of choice', rather than an 'alliance of necessity'. This is hardly the most stable foundation, and it is one which will require constantly to be ... reinforced ... For the Europeanists and Atlanticists alike, a vote of confidence in this evolving institution would be a rational decision. (Cornish, 1997: 115)

It is the contention of this author that the primary basis for that rational decision can be found in the arguments advanced (in an earlier section of this discussion) for the maintenance of NATO's collective defence posture, although humanitarian-based collective security arguments are also of relevance.

The role of the OSCE

On the surface the OSCE is an impressive organization with a key security remit and 55 members from Vancouver to Vladivostok. Its area of operation covers continental Europe, Central Asia, North America and the Caucasus, and it cooperates with partners in the Mediterranean. It makes the claim that: 'In its region it is the primary instrument for early warning, conflict prevention, crisis management and post-conflict rehabilitation' (OSCE, 1999a). Again in its own words, it states that: 'The OSCE approach to security is comprehensive and co-operative. It deals with a wide range of security issues, including arms control, preventive diplomacy, confidence- and security-building measures, human rights, election monitoring economic and environmental security' (OSCE, 1999a). And 'the Organization is active in all phases of the conflict cycle, from early warning and conflict prevention to conflict management and post-conflict rehabilitation' (OSCE, 1999a).

The OSCE is and has been engaged in an impressive range of activities in support of its key aims. Its Charter for European Security, which was adopted at its November 1999 Istanbul summit, includes such field tasks as the verifying of and/or assisting in fulfilling agreements on the peaceful settlement of conflicts, the provision of support in the rehabilitation and reconstruction of various aspects of society after conflicts (paragraph 38), together with such police-related activities as police training (including the creation of police services with multi-ethnic and/or multi-religious composition 'that can enjoy the confidence of the entire population' (paragraph 44)). The Charter lists a number of political instruments that can be used by the OSCE in pursuit of its aims, including the dispatching of delegations from the organization's institutions to states, 'to provide advice and expertise for reform of legislation and practices' (paragraph 36). In addition, the OSCE has provided a central focus for conventional arms reduction processes within Europe. The Charter, for example, notes that the Treaty on Conventional Armed Forces in Europe, which has significantly reduced equipment levels, 'is being strengthened by adapting its provisions to ensure enhanced stability, predictability and transparency amidst changing circumstances. A number of States Parties will reduce further their equipment levels' (OSCE, 1999b).

The organization works hard to try and secure respect for human rights, the rule of law and democracy via the efforts of its Office for Democratic Institutions and Human Rights, the High Commissioner on National Minorities and the Representative on Freedom of the Media.

It also has strong supporters of the value of its monitoring role. In October 1999, for example, Christine Ellworthy claimed that everywhere the OSCE monitors went in Kosovo prior to their withdrawal the violence stopped. On this basis she further claimed that if the number of monitors had been increased one-hundred-fold, then they could have prevented war. The cost of such an operation, by her estimate, would have been only one-fifth of the cost of the conflict that followed. (In reply, NATO's Jamie Shea disputed her claims concerning the effectiveness of the monitors, stating that they were withdrawn because violence was in the process of breaking out (Ellworthy and Shea: 1999). His conclusion is supported by David Travers (who has provided the UN chapter within the present volume).

However, despite the impressive rhetoric, and the fact that it undoubtedly has done extremely valuable work in each of the above (and additional) respects, to the extent that each particular situation in which it has been involved has permitted, the OSCE is in reality seriously constrained by three main factors. The first of these is the need to obtain consensus among all of its member states when making key decisions, a huge task when one considers the difficulties which NATO experienced over Kosovo with only 19 members. Second, it is confronted with serious differences of interpretation of East–West security issues and how they should be handled. These have been most visibly on display recently over Russia's Chechen war (Black, 1999: 2). Third, while NATO's new Strategic Concept appears to recognize clearly the role and value of such integral components of the new Europe's strategic architecture as the OSCE, the relationship of the two is in fact determined by the extent to which the alliance sees it as being potentially useful in any particular context. The same is true of the OSCE's relationship with Russia, as was emphatically demonstrated by the way that the organization was treated by the Russian military in December 1999 when it tried to advise restraint in the use of force against the Chechen rebels.

The OSCE is at its weakest in situations where Europe's major military powers (including the USA by virtue of its continuing military presence and leadership within Europe) have decided that they wish to use force for peace-making or peacekeeping, or where they are already using force, or have decided simply to ignore or sideline it on other matters of its prime concern. Its highly conditional status in this respect is illustrated in paragraph 46 of the Charter, which states that: 'we confirm that the OSCE can, on a case-by-case basis and by consensus, decide to play a role in peacekeeping, including a leading role *when participating States judge it to be the most appropriate and effective organization* ... .'(OSCE, 1999b: my emphasis).

In other words, particularly given the difficulties in obtaining consensus among so many greatly diverse states, never mind Russia and the West, the OSCE's scope for involvement in such activities as peacekeeping is not large. The West is particularly keen to avoid the Russian veto on its operations that would ensue if they were to be conducted under an OSCE command rather than a NATO one. The OSCE's scope in the field of collective defence, as defined within paragraph 16 of its Charter, is so vaguely defined as to be almost irrelevant. But even where such seemingly uncontroversial and potentially tremendously useful activities as conflict prevention via the monitoring of peace agreements are concerned, the organization is entirely dependent on the say-so of the major military powers.

In short, the OSCE does have some crucial European security functions with regard to conventional arms control and by virtue of the simple fact that it is the only security organization which provides a truly pan-European/transatlantic forum for debate and trust-building. It is engaged in a large range of middle-range and minor security-enhancing activities, such as election monitoring and police training, many of which go largely unnoticed by the Western press, but which at the very least help improve European security around the margins. While peacekeeping, defence and collective security matters seem very much to be dominated by Russia and NATO, with the OSCE's main potential role being limited to that of providing authorization for particular operations where this seems appropriate, it could be argued to have a potentially highly significant role in the fields of peace-monitoring and the prevention of conflict by non-military means. Given the huge economic and environmental costs of the Kosovo war, there may now at least be a small chance that ideas on monitoring, such as those espoused by Ellworthy above, might be given a fair trial in future crises. However, there are not any immediately visible signs that this might be the case.

Note

1. American official sources contradict each other on this. General Clark says that a ground attack would have followed (NATO, 1999e), while Strobe Talbott claims that it would not.

CHAPTER FIFTEEN

The United Nations in the former Yugoslavia

With special reference to its cooperation with European and transatlantic organizations

David Travers

Introduction

The Socialist Federal Republic of Yugoslavia was a multi-ethnic state of six republics: Bosnia Herzegovina, Croatia, Macedonia, Montenegro, Serbia and Slovenia. Apart from Slovenia the ethnic distribution seldom coincided with the internal boundaries. The Federal Republic started to dissolve violently in June 1991, bringing war to the continent of Europe for the first time since the Greek Civil War of 1945–48. The Serb-dominated Federal Army failed to prevent the secession of Slovenia and Croatia, but then attempted to help the Serb communities in Croatia and in Bosnia Herzegovina carve out new Serb states which would be linked to the parent republic. A fourth war was to break out in the Kosovo province of Serbia, in March 1998, when a liberation army of ethnic Albanians fought to achieve independence.

These secessionist, civil, territorial and international wars were to present the international community with what at times seemed to be insurmountable problems. There were ethnic and religious conflicts, deep-seated animosities, deliberate mass displacements of population, widespread and persistent violations of human rights, irresponsible armed bands as well as troops deliberately attacking peacekeepers and aid workers, and extensive physical destruction. The political and military leaders lacked commitment and good faith and repeatedly violated agreements that they had freely entered into. They had little desire to reach any political settlement if they believed that continued violence was advantageous to them. And yet there was persistent pressure from the media and public opinion in many states for something to be done to which international decision-makers felt they had to respond.

One of the ways that they chose to make that response was through the United Nations (UN). What is often foremost in the minds of many of Europe's citizens now is that the UN apparently failed in its efforts to bring about a peace deal during the Bosnian conflict, leaving the central role ultimately to the USA, and was effectively sidelined throughout NATO's sustained bombing operations against Serbian targets during the Kosovan campaign. The truth about the UN's role in the former Yugoslavia is somewhat more complicated than that, however. It was, and is, far larger than most people outside the military, diplomatic and specialist academic communities realize. It has been multi-faceted and in some respects impressively successful. Almost imperceptibly, the UN has become an integral part of the peace and security architecture of Europe at a regional level in a way that was not previously the case. Within the former Yugoslavia it is, or has been, involved in peace-making, peacekeeping, the administration of international justice and territorial administration, in addition to its humanitarian assistance role. Its work is interwoven with that of NATO, the OSCE and the EU, and it has proved to be a crucial partner of these bodies in a number of respects. The intention here is, unapologetically, to paint something of the 'big picture' of the UN's role in the former Yugoslavia, while acknowledging that to attempt to do this within the confines of a single chapter is to have to cover some parts of the canvas with broad brush strokes. However, the author's belief is that what is lost in some of the detail will be more than made up for by the communication of a fuller idea of the scale of the UN's activities. An attempt to draw out some of the key implications of the UN's Balkan involvement will be made at the end of the chapter. Our 'grand tour' begins with the UN's role in Balkan peace-making.

Peace-making

Bosnia

It might have been anticipated that in a continent rich in institutions, either the European Community, the Conference on Security and Cooperation in Europe (CSCE), the WEU or NATO would have been able to prevent or curb the violence in Yugoslavia. But it was not to be. The European Community, with the assistance of the Conference on Security and Cooperation in Europe (CSCE) and the WEU, took the lead, believing that although Yugoslavia had now lost its Cold War strategic significance, it remained a European problem politically, historically and geographically. The Community, however, was handicapped by the still embryonic nature of its foreign policy machinery, the need for unanimity, the absence of its own armed forces, a lack of political will, inconsistent policy, and a perceived lack of impartiality by some of the parties. And after its initial success in negotiating the ceasefire in Slovenia it was unable either to stop the violence in Croatia, despite its troika missions, unarmed ceasefire monitors and sanctions against Serbia, or to solve the crisis within the framework of the initial meeting of the Conference on Yugoslavia that its special envoy Lord Carrington had summoned to discuss a new confederal constitution and democratic institutions for the republics.

In September 1991 the Community sought the assistance of the Security Council of the UN, which, meeting at ministerial level, on 25 September, unanimously adopted resolution 713. This called on all states to impose immediately a general and complete embargo on all deliveries of weapons and military equipment to Yugoslavia. The Council commended the Community's efforts to restore peace and invited the Secretary General to offer his assistance to the parties to secure a ceasefire. The Secretary General appointed Cyrus Vance as his personal envoy to Yugoslavia. Lord Carrington then continued to seek a political settlement for the whole of Yugoslavia, while Cyrus Vance sought a durable ceasefire in Croatia; the establishment of the necessary conditions for, and the deployment of a UN peacekeeping force. This force was to be an interim arrangement to create the conditions of peace and security required for the negotiation of an overall settlement of the Yugoslav crisis. This became known as the Vance Plan for Croatia

On 15 January 1992 the members of the European Community recognized Slovenia and Croatia as independent states. Recognition was of immense importance. What had been previously internal administrative boundaries were now international frontiers. What had been previously a civil war between Croatian armed forces and the Serb-dominated Yugoslavian Federal Army that had helped the Croatian Serbs to create a mini state in Croatia would, if re-ignited, become an international and civil war. And it meant that Lord Carrington's quest for a confederation of democratic independent republics, which had been the community's previous policy, was now doomed. (Wilson, 1994: 142–8; Eknes, 1995: 112–14; Durch and Schear, 1997: 199–206)

The principal problem faced by the mediators now was that of how to find a negotiated settlement for Bosnia where, even before recognition had been granted, there was a civil war, a war for territorial gain and outside support from first Serbia and then, from May 1992, Croatia, for their respective Bosnian communities. This was considered first by the European Community and then by the International Conference on the Former Yugoslavia (ICFY) that was established in August 1992, with its headquarters in Geneva. The Conference was intended to be a permanent negotiating forum for seeking a political solution to all the problems of the former Yugoslavia. EC and UN envoys jointly chaired it. The two mediators had to decide whether Bosnia was to continue to exist as a state: what would be the relationship between the central and the internal governments; what principles would be used to draw the internal ethnic boundaries; and what ties might exist between the Bosnian Croats and Serbs and the neighbouring states. But the mediators represented institutions whose members were usually unable to find a common policy. They had none of the resources that states might use in mediation. They had only their diplomatic skills. The international community was not prepared to use force to reverse Bosnian Serb territorial gains once these had occurred. It was prepared only to use condemnatory resolutions and sanctions. The arms embargo, which reduced the Bosnian Government's ability to defend its people and territory, was to be maintained. And the two states whose influence would have been invaluable – the USA who had influence with the Muslims and the Croats and the Russian Federation whose leverage lay with the Serbs – were not then prepared to play a major diplomatic role.

The first attempt was the Vance–Owen Plan which was published in January 1993. This maintained the unity of Bosnia. It created ten federal ethnic territories with a loose central government. It was accepted by the Bosnian Muslims and the Bosnian Croats but was rejected by the Bosnian Serbs, who would have had to relinquish forcibly acquired land. The USA, however, still believed that it rewarded the Serbs and moreover was unworkable. The second attempt was the Owen–Stoltenberg plan. This proposed a union of three republics within the state of Bosnia in which the Muslim majority Republic should have a minimum of 33.3 per cent of the territory; the Croat majority Republic should have 17.5 per cent; and the Bosnian Serbs 49.2 per cent. But this proposal was rejected by the Bosnian Parliament (Eknes, 1995: 119–21).

Two important developments occurred in 1994. The USA persuaded the Bosnian Muslim and the Bosnian Croat leaders to create a Federation within the Republic of Bosnia and then to establish a confederation between the Federation and the Republic of Croatia. And in April a Contact Group was established consisting of France, Germany, Russia, the UK, the USA, the European Commissioner for Foreign Affairs and the co-chairmen of the ICFY. This group provided a map that was similar to the last EC-UN plan. But the Bosnian Serbs again rejected it. The Security Council then strengthened the sanctions that had already been imposed on the Bosnian Serbs.

In November 1995, however, the Bosnian war ended after exhaustive negotiations at Dayton, Ohio, led principally by Richard Holbrooke of the USA, supported by members of the Contact Group. The UN, however, was not represented at Dayton. These talks drew on political principles that Holbrooke had already agreed with the Foreign Ministers of Bosnia Herzegovina, Croatia and the Federal Republic of Yugoslavia at negotiations in Geneva: that Bosnia would remain a sovereign state within its present borders; that there would be two substantially autonomous entities within Bosnia: the federation and Republika Srpska; that each entity had a parallel right to create associations or special relationships with neighbouring states; and that there should be a 51 per cent–49 per cent split of territory. A heavily armed NATO-led force of 60,000 troops would replace UNPROFOR to implement the military aspects of the peace agreement, while the High Representative and a range of organizations, including the UN, would implement the civilian aspects. These arrangements were authorized by Security Council resolution 1031 of 15 December 1995.

The Dayton Peace Plan negotiations succeeded for both political and military reasons. The USA was now prepared to recognize the Serb Republika Srpska and was prepared also to accept a territorial division that was more likely to obtain Serb support. The USA knew that, in the event of the negotiations failing, the UK and France were likely to withdraw their troops from UNPROFOR in Bosnia. The military balance also had been fundamentally altered shortly before the Dayton deal. In Croatia three of the UN protected areas populated largely by Serbs were quickly overrun by the Croatian Army in May and August. In Bosnia after a mortar attack on a Sarajevo market place on 28 August NATO launched 14 days of air strikes intended to destroy the Bosnian Serb air defences and capacity to launch and sustain a military campaign. UNPROFOR lost its impartiality. The artillery of the Rapid Reaction Force that had been supplied by France, the UK and the Netherlands attacked Bosnian Serb positions and helped to lift the siege of Sarajevo. And the Bosnian Croats supported the Bosnian Government offensive, which resulted in the collapse of the Bosnian Serb Army in Western Bosnia in September. As a result of this development and the fighting around Sarajevo, the Bosnian Croat Federation increased their territorial share from 30 per cent to just over 50 per cent of Bosnia, which was similar to that envisaged in earlier peace plans. The Bosnian Serbs faced for the first time the prospect that they might lose all their territorial gains. This major psychological factor contributed to the settlement (Bilt, 1998).

What is most crucial about the Dayton Agreement, perhaps, is that while the UN had played a prominent role in Bosnia during the conflict, through a variety of means, it was the US superpower that played the most critical role in making the peace. Ultimately, once the Americans had become seriously involved, the limits of possible further UN involvement were clearly drawn. The Russians and the Western Europeans also found their role heavily circumscribed at Dayton. The UN, however, was sidelined not just because of the presence finally of determined US diplomatic muscle, but because of a perception held by many that, along with the EU, it had failed in earlier attempts to bring about peace. However, having said all of this, as will be seen in a later section of the chapter, there is also a view that while the UN was the absent guest at the final feast, its sanctions had begun to really bite before hostilities ended, and it is quite possible that it played an important role ultimately, along with the other factors mentioned above, in helping force Milosevic to accept an agreement.

Kosovo

The international community's response to the crisis in Kosovo, which began in March 1998, was developed through a variety of institutions: the Contact Group, the Security Council, the European Union, NATO and the Organization for Security and Cooperation in Europe (OSCE). The aims were to stop the violence in Kosovo, to create conditions which would allow for the safe return of the refugees and displaced persons, to monitor developments in Kosovo and to encourage a political settlement that would allow Kosovo to have the largest possible degree of autonomy within the Federal Republic of Yugoslavia.

The international community used a range of methods in attempting to achieve these aims. Envoys from the Contact Group, the EU and NATO negotiated agreements with the Federal Government on monitoring missions, access for humanitarian organizations, reductions of armed forces and restrictions on military activities in Kosovo. The UN's role was a supportive one. The Security Council declared that the situation in Kosovo was a threat to the peace; called for a ceasefire; and received regular reports from the Secretary General, who drew upon information from monitoring missions, UNHCR and other institutions, to detail the extent to which the Federal Government and the KLA were complying with Security Council resolutions. The Security Council imposed an arms embargo and the Contact Group, except for Russia, and the EU, imposed economic sanctions. (And NATO threatened twice to use force against the Federal Government to ensure that negotiations were successfully completed and agreements maintained.) However, when the crucial question of the possible use of force came up (after the failure of the Rambouillet talks and the Holbrooke mission to Belgrade), it was graphically illustrated how little had come of the beginning-of-the-decade hopes of some for a New World Order centred around a revitalized and freshly empowered UN, freed at last from the straitjacket of Cold War politics. Very simply, NATO chose to use substantial military power against the Serbs without any authorization from the Security Council, leading Russia and others to accuse it of being in breach of the UN Charter. It chose to act in this way, in declared furtherance of humanitarian principles, because it knew that it would not obtain Security Council authorization, most particularly because of the staunch opposition of the Russian Government to the use of force against the Serbs. The various postulated machinations and calculations of interest that underlay the Russian position are complex and should not be underplayed, but, for the purposes of this chapter, it is sufficient to note that Russian opposition derived from a number of factors, including: traditional links with the Serbs; anger at the extension of NATO's military muscle into what had previously been part of Russia's 'back yard'; a desire not to be seen domestically to be acting as a Western 'poodle', especially in the light of the unpopularity amongst the Russian electorate of the so far failed attempt to make them prosperous via the introduction of key aspects of Western-style capitalism; and a real fear of the possible future implications for Russia and the other successor states of such a flexing of Western military muscle so close to their own territories.

What all of this means in practice is that, where peace-making is concerned, the UN, like the OSCE (see Chapter 14), remains hampered by the radically different interests represented by its key decision-makers and the fact that each has a veto. In effect, the Security Council has no meaningful role in deciding on the appropriateness of European peace-making operations – particularly those involving the use of force – unless not only Russia and the transatlantic permanent members, but also China, agree that it should. Its relevance remains to be decided on a case-by-case basis. While Russia was crucial in helping bring about a conclusion to the military hostilities, it was NATO power, unauthorized by the UN, that had played the key role in pushing Milosevic towards an agreement.

Arms embargoes and economic sanctions

Having examined the UN's role in peace-making with regard to two specific territorial areas within the former Yugoslavia, we will look at two prominent instruments which the UN has used within the Balkans to try to further its peace-making efforts, namely arms embargoes and economic sanctions.

On 25 September 1991, at the outset of the Yugoslav troubles, the Security Council imposed a general and complete arms embargo on the Federal Republic of Yugoslavia. On 30 May 1992, after violence had spread to Bosnia Herzegovina, wide-ranging mandatory trade and financial sanctions were imposed against the Federal Republic, which now consisted only of Serbia and Montenegro. The resolution banned all international trade, including the movement of funds for any purpose other than medical supplies and foodstuffs; air travel to and from the Federal Republic; maintenance of aircraft; sports exchanges; scientific and technical cooperation; and cultural exchanges and official travel. The intention of the Security Council was that the federal economy would be progressively damaged, and the state isolated, if the government in Belgrade did not heed the demands of resolution 952. These demands were: that it cease all forms of assistance to the Bosnian Serbs and support a negotiated settlement in Bosnia Herzegovina. Subsequently sanctions were tightened against the Federal Republic and extended to the territory controlled by the Bosnian Serbs in Bosnia Herzegovina when the Bosnian Serbs refused to cease fighting and to accept the Owen/Vance plan. And when the Bosnian Serbs failed to sign the Contact Group Plan the Security Council applied similar sanctions to those against the Federal Republic.

But at the same time, the Security Council on 23 September 1994 decided to suspend some of the sanctions against the Federal Republic for consecutive periods of 100 days if the Secretary General could certify that the authorities were effectively implementing their decision to close the border with Bosnia Herzegovina, cutting off their links with the Bosnian Serbs. On 22 November 1995, the Security Council suspended indefinitely the sanctions against the Federal Republic. Sanctions against the Bosnian Serbs were suspended on 27 February 1996, when it was established that their armed forces had withdrawn behind the zones of separation created by the Dayton Peace Agreement. The sanctions against both were finally withdrawn on 1 October 1996, when the OSCE certified that fair elections had taken place in Bosnia Herzegovina. Similarly the Security Council decided that there would be a phased lifting of the arms embargo when and if the parties to the Dayton Agreement fulfilled certain conditions. The embargo was finally terminated on 18 June 1996.

A number of regional organizations helped to enforce the UN arms embargo and economic sanctions. In December 1992 NATO Foreign Ministers decided that the alliance was ready to support UN peacekeeping operations. This decision, like a similar one from the WEU, was perhaps an attempt to demonstrate the continuing relevance of a military organization post-Cold War when its original purpose appeared to have disappeared. NATO, however, first assisted the UN in July 1992 in the Adriatic, when it began to monitor, and in November, when it joined WEU naval forces to enforce the arms embargo and economic sanctions. In April 1993 the enforcement operation was extended when the Security Council banned all commercial maritime traffic in the territorial waters of the Federal Republic. And with the agreement of the Government in Tirana the joint force also operated in Albanian territorial waters.

NATO reported that, during the enforcement operation: the Montenegrin ports were closed; approximately 74,000 ships were challenged; nearly 6000 were inspected at sea; and just over 1400 were diverted and inspected in Italian and Albanian ports. No ship broke the embargo although six attempted to do so. These were five arms carriers and one oiler. They were seized and impounded (IFOR, NATO/WEU, 1996).

A second source of assistance was the unprecedented EC/CSCE (later EU/OSCE) sanctions assistance missions and the WEU/OSCE operation on the Danube. As early as June 1992 there was media and governmental scepticism about the ability of neighbouring states to impose effectively the arms embargo and economic sanctions against the Federal Republic. Romania appealed for advice and technical assistance. The Presidency of the European Commission – the UK – the European Commission and the USA organized fact-finding missions to Bulgaria, Croatia, Hungary, FYR Macedonia and Romania. As a result, sanctions assistance missions (SAMS), consisting of professional customs officers from member states in the EC and from Canada and the USA, were established in October in Bulgaria, Hungary, FYR Macedonia and Romania, and by February 1993 in Albania, Croatia and the Ukraine (for the Danube). The USA provided the missions with a fleet of ex-military 4 × 4 vehicles and the EC provided satellite communications, computers and other office equipment.

The missions helped the local authorities to enforce sanctions by providing training and equipment; by advising how illegal trade via rail, road, river and sea could be minimized; and by encouraging the prevention of breaches at border posts. And a further, rather delicate role emerged, when the head of missions reported on host-state enforcement effectiveness to participating governments, and to the communication headquarters: SAMCOMM in Brussels.

SAMCOMM was hosted by the European Commission – Directorate XX1 – Customs and Indirect Taxation. It was staffed by personnel from the EC, the USA and Switzerland. It coordinated and oversaw the SAMS; it received and disseminated information about the implementation of sanctions; it developed and recommended changes in the sanctions operational procedures; it constructed a data-base to manage the 10,722 suspected or actual breaches of sanctions, which were then notified to the relevant government for further investigation and possible judicial action; and it appointed a liaison officer to the UN Security Council Sanctions Committee in New York which had overall responsibility for these sanctions. This committee was in a continuous dialogue with SAMCOMM, from which it received regular evaluation reports, information about repeated violators and advice on which applications were unsuitable for the shipping of exempted goods.

In April 1993 the WEU created a Danube Patrol Mission of eight patrol boats manned with customs and police officers from riparian states and the WEU to halt and inspect all inward and outward marine shipping on the Danube, to verify their cargoes and destinations, and to ensure strict implementation of the arms embargo and economic sanctions. The patrols and the SAMS inspected more than 6600 vessels towing more than 40,000 barges and discovered over 400 violations.

Finally, in September 1994, the ICFY established a mission of international civil servants to verify that only humanitarian aid was being delivered from the Federal Republic to the Bosnian Serb controlled territory in Bosnia.

It is difficult to evaluate the direct effects of economic sanctions on target states. There is evidence, however, to suggest that sanctions were one of the factors that induced the Belgrade Government to cut its links with the Bosnian Serbs and support a negotiated settlement in Bosnia, particularly as this was done before the Bosnian Serbs' military position started to deteriorate in 1995 (Doxey, 1999: 37–40; OSCE, 1996: 106–11, 129–37, 159–70, 203–14, and 223–35; Fourth Freedom Forum, n.d.).

Finally, it is necessary in this section to turn to the Federal Republic of Yugoslavia's Kosovan involvement. On 31 March 1998 the Security Council imposed a mandatory arms embargo on the Federal Republic of Yugoslavia. The Secretary General was asked to recommend an integrated coordinating mechanism, which would prevent arms reaching Yugoslavia and the ethnic Albanians in Kosovo and provide reports to the Security Council Sanctions Committee. But the anticipated level of help from OSCE, NATO, EU, WEU and the Danube Commission was not forthcoming (presumably because the effect of the embargo would not be impartial). And Kofi Annan was reduced to recommending periodic meetings of the European institutions, UNPREDEP and the Secretariat to exchange information and to discuss practical problems arising from the monitoring of violations.

Peacekeeping

The UN Protection Force in the former Yugoslavia (UNPROFOR) was established by the Security Council resolution 743 (1992) of 21 February 1992 for an initial period of 12 months. The first mandate related to Croatia. It was extended to Bosnia Herzegovina in June 1992 and in December 1992 to the former Yugoslav Republic of Macedonia (FYR Macedonia). In March 1995 UNPROFOR was restructured into three separate operations: the UN Confidence Restoration Operation in Croatia; the UN Preventive Deployment Force in Macedonia; and the UN Protection Force in Bosnia and Herzegovina.

UNPROFOR in all three locations was initially based on standard UN peacekeeping principles: that the parties had given consent (in Bosnia the Bosnian Serbs never formally consented to the composition and the deployment of the force and in the case of FYR Macedonia only the consent of the host-government was sought); that the armed forces and other personnel would remain impartial and that they would use force only in self-defence; and that the operation could only succeed if the parties cooperated. But while the mandate in Croatia in some respects involved traditional peacekeeping, that in Bosnia involving the delivery of humanitarian relief, conflict mitigation and the protection of safe areas in the midst of a war was largely unprecedented and the preventive deployment in Macedonia was entirely new.

Croatia

The basic principle of the force in Croatia was that it was an interim arrangement to create the conditions for peace and security required for the negotiation of an overall settlement of the Yugoslav crisis. The force was to be deployed in areas of Croatia where the Serbs constituted the majority, or a substantial majority, of the population and where fighting had occurred. These areas were to be known as UN Protected Areas (UNPAs). They were divided into four: East, North, South and West in the areas of Eastern Slavonia, Western Slavonia and Krajina. They would be demilitarized and all armed forces within them would be either withdrawn or disbanded. UNPROFOR would secure any heavy weapons that remained in the UNPAs. The Federal Army would withdraw from the whole of Croatia. The local authorities' functions would be supervised by UN police and civilian staff. Once public order had been restored, the displaced Croats could return and be protected from intimidation and violence from within, and the Serbs living within the UNPAs could be protected from attack by the Croatian Army from without by the UN military, police and civilian presence.

The mandate was also extended to include, with the help of the EU mission, monitoring functions in the Serb-controlled areas of Croatia lying outside the UNPAs: the Pink Zones; to undertake immigration and customs functions where the boundaries of the UNPAs coincided with Croatian international frontiers; to monitor the demilitarization of the Prevlaka Peninsula; and to oversee the ceasefire agreement that was reached in March 1994 after fighting had occurred in January and September 1993.

UNPROFOR had only partial success. It observed the withdrawal of the Federal Army from Croatia. It monitored the demilitarization of the Prevlaka Peninsula. But it was unable to implement the Vance Plan partly because the force was too small, partly because of its slow deployment, partly because the underlying political problem of who ruled the Serb communities within Croatia was not settled, and partly because the parties refused to cooperate. The protected areas were not demilitarized and the displaced were unable to return. The Force therefore helped to maintain the ceasefire, protected minorities where it could and provided humanitarian sustenance.

At President Tudjman's insistence in March 1995 the force was re-named the UN Confidence Restoration Operation (UNCRO), reduced in size and partially redeployed. But in May and August the Croatian Army seized Sector West and the Krajina region. The peacekeepers, after performing humanitarian and human rights missions during and after the fighting, were withdrawn from these areas. But an element of the force remained in Eastern Slavonia which was the last Serb controlled territory in Croatia. The UN helped to negotiate an agreement between the Croatian Government and the Croatian Serbs which would lead to the peaceful integration of the territory into Croatia. The UN was requested to administer the territory. UNCRO terminated on 15 January 1996 (Durch and Schear, 1997: 206–33; Eknes, 1995: 116–17; Eknes, n.d.: 16–21; United Nations, 1994; Wilson, 1994: 148–54).

Bosnia

The UN force in Bosnia faced considerable difficulties throughout its deployment from June 1992 until December 1995, yet its record is far more successful than its critics allow. First the force – which was initially composed primarily of NATO forces – was despatched to a war zone where none of the necessary conditions for peacekeeping existed. The force was expected to secure and operate Sarajevo Airport, and to protect humanitarian workers and deliveries where no peace existed, where cooperation from the parties was uncertain and where the soldiers could use force only in self-defence. Then the force monitored the no-fly zone, weapons-exclusion zones and the UN six safe areas established by the Security Council. The force was permitted to use force in self-defence in reply to attacks against these areas, and to seek the assistance of NATO air power when necessary. It was also encouraged to maintain and supervise ceasefires between the parties and to use its good offices generally to help to contribute to the peace.

The first difficulty was that the Security Council had no strategic plan. The mandates were extended in response to public opinion, changing conditions on the ground and the varying views of the Council members, particularly permanent members. It failed to provide consistent political support. It did not always heed military advice nor address secretariat concerns when the clarification of ambiguous and contradictory resolutions was sought.

The parties' cooperation was also unpredictable and unreliable, partly because of the absence of effective government and partly because of large numbers of ill-disciplined and irresponsible armed groups. All the parties interfered with the work of the force, particularly the Bosnian Serbs. They hampered the delivery of humanitarian assistance by denying freedom of movement, preventing delivery to certain locations, stealing parts of the cargo and deliberately seizing or attacking peacekeepers, drivers and humanitarian workers. Yet the airlift to Sarajevo Airport was the longest such operation in history, carrying over 175,000 tons of humanitarian assistance – a large proportion of which was financed by the EC(EU). The airlift, air drops and the overland convoys, usually with UNPROFOR protection, enabled the UNHCR and its partners to support millions of people in Bosnia.

The force was never provided with sufficient manpower for the safe areas. It had to rely on the cooperation of the Bosnian Serbs and when this was withdrawn the international community was not prepared to intervene forcefully to prevent the fall of Srebenica and Zepa. Nor was UNPROFOR sufficiently endowed to monitor effectively the weapons-exclusion zones.

Finally the force successfully helped to maintain the various ceasefire agreements that were negotiated (Durch and Schear, 1997: 223–52; Eknes, n.d., 21–30; United Nations, 1994; Wilson, 1994: 154–7).

Preventive deployment in FYR Macedonia

The Security Council in December 1992, at the request of the Government of Macedonia (which was the only republic to secede peacefully), approved the deployment of its first ever preventive peacekeeping force along the borders with Albania and the Federal Republic of Yugoslavia. The initial purpose was to prevent violence spilling over into Macedonia. Its presence, along with that of the OSCE and the European Community monitoring missions, indicated that the international community had an important stake in the territorial integrity of the new state. The UN force commanders developed very useful relations with the military authorities in Albania and Serbia, which increased the transparency of the force's activities. The mission helped to defuse border incidents and to maintain communications between Macedonia and Serbia in the absence of diplomatic relations. Its monitoring reports were used to counter any suggestion that the republic faced immediate military danger. And the presence of US troops in the force, which would have increased the political price of any Serbian armed attack, may have deterred any remote possibility that still existed.

When it was clear that the more immediate threat was internal rather than external, the force assumed good office functions to help the Government maintain internal harmony. It worked closely with the ICFY and UNHCR on humanitarian issues and in promoting dialogue on human rights issues involving ethnic communities and national minorities. And the special representative of the Secretary General was able to obtain extra-budgetary funds, which were used to enhance the force's good offices' capabilities.

The force assumed a third role when it was asked to monitor and report on any breaches of the arms embargo imposed against Serbia and the KLA in 1998. But it did not have any authority to interdict and inspect the cross-border traffic. As the crisis in Kosovo deepened the force worked with the European Community Monitoring Mission (ECMM), the NATO Kosovo Verification Centre and the NATO extraction force that had been deployed in Macedonia. The force was withdrawn after a Chinese veto in the Security Council in February 1999 prevented the renewal of its mandate. China had objected to Macedonia developing ties with Taiwan (Eknes, n.d.: 31–3; Kuenning 1999: 238–52; United Nations, 1994 and 1999a).

Kosovo

When violence erupted in Kosovo the international community was represented by a small ECMM. In June 1998 the Federal Government rejected EU requests that the mission be enlarged. The Government was, however, prepared to accept additional diplomatic staff accredited to Embassies in Belgrade. The ECMM then became part of the new mission: the Kosovo Diplomatic Observers' Mission, which also included Russian, US, Canadian and Polish personnel. This mission was loosely organized and each participating state decided how many observers it would send. The observers monitored and reported on conditions in Kosovo and attempted to restore confidence between the Serb and Albanian communities. They had no executive functions, were unarmed and could not guarantee protection of the displaced. The relatively small size of this mission, Serbian and occasional KLA opposition and the difficulties of maintaining continuous surveillance throughout Kosovo, limited its influence (Sweden, Permanent Mission to the United Nations, 1998: 2).

The Diplomatic Mission was in turn absorbed into the OSCE Verification Mission (VM), which was endorsed by the Security Council on 24 October 1998 and created by the OSCE Permanent Council on 26 October 1998. The OSCE, although it had not previously mounted a large-scale field mission, was chosen because a NATO mission would have been opposed by Belgrade and Russia and because there was still a perception that the UN had failed in Bosnia. The mission, which was to last for a year in the first instance, was to be composed of up to 2000 seconded staff from OSCE states.

The mandate of the mission was to verify the Federal Republic's compliance with Security Council resolutions 1160 and 1199; to verify the maintenance of the ceasefire, and monitor the movement of forces; to provide assistance with the return of the refugees and displaced people; to supervise elections; to help in forming elected bodies and internal self-government and police forces; and to promote human rights and democracy-building.

The mission faced difficulties in fulfilling its mandate. Although the Diplomatic Monitoring Mission became the initial core of the KVM, the small OSCE secretariat found it difficult to recruit and speedily deploy the necessary unarmed verifiers. The Federal Government may have felt that OSCE member states did not regard the mission as a major priority. It waged a propaganda war against the mission through state-controlled media, which often stimulated local civilian opposition. The media claimed that the mission was partial because an American led it, because it was collecting military information for possible use by NATO and because it was encouraging the KLA. The Government used various ploys to delay the arrival of verifiers and their equipment. It refused landing rights. And it allowed the armed forces and the police to intimidate the verifiers and to place areas out of bounds to them.

The mission was unable to verify the ceasefire because both sides continued to fight. The KLA stated that it was not a party to the agreement which, moreover, the Serbs were violating. It needed to fight to achieve independence. The Serbs claimed that they had to respond to attacks on their villages and armed forces.

The mission therefore adjusted to these conditions. It attempted to become a calming presence by developing contacts with both parties and by patrolling in vivid orange vehicles. It placed these vehicles repeatedly in the middle of localized fighting, relying on the parties' knowledge that the verifiers were unarmed and that if they were injured the guilty party would lose international sympathy. Then it attempted to persuade the parties to cease fighting and restore and maintain the ceasefire. This helped to reduce the occasions on which the Serb forces could use large-scale violence for ethnic cleansing and to a degree enhanced the security of the Albanian population. The mission also investigated violent incidents, and secured the release of hostages. It assisted nongovernmental organizations' in their humanitarian activities. And its impartial reporting kept the international community informed about the political, humanitarian and security conditions in Kosovo.

The mission, however, was withdrawn from Kosovo on 20 March 1999. The increased military activities of the government forces had prevented it from fulfilling its tasks. It did not have to call on the NATO extraction force based in FYR Macedonia, which had been specially created in a unique agreement between the two organizations, to protect the emergency withdrawal of the mission. The KVM then worked in Macedonia and Albania, cooperating with the OSCE missions there and assisting the UN and nongovernmental organizations' humanitarian assistance programmes as they struggled to cope with the unprecedented numbers of Kosovar Albanian refugees fleeing from ethnic cleansing.

Finally, NATO on 15 October signed with the Federal Government an agreement that permitted unarmed alliance flights over Kosovo, during which the Federal Armed Forces were not permitted to use their radar systems. The flights were to supplement the reporting of the VM and to establish the extent to which the Federal Government was conforming to the security force reductions that it had agreed with NATO (Moore, 1999; North Atlantic Assembly, 1999; Walker, 1999).

The use of force for other than specific peace-making purposes

NATO and the use of air power during the Bosnian conflict

NATO cooperated with the UN in three ways. The Security Council established a no-fly zone over Bosnia Herzegovina on 9 October 1992. This was an attempt to neutralize the Serb advantage in fixed-wing aircraft. UN and European Community personnel monitored the zone from airfields and civilian air traffic control centres in Croatia, Bosnia Herzegovina and Serbia while from November NATO used monitoring aircraft in orbit over the Adriatic Sea and Hungary. NATO regularly passed information on any possible violations to the UN. On 31 March 1993 the Security Council authorized the enforcement of the no-fly zone which was now to include rotary-wing aircraft. NATO began its enforcement operation on 12 April 1993.

On 28 February 1994 four Bosnian Serb aircraft violating the zone were shot down. This was NATO's first ever combat operation. By 20 December 1995, when the UN peacekeeping role in Bosnia ended, NATO had flown nearly 100,000 sorties. But it had proved very hard to prevent violations by helicopters, which were difficult to detect; and continuous air combat missions over the zone were no long maintained after the Bosnian Serb air defences shot down a US F16 in June 1995. The Security Council resolution did not permit these to be attacked unless they were a direct threat to NATO planes.

The second way in which NATO assisted the UN was in offering from June 1993 close air support for the self-defence of UNPROFOR troops in Bosnia Herzegovina. This was later extended to troops in Croatia. The support was successively provided at the request of the UN on three occasions: 10 and 11 April 1994; and on 11 July

1995 and 9 October 1995 to protect UN personnel in Gorazde, Srebrenica and Tuzla from Bosnian Serb attacks.

The third form of assistance was air strikes against pre-selected targets. The UN requested NATO to authorize air strikes to deter attacks against the safe areas. NATO, without the express authority of the Security Council, established weapons-exclusion zones around Sarajevo in February 1994 and Gorazde in April 1994, which it expected UNPROFOR to oversee. It then warned the parties that air strikes would be implemented if the zones were violated. On 5 August 1994 NATO attacked Bosnian Serb weapons in the Sarajevo exclusion zone. On 22 September NATO struck a Bosnian Serb tank following an attack against an UNPROFOR armoured car. NATO bombed the Ubdina airfield in Serb-held Croatia on 21 and 23 November 1994, after it had been used for air attacks against the Bihac safe area, and attacked surface to air missiles in western Bosnia Herzegovina and the Krajina region of Croatia. (There were also similar protective strikes against air defences in Serb-held Croatia in August 1995 and in Bosnian Serb territory in October 1995.) On 25 and 26 May air strikes were made against Serb ammunition dumps at Pale because of violations of the exclusion zones and shelling of the safe areas.

After a major ministerial meeting held in London on 21 July 1995 the alliance initiated planning to ensure that NATO air power would be used in a timely and effective manner if the remaining safe areas were threatened or attacked. On 30 August following a Bosnian Serb mortar attack on Sarajevo two days earlier, NATO, with the approval of the UN Force Commander in Bosnia Herzegovina, started a bombing campaign to reduce the threat to Sarajevo and to deter any further attacks on the safe areas. The bombing was halted on two occasions but then resumed when the Bosnian Serbs failed to comply. On 20 September the two commanders concluded that their conditions had been met and the air strikes were halted.

The use of air power in support of a peacekeeping operation created difficulties both within and between NATO and the UN. The UN was concerned about preserving the primacy of the Security Council in maintaining international peace and security; maintaining its peacekeeping principles, particularly impartiality and the use of force in self-defence; delivering its humanitarian mandate, which could be achieved only with the consent of the parties, which could be withdrawn if the Bosnian Serbs believed that the organization was now at war with them; and protecting its personnel. This concern was particularly heightened after the bombing of the Ubdina airfield and the Pale ammunition dumps, when the Bosnian Serbs retaliated by taking UN personnel as hostage and using them as human shields. NATO, however, was fearful that its reputation and credibility as a war fighting machine was being eroded by UN constraints on the use of air power. It therefore gradually whittled away the UN civilian control element of the dual key decision-making process and moved from assisting the UN to taking over the final stage of the UNPROFOR operation in Bosnia (Annan, 1993, 1–2, 4–6; IFOR, NATO/WEU, 1996: 2–5; Schulte, 1997a; Schulte, 1997b: 1–2; United Nations, 1999b: paras 482–3).

The UN and the administration of international justice

The International Criminal Court for the former Yugoslavia

The Security Council, in resolution 827, of 25 May 1993, established the International Criminal Tribunal for the former Yugoslavia (ICTFY). It is located in The Hague, in the Netherlands. It is mandated to investigate and prosecute persons alleged responsible for serious violations of international humanitarian law committed on the territory of the former Yugoslavia since 1991. The ICTFY has authority to prosecute in four areas: grave breaches of the 1949 Geneva Conventions; violations of the laws or customs of war; genocide; and crimes against humanity. Since its inception, the ICTFY has publicly indicted 91 individuals. Six accused have died; charges were dropped against 18 others; and one person, having been tried, is now serving his sentence. Thirty-four are currently in proceedings before the ICTFY and 32 publicly indicted accused remain free, mostly in the Republika Srpska and the Federal Republic of Yugoslavia (International Criminal Tribunal for the former Yugoslavia, 1999d).

Yet, like other international institutions, the ICTFY cannot work without the assistance of states and international bodies. It requires adequate financial resources; it needs help in investigating alleged international crimes and in executing arrest warrants. And it also needs political support to deal with those states that persistently ignore its requests and the legal orders. The Security Council, despite repeated pleas from the President and the Chief Prosecutor, has failed to address the non-compliance of the Federal Republic of Yugoslavia. In refusing to surrender those indicted, Serbia has become a 'safe' haven for those accused of serious war crimes in Bosnia and Herzegovina, Croatia and Kosovo. Until the indicted face the prospect of arrest, trial and possible conviction, it will be difficult to break the cycle of immunity in parts of the former Yugoslavia. Furthermore, until victims or their families believe that they can receive redress, reconciliation will be delayed and the peace process will be even more difficult to achieve.

A further problem was that Croatia, also, was withholding cooperation. It claimed that the ICTFY had no jurisdiction to investigate the operation of its armed forces in operations Storm and Flash in 1995, when they overran UN Protected Areas in Croatia. But the ICTFY would not be successful if states were permitted to dictate to the independent prosecutor what events should and should not be investigated (International Criminal Tribunal for the former Yugoslavia, 1999e).

But this is not to underestimate the importance of the ICTFY. It is now functioning. It is capable, within the resources made available by the UN and individual states, of investigating alleged crimes, of conducting trials according to agreed legal rules, of obtaining and protecting witnesses and jailing those found guilty. And it is developing international criminal law. Its decisions 'make substantial findings on myriad legal issues, most of which have never before been considered by a court, or which have not been subject to legal review for decades' (International Criminal Tribunal for the former Yugoslavia, 1998, 1999a).

During the Kosovo crisis the ICTFY attempted to deter possible war crimes by giving publicity to its trials and to the Federal Republic of Yugoslavia's violations of international law. The Prosecutor announced that she would investigate alleged international crimes in Kosovo. She established temporary operational bases in

Albania and the FYR of Macedonia. She was permitted to recruit up to 300 gratis personnel from member states to undertake specialized forensic work in Kosovo once KFOR was deployed. She issued indictments against five leading political and military figures in the Federal Republic of Yugoslavia, including President Milosevic – the first ever issued by the ICTFY against a Head of State during a current armed conflict. Each person was accused of three counts of crimes against humanity and one count of violations of the laws or customs of war. And she announced later that she had received reports of 529 gravesites; that about one-third of these had been examined and that work had been completed at 195 sites. A total of 4266 bodies had reportedly been buried in those sites; 2108 had been exhumed (International Criminal Tribunal for the former Yugoslavia, 1999a and e).

The UN and international administration

There have been three major examples of international institutions administering parts of the former Yugoslavia: Eastern Slavonia, Dayton and Kosovo. It is a little early yet to make any firm judgements on the latter, so the first two only will be examined here.

Eastern Slavonia

The UN transitional administration for Eastern Slavonia, Baranja and Western Sirmium was established by Security Council resolution 1037 (1996) of 16 January 1996. This was in response to a request from Croatia and the Croatian Serbs – the parties to the Basic Agreement – for an international force to maintain peace and security and assist in the implementation of the Basic Agreement during a transitional period of a maximum of two years.

The major tasks of UN transitional administration for Eastern Slavonia (UNTAES) were to assist in the demilitarization of the region; to facilitate, with UNHCR, the voluntary and safe return of refugees and displaced persons; to reintegrate civil administration and public services; to establish a temporary police force; to cooperate with the ICTFY; to organize elections; to monitor respect for the highest standards of human rights; and to promote an atmosphere of confidence among all local residents.

This mission was largely a success. The region was peacefully reintegrated; elections were held; a multi-ethnic police force was established, whose standards of policing, even critics conceded, were higher than in other parts of Croatia. (But opinion differs on how many Serbs left the region during the transition and the extent to which there was a flourishing, democratic, multi-ethnic society.) This success can be attributed to a number of factors. There was a negotiated agreement between the Croatian Government and the local Serbs, which both wanted to see implemented, although there were considerable fluctuations in the degree of cooperation offered to the UN. There were two vigorous UN administrators, both from the USA, who were given reasonable resources to fulfil a carefully defined mandate; there was a clear time limit; and there was political support from major states. The military force quickly established a robust reputation. Moreover, the force had the support of IFOR and SFOR. If there was any significant military threat to the region that was beyond the capacity of UNTAES to contain, SFOR could order NATO close air support. A NATO air liaison cell and an SFOR liaison cell were located in UNTAES Headquarters to coordinate this support. And regular close air support exercises were held to indicate to the parties that this was a credible threat (Klein, 1997: 19–24; International Crisis Group, 1996a: 1–5).

When UNTAES left in January 1998 a small UN police mission remained until October to monitor the performance of the local police, particularly in relation to displaced persons. This was replaced by a counterpart from the OSCE mission. The OSCE mission in Croatia was first deployed in 1996. In June 1997 its mandate was enlarged to include helping with the return of refugees and displaced persons and with minority rights protection – tasks which it shares with UNHCR: they have a common secretariat as part of a liaison office, a common monitoring database and make common demarches to the authorities (OSCE, 1999c: 9). The mission has a large presence in the areas formerly controlled by the United Nations. But doubts have been raised about its efficacy (Human Rights Watch, 1999).

The Dayton Agreement

The aims of the Dayton Agreement were to end the war in Bosnia Herzegovina, to return the refugees and the displaced and to create a new democratic state of two multi-ethnic political entities. The ceasefire has been maintained, the forces separated and heavy weapons impounded, and conditions created in which there has been internal and external investment and reconstruction. But there are still foreign troops, armed groups and war criminals at large. There has been very little arms control. Democratic elections have been held by the OSCE, but these have generally resulted in nationalist parties being returned to office. Indeed, there is no major party which is capable of obtaining support from across the two entities on political rather than ethnic grounds. The entities determine how much influence the Central Government wields. The human rights provisions have been largely ignored. Refugee returns have been very disappointing and the UN has faced enormous difficulties in attempting to improve the behaviour and performance of the police forces.

The military aspects of the agreement have been reasonably well implemented because NATO had been planning for such an operation since 1993. The mandate was clear and achievable. The parties granted the force the legal authority to execute its mission. UNPROFOR provided assistance in the initial stages. The UN Force Commander became the Deputy Commander of IFOR and 18,500 troops and most of the infrastructure, equipment and assets were transferred from UNPROFOR to IFOR. The parties cooperated and very little military action was required. And the operation was supported across the international political spectrum (Schulte, 1997a: 31).

The civilian parts of the agreement have been more difficult to implement. The High Representative from the EU was not initially provided with sufficient staff, resources and legal authority. He had no control over the civilian implementing institutions, including the OCSE, the UNHCR and the UN. Indeed the extent to which these institutions were rivals or partners depended largely on the personal relations of the Secretariats. The military decided whether and to what extent they would help. And implementation had to take place within the context of the old communist political and economic system, which appears to have been reinforced by international aid and by democratic elections.

The parties whom the High Representative was helping to execute the agreement were not reconciled after the war. The Croats and the Serbs were still seeking union with Croatia and Serbia, but by peaceful obstruction rather than by military means. The pace of implementation was determined by the speed with which agreement was reached among the often obdurate politicians and officials. The High Representative could only plead, persuade and cajole. And so the 1997 Peace Implementation Councils increased the authority of the High Representative. He could now remove obstructive officials and impose the solutions which the politicians, having been given sufficient time, had failed to achieve. Many of the successes of the agreement have been imposed. But it is anticipated that the international community will have to continue to support Bosnia for a considerable period because if that support, particularly the military, were withdrawn then war would return (Klein, 1999; International Crisis Group, 1996b: 1–15; 1998a: 1–6; 1998b: 1–9; 1999a: 1–3, 5–7 and 16–20; and 1999b: 1–51)

Conclusions and future

In its 'grand tour' of the UN's role in the former Yugoslavia, this chapter has examined a variety of aspects of the UN involvement in attempts: to seek negotiated settlements to the various conflicts involved; to prevent the violence spilling over into neighbouring states; to mitigate the effects of the war on civilians; and to maintain the restored peace. All of the above activities resulted in the UN's largest and most complex peacekeeping operation ever, and unprecedented cooperation with European or European-based regional organizations to share the diplomatic, material and financial burden and to gain access to resources, particularly military, that the UN did not possess. There was cooperation in peace-making, peacekeeping, humanitarian programmes, bringing to trial those suspected of war crimes, sanctions, military coercion, administration and the reconstruction of war-torn societies. What there has been space to demonstrate only partially here is the fact that in practice, cooperation was not always easy because, on occasions, the organizations lacked political leadership from their major members; because regional institutions wanted to emphasize their own autonomy; because, at times, the regional organizations did not work under the authority of the Security Council; because sometimes there were institutional cultural clashes; and because regional bodies were unable to carry out UN requests.

If one were to try and draw up a profit-and-loss account for the UN's Balkan involvement, one might note, on the profit side, the previously mentioned evidence that UN sanctions may well have been important ultimately in helping to bring Milosevic to the negotiating table over Bosnia, together with the apparent success of the Macedonian preventive force, the fruitful cooperation between NATO, OSCE, EU and WEU and the UN over the enforcement of economic and arms sanctions during the Bosnian conflict, the success of the UN transitional administration for Eastern Slavonia, Baranja and Western Sirmium, and the way in which the ICTFY is developing international criminal law and establishing an embryonic European legal deterrent against the inhuman excesses that characterized the Balkan conflicts of the 1990s. On the loss side of the ledger, it would be necessary to acknowledge such things as: the way in which NATO gradually elbowed away the UN civilian control element of the dual key decision-making process and moved from assisting the UN to taking over the final stage of the UNPROFOR operation in Bosnia; the number of war criminals who so far have eluded the clutches of the ICTFY; the damage which has been done to the UN's potential role as a peace-broker in Europe by what by many was seen as its failures during the Bosnian conflict; the way in which the Chinese exercise of its veto concerning the Macedonian force (on irrelevant grounds of self-interest relating to Taiwan) showed the limitations that operate concerning the UN's peacekeeping role in Europe; and the way in which the firm Russian opposition to the use of the military against Serbia during the Kosovan conflict demonstrated the limitations on the UN's role in deciding on the appropriateness of the use of force for peace-making in Europe.

If an attempt were to be made to try and draw all of this together in terms of its present and future implications for the UN's role in Europe, then the picture that would emerge, unsurprisingly, would be something of a mixed bag. In short, the above summary demonstrates that the UN is now doing, or has recently done, a number of things in Europe that have aided significantly the peoples of the Balkans through preventing conflicts, helping to bring them to an end, facilitating the transition towards a more civilized society and introducing legal remedies, no matter how embryonic, where previously none existed. It is easy to remember the horrendous failures, such as the disaster at Srebrenica (not mentioned here as it has been exhaustively covered elsewhere), but the successes, while undeniably limited, are prizes worth having, both for the peoples of the former Yugoslavia and for the progress of Europe's still greatly unperfected civilization as a whole. The downside is that so long as the veto remains within the Security Council, and so long as the permanent members continue to have significant divisions of interest on matters such as the Balkan Question, there will be severe limitations on the extent to which the UN can play both a central and an effective role in the maintenance of peace and security within Europe's troubled regions. Despite this, however, and even though it has many faults, the UN seems now to have established itself as a credible, if junior, player within Europe's overall peace and security architecture.

CHAPTER SIXTEEN

The European Union and Central and Eastern Europe

Karen Henderson

Nowhere is the new Europe more obviously in transition than in Central and Eastern Europe. Here, transition takes many forms. Within each state, the entire political, economic and social structure has undergone a profound transformation throughout the 1990s. Yet it is an incomplete transition. Politically, democracy is nowhere fully consolidated, though some of the 'new democracies' have proceeded further down this path than others. Economically, the move towards a market economy has progressed much faster in some states than others, although even the most advanced still face some formidable challenges. Socially, citizens have confronted huge changes in their everyday life and their status in society, and many remain deeply insecure about what the future will bring.

At the same time, state borders have changed, so that the eastern half of the map of Europe has undergone its most radical alteration since 1918. In 1989, the communist part of Europe comprised a mere nine states: the Soviet Union, its six Warsaw Pact allies (Bulgaria, Czechoslovakia, the German Democratic Republic, Hungary, Poland and Romania), and the independent communist states of Albania and Yugoslavia. By 1999, the original nine had divided into almost 30. The three communist federations – Czechoslovakia, the Soviet Union and Yugoslavia – had disintegrated and left their constituent republics as sovereign states. In the case of the former communist Yugoslavia, the process of dissolution was still incomplete, with the eventual status of Kosova and Montenegro very much in question. Only the German Democratic Republic had simplified Europe's map by disappearing through incorporation into a united Germany, but problems still remain unresolved (see Chapter 7).

Defining the new Europe

Just as crucial, however, for the new Europe was the fundamental question 'What is Europe?' The old Europe reflected a bipolar world, and was divided in two between the 'first world' of western states, and the 'second world' of communist states. Behind this primary divide were less important sub-divisions. All of the western states were in the Council of Europe; some were in the European Union (EU), some were in NATO, and some were not; yet all were joined by the phrase 'western democracies'. On the eastern, communist, side, some nations were in the Soviet Union; others lived in Soviet satellite states; and some were in communist states outside the Soviet orbit. The Soviet Union was technically a Eurasian state, with a geographical border between continents running along the Ural Mountains east of

Moscow, but this did not alter its position as the leading power in the communist Europe. The only international organization in Europe which included both halves of the divided continent was the Conference on Security and Cooperation in Europe (CSCE), established in 1976. This encompassed all European states with the exception of Albania, as well as the USA and Canada.

In the 1990s, the definition of Europe underwent fundamental but incomplete changes. As the bipolar divide between communism and democracy disappeared, the importance of membership of international organizations in defining the new Europe increased. The criteria for determining membership of European organizations also assumed a vital significance. The only inclusive organization was the CSCE (from the end of 1994 the Organization for Security and Cooperation in Europe – OSCE), which embraced all its former members, including the non-European Soviet successor states, and accepted Albania in 1991. Other bodies, such as the Council of Europe, the EU and NATO, had their own, subtly different sets of democratic hurdles which prospective members had to overcome. As a result, what gradually occurred, in the course of the 1990s, was a process of differentiation between post-communist countries that had previously been considered one bloc. An illustration of this differentiation can be provided by looking at the fate of the three communist federations. The rationale – one could say inevitability – behind their disintegration becomes clearer if one examines the varied progress of their successor states in joining the new Europe.

This is most obvious in the case of the Soviet Union. At one extreme, the five Soviet republics in Central Asia and the three Caucasian republics have been largely excluded from 'Europe' in its geographic definition and do not belong to Council of Europe, although the Caucasian republics did obtain 'special guest status' in 1996 (Croft *et al.*, 1999: 144). Four former Soviet republics – the largely Slavic and orthodox states of Russia, Ukraine and Belarus, as well Moldova, with its strong Romanian cultural influence – are accepted as being European and are (with the exception of the pariah state Belarus) part of more inclusive European structures such as the Council of Europe. They have yet, however, to apply for EU and NATO membership. On the other hand, the three Baltic states (Estonia, Latvia and Lithuania), which were all independent in the inter-war period and are largely Protestant or Catholic by religion, are among the ten Central and East European countries (CEECs) which are included in the EU's accession process. One of them – Estonia – is even among the first group of five post-communist states to enter detailed negotiations on EU membership, together with the Czech Republic, Hungary, Poland and Slovenia. All the Baltic states are also considered credible applicants for membership of NATO. By the end of the millennium, the thought of states as different as Estonia and Tadzhikistan once having shared a government seemed almost unreal.

The former Yugoslavia also demonstrates marked divergence between republics in their post-communist fortunes. The most western of them – Slovenia – has achieved one of its major goals when it declared independence in 1991. It has reasserted its central European identity, and was included in the first group of CEECs to enter negotiations on EU accession. The rest of the former Yugoslavia is far behind. Croatia, which was embroiled in an often bloody struggle for its territorial integrity for most of the 1990s, remains more advanced economically than much of the post-communist Europe, and vehemently rejects the label 'Balkan'. Yet it is considered suspect in its democratic development and is not yet accepted as a credible candidate for the EU and NATO, and was only admitted into the Council of Europe in 1996 – after the much more backward Russia. The multi-ethnic and chronically war-damaged Bosnia and Herzegovina remains a politically and economically vulnerable state supervised by UN forces. Macedonia is internationally admired for its relative stability in the most adverse of circumstances (it is multi-ethnic and partly surrounded by states involved in military conflict), yet it is still excluded from the EU accession process. The remainder of the former Yugoslavia is notionally recognized on an international level as belonging to something called the 'Federal Republic of Yugoslavia' (FRY) – an entity whose government is recognized only in Serbia, and rejected by both Montenegro and Kosova, over which it claims sovereignty. The international pariah status of Serbia and the so-called FRY was cemented in May 1999 when the presidents of both were indicted as war criminals. 'Yugoslavia' does not belong to the Council of Europe, and even its OSCE membership has been suspended.

The final communist federation, Czechoslovakia, divided peacefully and legally at the end of 1992 into the Czech Republic and the Slovak Republic, both of which still share much in common in terms of their constitutional structures and standard of living. Yet divergent internal political and economic developments in the two states in the mid-1990s led to only the Czech Republic and not Slovakia joining NATO in its first eastern enlargement of March 1999 and being accepted for negotiations on EU accession in 1997.

However, amid all the divergent developments in the formerly communist part of Europe, changes within Western Europe should not be forgotten. While the former communist states have diverged in their paths of development, Western Europe has become more closely integrated. The role of the EU has increased as more west European states have joined. After the fourth EU enlargement of 1995, Switzerland and Norway remain the only major west European states outside the EU. In the south-east of the continent, Cyprus and Malta are negotiating accession, while Turkey – like Russia, a state geographically on Europe's dividing line – has applied for membership, but not yet been accepted into the accession process. Increasingly, therefore, the EU has come to embody the new Europe which is expanding into the east of Europe. It is the most multi-faceted of all international organizations, embracing not only democratic procedures and foreign and security policy, but also economic integration and legislative harmonization in a wide range of areas. Most importantly, it is the only European structure which has a profound effect on the intricacies of citizens' everyday lives in the member states (see Chapter 2).

The remainder of this chapter will look at the various dimensions of transition in Central and Eastern Europe largely in terms of both the transitions of the political, economic and social systems within formerly communist states and the redefining of the meaning of Europe. Crucially, too, the process of EU eastward enlargement tests the commitment of existing EU member states to creating the new Europe. Two major questions arise: are the CEECs ready for the EU, and is the EU ready for new members who for more than 40 years were part of a very different Europe? Since the focus of this chapter is developments in the CEECs, most attention will be paid to the first question. But before looking at these complex issues, it is useful to review how far the EU and the CEECs have progressed towards union on a formal level, and what membership criteria are being applied.

The stages of EU eastward enlargement

The revolutions of 1989 came to many as a surprise. Perhaps this should not have been the case. In Poland and Hungary, the most liberal of the Soviet bloc states, changes had been taking place gradually throughout the decade. They were given renewed impetus when Gorbachev came to power in the Soviet Union in 1985 and removed some of the external constraints that had previously restricted the room for manoeuvre of reform-minded communist leaderships. By the end of 1989, the Strasbourg European Council, reacting to reform in the CEECs as a whole, singled out Poland and Hungary when it created the PHARE programme, an acronym where the 'PH' reflected its intention to provide assistance to restructuring the economies of Poland and Hungary (Mayhew, 1998: 15). But the revolutionary events in the rest of the Soviet bloc had already overtaken this division of the CEECs into those who had embarked on a reform process and those whose leaderships were still locked into the thought patterns of Soviet orthodoxy. One very graphic illustration of the enormously rapid changes came on 29 December 1989, when the Czechoslovak Parliament elected Vaclav Havel, a renowned dissident who had been imprisoned by the regime earlier that year, as their state President. Even more dramatic – though less comforting from a democrat's viewpoint – had been the summary execution of the tyrant Ceaucescu in Romania four days previously. And on the streets of East Germany, the crowds whose protracted demonstrations against their oppressive rulers had led a hard-line but increasingly confused regime to open the Berlin Wall almost by accident on 9 November 1989 had already begun the call for German unification.

By the end of 1990, the European Community had adapted to what was now recognized as the total collapse of Soviet-style communism in the satellite states. The German Government had grasped the window of opportunity provided by Gorbachev and the capitulation to public protest of the East German communists, by welcoming the new *Länder* of the GDR into the Federal Republic of Germany on 3 October 1990. The first of the communist states had therefore joined the European Community through a process of self-dissolution. It was a unique form of enlargement never to be repeated. The East Germans gave up their state sovereignty in its entirety and gradually accepted westerners in leading positions in politics, the state and many professions; and in turn, the West Germans provided them with a level of financial and infrastructure support unimaginable in other enlargements. The welcome offered to the remaining post-communist states by the EC was far more modest. By September 1990, the PHARE programme had been extended to cover Bulgaria, Czechoslovakia, Romania, and also Yugoslavia, which by 1990 was carrying out multi-party elections in each of its constituent republics.

The relationship between the EC and the CEECs was gradually formalized. The trade and cooperation agreements signed with them from 1988 onwards were gradually replaced by the Europe Agreements, a special form of association agreement for post-communist states. These were signed first in December 1991 with Czechoslovakia, Hungary and Poland, the three states which had formed themselves in February 1991 into the Visegrad group, which aimed at regional cooperation as a means of achieving a 'return to Europe' (Hyde-Price, 1996: 122–31). Their selection for the first Europe Agreements reflected the common assumption of the period that these three (later, with the division of Czechoslovakia on 31 December 1992, four) central European states were the most natural candidates for EC membership. Europe Agreements were also signed with Bulgaria and Romania in early 1993 (Henderson, 1999: xviii).

The next major milestone in EU enlargement was the Copenhagen European Council of June 1993. Here, the decision in principle that the EU should enlarge eastwards was taken, as expressed in the Presidency conclusions:

> The European Council today agreed that the associated countries in Central and Eastern Europe that so desire shall become members of the European Union. Accession will take place as soon as an associated country is able to assume the obligations of membership by satisfying the economic and political conditions required.
>
> Membership requires that the candidate country has achieved stability of institutions guaranteeing democracy, the rule of law, human rights and respect for and protection of minorities, the existence of a functioning market economy as well as the capacity to cope with competitive pressure and market forces within the Union. Membership presupposes the candidate's ability to take on the obligations of membership including adherence to the aims of political, economic and monetary union.
>
> The Union's capacity to absorb new members, while maintaining the momentum of European integration, is also an important consideration in the general interest of both the Union and the candidate countries. (European Commission, 1993b: 13)

This declaration is quoted at length because it is the clearest single statement of the EU's two major caveats regarding enlargement. First, although it unambiguously states that accession of the CEECs shall take place, it relates this to the readiness of the applicants for membership. The conditionality of the offer of membership is made explicit in the three specific demands commonly known as the 'Copenhagen criteria'. These are political criteria, economic criteria and the ability to assume the obligations of membership (that is, adopting the *acquis communautaire* – the entire body of EU laws, regulations and agreements). The second caveat – that the Union should have the capacity to absorb new members – refers to the need of the EU to reform itself, both in terms of budgetary issues, and its structures of decision-making (see Chapters 2, 3). These are the two major themes that continued to underlie the dynamics of the accession process throughout the 1990s and which will endure into the new millennium.

Yet the shape of the new Europe continued to change for the rest of the decade. The EU's original focus on the Soviet satellites which had escaped Soviet dominance in 1989 gradually diminished. Two years after Copenhagen, in June 1995, Europe Agreements were signed with the three most advanced former Soviet republics, Estonia, Latvia and Lithuania, which had become independent in 1991, and also with Slovenia, the sole Yugoslav successor state to have escaped largely unscathed from the new Balkan wars. At the same time, one of the original front-running central European 'Visegrad four' candidates – the newly independent Slovak Republic – began to show alarming signs of diverging from the reform path it had formerly shared with its neighbours. Its Government began, from November 1994 onwards, to receive démarches from the EU about failings in its domestic democratic development (Henderson, 1999: 221–40).

On the more practical side of EU enlargement, the ten CEECs with Europe Agreements began formally to submit applications to join the EU, starting with Hungary in March 1994, and ending with Slovenia in June 1996. The EU, for its part, agreed a pre-accession strategy for applicant states at the Essen European Council meeting of December 1994 (European Commission, 1994b), and produced a White Paper on the integration of the CEECs into the internal market which was approved at the Cannes European Council meeting of June 1995 (European Commission, 1995b). In December 1995, the Madrid European Council session asked the European Commission to prepare its opinions (*avis*) on the CEECs' applications for membership.

The Commission's opinions on the CEECs, which were published as part of the more extensive *Agenda 2000* documents on the future of the Union in July 1997, were the next major turning point for the enlargement process (European Commission, 1997a). The Commission's opinions clearly split the ten post-communist applicants into two groups. It was recommended that accession negotiations should begin with five states, the Czech Republic, Estonia, Hungary, Poland and Slovenia, as these were considered capable within the short or medium term of fulfilling the 'Copenhagen criteria' (European Commission, 1997a: 57). Among the remaining five, Slovakia stood out as the only state rejected for failing to meet Copenhagen's political criteria relating to democratic development. This was important, because the principle was established whereby states had to fulfil the political criteria *before* negotiations commenced, whereas with the other criteria, it was sufficient if a country appeared able to satisfy them in the short to medium term (Henderson, 1999: 222–4). However, the Commission also stated that it would 'regularly report on progress to the European Council', and that the first of these reports would be submitted at the end of 1998 and then on an annual basis thereafter (European Commission, 1997a: 53). This effectively amounted to a statement that the Commission would update its opinions every year (Croft *et al.*, 1999: 60).

The Luxembourg European Council session of December 1997 largely concurred with the Commission's judgements. It decided that it would 'launch an accession process comprising the ten central and east European applicant states and Cyprus', and also that it would 'convene bilateral intergovernmental conferences in the spring of 1998 to begin negotiations with Cyprus, Hungary, Poland, Estonia, the Czech Republic and Slovenia on the conditions for their entry into the Union and the ensuing Treaty adjustments' (European Commission, 1997b: 9–10). Although the governments of the EU member states agreed with the Commission's selection of the first five CEECs eligible to negotiate EU accession, they did not wish to totally exclude the other CEECs from any chance of accession. The European Council had already concluded that accession negotiations with Cyprus should commence six months after the end of the Intergovernmental Conference, which finished in Amsterdam in July 1997. The total number of states beginning negotiations in 1998 was thus six, although the complications of Cyprus's status as a divided island were not underestimated.

However, in the course of 1998-99, two sets of developments substantially amended the possible scope of the future EU enlargements. The first related to developments within the candidate states. Among the first group of states which began negotiating membership at the end of March 1998, two states – the Czech Republic and Slovenia – began to lag behind the others in the transposition and application of the *acquis*. This was noted in the first 'progress reports' (that is, updates of the Commission opinions) issued in November 1998 (European Commission, 1998a). The same set of reports highlighted the particular progress and momentum of change made by Latvia, which, if maintained, would enable the Commission to propose the opening of negotiations before the end of 1999. Some favourable comments were also made about Lithuania, the other Baltic state which had remained outside the accession negotiations in which Estonia was included.

Perhaps more significant, however, were two elections in the autumn of 1998. The first took place in Malta in early September 1998, and returned a Government which immediately informed the EU Presidency that it wished to reactivate Malta's membership application, which the previous Maltese Government had suspended in October 1996. The European Commission duly presented a new, and favourable, opinion on Malta in February 1999 (EC Commission, 1999c), and the 'screening' process of its legislation started almost immediately. The second significant elections took place in Slovakia in late September 1998, when the participating parties agreed to make good the democratic failings of its predecessor, which had 'decoupled' Slovakia from the other three Visegrad states in fulfilling the country's aspirations to join the EU. The Commission's verdict on its success was initially delayed until the next progress report in October 1999, and then a decision was to be reached at the Helsinki European Council meeting in December 1999. The outcome is unknown at the time of writing.

The second set of developments related to far more tragic events. The three-month NATO campaign in Kosova and Serbia from March to June 1999, and the barbaric reprisals of Serbian forces against the Albanians of Kosova, shocked Europe to the core as approaching a million refugees poured over Kosova's borders into Macedonia, Albania, and also, to a lesser extent, Montenegro. This affected the EU's conception of the new Europe in two ways. Firstly, there was appreciation of the contribution made to NATO's efforts by the reform-minded governments of Bulgaria, Romania and Slovakia, whose countries had – unlike the Czech Republic, Hungary and Poland – been unwillingly excluded from the first round of NATO eastward enlargement in March 1999, and who had likewise been excluded from starting accession negotiations with the EU. Secondly, there was a heightened awareness of the fact that the stability of Europe as a whole depended on the cooperation of every single state in the continent. Whether as potential aggressors or as allies, all of them mattered.

The EU responded to Kosova in two ways. Firstly, it created the Stability Pact for South Eastern Europe in July 1999, which acknowledged that economic aid to every European state, and not just to the EU's candidate states, was of vital importance. Secondly, the second set of annual 'progress reports' issued in October 1999 strongly emphasized the inclusive nature of the EU's enlargement ambitions. The Commission recommended to the Helsinki European Council meeting in December 1999 that 'accession negotiations should be opened in 2000 with all candidate countries which meet the political criteria for membership and have proved to be ready to take the necessary measures to comply with the economic criteria (i.e. Bulgaria, Latvia, Lithuania, Malta, Romania and Slovakia) (EC Commission, 1999d: 28). It also recommended that Turkey, which had expressed its wish to be a candidate country, should 'now be considered as one', although negotiations could only be opened once the political criteria were met. Turkey was the thirteenth state, along with the ten CEECs and Cyprus and Malta, which had formally applied for EU membership, but received a negative opinion from the Commission in 1990 (Preston, 1997: 215). Finally, the Commission called for a 'wider vision on the relations with countries of the former Yugoslavia and Albania on one hand, and Russia, Ukraine, the Caucasus and Maghreb countries on the other' (European Commission, 1999b).

Amid this wider vision, however, two principles were upheld. The first was that established in the original 1997 Commission opinions on the CEECs, namely, that fulfilling the Copenhagen political criteria was a precondition for starting accession negotiations. While Latvia, Lithuania and now Slovakia were cleared unconditionally in terms of their readiness for negotiations, conditions were placed on Romania's starting accession negotiations regarding the situation of children in institutions. Conditions were also placed on Bulgaria, though these proved the exception to the rule, as they related to issues of nuclear safety (EC Commission, 1999a: 36). In the case of Turkey, specific reference was made to the issue of human rights, which was why there was no question of opening negotiations (EC Commission, 1999a: 11).

The second principle was that of differentiation, which had been increasingly articulated since the beginning of 1999. It was emphasized yet again that 'the EU must ensure that candidate countries fulfil all Copenhagen criteria before being admitted as member states to the EU'. However, the Commission simultaneously espoused the notion that each country should 'progress through the negotiations as quickly as is warranted by its own efforts to prepare for accession' (EC Commission, 1999d: 28). This was clearly intended to allow for the possibility that some of the 'first group' of candidates might fall behind – for example, the Czech Republic, which had received two negative progress reports in a row regarding its legal preparations (EC Commission, 1999d: 10–11) – while others in the second group might catch up and overtake them. In technical terms regarding preparation for accession, which involved negotiating individually with each country on 31 chapters of the EU's *acquis*, it was established that chapters would not, as hitherto with the first group of states, be opened at the same time for all countries (European Commission, 1999d: 28–30). The overriding principle was, ultimately, one of merit. The fate of each country lay in its own hands, and depended on its own achievements.

Finally, the Commission fudged the issue of specifying dates for accession. Hungary, the most ambitious, and the most advanced of the CEECs, had repeatedly stated its desire to accede to the EU by 2002. Yet the Commission only recommended that the European Council should 'commit itself to decide from 2002 on the accession of candidates that fulfil all necessary criteria' (European Commission, 1999d: 32). While it appreciated that dates were important targets for keeping up the momentum of preparations within the candidate countries, the EU had no intention of making premature and unrealistic promises.

Attitudes to EU enlargement in the CEECs

For the post-communist states of Central and Eastern Europe, joining the EU is simultaneously a foreign policy and a domestic policy goal. Both are deeply intertwined. On a foreign policy level, EU membership represents a guarantee of security. This implicitly encompasses military security, for although – unlike NATO – the EU is not a military organization, an EU member state is in practice unlikely to be subject to aggression by an outside power. The EU also offers a degree of economic security since it provides structural aid and access to the markets and other economic structures in the richest part of Europe. Finally, the EU provides a sense of full belonging to Europe, including the many everyday links between citizens and the freedom of travel so long sought by those living in the eastern part of Europe.

In short, EU membership will cement the break from the Soviet Union and the rupture from all the negative features of the communist system externally imposed from the East. It ensures that the CEECs will never be in danger of being dragged back by force into the Russian orbit. The foreign policy element of EU membership is therefore both practical and symbolic.

In terms of domestic policy, the goal of EU accession impinges on most areas of life, since EU legislation encompasses issues as diverse as the protection of minorities and anti-discrimination legislation, standards of environmental protection, border controls, judicial practice and a myriad of technical and economic regulations. The requirements of joining the Single Market, and later the Economic and Monetary Union, are immeasurably more demanding for states emerging from a communist system than for those involved in any previous enlargement. The prospect of EU accession also has an impact on the employment market. It makes the state-aided retention of obsolete industries with large labour forces impossible. At the same time, it radically increases the employment opportunities for those (relatively few) professionals with the legal training necessary to transpose, implement and enforce the *acquis*, and in general for anyone with sound knowledge of EU languages. It requires the over-sized, incompetent and poorly paid state bureaucracies to create – in times of economic hardship and strict budget restraints – the incentives necessary for recruiting and retaining high-calibre civil servants able to cope with the exigencies of EU legislation and adaptation processes. It also means that ordinary citizens, already reeling from effects of the changes in the economic system on their family life and the removal of the low-level but universal provision of all sorts of social and welfare benefits, are additionally adversely affected by the removal of massive state subsidies on heating, rent etc. Preparing for EU membership forces the pace of post-communist change by providing a model which can, and must, be followed.

In other words, EU accession is important for domestic politics not merely because preparation for membership changes the rules and regulations of everyday life, but also because these changes are part of the post-communist transformation to which many (but not all) citizens aspire.

In the CEECs, the strongest supporters of EU membership are usually the people who are most strongly in favour of rapid economic, political and social reform, rather than by those who are inspired by grander European notions of a united continent. A desire for EU membership implicitly entails a rejection of the communist past. Many publications in the CEECs about joining the EU concentrate not on the complexities of EU internal structures and the difficulties these present, but on the achievements of specific states which have been transformed into a normal European democracy with a market economy. When the CEECs talk about the EU, they talk primarily about themselves. The EU issue is an integral part of the domestic political debate, rather than just one contentious political issue among many.

For this reason, domestic political battles in the CEECs may yet impinge on the speed and sequencing of the EU's eastward enlargement. The least likely scenario is rejection of membership by a CEEC. It is improbable that any state will be forced to delay accession because, having successfully negotiated membership terms, it encounters a negative reaction when its government puts the issue to the citizens in a referendum. Indeed, the general willingness of the governments in the candidate states to agree that a referendum should be held prior to joining the EU reflects their confidence on this matter. This is most notable in the case of Czech and Slovak politicians who considered it acceptable to divide Czechoslovakia without seeking public consent, yet have no objections to a referendum on joining the EU.

Public opinion polls have, over many years, consistently shown majority support for EU membership in the CEECs. They also indicate that the EU enjoys greater popularity than NATO. The European Commission's *Central and Eastern Eurobarometer* survey showed that in late 1997, 60 per cent of citizens in the CEECs stated that they would vote in favour of EU membership and 8 per cent against, with the remainder undecided or not responding. The equivalent figures for NATO support were 52 per cent in favour and 10 per cent against (European Commission, 1998b). These averages are, admittedly, somewhat distorted by the fact the two states with the highest level of support for EU (and NATO) membership, Poland and Romania, are also the two largest, and together contain nearly 60 per cent of the entire population of Central and Eastern Europe. These are two very different countries, geographically, politically and economically, and their shared enthusiasm for European integration tends to suggest that Poles and Romanians are influenced less by positive objective assessments of the benefits of EU membership and more by their extremely negative experiences of the communist period. Over the decades, the Poles displayed the greatest distaste for and opposition to the communist regime, while Romania in the final years of Ceaucescu's rule suffered, after Hoxha's Albania, the most repressive and inhumane regime in communist Europe.

In other words, it is once again domestic attitudes to post-communist reform rather than specific aspects of EU membership which dominate public attitudes to enlargement in the CEECs. However, the most important fact about public opinion is that even in the least enthusiastic candidate state (which, in the 1998 *Eurobarometer*, was Estonia), there were two and a half times more supporters than opponents of EU membership. Domestic public opinion polls in most states tend to show somewhat lower support for the EU than the Commission's findings, but nonetheless the CEECs are firmly in favour of EU membership.

The reason for the high support for EU membership among citizens of the CEECs is the fundamental belief that there is no alternative because this is where they belong. When asked in the *Eurobarometer* surveys where the future of their country lies, the most common answer in each state is normally 'the European Union', with the major exception being a Romanian tendency to prefer the United States (European Commission, 1998b). The strength of their conviction about the future relates to CEEC understanding of the past: the EU is where they would have been *if* they had not been subjected to Soviet-style communism.

The compliance of the CEECs in trying to meet the complex demands of adopting the EU *acquis* in all its minute details is thus explained in part by the fact that it is viewed not as the *diktat* of an alien force, but as a useful model worth emulating in order to put themselves back on the correct path of development away from the retardation they suffered under their past Soviet invaders. Where political parties oppose EU membership, it is usually because they have a differing view of what their country would have been like without the communist experience. Like the Slavophiles in Russia, they believe that their country has specific characteristics which make it different from Western Europe.

EU enlargement could, therefore, be impeded if any candidate state returned to power a governing coalition which did not have as its goal the construction of a democracy conforming to a west European pattern. This risk is present most notably in Bulgaria, Romania and Slovakia, where the major opposing forces led until 1996 (Romania), 1997 (Bulgaria) and 1998 (Slovakia) governments which did not pursue democratic and economic reform policies meeting the approval of the Western democracies. It may be argued that in these cases, it is particularly important to expedite negotiations with the current reform-minded governments. Such a course of action on the EU side increases the likelihood that, if the opposition should return to power, the democratic conditionality of EU accession will constrain any new government's tendency to diverge substantially from a Western-oriented reform path.

The final area where the CEECs' domestic politics may delay EU enlargement relates to specific contentious issues in accession negotiations. The government of a candidate state may be encouraged to adopt a 'tough' stance – and thereby slow down negotiations – if public opinion on any point is strong enough to allow political capital to be gained, by either the government or the opposition, through resistance to the EU's demands. *Eurobarometer* research indicates that there is some social structuration to positive and negative views on the EU. 'Decision-makers' (in academia, journalism, local and central government, parliament, non-governmental organizations and the private sector) generally have a more positive image of the EU than ordinary citizens, mostly because fewer are undecided, and fewer are more negative. More importantly, there is a general perception that farmers and low income groups have least to gain from EU membership, and these groups show lower (though still relatively strong) support for joining the EU (European Commission, 1998b). Support for the EU is also highest among those demographic groups generally considered to be the 'winners' from the post-communist transformation, such as youth and the better educated. Economic arguments prevail in support for the EU, so negotiating points relating to economic benefits are likely to be the most sensitive areas of accession negotiations, particularly where political actors have to battle at election time for the votes of citizens in low income groups.

Besides the economic arguments, other issues such as the loss of national sovereignty also hold some sway in the CEECs. These are conspicuous in Poland, and also the Czech Republic (Kucia, 1999). The right of foreigners to buy property, for which candidate states may demand transitional periods, are also sensitive issues, particularly in states such as the Czech Republic and Slovenia, which have two prosperous EU member states as immediate neighbours. Questions of relations with non-EU neighbours, and whether they will require visas, also gain in prominence as the prospects of accession increase. Hungary is anxious about contact with the Hungarian minority in Romania (and in Slovakia if it does not join the EU at the same time as Hungary), whereas Poland is worried about trade links over its border with Belarus, and the effects on the democratization process in its eastern, post-Soviet neighbours as a whole if EU enlargement increases their sense of isolation. The three Baltic states face difficulties in their close mutual cooperation if they do not all join the EU at the same time. So far, debate on individual issues in the accession negotiations is most developed in Poland. This is significant because Poland is the largest of the candidate states. With a population of 38.7 million (European Commission, 1999d: 46), it is also the only CEEC which will belong, together with Germany, the UK, France, Italy and Spain, to the group of larger EU member states. Poland's very size, plus its tradition of national assertiveness maintained throughout the communist period, gives it the confidence to be a demanding negotiating partner. Yet it means that the effect of compromise on the EU side could have a greater, potentially negative, impact on the current member states after its accession than was the case in Estonia, with its 1.4 million population. As EU accession approaches, the debate on the 'devil in the detail' of the *acquis* is likely to become livelier in other states as well. Since each passing year gives the applicant states extra time to improve both their comparative standard of living and their bureaucratic capacity, the EU has no particular need to make concessions.

The communist legacy

The backwardness of the CEECs is due to a large extent to the communist legacy, which still weighs heavily on them. It is this which makes the forthcoming EU enlargements so very much more demanding than previous ones. The three Copenhagen criteria were framed with this in mind.

Political criteria

If one looks first at the political criteria, these require the stability of institutions guaranteeing democracy. This has now generally been mastered to the EU's satisfaction in all the CEECs, but it was a considerable challenge for states that have been democracies for barely a decade. Since the first democratic elections around 1990, many have changed either their electoral systems or the method by which they elect a president. All have rather unstable party systems, and in three cases – Bulgaria, Romania and Slovakia – the major opposition groupings in parliament are unlikely to be acceptable negotiating partners for the EU, notwithstanding the fact that their membership applications were submitted by these forces when in government in the mid-1990s. Slovakia was excluded from the first round of negotiations largely because a Government with dubious democratic commitment was still in power in July 1997, whereas their counterparts in Bulgaria and Romania had been ousted from power in the 12 months before. Yet the fact that all three governments accepted election defeats, thereby leading to the alternation in power which is the lifeblood of a functioning democracy, is a positive sign.

Citizens' rights – and the rule of law which upholds them – is a further EU criterion, and one that was virtually ignored in the communist period. In concrete terms, most attention on the EU side has been paid to 'respect for and protection of minorities'. This is problematic in the rather ethnically diverse eastern part of Europe, and the difficulty has been exacerbated by the communist tendency to espouse formal, 'quota', representation of minorities which did not – as in communist politics as a whole – allow for the articulation of genuine group interests.

While considerable progress has been made in the treatment of the well-organized Hungarian minorities in Slovakia and Romania, both of which are represented by ethnic parties able to enter government, two other minority problems remain: that of Russians in the Baltic states, and the Roma who are numerous throughout the region, but particularly in Bulgaria, the Czech Republic, Hungary, Romania and Slovakia, where estimates indicate that they comprise some 5 per cent of the population. The Baltic states face the challenge of coping with a Russian minority which was still part of the ruling imperial power in the early 1990s. This means that the Russians are only just coming to terms with their status as a minority, and the attendant need to learn a state language with almost no international utility at a time when the acquisition of a Western language is a notable career asset. Their status is also questionable in the eyes of the majority population because few of them have been settled in the newly independent states for much more than a generation. Dealing with the Roma community present in many states is complicated by the fact that they are frequently viewed as a social underclass rather than an ethnic group. They usually lack organized political representatives, and discrimination takes place on some basic levels as a disproportionate number of their children are segregated from the educational mainstream in 'special schools' designed for children with special needs. Adult Roma are, partly in consequence of this, strongly represented in the least skilled end of the labour market, where unemployment has hit hardest in the transformation period. Post-communist societies are unpractised in the sophisticated anti-discrimination measures necessary to counter such entrenched disadvantage (see Sfikas and Williams, 1999).

A further area of difficulty iies in ensuring that the rule of law relates to the judicial system. Almost all EU reports on the CEECs emphasize in particular the need for training judicial personnel from judges to court officials, and the excessive delays involved in court cases. This is an area which has been badly affected by post-communist transition in two respects. Firstly, judges are normally very senior lawyers who have completed both a lengthy legal training and extensive experience in legal practice. Yet in the CEECs, it is inevitable that most candidates fulfilling these criteria have been trained during the communist period, where ideological criteria played a particularly prominent role in selection and advancement because of the politically sensitive nature of the activity involved. The top echelons of the legal profession therefore experience particular difficulties in distancing themselves from the 'old structures' of the disgraced communist regimes. The second problem is that the mushrooming of independent economic activity in the post-communist period has opened up a wealth of previously non-existent employment opportunities for lawyers in the private sector, many of which pay significantly higher salaries than state employment. This further depletes the pool of talent from which the judiciary can recruit. Consequently, a government determined to improve the administration of justice in its country faces very substantial practical problems in implementing its goals.

A final political problem in the CEECs is corruption. This was endemic in the communist period, when public accountability and transparent, user-friendly administrative procedures were virtually unknown. Official corruption flourished also because not only the entire apparatus of government and administration but also most of the economy were in state hands. Citizens had little possibility of changing the political system or amending specific examples of flawed legislation, or of lobbying publicly to counter official abuses. Consequently, they were accustomed to seeking through friends and contact networks personal solutions to problems with the authorities. This is an old habit which dies hard. It is easier for citizens to seek an individual solution to their difficulties with officialdom rather than mobilizing independent voices in non-governmental organizations which can push for change of the system as a whole for the good of all. The lack of a 'civil society' in communist states has left a legacy which makes it hard to counter corruption.

Several other factors exacerbate this problem. As with the judiciary, the civil service is severely affected by competition from the newly-formed private economic sector in recruiting the most competent managerial personnel. The fact that the state pays lower salaries increases the danger that its employees will be tempted by bribes and presents from a populace which was accustomed to this practice under communism. The lack of civil service codes in many states also leaves the obligations of public servants unclear, and means that they are offered no particular advantages over private sector employees in terms of career structure or job security. Since, under communism, almost everyone was employed by the state, there was no clear definition of the role of those working for the state administration. Finally, the removal of much of the economy from the state sector into private ownership has quantitatively increased the rewards available via corrupt practices. Rather than granting small individual favours, state employees involved in the privatization process can channel millions (of whatever currency is involved) into the hands of friends, family and clients.

Economic criteria

The second set of Copenhagen criteria relate to the economy, and evaluate both whether a functioning market economy exists, and whether a candidate state has the 'capacity to withstand competitive pressure and market forces within the Union'. The first criterion relates largely to the achievements of the candidate states in restructuring the economy and establishing the structures and mechanisms for regulating a free market. Success depends largely on the political will of candidate states and on the level of dedication to reform. By October 1999, the Commission concluded that a functioning economy existed in the six countries with whom it was negotiating accession, as well as Malta and Latvia. In the near future, Lithuania and Slovakia may be added to this list (European Commission, 1999d: 18). The second part of the economic criteria looks at the strength and viability of each state's economy, and whether it is likely to benefit from, rather than be damaged by, incorporation into the EU's Single Market. It is highly significant that only Cyprus and Malta were given a clear bill of health in this regard in 1999 (European Commission, 1999d: 19).

The most fateful economic problem for the CEECs is their low standard of living. Real GDP per capita levels allowing for the variable cost of living within the EU member states and the candidate states ranged from 68 per cent of the EU average in Slovenia to a mere 23 per cent in Bulgaria in 1998 (European Commission, 1999d: 46). Standard of living remains one of the most sensitive indicators of a state's capacity for joining the EU. It measures the likelihood that civil servants will earn such low salaries that they will be tempted to take bribes; it measures the state's capacity to invest resources in the improvement of inadequate state and judicial administration; it measures the likelihood that mobile elements in the labour force would be motivated to move to the EU and work for what locally are low wages in order to better their position at home; and it also measures the likelihood that any EU funding offered will appear so attractive that it will fall foul to corrupt allocation via clientelistic networks rather than neutral, objective criteria.

Membership obligations

The third Copenhagen criterion relates to a candidate state's 'ability to take on the obligations of membership'. By the time the Commission issued its second set of progress reports in October 1999, it made explicit that the adoption of the *acquis* involved 'a process of transposition, implementation and enforcement' (European Commission, 1999d: 20). The earlier tendency within the candidate states had been to concentrate on the formal procedure of harmonizing their legislation with that of the EU. What was crucial, however, was not whether they had the right laws on their statute books, but rather whether they were able to implement them in everyday life, and take appropriate measures against violations of the new legislation.

The difference between transposition, implementation and enforcement of legislation was particularly important because of the way that communist systems had operated in their terminal, degenerate phase. Communist systems were highly regulated. Unfortunately, regulation had reached a point where actual implementation and enforcement in everyday life was completely impossible. Citizens were therefore accustomed, in their professional and private lives, to conspiring at all levels in a pretence that the formal activity required by the regime was happening, while, below the surface, they just got on with sorting out their lives in the best way possible. It was the form and not the content of structures that mattered to the authorities.

Furthermore, because communist systems were highly centralized, with all decisions emanating downwards from the communist party leadership, many post-communist states are still experiencing difficulties in restructuring their systems of regional and local government in a way that permits meaningful devolution of power from the capital. Until they do so, they will have problems functioning effectively as EU member states.

The difficulty in applying the EU *acquis* in the CEECs is therefore one of making sure that real activity, rather than the pseudo-activity of communist times, accompanies the harmonization of legislation to EU standards. The citizens of Central and Eastern Europe are only too accustomed to having alien structures of rule imposed on them, and are adept at quietly undermining such structures. A major task of preparing for EU enlargement is thus ensuring that, while the *acquis* comes from an external source, it is internalized by the new member states and transformed into a functioning system that meets the needs of citizens in a complex, modern society.

Specific concerns about the capability of the CEECs to fulfil the Copenhagen criteria are compounded by other weaknesses of post-communist societies. There is a lively debate in the current EU member states about the 'democratic deficit' within the Union, and the fact that its decision-making procedures lack the transparency and accountability to which citizens are accustomed in domestic politics (see Chapters 2–3, 6). The CEECs, being new and inexperienced democracies with often underdeveloped civil societies, are unlikely to contribute to the solution of this problem. Their citizens are still struggling to find effective means of control over their own elites, and are likely to feel an even greater sense of alienation from the massively complex structures of the EU.

The challenges for the EU

Amid the multifarious challenges which EU accession poses for the CEECs, one should not forget the practical difficulties which enlargement creates for the current member states. These were addressed in detail in *Agenda 2000* (European Commission, 1997a).

Some of the problems are economic. Of the CEECs, only Slovenia – the only applicant not to have suffered 40 years of Soviet domination – is managing to catch up with the poorest of the member states, and more than half the CEECs have large agricultural sectors. Consequently, reform of the EU's Structural Funds for poorer regions, and of the Common Agricultural Policy, which together consume more than three-quarters of the EU budget, are required before enlargement (Ardy, 1998; Croft *et al.*, 1999; Grabbe and Hughes, 1998).

Other problems are institutional. The EU's decision-making procedures are unwieldy with the current 15 members, and threaten total gridlock if the number of member states exceeds 20. The issues which need to be addressed here are numerous: the weighting of votes in the Council of Ministers; the number of Commissioners in the European Commission, and their distribution between large and small states; the feasibility of rotating the Presidency if there is a large number of smaller states; and the number of MEPs in the European Parliament (Avery and Cameron, 1998; Croft *et al.*, 1999). All of these involve complex negotiation of interests between the current member states and the European Parliament, all of whom have a veto on the accession of each new member.

Finally, eastward enlargement is a politically sensitive area in the current member states. Some of the most challenging issues that have to be dealt with in the accession negotiations correspond to what emerge as the most emotive topics in public opinion polls. These include the chapter in the negotiations on justice and home affairs, which embraces such subjects as border controls, asylum procedures and police cooperation, and also the question of mobility of labour and the transfer of jobs to countries which have lower production costs. The European Commission's annual *Eurobarometer* surveys show that the transfer of jobs, as well as and drug trafficking and organized crime, feature most prominently among citizens' fears about EU integration and enlargement (European Commission, 1999a). Unless the commitment towards reintegrating the once divided Europe, which has been shown by member states' governments, can be effectively transmitted to their citizens, the chances of each applicant state's accession encountering last minute delays are increased. Again, the fact that each member state can exercise a veto on enlargement is of key importance.

Conclusions and future perspectives

Considerable uncertainty exists on two points: when the next enlargement of the EU will take place, and which, and how many, applicant states will be included. In terms of dates, the only certainty is that it will take place after 2002, although it also seems likely that it will occur by 2006. In terms of states that will be included, the only reasonably certain candidate among the CEECs is Hungary, which has consistently figured as a 'leader in the field' from the late 1980s onwards. From 1998 onwards, its most likely 'partner' in a next wave of enlargement appears to be a non-CEEC state – Malta. The other non-CEEC in the accession process, Cyprus, is two years ahead of Malta in the accession negotiations, but remains controversial because of the refusal of the Turkish Cypriot community to participate in the process. Poland, which was Hungary's original partner in the PHARE programme in 1989, has retained the admiration of the West for its consistent and successful reform efforts and its progress in consolidating democracy, but nonetheless presents more problems than Hungary. It is the largest of the CEECs, representing nearly 37 per cent of the total population of all ten CEECs; it has a problematically large, vocal and mobilized agricultural sector; and, while overall support for EU membership is strong, there is a genuine political debate over the complex implications of accession negotiations. Estonia has made most remarkable strides in becoming a frontrunner for EU membership, but still retains disadvantages from the legacy of its Soviet past, both in terms of a low (but increasing) standard of living, and the complications of dealing with a sizeable Russian minority, many of whose members do not benefit from citizenship. Slovenia and the Czech Republic have the highest standard of living of the CEECs, but their governments have not always demonstrated urgency in adopting the legislative measures necessary for accession. Slovakia, Latvia and Lithuania are disadvantaged by not having commenced accession negotiations in 1998, while Bulgaria and Romania lag behind notably in most areas of concern to the EU. Hence while Hungary appears unlikely to lose its leading position among the CEECs, and Malta looks well placed to catch up in the accession process, a variety of factors could prejudice the chances of the other applicant states in fulfilling the 'necessary criteria' by 2002.

Yet behind all these uncertainties, some points are also clear. A political commitment to EU enlargement has been made both by the current members and by the applicants. It may be delayed by practical and political problems emanating from states in either the eastern or western halves of Europe. Yet the momentum towards enlargement is too great for it actually to be stopped. A mutually agreed decision to reintegrate Europe has been taken. The alternatives of *either* broadening the EU by taking on new members *or* deepening it by increasing political and economic harmonization between the current member states no longer exist. Both must take place at the same time. This poses an enormous challenge of great complexity. Yet highly developed procedures exist for meeting this challenge. The key question on integration is no longer 'whether', but rather 'when' and 'how'.

CHAPTER SEVENTEEN

The New Russia: from Cold War Strength to Post-Communist Weakness and Beyond

Christopher Williams

For most of the twentieth century, the Soviet threat was the main concern of the West. In the words of one famous American specialist, George Kennan, the West needed to 'contain the spread of Communism' (cited in Ashton, 1989: 60). Hatred of communism and fear of so-called 'Reds under the beds' was ingrained in Western consciousness. Russia was so strong and powerful that it required a firm Western response and a substantial military arsenal to keep communism at bay. For most of the Cold War period the West tried to deal with Russia's strength, but since 1992, the situation has dramatically changed, the West is now having to deal with Russia's weakness. The key questions which scholars have been trying to answer since the early 1990s are: What are the main economic, political and social features of the new Russia? What kind of Russia would fit into Europe? Is a strong or weak Russia preferable? What sort of relationship does the West want with Russia? What attitude should Russia have towards the newly independent states? Who has gained and who has lost most in the last decade? This chapter seeks to explore the changes which have swept Russia since the collapse of the USSR in December 1991 and will examine the main challenges facing the country almost a decade on.

However, in order to understand current events we need to be aware of the communist legacy and of the evolution of the West's attitude towards Russia.

East–West relations, 1917–1985

It is impossible to explore this topic in great depth here so suffice it to say that between the 1917 October Revolution and the major changes made during Gorbachev's policy of *glasnost* (openness) and reconstruction (*perestroika*) in the 1980s, Russia's relationship with the West was highly problematical. The West fiercely opposed Lenin's socialist regime and heavily criticized Stalin's policies (forced collectivization (of agriculture), rapid industrialization, the Great Terror (in which up to 30 million died), and the signing of the Nazi–Soviet Pact in August 1939). After Germany was defeated in the Second World War, the world rapidly became split into two hostile camps when, in 1947, the Cold War broke out, dividing East and West on different sides of the Iron Curtain. For almost the next 40 years, with only intermittent periods of détente, Russia and the West were adversaries – the West set up the NATO Alliance and the European Economic Community (later Union) and Russia responded by establishing the Warsaw Pact and the Council for Mutual Economic Assistance (Comecon). East–West conflict was the order of the day –

initially there was a major disagreement over Berlin (1947–48) and Korea (1950–53) then Russian tanks rolled into Hungary and Poland in 1956, Russia successfully divided Germany into two by building the Berlin Wall in 1961 and a Third World War nearly occurred between Russia and the USA over Cuba in 1962. Vietnam also was a constant US–Soviet problem. One of several brief periods of détente was shattered when Soviet tanks entered the streets of Prague in 1968. This was followed by the Soviet involvement in Afghanistan (1979–88) and by riots in Poland in 1970 and by the problems of 1979–80 when Solidarity pushed the communist leadership to its limits (Williams, C., 1992).

All these activities tended to reinforce the West's view that Russia was a threat and that the Soviet leadership was expansionist in orientation and simply wanted to spread communism worldwide. Russia's abuse of human rights at home and throughout Eastern Europe was widely condemned by the West, and serious strains on superpower relations resulted from the USSR's ideological competition with the USA in Africa, Asia and Latin America. Russia's relations with the West simply went from bad to worse. From the early 1960s onwards both sides were engaged first in a space then in a nuclear arms race, with each country believing the other to have aggressive, expansionist tendencies. By the early 1980s, the American President Ronald Reagan summed up the West's view by referring to the USSR as an 'Evil Empire'. A strong military stance against Russia was deemed essential by the West as a nuclear deterrent and to prevent an all-out Third World War. The USA, under Reagan, set out to break the Soviet economy, and with it the USSR, by accelerating the arms race and introducing the Star Wars (or Strategic Defence) Initiative in 1983.

The impact of Gorbachev, 1985–1991

Fortunately, Mikhail Gorbachev came to power in March 1985. Gorbachev opened up Russia to the West by abandoning central planning and introducing the basic features of the market; abolished the Communist Party monopoly on power by implementing multi-party elections; withdrew Soviet troops from Afghanistan; called for an end to the arms race; did not intervene in the 1989 revolutions throughout Eastern Europe; and finally secured the end of the Cold War. Thus in a mere five years, Gorbachev had transformed the West's view of Russia. Even past arch-enemies of Russia, such as the former British Prime Minister, Margaret Thatcher, declared that she 'could do business' with Gorbachev. Gorbachev's reforms were widely applauded abroad, with chants of 'Gorby', 'Gorby' being frequently heard as he toured the major capitals of Europe from the mid- to late 1980s. However, the reaction to him at home was hostile. Many political and economic leaders, as well as members of the general public, thought that he had attempted too much, too soon (see Brown, 1997). Hard-line communist opposition also remained entrenched within key sections of the CPSU (Communist Party of the Soviet Union) and many thought that Russia was simply not ready to become 'like the West'. In August 1991, resentment towards Gorbachev and his policies, which had destabilized society, economy and polity, and meant that Russia was no longer in a position to put up a fight against the West, reached its peak and a coup d'état occurred (Dunlop, 1999). Although this coup failed, it only postponed the inevitable.

On 25 December 1991, the USSR finally collapsed and power in the Kremlin was passed from Gorbachev to Yeltsin.

The Yeltsin era, 1992–1999

The world changed dramatically in the 1990s. The American feeling of decline which was so prevalent in the 1960s and 1970s now gave way to a more confident, optimistic stance in the 1980s and 1990s in the aftermath of US victory over communism and in the Gulf War. Russia, meanwhile, had gone from strength to weakness as a result of the end of the Cold War and the collapse of communism. However, the end of the old bipolar world had also led to the emergence of an unclear new world order. In the early to mid-1990s, it seemed as if Western liberal democracy had triumphed as a role model and would spread quickly throughout the ex-USSR, thereby guaranteeing long-term peace and stability; but by the late 1990s the situation was markedly different. Whereas the West, especially America, was growing stronger and stronger, Russia had made an unsuccessful transition to liberal democracy. The key question now was: do Russia and the West have anything to fear from one another?

The re-emergence of mutual suspicions

In the past, Western fears regarding Russia focused on its perceived *strength*. Nearly 85 years after the 1917 October Revolution, this situation has dramatically changed. Now the West sees Russia as *too weak*; while Russia views the West as domineering. The West is now paying the 'price of victory', in so far as an unbalanced and destabilized Russia could have an adverse impact of the new world order and on East–West relations well into the twenty-first century. First we shall look at Western fears of Russia before examining the impact of Western policies on post-communist Russia.

Western fears

Western anxieties centre on the following issues: economic difficulties, political instability, ethnic conflict, terrorism, the nuclear threat, the rise of the mafia and what might happen after Yeltsin.

Economic collapse

Russia has been embarking on market reforms since the mid-1980s. This issue will be explored in the following chapter by Peter Anderson, so mention will only be made here of the fact that although many gains have been made since 1992 (the improved availability of a wide range of consumer goods; an increase in private investment (produced by easing restrictions on the size of land-holdings, on the percentage of foreign ownership in local firms and on the repatriation of profits); a thriving private sector (which consists of a mix of kiosk capitalism and large department stores); a decline in black market activity and currency speculation; falling inflation (from 900 per cent in 1992 to around 100 per cent by 1999) and the emergence of a small affluent business class), such progress has been achieved at great cost. At the time of writing, Russia's transition to the market economy seems by and large to have failed.

Russia's GNP has been in decline since 1989 (and fallen by around 47 per cent in the last decade of the twentieth century), production has plummeted, trade with the East (largely due to a lost East European export market) and the West is minimal, local industries are still adversely affected by a weak domestic market, enterprise closures have led to rising unemployment (currently at around 13 per cent of the economically active population) and Russia has a huge budget deficit. High interest rates (around 5 per cent per month) threaten Russia's ability to service its external debt (13 per cent of Federal expenditure), many people do not get paid, over one in three Russians are living below the poverty line and Russia has accumulated huge debts at home (US$60–80 billion) and abroad (around US$120 billion). In August 1998, the bubble finally burst. Russia was forced to devalue the rouble, the banking system collapsed, inflation skyrocketed, imports fell, output declined still further and most of society was badly affected. It was not so much that Russia now consisted of a society of 'rich' and 'poor', it was largely composed of 'have-nots' (see Table 17.1). According to EBRD (European Bank for Reconstruction and Development) transition indicator scores, Russia is rated around 2.5 out of 4 and therefore is only at the halfway stage (Wolf, 1999: 11).

From a Western point of view, the fear was 'contagion', namely that Russia's economic collapse might have *knock-on effects elsewhere*, either throughout the newly independent states, where this might threaten their economic integration, or in the West. Thus on the top of similar recent crises in Japan and Asia, the situation in Russia might make the international economic situation even more fragile. Finally, it was felt that this situation might derail Russia's experiment with the market. Most of these Western fears were not realized. Contagion was minimal. Poland and the Czech Republic, for instance, were able to ride out the crisis (largely because they were within the EU orbit), but in some cases (the Czech Republic), economic transformation did start to go wrong, but not for contagion reasons (Blazcya, 1999; Myant, 1999).

The declining economic conditions of the new Russia mean that it is likely to seek massive Western financial support to keep its economy afloat. Western anxiety about Russia's huge nuclear arsenal means that, despite recent financial scandals regarding aid and the ongoing Chechen war, such support is likely to be forthcoming, although not necessarily at the level Russia desires.

We shall explore the Russian perception of this situation below, so suffice it to say here that in Russia's eyes, its growing economic weakness and the prolonged recession, which is deepening as I write, together with a feeling that the West must share part of the blame for Russia's plight, is not likely to be quickly forgotten. Neither are growing Russian concerns about Western hegemony and economic power. A commonly held view in Moscow nowadays is that the West has won the Cold Peace, but only at Russia's expense.

Political instability

The second area of Western concern centres on Russia's political instability.

For most of the communist era, 1917–90, the Communist Party (CPSU) was very strong and enjoyed supremacy over state bodies in policy-making via the *nomenklatura* and the principle of democratic centralism. However, by the time Gorbachev took over power in 1985 political inertia was widespread and a major overhaul of the Russian political system was necessary. In spring 1990, Gorbachev abolished Article 6 of the 1977 Constitution granting the CPSU a leading and guiding role in Soviet society. This, on top of multi-party elections, significantly undermined CPSU hegemony. Gorbachev eventually created a USSR Presidency and was sworn in on 15 March 1990. Although these moves failed to solve Russia's problems, Yeltsin survived and was elected Russia's first President. On the eve of collapse in 1991, Russia was described as a ship sailing into the Bermuda Triangle. Since the political changeover, little has changed.

Table 17.1 Economic trends in Russia, 1991–1999

Indicator	*1991*	*1992*	*1993*	*1994*	*1995*	*1996*	*1997*	*1998*	*1999 (est.)*
Population (millions)	148.3	148.3	148.7	148.4	148.3	148.0	147.5	147.1	146.3[d]
No. of unemployed (as % of economically active population)[c]	—	3.59	3.95	5.43	6.41	8.9	9.3	11.0	12.4[d]
Real GDP growth (annual % change)	–5.0	–15.0	–8.5	–12.5	–4.1	–4.9	0.2	–4.8	3[f]
Wage arrears (as % of GDP)	80.9	1,094	978.5	368.0	184.3	20	26	28[b]	n.a.
External debt (billion $)	67.0	77.7	83.7	93.4	96.2	98.8	n.a.	250[b]	n.a.
Inflation (in % against previous year)	92.7	1,353	896	302	132	22	11	80	36
Budget deficit (as % of GDP)	2.9	3.0	5.0	9.9	2.8[d]	n.a.	n.a.	4.7[a]	3.2[d]
Number living below official poverty line (% of population)	n.a.	33.5	31.5	22.4	24.7	22.0	20.8	21.2	38.0[e]

Notes:

[a] Third quarter of 1998 over same period of 1997
[b] By late August 1998
[c] International Labour Organization definition
[d] January 1999 figure
[e] IMF forecast
[f] Russian Economic Trends/IMF forecast for 1999
n.a. Data not available

Sources:

Williams, Chuprov and Staroverov (1996), pp. 13–14; *Rossiya v Tsifrakh* 1998 (Goskomstat: Russia, Moscow, 1998), p. 25; 47, 79; *Economic Survey of Europe No.1 1998* (United Nations, New York, 1998), p. 46; *World Economic Outlook, May 1998* (IMF, Washington, DC, 1998), p. 34; A. Browne, 'Real straws that broke the Russian bear's back', *The Observer*, 23 August 1998, p. 4; M. Wolf *et al.*, 'Meltdown', *Financial Times*, 28 August 1998, p. 15; J. Grant, 'Moscow claims debtors owe it $148bn', *Financial Times*, 28 August 1998, p. 3; Vienna Institute for International Economic Studies, June 1998 Review on CEE region; C. Piggott, 'Bankers shore up their assets', *The European*, 31 August–5 September 1998, p. 10 *Statisticheskoe obozreniye* No.1 (28) 1999, pp. 7, 9, 16; J. Thornhill, 'Should we support Primakov?', *Financial Times*, 23 March 1999, p. 25; *Financial Times Russia Survey*, 30 April 1999, p. 11; *Ekonomicheskoe razvitiye Rossii* 6(3), (1999), pp. 5, 7, 10; M. Ellman, 'The Russian economy under Yeltsin', unpublished paper presented to the BASEES annual conference, Cambridge, 1–3 April 2000, pp. 6–7.

For the sake of simplicity, the post-communist period can be split into five stages: the first phase (January 1992–September 1993) witnessed the emergence of a Presidential Republic and the start of executive-legislative conflict; the second phase (December 1993–December 1995) saw the election of a new Parliament dominated by Yeltsin's opponents (especially the LDPR); the third phase (December 1995–June 1996) saw the rise of a new Parliament dominated by the CPRF together with Yeltsin's re-election as President; the fourth phase (July 1996–December 1999) saw the appointment and dismissal of five different PMs (Chernomyrdin, Kiriyenko, Primakov, Stepashin and Putin), the election of a largely pro-government Duma and Yeltsin's resignation as Russian President on 31 December 1999; and finally, the current phase (1 January 2000 onwards) saw Putin nominated as Acting President trying to end the war in Chechnya and to fight a successful presidential campaign.

Owing to space constraints, it is only possible here to highlight some of the key aspects and reasons for Russia's political instability. Firstly, Russia did not resolve its constitutional crisis. Secondly, this led to a dual power situation between Parliament and President. Thirdly, the constant shift in PMs, governments and bickering between the President (executive) and the parliament (legislature), brought Russia to the brink of disaster which culminated in the bloody events of October 1993 when Yeltsin used tanks to fire on his own White House. As a result, 145 people were killed and 733 wounded. Fourthly, although a new heavily amended constitution was put in place by referendum in December 1993, making Yeltsin a Gaullist type of President, this was followed by another disaster in the same month, when Yeltsin and the centrists suffered a major defeat at the hands of Zhirinovsky's Liberal Democrats in the 1993 parliamentary elections (see McFaul, 1994; Colton and Hough, 1998). Thus only 92 out of the 450 Duma members were supporters of Yeltsin and 56 out of the 172 elected to the Council of the Federation opposed Yeltsin's reforms (*Megapolis Ekspress*, 5 January 1994). Although this result sent shockwaves throughout Russia and the West, and Russia's reform-minded President suffered a number of setbacks (hence Yeltsin was unable to mobilize sufficient resources or the political will to counteract Duma attempts to block major economic and political decisions, such as the President's reform programme, changes to the Federal Budget, etc.), the new Russian political system was nevertheless adaptable and flexible enough to survive, largely because Yeltsin 'ruled by decree' (*Moskovskie Novosti*, 24–31 July 1994: 7). Fifthly, on top of this, Russia invaded Chechnya on 11 December 1994, lost and was forced to enact a Peace Settlement (via General Lebed) before the presidential election of 1996. (On the Chechen crisis, see Lieven, 1999.) The long-term outcome was greater attention devoted to the Near Abroad in Russian foreign policy and the launch of a second Chechen offensive in 1998–99. Sixthly, on 17 December 1995, Russia's second democratic elections to the Federal Assembly took place (see Belin with Clem, 1997). On this occasion, Yeltsin and the centrists suffered their second major defeat of the post-communist era, at the hands of Zyuganov's Communist Party, which received 22.3 per cent of the vote, followed by Zhirinovsky's LDPR, which got 11.1 per cent, Chernomyrdin's Our Home Is Russia, which gained 9.7 per cent, and finally, Yabloko, led by Yavlinsky, which received 7 per cent of the vote. Seventh, despite an ongoing war with Chechnya, growing discontent with Yeltsin's policies (see below), widespread concern about Russia's political inertia, serious economic instability, corruption, rising crime, declining living standards and so forth, leading some commentators to refer to Russia as a 'soft state' (Remington, 1997: 110), Yeltsin still managed to get re-elected in the summer of 1996 (see Hough, Davidhesier and Lehman, 1996; McFaul, 1997), as Table 17. 2 shows.

However, from the summer of 1996 until his resignation at the end of December 1999, Yeltsin's support was being gradually eroded due to widespread government scandals and accusations of corruption within the Yeltsin camp and even in Yeltsin's own family; Yeltsin's failure (through his government) to address Russia's main problems; his inability to combat organized crime (see below); and above all, by the 68-year-old's inability, due to ill health, to put Russia firmly back on track. Under Yeltsin, Russia's political system lacked the dynamism and innovation it needed to forge ahead, and the frequent shifts of personnel, many of whom were dismissed because they had allegedly failed to deliver but in actual fact were also seen as a threat to Yeltsin (thus the former PM, Primakov was seen as 'too presidential'), did very little to avert Russia's deepening economic and social crisis (see Nichols, 1999).

Table 17.2 1996 Russian presidential election results (percentage of overall valid vote)

Candidate	*First round, 16 June 1996*[a]	*Second round, 3 July 1996*[b]
Boris Yeltsin	35.3	53.8
Gennady Zyuganov	32.0	40.3
Alexander Lebed	14.5	n.a.
Grigory Yavlinsky	7.3	n.a.
Vladimir Zhirinovsky	5.7	n.a.

Notes:
[a] total valid vote 68.7 per cent
[b] total valid vote 68.8 per cent
n.a. not applicable.

Source: Adapted from *Vybory Prezidenta Rossiiskoi Federatsii. 1996. Elektoral'naya statistika* (Moscow: Ves'mir, 1996), pp. 128, 130.

The August–September 1998 crisis was a turning point. It meant that the new (rich) Russians (oligarchs) who have financed Russia's market transition for the last few years, suffered major financial losses. This had an adverse effect on Russia's political situation: firstly, by generating greater rivalry between Russian political elites (centred around the President and his rivals) and secondly, by contributing to the rise of regional elites in the Yeltsin era. However, it did little to correct what Thomas E. Graham calls Russia's 'weak centre – weak regions' syndrome (Graham, 1999: 5).

On top of economic crisis and political instability, the West has several other concerns about Russia.

Ethnic conflict, terrorism and the nuclear threat

One of the positive outcomes during the Cold War and the Arms Race, leaving aside the Berlin crisis of 1948 and the Cuban missile crisis of 1962, was a sense of relative stability, safety and security in the West because the danger of accidental war was minimal. In the East too, the same applied, although there was a greater degree of repression. Since the collapse of the Soviet Empire and the Warsaw Pact in the late 1980s, Russia itself, and especially its military, has been in a state of decay and disintegration. The Chechnya fiasco, 1994–96, was a symptom of a much bigger crisis in which soldiers and officers are demoralized, poorly paid, under-resourced and badly neglected.

However, the recent Chechen war of 1999 is important in three respects: firstly, because some ground has been recovered by the Russian military since the 1994–96 offensive; secondly, the war increased Russian tension with the West over its handling of the Chechens; and finally, the Chechen war overshadowed and strongly influenced the outcome of December 1999 parliamentary elections. For all these reasons, a brief discussion of the Chechen situation is essential.

The reasons for Russia's war with Chechnya remain largely unchanged from those in 1994–96, namely to reduce opposition to Russia in Chechnya, fear of the mafia, the desire to protect pipelines in the Black/Caspian Sea region, fear of Islam and the need to defend Russians living in the area and finally to prevent ethnic conflict spreading to other parts of the North Caucasus (see Menon and Fuller, 2000). The difference this time is that Putin has been more decisive than Yeltsin and public opinion has also been on his side. Thus recent surveys suggest that 48 per cent of Russians feel that Russia's actions were 'severe and decisive enough' whereas 29 per cent thought they were not so. Only 7 per cent thought the Russian response was 'too severe and hurried' (VTsIOM survey of 5–9 November 1999 cited at www.russiavotes.org/Duma_cur). Although 61 per cent of those surveyed thought that Chechens were 'getting what they deserved' and that the mission had been a success; 51 per cent were convinced that Russian actions in Chechnya in 1999 had been humane (VTsIOM survey of 5–9 November 1999 cited at www.russiavotes.org/Duma_cur). What Russians disliked most was Western criticism of its actions. Although 13 per cent of Russians appreciated that the West was simply trying to protect human rights and prevent further bloodshed, 20 per cent thought that the West misunderstood the 'real situation in Chechnya' and a further 46 per cent saw the West's reaction as an attempt to 'interfere in Russia's internal affairs' and to 'weaken Russia' (VTsIOM survey of 5–9 November 1999 cited at www.russiavotes.org/Duma_cur) Putin has largely ignored Western criticisms of his actions.

In addition, the fact that we have witnessed the erosion of political authority and state order, and the rise of ultra-nationalism, is also of great concern (Hanson and Williams, C., 1999; Williams C. and Sfikas, 1999), but there are other more serious dangers, namely ethnic conflict (especially in the Caucasus), terrorism (as the spate of bombings in Russia over the last few years and in particular in September 1999 show) and the potential misuse of nuclear weapons. These are all likely to add to Western fear of Russia now and in the future. However, providing all of this did not result in key parts of the nuclear command falling into the hands of extremists, the chances of any future wars between the West and Russia appeared to be minimal.

The West could, given Russia's recent resumption of war with Chechnya and its violation of their human rights, choose not to continue throwing good money after bad and stop providing Russia with funds. However, the West is likely to continue bailing Russia out in the immediate future for a number of reasons. Firstly, if Russia becomes an insolvent debtor, this will leave the IMF in trouble and secondly, perhaps most importantly, is the fact that Russia has 30,000 nuclear warheads, so it would be unwise for the West to turn its back on Russia, as an increasingly unstable Russia might lead to nuclear Armageddon. For this reason alone, the USA is likely to apply pressure on the IMF and other international organizations to continue granting loans to Russia. After all, the IMF alone has lent over $20 billion to Russia since 1992 (*The Economist*, 28 August 1999: 17). In fact on 30 March 1999, the IMF pledged US$1.4 billion to ensure that Russia did not go from crisis to catastrophe and a further $4.5 billion was agreed in August 1999 (*The Economist*, 28 August 1999: 18). Finally, the West is keen to keep Russia on the road to reform, as this is crucial to the maintenance of the Washington consensus and to the success of the new post-Cold War order.

Russia's mafia capitalism

On top of the above fears, Russia has gone from being a monolith dominated by the Communist Party to a country dominated by the (Red) mafia (see Vaksberg, 1991; Gurov, 1992, 1995; Handelman, 1994). This is due to Russia's past history of political corruption, the existence of a second (black) economy and the fact that criminal elements have already penetrated the Russian business sector. With the collapse of the Soviet system, the mafia has filled many of the resulting gaps. For all these reasons, contemporary Russia is now frequently compared to Chicago in the 1920s or to Sicily. Russia's organized criminals, like their Western counterparts, control prostitution, drugs, gambling, arms and also nuclear weapons. There are an estimated 9000 criminal gangs in Russia today. According to Russian estimates, criminal groups invest about 80 per cent of their money in legitimate businesses, control 25 per cent of the banks and 40 per cent of Russia's GNP. The state is powerless to stop them. The police (*milisia*) is overstretched, underpaid or corrupt because an estimated 90 per cent of Russian officials are said to be 'on the take'. As a result, one in four crimes remain unsolved (Ilynsky, 1996: 224–5). The August 1999 Bank of New York/Russian mafia money laundering scandal is only the tip of the Russian organized crime iceberg which extends across the globe. All in all, the future looks bleak and an expansion in the size and power of the mafia looks likely.

This, coupled with all the factors outlined earlier, is likely to mean that Western anxiety about the new Russia is here to stay for many years yet because the Cold Peace was short-lived. Therefore, the West may have won a few battles, but there are many more to come and the war between Russia and the West is far from over.

The end of the Yeltsin era and Putin's ascendency

Three other key issues – Yeltsin's resignation, Putin's rise to power, and the outcome of Russia's third parliamentary elections on 19 December 1999 – have dominated the Russian scene since the end of 1999.

Yeltsin's resignation

One of the biggest shocks was Boris Yeltsin's resignation on 31 December 1999. He stated that in the twenty-first century 'Russia needed new politicians and new faces' (Powell, 2000: 51). Yeltsin acknowledged the existence of many of the problems that are highlighted in this and the following chapter and asked Russian citizens for their 'forgiveness', because in Yeltsin's words 'our hopes have not come true, because what we thought would be easy turned out to be painfully difficult' (cited in Powell, 2000: 51). Yeltsin said he was pleased with the results of the December 1999 elections and felt that as 'Russia will never return to the past [and] will always be moving forward ... I must not stand in its way' (cited in Delahaye, 2000: 53). After eight years' rule, Yeltsin had left Russia in ruins. His leadership style was ambiguous, aggressive and based on his extended family circle and on the prominence of oligarchs. Yeltsin was only galvanized into action by one crisis after another (Sakwa, 1999). Early January 2000 VTsIOM public opinion poll surveys pointed to the following benefits of Yeltsin's rule: political freedom, no shortgages, restoring private property rights and ending communist rule; but these were more than offset by the following 'bad rights' resulting from Yeltsin's tenure: rising unemployment, economic decline, war in Chechnya, declining standard of living, organized crime, the collapse of the welfare state and loss of 'great power status' (VTsIOM survey of 8–10 January 2000 cited at www.RussiaVotes.org/Yeltsin).

Russia hoped that Yeltsin's replacement would be better able to govern Russia and to introduced more decisive policies to tackle Russia's ills (see Sakwa, 1999).

The new acting President – Putin

Vladimir Putin's rise to power has been astronomically rapid. The 47-year-old law graduate and ex-KGB Lt Colonel was born in St Petersburg in 1952. From 1990 to 1996, he worked with the late St Petersburg Mayor, Sobchak, before being transferred to Moscow in 1996–97 to work in the Presidential Administration. In July 1998, he was Director of the Federal Security Service (FSB, the successor of the KGB) before being made PM in August 1999. Yeltsin subsequently nominated Putin as his chosen successor until the new elections on 26 March 2000 (for more see *Ot Pervogo Litsa*, 2000, published in Moscow; Toomey, 2000 and Traynor, 2000). Since September 1999, Putin has edged ahead of all others in the popularity stakes. Thus only 5 per cent of voters favoured Putin in September but by December 1999, this figure had reached 51 per cent, well ahead of other candidates, such as Zyuganov (19 per cent), Primakov (9 per cent) and other Presidential hopefuls (whose support ranged from 2 to 5 per cent) (December 1999 VTsIOM pre-Duma result survey cited at www.russiavotes.org/Duma_cur).

Putin's popularity can be attributed to his strong stance on terrorism and Chechnya and on his ability to withstand criticism within Russia (for his bloodthirsty tactics, Napoleonic tendencies, etc.) as well as from the West (who are demanding a more humanitarian approach on the refugees wishing to flee the conflict zone). He has also tapped into Russian anxieties at a time of great uncertainty. As *Nezavisimaya Gazeta* put it: 'Russia has grown tired of reforms and longs for a bit of stagnation' (*Nezavisimaya Gazeta*, 28 October 1999). Although *Sevodnya* portrayed Putin as the new Iron Man of Russia, *Obshchaya Gazeta* was more accurate in attributing his appeal to a desire for 'efficient and competent authorities' capable of dealing with ethnic conflicts or economic problems (*Sevodnya*, 11 November 1999; *Obshchaya Gazeta*, 12 November 1999). In this respect, *Izvestiya* pointed out that: 'Putin promises realistic things; fulfils his promises and accepts full responsibility for the consequences' (*Izvestiya*, 13 November 1999). While these qualities are recognized by the electorate and across the political spectrum, Russians are still very concerned about increasing anarchy (62 per cent), the poor development of democracy (9 per cent), dictatorship tendencies (6 per cent) as well as inflation, low standards of living, jobs, no social guarantees, rising crime, corruption and terrorism. On the positive side, however, 24 per cent of those surveyed had 'no grievance' against Putin and his government. (See Table 17. 3.)

Table 17.3 Assessments of the Government's handling of Russia's ills under Putin's leadership, November 1999 (survey of 1600 respondents, 5–9 November 1999)

Problem not addressed	*Percentage of respondents highlighting this issue*
Inflation, declining incomes	25
Economic crisis, falling production	20
Jobs	18
Social protection	16
No solution to current crisis	14
Rising crime	14
Security or terrorism	10
Corruption	3
Acts in own interests	3
Acts in mafia's interests	2
Acts in interests of foreign capital	2
Other	3

Source: Adapted from VTsIOM survey cited at www.russiavotes.org/Duma_cur.

The December 1999 parliamentary elections

The current political landscape in Russia is rapidly changing. The eventual results for all the political parties making it past the 5 per cent threshold in the December 1999 parliamentary elections are given in Table 17.4.

The biggest surprises are the narrow Communist Party of the Russian Federation (CPRF) victory, the excellent performance of the pro-government party, Unity, which had only been in existence three months, together with that of the Union of Right Forces (SPS), and the relatively poor showing of Fatherland All-Russia (OVR). The success of Unity and the SPS can be largely attributed to Putin's backing. Furthermore because OVR was viewed by the Yeltsin camp as the new opposition instead of the CPRF, the Government launched a dirty tricks campaign, especially on ORT (Russian public television), against Luzhkov, and it seems to have worked well. The Zhirinovsky bloc and Yabloko seem to have held onto their voters, but the biggest loser in comparison to 1995 is Viktor Chernomyrdin's party Our Home is Russia, which seems to have virtually disappeared from the Russian political map. The overall outcome means that representatives of centrist and pro-reform parties now outnumber the old (CPRF) and new (OVR) opposition.

Table 17.4 Results of elections to Russian State Duma, 19 December 1999

Parties above 5% barrier	*Party leader*	*% of total vote*	*Seats in State Duma (out of possible 450)*		
			Party lists	*Single mandate districts*	*Total*
Communist Party of the Russian Federation (CPRF)	Gennady Zyuganov	24.29	67	48	113
Unity	Sergei Shoygu	23.32	64	8	72
Fatherland All-Russia (OVR)	Yevgeny Primakov, Yuri Luzhkov, Vladimir Yakovlev	13.33	37	30	67
Union of Right Forces (SPS)	Sergei Kirienko	8.52	24	5	29
Yabloko	Grigory Yavlinsky	5.93	17	4	21
Zhirinovsky bloc	Vladimir Zhirinovsky	5.98	16	1	17

Sources: Central Electoral Commission data, 29 December 1999 cited in *Novye Izvestiya*, 30 December 1999, p. 2; *Nezavisimaya Gazeta*, 30 December 1999, p. 1; *Sevodnya*, 30 December 1999, p. 2; *Izvestiya*, 30 December 1999, p. 3.

The most important legislation to be debated in the new Duma, when it resumes in mid-January 2000, includes land reform, the size and nature of the Army (including the possibility of making defence enterprises bankrupt), privatization, ratification of START-2 and new tax laws. *Nezavisimaya Gazeta* argues that the December 1999 election results mark Russia's 'awakening from hibernation' and it views the emergence of a new Duma loyal to the government as boosting the prospects for greater cooperation between the future President and his new Parliament on these and other issues (*Nezavisimaya Gazeta*, 23 December 1999). These election results also signalled that Putin won the first stage of the presidential campaign.

The March 2000 Russian presidential elections

What Russians wanted from the new President was stability (50 per cent), law and order (42 per cent), a decent life (31 per cent), social protection (22 per cent), equality and fairness (14 per cent) and wealth and prosperity (18 per cent). The creation of a powerful state (28 per cent) and the overall rebirth of a strong Russia (26 per cent) is seen as vital to Russia's future prospects. (VTsIOM survey of March 1999 cited at www.russiavotes.org/Duma_cur.) The person most favoured in Russian public opinion polls to restore order in Russia is Putin. As one pollster put it recently: 'Putin has given the Russians a chance to start shrugging off their inferiority complexes, a chance to begin to feel better about themselves' (cited in Franchetti, 2000: 22). This view is backed by a November 1999 VTsIOM poll, as shown in Table 17.5.

Table 17.5 Who can restore order in contemporary Russia?

Question	*Answer (per cent)*				
	a	*b*	*c*	*d*	*e*
Who would bring order quickly and efficiently to Russia now?	41	14	9	8	1

Notes:
a Putin; b Zyuganov; c Army; d Fatherland All-Russia; e Yeltsin.

Source: Adapted from VTsIOM survey cited in 'Russia's election', *The Economist*, 18 December 1999, p. 21.

What Putin needs to bear in mind, though, was that 58 per cent of those surveyed thought they were better off under communisim (i.e. before 1985), compared to 27 per cent who disagreed with this view (VTsIOM survey cited in 'Russia's election', *The Economist*, 18 December 1999: 21). Therefore, public expectations of better times are high.

The new presidential elections took place on 26 March 2000, three months ahead of schedule. This was a deliberate damage limitation exercise meant to reduce any potential adverse effects on Putin's popularity should the Chechen war go sour and to ensure that Putin and his team had no time to make any serious policy blunders. The results are shown in Table 17.6. As we can see, despite his lack of an electoral campaign (no TV or radio debates), Putin was able to become President outright at the end of the first round, unlike Yeltsin in 1996.

Table 17.6 26 March 2000 Russian presidential election results

Candidate	*Affiliation*	*First round results (% of overall valid vote)*
Vladimir Putin	PM and Acting President	52.9
Gennady Zyuganov	CPRF	29.2
Grigory Yavlinsky	Yabloko	5.8
Aman-Geldy Tuleev	Independent	3.0
Vladimir Zhirinovsky	LDPR Bloc	2.7
Konstantin Titov	Independent	1.5
Ella Pamfilova	For Civil Dignity Party	1.0
Stanislav Govorukhin	Independent	0.4
Yuri Skuratov	Independent	0.4
Aleksei Podberezhin	Spiritual Heritage	0.1
Umar Dzhabrailov	Independent	0.1
Votes against all candidates		1.9

Source: Final results given by the Central Electoral Commission on 6 April 2000 (cited at www.fci.ru).

Putin successfully beat all the other candidates. He had the advantage of being Prime Minister and Acting President but, taking no chances, he launched a dirty tricks campaign on his opponents (accusing Yavlinsky of being 'gay' for instance) and his campaign team arranged for other candidates of various persuasions to stand in order to split the vote for his nearest rivals. Moreover, Putin appears to have judged public opinion well in asking the voters to assess him on the basis of his deeds not false election promises. The results, shown in Table 17.6, are reminiscent of the Soviet era.

It is too early to tell what difference Putin might make. This is not simply because he has only been in office three weeks at the time of writing; it can also be attributed to his failure to publish a presidential manifesto. Dmitrii Medvedev, the head of Putin's campaign headquarters, explains this by stating that Putin and his future team needed more time to 'carefully consider' what was required and hence they were not keen to make hasty decisions (Medevdev, 2000).

All we are, therefore, left with, are the vague statements made in Putin's 'Open Letter' to voters of 25 February 2000 where he acknowledged poor past management and decision-making and stressed the following possible future policy goals:

- rebuild the Russian family, improve standards of living and restore national pride;
- eradicate crime, especially organized crime, and fight corruption partly via a stronger legal system;
- reduce the power of the oligarchs;
- eliminate poverty;
- protect Russia's national interests in security matters and foreign policy;
- introduce tougher state control over the economy to put it back on track (it is unclear as yet whether this will or will not mean a continuation of market reforms); and
- create a new Russia but 'not stifle democracy' in the process.

Since becoming President, Putin has:

- emphasized the need to protect individual rights;
- called for a free press;
- pledged to increase expenditure on the military; and
- stressed the need to create an equal and more trusting relationship with NATO (*BBC News*, 27 March 2000, cited www.monitor.bbc.co.uk).

The failure to deliver in the past cost both Gorbachev and Yeltsin their Presidencies, so Putin must walk the tightrope with care and hope that if he does fall, a safety net is in place. All current reports suggest that Putin is well aware of Russia's problems and what needs to be done to resolve them. For the time being, however, Putin is maintaining his liberal nationalist position which necessitates maintaining a delicate balance between respecting the basic principles of liberal democracy while trying to restore Russia's damaged national pride (Albats and Powell, 2000: 54). Meanwhile, the West is anxious about Putin because he has already granted Yeltsin immunity, been accused of orchestrating the alleged Chechen bombings in autumn 1999, stated that he intends to appoint ex-FSB personnel onto his staff and talked of a 'dictatorship of the law', indicating a possible hard-line approach in future. Early indications suggest that the future may be more difficult in comparison to the Gorbachev and even the Yeltsin era.

Russia's fears

As we saw above in the period 1917–85, the West's attitude towards Russia was highly problematical, but, under Gorbachev, things improved dramatically, and for most of the Yeltsin era East–West tension was minimal and relations were relatively smooth. However, in recent years, as the nationalists and communists gained ground in the 1993-95 parliamentary elections, there has been growing concern in Russian circles that the West was using its economic strength and political muscle in order to try and influence Russian policies, on the one hand, and to increase Western influence in the region, on the other.

From a Russian point of view, the West's strength in the post-communist era is now accompanied by a new and disturbing assertiveness, especially on the part of the USA. This is what Russians refer to as the rise of the 'new Pax Americana'. This Western domination of the new world order is already unbalancing the European and international arena and is likely to pose greater threats in the future. The absence of a countervailing power – due to the demise of the USSR and the Soviet Empire – means that the West is free to dominate other countries in economic as well as political terms. The West's strength, some Russian specialists argue, will ensure that its influence spreads throughout the world. This influence is being felt in many parts of the globe but especially in the old Soviet bloc (Truscott, 1997; Trofimenko, 1999).

Increasing Western strength and a corresponding increase in Russian weakness has meant that the West has been able virtually to dictate much Russian policy for at least a decade. The outcome of this situation is changing Russian perceptions of the West. For a time (1985–96), Russia trusted the West and had a great deal of faith in its policies. Key (though by no means all) Russian policy and decision-makers thought that the West was Russia's friend and wanted to help Russia overcome her problems and hence make a successful transition to Western-style capitalism. However, over time, and increasingly in the last few years, there has been a noticeable increase in anti-Western feelings in Russia. The initial feelings of euphoria and optimism about the future have now given way to scepticism and mistrust. In some Kremlin circles as well as outside the corridors of power, the West's solutions for Russia's ills are now deemed inappropriate. Experience since 1985, and especially since 1991, shows that the West's policies are not suited to the new Russia. As Table 17.1 shows, the *costs* of transition (based on Western economic principles and strategies) far outweigh any *benefits*, which are tangible for most sections of the Russian population. In Stefan Hedlund's view this constitutes 'predatory capitalism' (see Hedlund, 1999).

Because Western policies are not bearing fruit, anti-Western views are gaining ground in Russia. Russia sees NATO expansion and the Eastern enlargement of the EU as a serious threat to its security interests (see Black, 2000). Although a return to Soviet-style views of the West cannot be ruled out, we must not, however, exaggerate Russian fears of the West or their potential impact. Thus Russia is unlikely, at least on current indications, to respond in a violent way towards the West. At the same time, however, increased criticism of the West and of its policies on Russia should not be dismissed out of hand. Russia's loss of superpower status, its economic collapse, political instability and tremendous social problems (see below) have led many Russians to conclude that the West genuinely does not want to help them and that instead it would prefer to see Russia on its knees. Thus while visiting Moscow in July–August 1999, the author was told that the West's 'closeness' to Russia was nothing more than 'window dressing'. In reality, the West had no desire to get close to its former adversary, except to find out more about its vulnerability; rather it simply wanted to deceive Russia. This was the view held of the Soviet Union in the West in the early Gorbachev years; now the tables seemed to have turned. It was the West, not Russia, that could not be trusted. This position has led some Russians to argue that it is high time that Russia put its own national interests first and stopped bowing down to the West (Truscott, 1997; Trofimenko, 1999). While this view has yet to be fully articulated in Kremlin circles, the Kosovo/Balkan crisis in 1998-99 proved to be a turning point in Russian–Western relations. The West's heavy-handed reaction to the Serbs' treatment of the Albanians in Kosovo led to increased Russian criticism of the West and growing sympathy for the underdog – the Serbs (see Table 17.7). It is clear from Table 17.7 that the West made a grave mistake in almost totally ignoring Russia when NATO bombed Serbia. Thus in this March 1999 survey (shown in Table 17.7), 48 per cent of Russians blamed the USA and NATO for the Kosovo crisis and 90 per cent believed that NATO was not right to bomb Serbia for its treatment of Albanians. Finally, 74 per cent of those surveyed thought that this would have an adverse effect on Russia's relationship with NATO in future. The Kosovo crisis exposed the myth in Russia that the West was civilized and democratic. It is easy to see why Russia might fear the West and its ways (liberal democracy and market economics) if we look at the social consequences of Russia's transition. Here the myth of victory is exposed for all to see. There have been very few *real* victors in the new Russia. Economic collapse and political instability have had an adverse effect on the Russian population. Thus the political euphoria of 1991 has now given way to frustration because most Russians have lost out. Thus Russia's 'shock without therapy' strategy has resulted in a higher proportion of the low paid – OAPs, incapacitated and dependent persons, single parents and the unemployed – since the collapse of communism (see Williams *et al.*, 1996, Part II).

Social costs

As shown elsewhere, the consequence of the above has been an increase in the gap between rich and poor (with the ratio of incomes between the wealthiest and poorest rising from 4.4 in 1990 to 13 in 1998) coupled with a serious deterioration in the quality of life – declining birth rates, increasing deaths, poor health provision, declining education standards, the demise of the welfare state and so forth (Williams *et al.*, 1996). This, among other things, cost Yeltsin his job. Unless greater attention is devoted to these issues in future, the same fate might await Putin and Russia's reforms might also not succeed.

Conclusion and future prospects

The analysis in this chapter shows that Russia's progress on the road to Western-style reform is not irreversible. While it would be wrong to assert that 'everything was fine' between 1992 and 1998, and that Russia was experiencing an economic miracle, outward appearances suggested that things were not too bad and Russia seemed to be making slow, yet steady progress towards the market. Events since autumn 1998 indicate, however, that Russia (with the West's help) seems to have got it wrong. Shock therapy – the elimination of subsidies, open trade, convertibility of the rouble, rapid privatization – has produced one of the worst economic recessions with a correspondingly high level of social costs since the 1929 Wall Street crash. It looks as if Russia fooled the West by suggesting that economic stabilization had

Table 17.7 Russian attitudes to the Balkan crisis, March 1999

Question/Answer	*Answers as percentage of sample of 1600*	
	March 1998	*March 1999*
Question: *What do you think about the plight of the Albanians in Kosovo?*		
Internal Yugoslav issue	26	46
Concern of the West	64	22
No answer	28	14
Question: *What caused the Kosovo crisis?*		
Albanian separatism		13
Serbian cruelty		7
Aggressive response by USA and NATO		48
No answer		32
Question: *Do you agree that NATO was right to bomb Serbia?*		
Yes		2
No		90
No answer		8
Question: *What do you feel about NATO's attack on Yugoslavia?*		
Indignation		52
Anxiety		26
Fear		13
Understanding		2
Approval		1
Indifference		2
No answer		4
Question: *Did NATO have the right to attack Serbia without UN sanctions?*		
No		90
Yes		2
No answer		8
Question: *In what way do you think the Kosovo crisis might influence Russia–NATO relations?*		
Increase tension		41
Start a new Cold War		33
No answer		26

Source: VTsIOM survey of 27–30 March 1999 on Russian attitudes towards Kosovo cited in *Russkaya Mysl'*, 8–14 April 1999, p. 7.

occurred, when in fact the opposite was true. With the benefit of hindsight, Russia could perhaps have taken a much slower pace of reform and given equal attention to therapy and shock. However, a combination of the kinds of internal and external factors outlined previously left virtually no room for manoeuvre. As we have seen, the costs (poverty, unemployment, economic recession, political instability, the rise of the Far Right) have by far outweighed the benefits of transition. This has increased Western anxiety and led to the partial return of old Cold War attitudes towards post-communist Russia. This is by no means one-sided either, as Yeltsin's recent criticism of Western policy on Kosovo shows. While some Western criticisms of Russia might be well-founded, a portion of the blame must also be placed on the West as it encouraged Russia to go too far, too fast, too soon.

In political terms, Russia is an imagined democracy. As we saw earlier, Russia's balance sheet does not look very good after nearly a decade of 'shock therapy'. The economy has collapsed, Russia's politics is in disarray and the average Russian has seen their savings vanish, their real wages plummet and the value of the rouble decline by around two-thirds. Thus all Russians face an uncertain future.

Russia's political and economic turmoil is far from over. Debates in future are likely to focus on the direction of government domestic and foreign policy and in particular over what measures are required to restore (economic and political) stability, investment, growth and Western support.

In my opinion there are at least two possibilities during Putin's first presidential term (until 2004). In the best case scenario, Putin continues to pursue market reform and is helped in making and implementing successful new strategies by the loyal, pro-government Duma appointed in December 1999. This heralds an era of cooperation between the pro and anti-government forces. Putin takes control over his government through the promotion of ex-FSB staff and moderate reformers, then foreign investment returns, privatization continues, the banks adapt and economic stabilization is gradually ensured. By contrast, in the worst case scenario, Russia ends up losing the war against Chechnya, anti-government groups (such as the CPRF and Fatherland All-Russia) block the new President's policies, Russia objects more forcibly to EU and NATO's Eastern expansion (see Chapters 14, 16) and makes overtures to China. This exacerbates Russia's economic difficulties and increases the tension in Russia's relations with the West. Given the weakness of the centre, power gradually shifts towards the regions and Russia's relationships with the periphery will be increasingly based on inconsistent, unclear and unstable bilateral agreements. As a consequence conflicts spread to many regions of the Russian Federation with the recent turmoil in Chechnya and Dagestan only marking the beginning of Russia's disintegration. Also, according to this scenario, the power institutions (security services, military) revert towards greater authoritarianism and hard-liners come to power (Zyuganov, Zhirinovsky, Lebed, and the like). This leads to the rejection of Western solutions to Russia's economic ills (as advocated by the IMF, EBRD, World Bank) and the introduction of more protectionist policies to protect nascent capitalism, prevent rising unemployment and offer more social guarantees and thereby restore people's faith in the Russian state.

Although Western anxieties about Russia's uneven progress towards democracy are natural, both sides must keep their nerve. What is at stake here is the following: Russia's continued decline or slow recovery. The first option is in nobody's interest, as it increases the likelihood of Russian disintegration and might destabilize other neighbouring newly independent states. Surely the preferred alternative is the second option which would constitute a policy based on Russian–Western cooperation not Western diktat, which facilitate Russia's slow growth in the short term and recovery in the long term (Graham, 1999: 10–12). As Jan Nowak notes: 'present Russian policy [under Yeltsin is] . . . dictated more by frustration, hurt, pride and old habits than by reason . . . Russia no longer poses any *military threat* to the United States or NATO . . . [but] Russia is not yet reconciled to the loss of her Empire or Superpower status' (Nowak, 1999: 3).

The difficulty in future will be persuading the Russian electorate to have faith in the new 1999 Duma and the new President Putin, elected in March 2000. This is a tall order. Thus Putin himself noted just prior to his election: 'I have no right to say that tomorrow miracles will occur . . . If you raise people's hopes, disappointment is inevitable. I think additional difficulties lie ahead for me in that the level of [public] expectation is high' (Vladimir Putin speaking 27 March 2000, cited on www.news.bbc.co.uk). Peter Rutland concurs. He concludes that Russian reformers did 'better than one would have expected [in implementing shock therapy], but worse than one would have liked, and not well enough to save Russia from collapse' (Rutland, 1999: 6). The recent *Kursk* submarine tragedy and the Ostankino TV station fire are evidence of just how far Russia has declined.

In the next few years, both Russia and the West will need to reach a compromise and modify their policies and stances. This means the West acknowledging that its policies failed and also that, although in Western eyes Russia is a 'basket case', Russia's leaders, from Yeltsin through to Putin still 'regard Russia as a superpower' (Rutland, 1999: 11). In order to ensure that the cure is not deadlier than the illness and that past Western mistakes are not repeated in the year 2000 and beyond, the West might have to take a more backseat role in the years to come. This low-profile, yet supporting, role, might well pay off in the long term. The Russians for their part must also accept part of the blame for the lack of success.

However, if the West continues in a pig-headed fashion to still pursue the same 1992–98 policies in the future, then Russia might well reject capitalism (or what we currently call the Washington consensus) (see World Bank, 1996). This would be an undesirable outcome for all sides, as it might produce the outbreak of the third phase of the Cold War and make the world (including Russia) an unsafe place to live in once more. In Andrei Illianov's view the key issue in the twenty-first century will be whether Russia and the West view each other as adversaries, partners or allies (Illianov, 1997: 1). One can only hope that the latter rather than the former succeeds, so that greater peace and stability prevails in Europe in the new millennium.

CHAPTER EIGHTEEN

The Problems and Prospects of the Transition Economies

Peter J. Anderson

In this chapter, an overall assessment will be made of the current chaotic state of the Russian economy and of the medium-term prospects of turning the situation around. This analysis is intended to be complementary to Christopher Williams' chapter specifically on the overall problems and prospects of Russia, and sets out to cover in detail some of the economic issues that necessarily are addressed only briefly there. An obvious problem in trying to undertake such an exercise is the difficulty of getting accurate data on an economy which currently is significantly, although by no means entirely, criminalized or 'informalized'. (According to some estimates 55 per cent of capital and 80 per cent of voting shares in Russia's post-Soviet economy have been bought by Russian and foreign criminal elements (Yurlov, 1999: 86). In the absence of entirely reliable information, the decision has been made to use mainly Western data suppliers, but with Russian information used in addition. The Western sources are ones which the author believes to be accurate enough to create a picture of the overall state of the Russian economy that is near enough to the truth to be acceptably reliable. (Given that banks such as the Banca Commerciale Italiana use the same sources as reliable outside referents for the problematically partially criminalized Italian economy, their trust would seem to be a useful 'character reference'.) Their accuracy can be broadly cross-checked by consulting such Russian sources as former Russian Government senior advisor Vladimir Andrianov's *Russia in the Global Economy*[1] or, for example, the more limited data provided by Felix Yurlov (Yurlov, 1999). The conclusions drawn from much of the statistical data used here will be found to be mostly in close alignment with those which Andrianov draws from the data used in his own very detailed economic analysis, and, indeed, where relevant, such correspondences will be pointed out in the text.

Additional data, providing a more long-term view of the Russian economy, can be found in the previous chapter showing economic trends in Russia since 1991.

Some of the key economic problems and prospects of three Central and Eastern European economies – the Czech Republic, Poland and Hungary – will be discussed also, including the still very substantial gap in economic performance that exists between them and the European Union (EU) states. Particular attention will be given to those aspects of the economies of these Eastern European states which might be most affected should they succeed ultimately in joining the EU, as currently they intend. This part of the chapter obviously will link directly with Karen Henderson's discussion on future EU enlargement. However, it should be noted that, given the limited space available within the book, most of this chapter is given over to the Russian economy, because Russia remains a far more important determinant of world political and economic outcomes than any of these states.

Finally, it should be emphasized that the collapse of communism within Europe does not mean that this chapter will start from the premise that present-day capitalism in its most common forms has not only been triumphant in the struggle between East and West, but should and will be able to impose itself on the Russian Federation, as the main inheritor of the mantle of the former Soviet Union, without regard to the preferences of the Russian people. What will be shown is that Russia's unique cultural, economic and political circumstances mean that just because particular versions of an economic ideology have been shown to work relatively well in the West does not automatically mean that they will be suitable for the Russian Federation, either now or within the foreseeable future.

The one-legged bear: the problems and prospects of the Russian economy

The scale and detail of Russia's economic problems

Many of the surface economic characteristics and problems of Russia are easy enough to identify. In terms of its relative size, it is at first sight a considerable entity, ranking as Europe's sixth largest economy after Germany, France, Britain, Italy and Spain. However, the fact that Russia has a far larger population than any of these individual economies, and one that is highly educated and highly skilled, suggests straight away that all is not as it should be in terms of a state formerly regarded as the core of one of the world's two post-1945 superpowers. This impression is confirmed fully when the GDP figures for (for example) Germany and the EU as a whole are compared with those of Russia (see Table 18.1).

In terms of natural resources, something of Russia's *tremendous economic potential relative to the poverty of its performance* during the 1990s becomes apparent (Andrianov, n.d., accessed 1999). For example, it has significant coal deposits and more of the world's oil reserves (5 per cent) than the rest of Europe put together, and its daily production in terms of barrels is far in excess of that of its nearest European rivals, Norway and Britain (*Economist*, 1999b: 56), comprising 22 per cent of the world's total (Yurlov, 1999: 95). Even more dramatically, Russia has natural gas reserves that are almost seven times larger than those of the rest of Europe combined, and which account for 33 per cent of the world's total (*Economist*, 1999b: 56). Its natural gas production (million tonnes of oil equivalent, 1997), at 477.9, is around six times that of Britain, its nearest European rival (*Economist*, 1999b: 56). In addition, Russia has economically significant reserves of other minerals, such as iron ore, gold and platinum. Exports of cut and uncut diamonds are also important, with Russia producing 25 per cent of the world's total (Yurlov, 1999: 95).

However, the very prominence of exports such as the above *itself demonstrates* a key continuing weakness in Russian economic performance, namely the fact that most of its exports other than armaments contain, as Alan Smith noted back in 1993 (Smith, 1993: 78–9), a high raw material content and a low industrially processed content. Its weakness in the field of industrial exports is perhaps most vividly demonstrated by its performance with regard to automobiles. Despite the fact that

Table 18.1 Selected economic indicators for post-communist Russia

GDP ($bn at 1997 market exchange rates) (*Economist*, 1999b: 44)
Russia: population 148.13m, 1996 (*Economist*, 1999b: 28) – **450**
The European Union as a whole – **8093**
Germany: population 81.92m, 1996 (*Economist*, 1999b: 28) – **2041, over four times** as large as that of Russia

GDP per head ($) 1997 (*Economist*, 1999b: 48)
Ireland came 14th in a GDP per head league table of 26 European states, with a figure of **20,605**
Russia, a state massively larger in terms of both territory and population, came in at 26th with a figure of **3037** – just under **a seventh** of Ireland's

Emerging markets' foreign reserves ($bn), June 1999 (*Economist*, 1999h: 180)
Russia – **8.2**
China – **150.6**
Singapore – **73.8**

Interest rates (1998) (*Economist*, 1999b: 98–9)
(1) Central Bank discount rate
Russia – **60.00 per cent**
Germany – **2.50 per cent**
Britain – **7.50 per cent**
(2) Money market interest rates
Russia – **75.10 per cent**
Germany – **3.47 per cent**
Britain – **7.19 per cent**

Inward investment (inflows, $m, 1996) (*Economist*, 1999b: 130)
Russia – **1,800**
Britain – **30,053**
France – **20,809**
Belgium – **13,920**

Average earnings, $'000, 1997 (*Economist*, 1999b: 130)
(1) Skilled worker
Russia – **3.6**
Switzerland – **39.7**
United Kingdom – **21.6**
(2) School teacher
Russia – **0.8**
Switzerland – **51.7**
United Kingdom – **23.8**
Ireland – **24.7**
(3) Department managers
Russia – **5.2**
Switzerland – **73.5**
United Kingdom – **30.8**
Cyprus – **24.2**

the Soviet Union in its heyday maintained a massive military vehicles construction capability, it was unable to establish itself as a producer of quality private motor vehicles for export. Even now, in spite of investments by major foreign motor manufacturers, for example, Russia produced only 911,000 cars in 1997 (as compared to the 4,678,000 manufactured by Germany in the same year) and made little impact in Western export markets (*Economist*, 1999b: 116). During 1998 and 1999 Russian motor vehicle exports to Britain were non-existent.

Russia's industrial weakness is a particular problem, given that industrial output accounts for 39 per cent of its GDP (*Economist*, 1999b). It is unrepresented in the top 40 (by sales) of Europe's biggest companies, although Gazprom was the continent's sixth most profitable company and its second largest employer in 1997 (*Economist*, 1999b: 120–1). It is only really in the field of armaments exports that it ranks currently with the world leaders of industrial production. In 1996, for example, the Russian Federation ranked as the world's fourth largest arms exporter, with 9 per cent of a global trade worth $39.9bn.

In terms of foreign direct investment, Table 18.1 shows that Russia has performed extremely poorly, and, given the dire need of investment for the modernization of many of its industries, this in turn might reasonably be assumed to be a key part of the reason for its poor industrial exporting performance. The OECD has argued that Russia's poor performance in attracting foreign investment has been due to, 'the fluidity and arbitrariness of the tax regime, uncertainties surrounding property rights ... concerns about the predictability and stability of laws and regulations affecting FDI' (OECD, 1998b: 10). The money laundering and other financial corruption scandals revealed during 1999 are likely to act as further disincentives to legitimate foreign investors. The OECD has further noted that: 'Over the past several years, declines in investments have consistently outpaced falls in output, and they still show no signs of bottoming out' (OECD, 1998b: 11). Table 18.1's interest rate section shows how unattractive Russia was as a place to borrow money during the late 1990s, thereby emphasizing even more the difficulties facing would-be industrial modernizers.

As far as financial services are concerned, Russia is unrepresented in the top 45 of Europe's banks (calculated by capital, $m 1997, *Economist*, 1999a: 122–3), and was again unrepresented among the continent's top insurance companies (*Economist*, 1999b: 125). It does at least register in the tourism league tables, having had the tenth highest earnings in Europe prior to the Moscow and St Petersburg bomb blasts of 1999. However, this is somewhat put in context when it is realized that Central and Eastern Europe together earned only 8 per cent of the continent's total tourism cake in 1997, while the EU states together took 79 per cent of the earnings.

On top of the fact of Russia's general economic weakness is the problem of gross inequality of wealth distribution. Gray notes that:

> In all, around 45 million people have fallen into poverty since the transition to a market economy began in Russia in 1991. At the same time, 'New Russians' who profited from market reforms – between 3–5 per cent of the population ... – had an average monthly income of between $500 and $100,000 in 1995. (Gray, 1999: 147)

Yurlov's estimates of the number of beneficiaries of the reforms are a little more generous, putting the figure at 10–15 per cent of the population (Yurlov, 1999: 85).

For the unprivileged many, while unemployment remains relatively low by the standards of Europe as a whole, wages are poor and are simply not paid at all when the government or particular firms get into serious financial difficulties. Table 18.1 shows how bad the situation is for many of those outside the relatively small, privileged economic and criminal elite.

To add to the woes of low wage earners, during the period 1992–97, average annual consumer price inflation in Russia was 188.5 per cent, as compared to 16.9 per cent in the Czech Republic, 5.9 per cent in Portugal and 3.2 per cent in Britain (*Economist*, 1999b: 79). On top of this, by 1998, agricultural production had fallen 40 per cent since the inception of Yeltsin's republic (Yurlov, 1999: 86).

It did look initially as though a flourishing new entrepreneurial middle class would emerge within the post-communist economy and help to create the kind of home-driven growth that would have reduced the above problems significantly, but: 'To the dismay of most of them, they encountered a total lack of government support, faced exorbitant taxes, confronted mafia interference and ran into insurmountable corruption of government officials' (Yurlov, 1999: 84). Many gave up in the face of such obstacles and many more were ruined by the debt default and the plunge in the value of the rouble during 1998 (Yurlov, 1999: 88). Ultimately, 50 per cent of the Russian economy fell under the control of around only a dozen individuals (Yurlov, 1999: 84).

As far as government finances are concerned, the situation also is deeply problematic. In Christopher Williams' chapter on Russia it was explained that the Federation's Government is not very successful in the essential business of collecting taxes. 1997 figures reveal the consequences of this, in that they show the Government of Russia to be raising \$55.78bn in annual revenue, compared to the \$742.67bn, 648.13bn and 403.60bn raised by the much smaller states of Germany, France and Britain respectively (*Economist*, 1999b: 86). The OECD has pointedly noted the popular enthusiasm for tax evasion in Russia, and the failure of increased numbers of taxes, rules and penalty levels to curtail this (OECD, 1998b: 8). The OECD believes, that the increased number of tax rules and laws to try and cope with all of the above is discouraging investment, further adding to Russia's difficulties (OECD, 1998b: 8).

In 1996, Russia's external debt stood at \$124.8bn (*Economist*, 1999b: 91). The OECD has noted that during that year the servicing of the debt accounted for 30 per cent of federal budget expenditure, and amounted to more than two-thirds of the 8 per cent GDP federal budget deficit (OECD, 1998b: 7). Its paltry foreign reserves are shown in Table 18.1.

The IMF's latest available World Economic Outlook (at the time of writing in September 1999) appeared to offer a brighter prospect than all of the above, in that while forecasting zero percentage GDP growth for Russia during the remainder of 1999, it foresaw an improvement to around 2 per cent during 2000. However, the low Russian economic starting point somewhat limits any hint of excitement that such a prospect might create, and it should be noted that China, South Korea, India and Mexico were all seen as being likely to far outstrip Russia's performance during the same period (*Economist*, 1999h: 180).

To return to the comments made at the beginning of the chapter, Andrianov notes that as well as problematically poor relative rates of performance in such areas as

GDP, GDP per capita, poverty levels, foreign debt, investment and the prevention of corruption (all mentioned above), Russia has additional problems with such things as the rate of government expenditure on science, education and public health services: and poor relative ratings on the human development and quality of life indexes (Andrianov, n.d., accessed 1999) (see also Yurlov, 1999: 83–5).

It is symbolic of the generally unencouraging Russian economic environment of recent years that Simon Commander should note in April 1999 that anecdotal and statistical evidence, 'suggests that barter has become the dominant method of transacting in Russia and, to a lesser extent, a feature of a number of other countries of the Former Soviet Union' (Commander, 1999: 19–22). Barter is only partly goods for goods in the Russian Federation. Other transactions include, 'money surrogates – promissory notes ... issued by enterprises, banks or government with specified maturities and discount rates' and 'offsets or *zachety*', which involve the exchange of debts for goods (Commander, 1999: 19). The latter have been used most frequently for transactions between firms, 'firms and tax authorities ... firms and utilities and government' (Commander, 1999: 19).

High interest rates, together with the fact that high yields on treasury bills (GKOs) meant that banks were prepared to lend significantly less to private firms and significantly more to the government during 1997 and 1998, led firms to start looking increasingly to trade credit instead of bank credit (Commander, 1999: 20).

In Commander's view, while barter has been of benefit to Russian firms, it has also helped prevent the restructuring of the Russian economy by weakening competition and has so distorted it that: 'Accounting prices now have little to do with cash values: inflated barter prices exaggerate the revenues of manufacturing enterprises, while distorting business decisions and fostering corruption' (Commander, 1999: 21). The role that barter now plays in the daily lives of many ordinary Russian citizens also should not be forgotten. This was most farcically emphasized when workers in a Russian pickle factory found during 1998 that their employer had run out of all means other than the pickles which the factory produced with which to pay them.

To sum up, Russia's economic situation at the end of the 1990s is best described with the only word that will fit the picture: dire.

The causes of Russia's economic crisis

There is not complete agreement on how precisely Russia has arrived at its current parlous economic situation. This is hardly surprising, given the different ideological starting points of many of the parties to the debate. One of the most commonly cited causes of Russia's weakness is its economic inheritance from the now defunct Soviet Union, a state whose economy was characterized by a crippling degree of rigidity, a lack of competitive pressures, corruption, too little attention to product quality, a failure to modernize in order to be able to compete with the West, and a damaging, massive diversion of crucial investment and research and development resources into the build up and sustenance of a superpower armoury. Externally, this led to a situation where

> the trade structure of the Soviet Union resembled that of a relatively backward Third World country dependent upon fuels, raw materials, precious metals, wood and lumber for 95 per cent of its exports to the industrial West. Its major industrial exports to non-

socialist countries consisted of armaments, frequently delivered on credit to Third World countries. (Smith, 1993: frontispiece)

Before the government of the newly independent Russian Federation could do anything else, it had to try and recover the economy from the years of Soviet mismanagement and the consequences of the failed Gorbachev reforms of the 1980s.

But whatever the Soviet inheritance, many writers have argued that its ill effects have been more than added to by those who have come after the last Soviet Government. With regard to the general chaos of the domestic situation, for example, the OECD noted in its 1997/98 economic survey that serious problems existed with regard to the raising of taxation, government and corporate governance, a predominance of insider-controlled enterprises, financial markets that are only poorly developed, a decline in enterprise profits and liquidity, and various micro-level incentive problems, and concluded that, together, these had, 'hindered restructuring and contributed to further declines in investment activity' (OECD, 1998b: 2). It noted also problems with regard to small businesses and commercial banks. While observing that steps could be taken to try and deal with these problems through legislative means, it pointed out that little in the way of the necessary practical measures had materialized. It concluded that the failure to solve the above problems by legislative means, together with a general indecisiveness in policy-making, was due to a 'fundamental antagonism between the executive and legislative branches of the Federal Government' (OECD, 1998b: 3). This points towards a crucial conclusion, namely that one of the key domestic problems for the economy has been the nature of Russian governance. In 1998, Edward Lucas stated that the central government was: 'rendering the currency worthless, extorting unfair taxes, confiscating export revenues and strangling imports . . . ' (Lucas, 1998: 58).

In the eyes of many analysts, by 1998/99, Russia under Yeltsin seemed to have lost any coherent sense of direction economically. It appeared to be a ship listing almost motionlessly in the water, weighed down by corruption and suffering from a constant change of captains. Its gradual transition to this state perhaps had been marked by two symbolic moments, each of which had dented severely Russia's embryonic economic credentials in the eyes of the developed world. First, in 1993/94 Yeltsin finally had to acknowledge that the shock therapy introduced in the wake of the Soviet collapse was unworkable in the Russian context. Thenceforth, it was effectively abandoned. Second, as a result of the globalized world economy – the same globalized economy that allegedly has been used so successfully by corrupt government officials to engage in money laundering – Russia was forced to default on its debt in 1998. This was most particularly due to the impact of the Asian slump that year on oil and other commodity prices, which both hit Russian revenues badly and caused investors to lose confidence in emerging markets. Russia's already limited chances of attracting significant inputs of foreign commercial capital were hit badly by these two events.

If the Asian slump that helped occasion the Russian debt default at least was out of the government's control, being as it was a consequence of a globalized economy, the policies of the dominant powers and institutions within that economy also are external factors that, certainly in the eyes of many of the Russian electorate, should take a significant part of the blame for economic failure away from Russia itself. A number of prominent Western authors agree with them to one extent or another. Writing at the beginning of the 1990s, for example, Alan Smith stated that the response of the West to the problems confronting Russia in the months following the collapse of communism lacked vision. He noted that:

> The economic conditions attached to IMF-backed assistance (the satisfaction of which western powers have accepted as prerequisites to additional bilateral aid) have been virtually impossible to achieve under Russian conditions and have raised the genuine question for many Russian citizens of whether the cure is worse than the illness and have badly undermined the reform process. (Smith, 1993: 237)

Writing in 1999, John Lloyd stated that:

> The West has lost the goodwill it had in 1989/90. Instead of helping to develop the civil society and functioning government that capitalism needs, they rushed through a botched privatisation. They spoke only to a westernised elite – ignoring the society that we wanted to democratise and imposing values without allowing local ownership. (Lloyd, 1999: 4)

However, to return in more detail to a point alluded to above, whatever the desirability or otherwise of particular conditions forced on Russia by Western-dominated institutions during the Yeltsin years, it could be argued that one of the most fundamental problems facing Russia was the shared assumption, initially both within key sections of the Yeltsin leadership and the West, that a Western-style economic model would be the best solution to Russia's economic problems. John Gray is one of the most eloquent advocates of this point of view. He argued, for example, that:

> Russia has been the site of two experiments in western utopianism during this century. The first was Bolshevism . . . The second was shock therapy. Implemented briefly in the aftermath of the Soviet collapse, shock therapy aimed to construct a free market in post-communist Russia. It produced instead a species of Mafia-dominated anarcho-capitalism. Both utopian experiments had enormous human costs. Both were failed modernizations guided by western theories or models that had little relevance to Russia's history and circumstances. (Gray, 1999: 133)

Back in 1993, Smith noted two polar views on the appropriateness of Western market reform models for Russia. He outlined first the Slavophile perspective, in which Russian and Slav people in general are so different from all other ethnic groupings in the West and elsewhere that the prescriptions for economic success which have been applied in other parts of the world, such as market capitalism, will not necessarily work in the case of the Russian Federation:

> The counter argument is that the Russian economy is inherently similar to other economies, and subject to the same economic 'laws' as other economies and that Russia should pursue policies that are broadly similar to those pursued by successful newly industrialising economies that have embraced a free market philosophy and accepted substantial foreign direct investment. (Smith, 1993: 236)

He concluded that the truth most probably sits somewhere between these two views. It is this perspective which seems most convincing here, if the differences of the Russian people from others are seen in terms of their economic, political and wider cultural history and the distinct structures and modes of thought which this has produced over the centuries. It is, for example, surely bizarre to expect that a society which for most of the present century was run via a central command economy should be able instantly to reorientate itself towards the complex demands of such a radically different system as free market capitalism. Nevertheless, given that capitalism is 'the only game in town' as far as available and tried economic prescriptions for helping Russia pull itself out of the mire are concerned, it is not unreasonable to argue that a version of capitalism appropriate to the specific needs of Russia – and credibly saleable to the Russian electorate – is what is now needed to help rescue an increasingly desperate situation. It could be argued convincingly to have been the past failure of the West and successive Russian governments to come up with such a version that is in large part responsible for the economic calamity of the present. However, the other failures of the Russian government outlined above should also be borne in mind in this regard, as should the problematic economic inheritance from the former Soviet Union. In addition, and finally, four very distinct characteristics of the economy of the Russian Federation need to be mentioned in their own right as part explanations of the current parlous state which the country finds itself in.

Firstly, one of the biggest of all problems of the economy is the previously mentioned phenomenon of corruption which, Gray claims, is a continuity from Soviet days rather than something new (Gray, 1999: 153–4). Others, such as Yurlov, see Western influence as having greatly worsened the problem (Yurlov, 1999: 86) not least because it is clear that corruption runs not only through mafia-penetrated enterprises, accounting for a significant amount of economic activity, but up into the highest levels of the government. It is a problem not just because of the money that it takes out of sectors of the economy important for the overall process of regeneration, or because of the embarrassment caused to the Russian state by the past disappearance of significant amounts of assistance provided by the international community, but, as pointed out previously, because of the serious disincentive which it provides for foreign direct investment and economic assistance. In September 1999, it was already becoming a serious complaint of Republican hard-liners in the run-up to the presidential elections that US assistance to Russia was ill-advised, given the level of corruption now prevalent within that state. Concern had been increased significantly by revelations in August that the Russian mafia had penetrated the Bank of New York, which it was using to facilitate its laundering of money obtained dishonestly from within Russia. A report in the *New York Times* suggested that up to $10 billion dollars might have been laundered through the bank (*Guardian*, 20 August, p. 14). By late September the American *Time* magazine was running a major story on the scandal which suggested strongly that it was not just the mafia, but people at the highest levels of the Russian Government who were involved in looting billions of dollars from private companies and the Russian exchequer. This was on top of serious allegations about a credit card scandal involving Yeltsin and his immediate family (Quinn-Judge, 1999: 42–5).

Secondly, another problem arises from the costs of the major wars which Russia has been involved in during recent years. The first Chechen war was wasteful in every sense and the second round of the conflict that began during 1999, while popular with much of the electorate, was clearly a hugely expensive venture. These are drains on the economy which the Russian Federation can ill afford.

Thirdly, there are in addition the continuing costs from the massive chemical, mineral and radioactive contamination problems which Russia inherited from the criminally negligent Soviet period. The expense of clean-up operations is well beyond the resources of the Russian state and assistance from other actors, such as the Government of Norway, has been crucial in trying to deal with at least the most immediately dangerous aspects of the problem.

Fourthly and finally, there is the problem of Russia's enormous crime rate, including a spectacularly high murder toll of the economic elite. The fact that some Western oil company employees feel so insecure in terms of their personal safety that they live in fortress-style compounds while in Russia demonstrates vividly how much Russia's image as the 'Wild East' detracts from its attractiveness as a place for foreign direct investment.

Future prospects of the Russian economy

The last point made by Smith above takes us neatly into a consideration of Russia's future economic prospects. Gray's anticipation of the most practical future pathway for the Russian economy dovetails with Smith's conclusion above. Going against many conventions, he argues that:

> Over time, perhaps spanning more than a generation, Russia's post-communist anarcho-capitalism is likely to evolve into something akin to the highly successful state-led Russian capitalism that generated the rapid economic development of Russia in the last decades of the Tsarist regime. (Gray, 1999: 152)

This is not to say that Gray ignores the many downsides of the Tsarist system. In fact he outlines these in some detail. But he does make a strong argument for the mode of capitalism then operating as being of more relevance to Russian society than its modern Western counterpart. This is most particularly the case because the failure of shock therapy has meant that full-blown Western-advocated models of market capitalism simply will not be accepted by the Russian people, as, he argues, was demonstrated by the parliamentary and presidential elections that occurred between 1993 and 1996 (Gray, 1999: 161), and because experience has now clearly shown that without a strong, effective state, market capitalism becomes just another system of exploitation (Gray, 1999: 151). However, for the above scenario to come about he believes that an essential precondition is a renovation of the institutions of the Russian state. He argues that:

> Without the institutions of a modern state the umbilical cord that connects Russian capitalism with the former Soviet Union and the mafia cannot be severed. Until it has a strong, effective state, Russia will not have a genuine market economy but rather a kind of criminal syndicalism. Until Russia has solved its Hobbesian problem it cannot be a modern state. (Gray, 1999: 165)

Andrianov, while agreeing by implication with the need for strong government, argues that a future reform programme for Russia must be based on a fundamental platform of sustainable development (Andrianov, n.d., accessed 1999).

Smith argues, by implication, that whatever the economic system in place in Russia, large-scale Western assistance is likely to be necessary to help place the Federation's economy on the road towards recovery. He argues that this is very much in the West's long-term security and economic interests (Smith, 1993: 218–37).

In its 1997/98 survey, the OECD summed up its view of Russia's prospects as follows:

> Macroeconomic prospects largely hinge on how decisively structural reforms are pushed through. If the most is made of the current window of opportunity, the foundations for durable and robust medium-term growth can emerge, given Russia's rich human and natural endowments. In the shorter run, financial stabilisation urgently needs to be consolidated. This requires persevering with an ambitious monetary policy, streamlining the tax system, and phasing out blanket subsidies for housing and other services, replacing them by more targeted forms of assistance. The revival and sustained growth of the economy should be promoted through renewed efforts to enforce the rule of law, enhance competition, improve the budgetary process, strengthen capital markets, facilitate bankruptcies and liquidations, reform the tax system, and attract foreign investment. Those are no doubt tall orders, but the Russian government itself has acknowledged that less would not do. In the absence of such bold and comprehensive moves, output and living standards would continue to stagnate at today's low levels. (OECD, 1998b: 22–3)

The phrase 'bold and comprehensive' is of course the key one here. Whether or not it is intentional, there is a clear implication of the same conclusion as that reached by Gray, that without a strong state there is little chance of achieving any meaningful improvement in Russia's economic situation. The question then becomes one of how is this to be achieved in a Russian context? Gray believes that a possible way in which this may come about is through a growing fear of another 'Time of Troubles', 'the period of anarchy and civil war in the late sixteenth century whose historic memory lives on in Russian song and folklore' which 'will act as a catalyst for a strengthening of the Russian state. The criminalization of Russian capitalism today will trigger demands that the regime of extensive presidential authority that Yeltsin inaugurated be further extended' (Gray, 1999: 158). He does not believe that this will necessarily lead to an undemocratic mode of government, citing pre-existing models of democratic state strengthening such as De Gaulle's France. Whether the influence of leaders such as Putin ultimately will lead in this direction is something that time alone will tell. Whether even a democratic strong state will lead to the adoption of a form of capitalism that is relatively benevolent to the poor as well as the rich is yet another question that only time will answer satisfactorily.

In short, and unsurprisingly, everything in the end comes down to the possibility of finding not only an appropriate economic model for the development of the Russian economy, but an appropriate political system to support and nurture it. Given that politics is a complex interplay of many diverse factors and interests, there can be no more than a hope that Russia will find these essential things. It is possible that the above kind of scenario might lead to a strong leadership that remains democratic, but there can be no guarantee of this. Should Russia's actual and feared troubles become too great, there is always the possibility of someone attempting to take over with military backing, and the history of the economic competence of many past and present military-backed regimes across the world is not a promising one. At the time of writing, there was no shortage of Russian politicians warning of such a possibility as the run up to the presidential elections began, although some of the rhetoric was no doubt as much electoral scaremongering as anything else.

In many ways, a lot depends on the range of credible economic alternatives facing Russia. While there is still an active communist party in the country, it is difficult to see it winning an electoral majority in the foreseeable future, given the exposure of its many serious, and in some cases, disastrous, economic failings during the Gorbachev era. Given that Russia exists now within a globalized liberal capitalist economy, the only viable alternatives, unless and until the economic thinking underlying that economy changes, are various forms of capitalism. Given also that there apparently is serious disillusionment with the USA and the West as a result of the failure of Western capitalist models to solve Russia's problems, the NATO bombing of Serbia and the American reactions to the August/September 1999 money-laundering revelations (Quinn-Judge, 1999: 42–5), it is unlikely that a Western preferred, or certainly an American preferred, model of capitalism and democracy is what many within the Russian electorate will want. This therefore would seem to make the scenario pointed to by Gray the most likely of the available alternatives. The alleged terrorist bombings and the strong Russian military response to them of the Putin Government during August/September 1999 would certainly seem to suggest that the idea of the 'Time of Troubles' and a possible strengthening of the Russian state in response to them together form a credible scenario by which that possibility might be realized.

However, this conclusion must be no more than a snapshot of the possibilities inherent within the ever-changing interplay of Kremlin political interests. It is not possible to make a prediction that is any more certain than the above for the simple reason that there are too many unpredictable variables at work within post-Soviet Russia. Indeed, as has been seen already in Christopher Williams' chapter on Russian politics, consideration of other variables than those examined here can produce a range of alternative predictive scenarios. What can be said, however, is that (thinking back to Smith), no matter how unpopular the West currently may be, its help, both directly and through such bodies as the IMF, could well be crucial in helping Russia avoid sinking to the point economically where democracy in any meaningful form becomes untenable and the doors to the Kremlin become open to extremists. John Lloyd, when analysing current American reactions to Russia's various financial crises, notes that:

> Instead of understanding that we need to engage in a more sensitive way, most US commentators are calling for disengagement – a fast track towards Russian collapse. Many in Europe, especially in Germany, are starting to learn the lessons and seek new approaches. The EU now needs to move beyond the rhetoric of common strategies and Russia as Europe's natural partner. That means concrete assistance on major policy challenges such as avoiding bankruptcy and restoring the cash economy. (Lloyd, 1999: 4)

The last word should perhaps be given to Yurlov, who argues that what Russia needs are 'reforms that will not only use international experience, but also take into account the specific features of Russia, its spiritual and cultural traditions, and its ethnic pluralism' (Yurlov, 1999: 95). It is not intended to say anything more on the book's core theme of threats to democracy here in order to avoid duplication of material covered in the chapter on Russia as a whole.

Ultimately it is up to readers obviously to make their own minds up as to how convincing they find the thoughts offered within this chapter on the future prospects for Russia's economy. It is now necessary to move on and analyse the current economic situation of some of Russia's near neighbours, Poland, Hungary and the Czech Republic.

In between two giants: the Eastern European economies

The massive task of trying to squeeze the proverbial 'quart into a pintpot' which confronts the authors necessarily when trying to cover the enormous topic of 'Europe in transition' means that choices of primary and secondary focus have to be made. Russia's size and overall strategic importance mean that inevitably it must take up most of this chapter. Undesirable academically though it may be, it is possible here only to cover briefly a small selection of Eastern European states. In deciding how to make such a selection, it should be noted that what is emerging in the East is clearly a two-speed Europe, one in which there is a clear demarcation between those states most likely to be admitted to the EU during its next enlargement, namely Poland, Hungary, the Czech Republic, Slovenia and Estonia, and those who will have to wait longer, in some cases, possibly, considerably so, before their economies and/or polities come sufficiently close to the minimum standards required by the Union before admission can be granted, such as Bulgaria and Romania. It would seem most sensible to concentrate on the three largest of the current 'first wave' applicants, Poland, Hungary and the Czech Republic (Estonia and Slovenia, the other two 'first wave' Eastern states, both have less than two million people). As an indication of the importance of these three states, it can be noted that in 1997 the World Bank reported that 80 per cent of the foreign direct investment in Central and Eastern Europe had gone into them. (It noted also that the sectors into which the investment had gone were services and the motor vehicle and food processing industries.) (Hockman and Djankov, 1997: 472.)

However, in choosing the above necessarily limited focus, it is important to remember that the relative success of the three chosen states makes them amongst the notable exceptions rather than the rule in the Eastern European region, and that their own relative economic backwardness in Western terms is far exceeded by some of those states who have been left out of the EU's first wave enlargement negotiations. As was noted in Karen Henderson's chapter, Eastern Europe as a whole still has a considerable way to go before it begins to catch up with Western living standards and this should be kept in mind constantly throughout the discussion which follows. In this regard, it is instructive to look at recent IMF figures (Woodall, 1999: 105) for the proportion of world GDP enjoyed by the *entire* former Soviet bloc. They show that the latter's share of 4.8 per cent is dwarfed by the 20.4 per cent held by the USA, the 19.8 per cent credited to the EU, the 7.7 per cent attributed to Japan, and the 8.8 per cent of Latin America.

The current economic situation of Poland, Hungary and the Czech Republic

As far as the three key states to be examined here are concerned, 1997 figures for the Czech Republic, with a population of 10.2 million, showed it to have an overall GDP of $52bn, with a GDP per head of $5,076 (*Economist*, 1999b: 44 and 48). Available figures suggest that its GDP growth rate has been in marked decline since the impressive 1995 figure of 6.36 per cent, partially at least as a result of political instability. In 1998, GDP slightly contracted by 0.51 per cent (EIU, 1998: 89). Its relative economic backwardness within Europe, even as one of the stronger of the former Eastern bloc economies, is shown by comparing its GDP with that of

Belgium, an EU state with an identically sized population, which in the same year had a GDP of $242bn. The massive gap between the two economies is further demonstrated when Belgium's GDP per head figure of $23,864 is compared with the Czech Republic's figure of $5,076 (*Economist*, 1999b: 44 and 48).

Poland's GDP of $135bn, and GDP per head of $3,508 for a population of 38.7 million compares with similarly sized Spain's (population 39.4 million) GDP of $531bn and GDP per head of $13,391 (*Economist*, 1999b: 44 and 48). Given that Hungary is almost identical in population size to Belgium and the Czech Republic, its GDP figure of $37bn and its GDP per head of $3,647 (*Economist*, 1999b: 44 and 48) are most usefully compared to the considerably much more impressive figures of the former.

What stands out immediately is that the GDP per head figures of each country are noticeably but not dramatically greater than those of Russia. The 'score' of even the weakest of the three in GDP per head terms, Poland, is nevertheless over twice that of Ukraine, over a third larger than that of Romania, Bulgaria and Lithuania and well over 50 per cent greater than that of Latvia (*Economist*, 1999b: 49). However, what is equally apparent is that while these figures might be mildly impressive in Eastern European terms, they are drastically inferior to those of key equivalent sized (in population terms) EU states. Furthermore, the 'best of the bunch', the Czech Republic's GDP per head figure of $5,076, is less than half that of the EU's second poorest state, Greece, and only comes 'within shooting distance' of the very poorest of the 15, Portugal, with a GDP per head figure of $9,610. It is in entirely another galaxy from tiny Luxembourg's figure of $37,132.

Looking at the figures for direct foreign investment into each of the three selected economies, a key indicator of growth possibilities in the post-communist east, the latest figures available in 1999 (for 1996) showed the Czech Republic, Hungary and Poland to have attracted sums of $1,200m, $1,982m and $5,196m respectively. While these figures are far behind the comparable figures of the EU's star performers, Britain, France and Belgium, they are quite respectable in comparison to those of a number of other EU states, and are far better than those for Russia ($1,800m), given its much larger population size (*Economist*, 1999b: 130). It has been mentioned already also that 80 per cent of the foreign direct investment in Eastern and Central Europe has gone into these three states. One of the key incentives for such investment levels can be seen by looking at the earnings of employees in each of the three states. Referring back to the several categories of employment detailed in Table 18.1 earlier, while there is a marked improvement on the very low wages offered in Russia for school teaching (in the case of all three states), and departmental management (in the sole case of the Czech Republic), all three economies offer lower wages than Turkey in all of these employment categories and for other types of work such as secretarial duties (*Economist*, 1999b: 108–9). Furthermore, Philippe Martin has noted that, even when non-wage costs are included in labour costs, the most expensive of the three states in terms of labour costs is still less than half as expensive as Portugal, the EU state with the cheapest labour costs (Martin, 1996: 96, footnote 1). Such low wage rates and overall labour costs would seem likely to have been one of the key factors which have attracted Western, and in particular German, investors into these states, together with such things as a readily available skilled labour force. However, this does not explain why such investment should not have been attracted instead to even lower cost Russia, with its at least equally skilled workforce. In this regard, it has been suggested that such factors as a greater proximity to the EU's key markets, with a consequent lowering of transportation costs, and perhaps crucially, a much smaller problem of corruption and a much greater level of perceived stability within, in particular, Catholic Poland (by far the largest recipient of such investment within the former Eastern bloc), have been decisive. Volkswagen of Germany's flagship investment in (and remarkable turnaround of) Skoda in the Czech Republic is symbolic in this regard, although the Czech Republic's record on political stability has been somewhat less than perfect in the years since the investment was first attracted. Volkswagen seems to have been lured also by the Czech Government's guarantee that import tariffs on passenger cars would be kept at 19 per cent for a minimum of four years (Martin, 1996: 584).

Therefore, key aspects of the economies of these three states are impressive relative to Russia and much of the rest of Eastern Europe, but available figures show that they remain still far behind the economies of the EU states in terms of their overall wealth.

The economic problems and prospects of EU membership

Given all of the above, it is easy to see why the enlargement question has been such a thorny issue in the EU. To elaborate very briefly on Karen Henderson's earlier observations, Germany and Austria in particular have an ambiguous attitude towards enlargement, on the one hand welcoming it enthusiastically on the grounds of its potential long-term stabilization of Europe, but on the other fearing 'an influx of cheap labour' from the East (Cottrell, 1998: 41–2 and 'anonymous' government sources). Those EU states which traditionally have benefited significantly from the regional and structural funds and the Common Agricultural Policy (CAP) also have been afraid of losing money as the need arises to spread EU funds more widely once the prospective new members join, and reassuring them in this regard was one of the key concerns during the Agenda 2000 negotiations (Galloway, 1999: 9–36). The considerable implications for the CAP, for example, can be seen when it is noted that, as a percentage of GDP, agricultural output in the Czech Republic, Poland and Hungary accounted for 6, 6 and 7 per cent respectively compared to 2, 2 and 1 per cent in France, Britain and Germany respectively (latest figures available in 1999 (*Economist*, 1999b: 50).

Nevertheless, for the political and economic reasons examined in Karen Henderson's chapter, membership of the EU has become the key goal of the economic policy of all three states. Up until the end of 1989, the majority of Eastern and Central European states traded mostly with the Soviet Union and with each other. After the fall of the Berlin Wall and the collapse of communism, their trading patterns became reoriented towards the West, to the extent that by 1996, 50–80 per cent of their exports went to the West and 70–80 per cent of their imports came from it (Hockman and Djankov, 1997: 473). A significant proportion of Eastern European exports to the EU consists of components and materials which have been sent to the East by firms within EU states for processing and which are then exported back to the EU as finished products. Industries with a significant involvement in this trade include those producing footwear and leather, textiles and cloth, precision instruments, furniture and electrical machinery (Hockman and Djankov, 1997: 471–87).

As the World Bank has noted, the situation now is one in which: 'The European Union is by far the largest trade partner – and direct investor in – the Central and Eastern European countries' (Hockman and Djankov, 1997: 477). The three 'chosen' states have been at the vanguard of the re-focusing of trade on the EU, and their decisions to do this, together with their determined attempts to gain early membership, are clearly moves that have been made in anticipation of considerable consequent benefits. These include, for example, the prospect of *significant increases* in inward investment as a result of the political and economic stability associated with EU membership and their membership of the Single Market, together (as Henderson has noted) with the prospect of *securing long-term political stability* as a result of the restraining effect of EU 'club membership'; the prospect of improving long-term economic *growth prospects*, both as a result of the receipt of EU internal aid and of full membership of the Single Market; and the prospect of *achieving greater currency stability* should the euro succeed over the longer term and the new members eventually qualify for (and choose to apply for) membership of the euro zone.

However, it needs to be realized that there are also sizeable potential costs attached to membership, should the three states secure it. Faced with an increasingly hard-line stance from the EU's representatives as the enlargement negotiations progress (Taylor, 1999b: 9), the favourability or otherwise of the economic deal that the three states get at the end will depend very much on their ability to horse trade and thus water down some of the aspects of membership that at the moment look likely to be quite costly for them. These arise from the relative weakness of the Eastern economies and the fact that the rules that they will have to accept on joining have been designed for wealthier economies used to operating on different economic lines. In May 1999, for example, Simon Taylor noted that the areas of the economic negotiations then at the centre of controversy

> are ones which involve sectors crucial to the applicants as they try to cope with the social impact of restructuring their heavy industries to meet the competitive challenges of being part of the EU economic zone. They are also sectors in which existing member states are determined that their domestic industries will not be undermined because factories in the new member countries enjoy state support. In the discussions on state aid, for example, both Poland and the Czech Republic have asked for a special clause in their accession treaties which would allow them to protect industries if cutting off support would have a serious social impact on the sector concerned ... Union governments are adamant, however, that the existing state aid rules already take into account differing levels of economic development and no extra concessions are necessary. (Taylor, 1999b: 9)

Furthermore, one of the outcomes of the EU's March 1999 Agenda 2000 agreement on financial reforms for the Union, including those necessary to facilitate enlargement, has been that:

> an important political signal has been sent to the applicant countries queuing at the Union's door that, in the context of a single currency in which the applicants are all aspiring participants, enlargement of the Union will have to take place within tight budgetary constraints. (Galloway, 1999: 33)

As the above and other sobering developments have occurred, the effect has been to concentrate the minds of the three states increasingly on the costs side of the enlargement equation and the need to try and minimize it. In May 1999, for example, Hungary's worries were demonstrated by its insistence that speculative Western firms and individuals should be prevented from buying up its farmland until ten years after it has achieved full EU membership. It and other states have also been having problems with the Union's insistence that their external tariffs must be brought into line with EU levels when they become members. Some of the applicants have also been coming under EU pressure to break up large state energy monopolies (Taylor, 1999b: 9). There is also the fear that the Union's previously mentioned attitude on state aid might cause considerable social dislocation and political dissatisfaction, and that, just as it is possible that the applicant states' economies might benefit from the proverbial 'cold shower' of competition resulting from full membership of the Single Market, sectors within them might also drown.

Finally, the huge gaps between the economies of Poland, Hungary and the Czech Republic, and their wealthy Western neighbours, that were demonstrated in the statistical comparisons at the beginning of this section should be recalled throughout any consideration of the economic future of these states. They illustrate graphically just what an enormous leap it is that they are attempting to make in joining the EU and are suggestive in themselves of the very substantial adaptations that they will have to make in becoming full members. All of the applicant states are already in receipt of pre-accession financial assistance under the EU's PHARE programme, with 70 per cent of the assistance provided going towards the reduction of structural, sectoral and regional imbalances, and this is taking up some of the initial burden of the adjustment process. However, something of the daunting scale of readjustments to come and their potential social impact can be seen from the outcome of recent negotiations between the EU and Poland over steel. These resulted in Poland cutting its tariffs while simultaneously restructuring its steel industry, with the loss of 40,000 jobs – nearly half the current workforce (Allen and Smith, 1999: 95).

Future economic prospects for the three Visegrad states

So, given this proverbial mixed bag of costs and benefits, risks and opportunities for the three states examined here in their chosen path of securing full EU membership, what are their likely prospects economically within the foreseeable future, prior to and after accession?

One of the rosiest forecasts was made at the end of 1998 by Mathew Valencia. He saw Poland's prospects as being particularly bright as a result of its now established position as the largest recipient of foreign investment in the region and the most dynamic market. He pointed to the impressive growth rate of 6 to 7 per cent of recent years, and believed that growth would remain healthy, although his conclusion was that its 1999 rate would not quite reach its previous heights. He saw also improved prospects for the Czech economy after its then recent decline in growth rates, believing that it would harvest the benefits of restructuring which a recent currency crisis had forced on the country's companies and of an improved system of financial regulation. He also believed that the leading East European states would benefit from other reforms by then in place, 'such as strengthening their banking systems, making labour practices more flexible and clamping down on cronyism' (Valencia, 1998: 56). He was encouraged also by the way in which these states have ended their reliance on Russia. He concluded that not only would this offer them some protection against economic turbulence in Russia, but that it would in future mean that their economic fate will 'depend on how immune the EU can remain from global turmoil and on the success of the euro, as much as on their own economies' (Valencia, 1998: 56). His optimism, as expounded in 1998, appears to have been rather 'over the top', but not dramatically so. IMF forecasts available in September 1999 project GDP growth rates during the year 2000 of around 5 per cent, 4.4 per cent, and 1.6 per cent for Poland, Hungary and the Czech Republic respectively. These forecasts are up on the 3.8 per cent, 3.8 per cent and 0 per cent actually achieved by these states in the previous months of 1999. These latter figures represent a noticeable but not disastrous decline on their 1998 equivalents for both Hungary and Poland, but a small improvement for the Czech Republic (*Economist*, 1999h: 180). The IMF's optimism suggests an underlying confidence in the basic relative economic soundness of the three states on the part of one of the world's key economic institutions, and this would seem to be backed up by other figures covering the previous 12 months available at the same time (*Economist*, 1999h: 180). What it does not suggest, however, is any belief that their attempts to catch up economically with their Western neighbours will produce any great advances within the immediate future.

Even when these three states eventually join the EU, it will be some time before they will become eligible to participate fully within all of its dimensions. Even if they decide that they would definitely like to participate in EMU, their economies currently are a long way from the point where they would be strong enough to do so. What this means of course, is that the Eastern European states initially will be in the outer layer of a three-speed EU, where the first layer consists of those states within European Monetary Union (EMU), the second consists of those like Britain who could be but so far have refused the offer, and the third consists of those who are as yet too economically weak to participate.

Equally, while there will be some real immediate benefits from membership in terms of assistance from various EU internal funds, the costs in terms of labour-shedding adjustments and environmental reforms are likely to be considerable. While the Single Market offers notable opportunities, full membership of it also presents a considerable challenge in terms of increased competition for some enterprises. The enhanced funding access and increased competition *may* act as a much needed stimulus to drive the three economies forward towards ever greater success. But at the same time, as has already been made clear, there look likely to be rigid ceilings on funding and some enterprises could simply find the increased competition too much for them.

On the other hand, if the euro is a success and the EU economy as a whole prospers during the next few years, the Eastern European states could benefit greatly from their membership. The confidence that economic success will engender should stimulate investment, and Poland, the Czech Republic and Hungary, with their labour cost advantage, the long-term political stability that membership should encourage, and their new position within the EU's boundaries, are likely to become even more attractive locations for such investment than they are currently.

Therefore, membership of the EU is something of an economic gamble. If it works, it should be of real benefit to the economies of the three states, providing they are run responsibly by their governments. But against the arguments of those who are worried about what happens if it does not work is the simple fact that, in reality, the three have little choice but to move towards membership. Their position sandwiched between Russia and the EU means that their economic fortunes are going to be heavily affected by one or the other. Russia's economic weakness makes it a poor bet as an economic senior partner and the EU a profoundly sensible one. Having recognized this and reoriented their trade towards the latter, the three are faced with the realization that their Western neighbour is so large and powerful that the only way in which they can maximize their effectiveness in trying to influence its policies in a manner favourable to themselves is through full membership. This, of course, would give them representation within both the Council of Ministers and the European Parliament, the two key elected decision-making/influencing bodies at the EU's heart. Equally, in an increasingly globalized world economy, the voices of the three states on their own are almost completely inaudible in the key councils of world economic decision-making. Membership of the EU, on the other hand, gives them direct influence and representation on one of the world's three leading economic players.

While the relative backwardness of their own economies is likely to result in painful initial adjustments and costs when they join the EU, the overall likely benefits of EU membership in terms of increased influence over the European and global economies means that it is something they cannot really afford to turn down should it be offered. Politically, of course, membership is seen also as a crucial means of securing the newly acquired democratic status of these states against a range of possible threats, but this is something that has been discussed already in Karen Henderson's chapter.

Notes

1. Full details and a full text copy of Vladimir Andrianov's study can be obtained by emailing andrian@host.cis.lead.org. A summary version can be viewed at ntserver.cis.lead.org/infores/andian.

Conclusions

Peter J. Anderson, Georg Wiessala and Christopher Williams

A large number of conclusions have been drawn within the various preceding chapters concerning the problems and prospects of the new Europe and the European Union, as they begin the twenty-first century. Just looking across a sample range of these, *New Europe in Transition* has demonstrated not only the rich diversity of Europe, but also the consequent enormous complexity of the ongoing European integration project. We have shown the following:

- Firstly, the serious problems of the largest state outside that project, Russia. We have also identified possible solutions to at least some of its current difficulties.
- Secondly, in the chapter on NATO and the OSCE, we have shown how closely interwoven with the USA Europe's fate remains.
- Thirdly, we have illustrated something of the all-pervasive nature of the globalization process within present-day Europe, but also demonstrated that it is uneven in its impact and not irreversible.
- Fourthly, we have revealed not only how this phenomenon is driven by Western modes of liberal capitalism and technological development, but also how, ironically, it is threatening the liberal democracy for which the Western European states fought the Cold War.
- Fifthly, this book suggests that Western-style democracy, and the attempts that Russia has been making to move towards some form of stable democratic pluralism of its own, are faced with a number of significant threats over and above that of globalization.
- Sixthly, *New Europe in Transition* demonstrates that there is a significant difference between Anglo-Saxon and Western European models of the welfare state. This helps divide the largest member states of the EU, thereby perpetuating the exclusion of Britain from 'the heart of Europe'. The book shows how, in a continent of great wealth, there are still areas of enormous poverty.
- Lastly, we have illustrated something of the depth of the problems of corruption and organized crime within two of Europe's biggest states, together with the consequences for the EU following from the exposure, in 1999 and 2000, of deep corruption at the heart of the Commission, one of its own central institutions.

It is not intended here to restate and 'organize' the conclusions reached by various contributors. Instead, we wish to draw out the editors' perceptions of the *broad outlines* of the transition which Europe is currently undergoing. Some features of this process are relatively new, such as the attempts of the Eastern and Central European states, through accession negotiations and a structured Pre-Accession

Strategy, to begin integrating economically, politically and socially with their giant EU neighbour; the uncertain steps which Russia continues to take in the direction of a meaningful democracy; or the incremental development of a new, proactive and interventionist stabilizing role within Europe for NATO. On the other hand, there are some features, such as the slow but continuing progress towards deeper European union amongst the existing EU states, despite a wide range of problems that appear to threaten seriously the success of that project, that have acquired the status almost of 'old friends' for analysts of the European scene. Some aspects of Europe's transition have an almost illusory character, as in the case of the apparent move, since the 1999 Cologne summit, towards greater military muscle and an enhanced role for the Europeans within NATO, which, as in the past, has not so far been backed up by anything like the necessary resources to make it viable.

All in all, certain changes are beneficial, while others are potentially destructive. Hence, globalization has helped both to strengthen economies such as Britain's, via the locational decisions of multinational business corporations, and, in a different manifestation, to threaten states' abilities to manage their own economies successfully, because of increased levels of unpredictability. This was shown in the case of the 1997/98 financial crisis, which started in Asia, but ended up impacting seriously on parts of Europe, most particularly Russia, but also Italy, as the relevant chapters demonstrate. Some aspects of change appear to be pushing Europe towards a crisis point. One does not have to be a resurrected Marxist, for example, to believe that the liberal capitalism that currently dominates Europe is heading rapidly towards a position where a number of very fundamental questions will have to be addressed in the not-too-distant future, to avert catastrophe.

To try and predict in any *scientific* sense how all of this might interact to shape the Europe of ten or twenty years from now would be a ridiculous exercise. Political science simply does not have the appropriate methodological tools available. For example, most political pundits and analysts were taken by surprise by the rapid collapse of the Soviet Union and the speedy dissolution of its Eastern Empire. While the disintegration of Yugoslavia in the years following the death of its strongman, Marshal Tito, was much more widely predicted, the subsequent Balkan role of NATO was not foreseen by most until recently. This was because the *full extent* of the sharp decline in Russia's military and political influence within the region – a key development in permitting Western offensive military action in Bosnia and Kosovo – had not been properly anticipated. Equally, many analysts regarded the prospects of European Monetary Union (EMU) proceeding according to schedule with the likes of Italy on board, as a rather poor prospect. Those who spent the years of Boris Yeltsin's rule of Russia trying to predict what he would do next often ended up with the proverbial egg on their faces. In other words, the predictive tools available to social scientists are just not substantial or refined enough to provide anything more than rough estimates of the way many of Europe's complex relationships will develop over the next few years. Therefore, the projections made below are well informed but rather impressionistic at this early stage of the new millennium.

As suggested in Part II of the book, despite its many problems and failure to respond adequately to public expectations of democratic accountability, the EU is likely to survive and to continue making slow progress towards greater integration. In a year (2000) that has seen the inauguration of another Intergovernmental

Conference (IGC), tasked with contributing to the shaping the Union of the future, the ongoing debate about reform – root-and-branch or dealing with the 'Amsterdam leftovers' alone – has only just begun to demonstrate that some lessons have been learnt from the demise of the old Commission in 1999. Further than that, it has shown that the EU continues to be pulled in two directions at the same time. While comprehensively seeking to restructure itself, its policies, priorities and institutions on the inside, it has also emerged as a potentially stronger and more assertive force in the international arena. Wide-ranging reorganization and new appointments, not only inside the Commission, have illustrated the link between internal overhaul and external muscle and credibility. A more self-assured and outspoken European Parliament, changed in its political composition, is again shifting the goalposts of the institutional balance of power, moving in the process many standards and parameters of accountability and openness in the entire rebuilding of the EU. There is no choice for the Union but to continue on this path and it will do so, while trying simultaneously to deal with a variety of economic and political problems occasioned by the historical priorities of the 1990s, the third stage of EMU and the gradual absorption of new members from Eastern and Central Europe and elsewhere. Individual European states, with the possible exception of Germany, are simply too small to hold their own economically and politically in a world where not only is there already the huge American economic superpower, but also a newly emerging Chinese counterpart, as well as the existing currently troubled Japanese economic giant.

NATO equally is likely to survive, not only because of the USA's role as a superpower for the foreseeable future, and a majority American elite preference to see some protection for US investments and influence in Europe kept in place, but also because of the Europeans' own realization that without the Alliance, some of Europe's old instabilities could re-emerge. In addition, as long as Russia retains a superpower's nuclear armoury and remains unpredictable concerning future degrees of hostility or friendship towards the West, there are likely to be strong lobbies within the elites of both the USA and the European states in favour of keeping the Alliance in place as a guarantee against any potential future Russian aggression.

On top of all of this, two further scenarios are causing concern among the European policy elite. The first is that major new centres of global military power capable of threatening European interests will arise in the world during the twenty-first century, most particularly in the case of China. The second is the likely emergence of a number of new nuclear weapons states with unpredictable regimes and the capability of striking European interests and capitals during the next ten years or so. These additional factors are likely to make individual European states feel insecure without a major nuclear armed alliance to guarantee their safety. What is less certain is how much of the NATO burden of personnel, equipment and general expenditure the Europeans will be carrying in ten to twenty years, or whether their role in Alliance decision-taking will increase substantially. While they have a tradition of failing to deliver on defence spending as far as the Americans are concerned, it is quite likely that pressure for this situation to change radically will increase significantly should the USA find itself facing greatly increased economic competition from the New Pacific over the next few years.

The chapter on Russia has made it clear that attempting to predict its future over the course of the next year is difficult enough, without trying to extend the exercise to ten years or more. But what would seem likely to us is that Russia will gradually stabilize in the direction of a democracy still largely centred on a strong Presidency, but with a more supportive Parliament. It would also seem possible that much of the criminalized element of the Russian economy will gradually 'turn respectable' and conventional once their economic power is consolidated, if only to avoid the counter-measures that are likely to be introduced against them within the global economy as a whole, and the now neighbouring EU, if their current modes of operation continue. Furthermore, as that power consolidates, they are likely to have a decreasing need of criminal methods to enhance and protect their wealth, particularly if, as is quite possible, a strong Presidency emerges which sets in place a state apparatus effective enough to uphold and implement the rule of law. This does not mean that corruption or organized crime will disappear altogether, but simply that the latter is likely to be significantly curtailed. As far as the Russian economy is concerned, as the chapter on transition economies suggests, a strong Russian leadership is likely to try and establish a strong state. Within the latter, factors such as Russia's enormous resources in terms of raw materials, its educated and skilled workforce and the emergence of an embryonic entrepreneurial class might prove to be crucial in kickstarting Russia's economic growth process, providing the right guarantees can be put in place by the new President in the next few years. This will take some time, given the ground that has been lost and the enormous economic and social damage done during the 1990s. Whether such an economically recovering Russia would be friend, foe or neutral towards its European neighbours will probably depend on whether Russia's new, 'strong leadership' seeks to be independent from the more prosperous West, or views Western largesse to be crucial to economic regeneration.

For the Eastern and Central European states, their future is likely to be governed most by their success or failure in gaining admission to the EU and subsequently making something of that membership economically. EU and/or NATO membership will guarantee their security for as long as NATO remains an effective alliance, given that both organizations are regarded as drawing a formal Western line of influence around those who attain membership. Economic prosperity, however, can only be partially generated by Western assistance. The biggest effort has to come from within the societies themselves, and that requires not only effective governments with sufficient authority to carry the appropriate economic measures, but populations that are able and willing to adapt to the cultural and economic changes that are necessary.

This is not to say that those changes should coincide completely with those being advocated currently by the EU. As pointed out earlier, it looks likely that liberal capitalism will move towards one or more points of crisis during the present century. Like the now largely defunct Soviet-style Marxist-Leninist economic systems, capitalism in its present form is leaving too many questions unanswered in too many states, those in Europe included. The continuing consolidation of economic activity in the hands of a limited number of global corporations is placing the core notions of competition and the value of individual initiative under increasing strain. It is making it increasingly difficult for European states to control their own economies to the extent that the more interventionist of them would like. It is also impinging on the most fundamental aspects of human existence by threatening people's ability to make basic choices about the food that they eat and the threats to their health that they are willing to tolerate, as was very much in evidence during the debate over the activities of the American Monsanto corporation in Europe during 1998 and 1999. Social injustice and inequality still exist in most parts of the new Europe and liberal capitalism has therefore not as yet provided an adequate answer to these and related social problems. On top of all of this is the impending 'greying of society' referred to in the chapters on Italy and Germany, which is going to exert tremendous pressures on the health and welfare systems of Europe's states during the first half of the new century. Together these problems inevitably will force a reassessment of how economics should be 'done' in Europe. The result may simply be an incremental rejigging and overhaul of existing liberal capitalism to try and produce something more appropriate to the needs of the new century. Or it may lead to the development and adoption of new economic ideologies. As yet, liberal capitalism appears without an alternative to really challenge its dominance.

We would like to re-emphasize that, while the above projections might be well-informed, they are subject to a number of imponderable variations, such as the sudden collapse of communism at the end of the 1980s and Boris Yeltsin's surprise resignation on New Year's Eve 1999. The scenarios outlined here represent only one of many possibilities, but it will be interesting to see, in five, ten or more years, in how many respects our projections regarding the problems and prospects of the New Europe in Transition have been verified or contradicted.

Bibliography

Abrahamson, P. (1998) 'Combating poverty and social exclusion', in W. Beck, L. van der Maesen and A. Walker (eds), *The Social Quality of Europe*, Bristol, Policy Press.

Abrahamson, P. and Hansen, F.K. (1996) *Poverty in the European Union*, Strasbourg, European Parliament.

Adonnino (Pietro) (1985) *A People's Europe: Report from the* ad hoc *Committee, Bulletin of the European Communities*, Supplement 7/85.

Agenzia Giornalistica Italia (2000a) 'D'Alema says Amato is critical and self-critical', *Oggi in Italia*, 7 January, www.agenziaitalia.it/comunicazione/demo2/index.

Agenzia Giornalistica Italia (2000b) 'Cosutta supports Amato's focus on Alliance, not individual', *Oggi in Italia*, 7 January, www.agenziaitalia.it/comunicazione/demo2/index.

Albæk, K. and Sørensen, B.E. (1998) 'Worker flows and job flows in Danish manufacturing, 1980–91', *Economic Journal*, 108, 1750–71.

Albats, Y. and Powell, B. (2000) 'Moscow's man to watch', *Newsweek*, 10 January, p. 54.

Albert, M. (1991) *Capitalisme contre capitalisme*, Paris, Seuil.

Aliboni, R. and Greco, E. (1996) 'Foreign policy re-nationalization and internalism in the Italian debate', *International Affairs*, 72 (1), 43–51.

Allen, D. and Smith, M. (1999) 'External policy developments', in G. Edwards and G. Wiessala (eds), *The European Union: Annual Review*, Oxford, Blackwell, pp. 9–36.

Almond, G.A. and Bingham Powell, G., Jr (1978) *Comparative Politics*, Boston, Little, Brown.

Alonso Zaldivar, C. and Castells, M. (1992) *Spain beyond Myths*, Madrid, Alianza Editorial.

Alter, K. (1998) 'Who are the masters of the Treaty? European governments and the European Court of Justice', *International Organisation*, 52 (1), 125–52.

Amodia, J. (1998) 'Politics in contemporary Spain: Establishing and consolidating a new democracy', in T. Lawlor and M. Rigby (eds), *Contemporary Spain*, Harlow, Longman, pp. 3–45.

Andersen, H.W. (1982) *Dansk Politik I Går og I Dag*, Copenhagen, Fremad.

Anderson, B. (1991) *Imagined Communities*, London, Verso.

Anderson, C. (1995) 'Economic uncertainty and European solidarity revisited: Trends in popular support for European integration', in C. Rhodes and S. Mazey (eds), *The State of the European Union: Volume 3 Building a European Polity?*, Harlow, Longman.

Anderson, P.J. (1996) *The Global Politics of Power, Justice and Death*, London, Routledge.

Anderson, P.J. and Weymouth, A. (1999) *Insulting the Public? The British Press and the European Union*, Harlow, Longman.
Anderson, S., and Eliassen, K. (eds) (1996) *The European Union: How Democratic Is It?*, London, Sage.
Andrianov, V. (n.d., accessed in December 1999) *Russia in the Global Economy* (chapter-by-chapter detailed summary of conclusions), ntserver.cis.lead.org/infores/andian.
Annan, K.A. (1993) 'UN peacekeeping and co-operation with NATO', *NATO Review*, 42(5), 3–7.
Ardagh, J. (1999) *France in the New Century: Portrait of a Changing Society*, London, Viking.
Ardy, B. (1999) 'Agriculture, structural policy, the budget and eastern enlargement of the European Union', in K. Henderson (ed.), *Back to Europe: Central and Eastern Europe and the European Union*, London, UCL Press.
Ariztegui (1993) 'La politica monetaria', in J.L. Garcia Delgado (ed.), *España economía*, Madrid, Espasa Calpe, pp. 1123–48.
Armstrong, K.A. (1998) 'Legal integration: theorizing the legal dimension of European integration', *Journal of Common Market Studies*, 36(2), 155–74.
Ashton, S.R. (1989) *In Search of Detente: The Politics of East–West Relations Since 1945*, London, Macmillan.
Avery, G. and Cameron, F. (1998) *The Enlargement of the European Union*, Sheffield, Sheffield Academic Press/UACES.
Banco de Portugal (1994) *Report of the Directors and Economic and Financial Survey for the Year 1993*, Lisbon, Banco de Portugal.
Banco de Portugal (1998) *Relatorio do Conselho de Administracao 1997*, Lisbon, Banco de Portugal.
Banco de Portugal (1999) *Relatorio do Conselho de Administracao 1998*, Lisbon, Banco de Portugal.
Bandrés, E. (1993) 'Las infraestructuras, politicas y realizaciones', in J.L. Garcia Delgado (ed.), *España economía*, Madrid, Espasa Calpe, pp. 1051–70.
Banca Commerciale Italiana (1999) *Views on the Italian economy*, 4 November, www.bci.it/ufficio-studi/vie/evie.pdf.
Barreto, A. (1994) 'Portugal, a Europa e a democracia', *Analise Social*, 29(129), 1051–69.
Barreto, A. (1995) 'Portugal na periferia do centro: mudança social, 1960–1995', *Analise Social*, 30 (134), 841–55.
Barreto, A. (ed.) (1996) *A Situacao Social em Portugal 1960–1995*, Lisbon, Instituto de Ciencias Sociais, Universidade de Lisboa.
Beck, W., van der Maesen, L. and Walker, A. (eds) (1998) *The Social Quality of Europe*, Bristol, Policy Press.
Belin, L. with Clem, R. (1997) *The Russian Parliamentary Elections of 1995*, New York, M.E. Sharpe.
Beyers, J. and Dierickx, G. (1998) 'The working groups of the Council of the European Union: supranational or intergovernmental negotiations?', *Journal of Common Market Studies*, 36 (3), 289–317.
Bilt, C. (1998) 'Holbrooke's history: Review article of "To end a war" ', *Survival*, 40 (3), 187–91.

Bird, C. and Vulliamy, E. (1999) 'Serbs attack as monitors leave', *Observer*, 21 March.

Bjørn, N.H. and Brixen, P. (1998) 'Handel og velstand: Udviklingslinjer I den internationale varehandel', *Politica*, 30 (1), 8–23.

Black, I. (1999) 'Angry Yeltsin berates west', *Guardian*, 19 November, p. 2.

Black, J.L. (2000) *Russia Faces NATO Expansion: Bearing Gifts or Bearing Arms?* Maryland, Rowman & Littlefield, Lanham.

Blair, A. (1999a) *Speech at the Lord Mayor's Banquet*, Guildhall, London, 22 November, www.number-10.gov.uk/public/info/r.../Speech_display.asp?random = 3657&index = .

Blair, A. (1999b) *Speech at the Launch of the Britain in Europe Campaign*, BFI Imax Cinema, London, 14 October, www.fco.gov.uk/news/speechtext.asp?2886.

Blazcya, G. (1999) 'Poland – how immune to economic and financial contagion?', Paper presented to the BASEES annual conference, March, Cambridge.

Blitz, J. (1999) 'Italy to vote on poll reform', *Financial Times*, 17 April/18 April, p. 3.

Boix, C. (1998) 'El gobierno de la economía, naturaleza y determinantes de la política económica en España', in R. Goma and J. Subirats (eds), *Políticas públicas en España*, Barcelona, Ariel, pp. 39–54.

Bravo, O. (1989) *Economia Portuguesa*, Oporto, Porto Editora.

Bretherton, C. and Ponton, G. (1996) *Global Politics*, Oxford, Blackwell.

Bretherton, C. and Vogler, J. (1999) *The European Union as a Global Actor*, London, Routledge.

Brown, A. (1997) *The Gorbachev Factor*, Oxford, Oxford University Press.

Brown, P. and Meikle, J. (1999) 'Danes steal a march on home market: British producers defend "fine-tuned system" as Scandinavia mounts challenge', *Guardian*, 8 September, p. 8.

Brundtland, A.O. (1966) 'Nordisk balance før og nå', *Internasjonal Politikk*, 5, 491–541.

Brundtland, G.H. (chair) (1987) *Our Common Future: The World Commission on Environment and Development*, Oxford, Oxford University Press.

Bruto da Costa, A. (1998) *Exclusoes Sociais*, Lisbon, Gradiva.

Buzan, B., Kelstrup, M., Lemaitre, P., Tromer, E. and Waever, O. (1990) *The European Security Order Recast: Scenarios for the Post Cold War Era*, London, Pinter.

Cameron, D.R. (1996) 'National Interest, the Dilemmas of European Integration, and Malaise', in J.T.S. Keeler and M. Schain (eds), *Chirac's Challenge: Liberalization, Europeanization and Malaise in France*, New York, St. Martin's Press, pp. 325–82.

Cameron, P. (1999) *European Foreign and Security Policy – Past, Present and Future*, Sheffield, Sheffield Academic Press/UACES.

Cannan, C., Berry, L. and Lyons, K. (1992) *Social Work and Europe*, Basingstoke, Macmillan.

Carreira, H.M. (1996) *As Politicas Sociais em Portugal*, Lisbon, Gradiva.

Castles, F.G. (1995) 'Welfare state development in Southern Europe', *West European Politics*, 18 (2), 291–313.

CDU/CSU Fraktion des Deutschen Bundestages (1994) *Berlegungen zur europaischen Politic*, Bonn.
Centre for Economic Policy Research (1995) *Flexible Integration – Monitoring European Integration 6*, London, Centre for Economic Policy Research.
Charlot, J. (1971) *The Gaullist Phenomenon: The Gaullist Movement in the Fifth Republic*, London, Allen & Unwin. Translated from the French by M. Charlot and M. Neighbour.
Cini, M. (1996) *The European Commission: Leadership, Organisation and Culture in the EU Administration*, Manchester, Manchester University Press.
Cole, A. (1998) *French Politics and Society*, London: Prentice Hall.
Collins, R. (1994) 'Unity in diversity? The European Single Market in broadcasting and the audiovisual, 1982–92', *Journal of Common Market Studies*, 32 (1), 89–102.
Colomer, J.M. (1999) 'The Spanish "State of Autonomies": Non-Institutional Federalism', in *Politics and Policy in Democratic Spain*, London, Frank Cass, pp. 40–52.
Colton, T.J. and Hough, J.F. (eds) (1998) *Growing Pains: Russian Democracy and the Election of 1993*, Washington, DC, Brookings Institute Press.
Commander, S. (1999) 'Barter in Russia', *Economic Outlook*, 23 (3), pp. 19–22.
Cooper, T.M. (1995) 'Convergence and competitiveness: the Spanish situation', in T.M. Cooper (ed.), *Spain in Europe*, Leeds, Trinity and All Saints College, pp. 101–34.
Confindustria (1992) *Confindustria per la modernizzazione, Proposte ed intese 1992–1995*, Rome, SIPI.
Corkhill, D. (1993) *The Portuguese Economy since 1974*, Edinburgh, Edinburgh University Press.
Corkhill, D. (1996) 'Portugal votes for change and stability: the election of 1995', *West European Politics*, 19 (2), 403–9.
Corkhill, D. (1999a) *The Development of the Portuguese Economy: A Case of Europeanization*, London, Routledge.
Corkhill, D. (1999b) 'Portugal's 1998 Referendums', *West European Politics*, 22 (2), 186–92.
Cornish, P. (1997) *Partnership in Crisis*, London, Pinter/RIIA.
Costs, F.S. da (1997) 'Conferencia Intergovernmental', *Europa – Novas Fronteiras*, November 1997, pp. 22–30, Lisbon, Centro de Informacao Jacques Delors.
Cottrell, R. (1998) 'Lots to be doing in Europe', in The Economist Intelligence Unit (ed.), *The World in 1999*, London, The Economist Group, pp. 41–2.
Council of the European Union (1999) *Helsinki European Council: Presidency Conclusions*, Luxembourg, Office for Official Publications of the European Communities.
Cox, R. (1997) 'Democracy in hard times: economic globalisation and the limits to liberal democracy', in A. McGrew (ed.), *The Transformation of Democracy*, Cambridge, Polity Press/Open University.
Cram, L., Dinan, D. and Nugent, N. (1999) *Developments in the European Union*, Basingstoke, Macmillan.
Criddle, B. (1993) 'The French Referendum on the Maastricht Treaty, September 1992'. *Parliamentary Affairs*, 46 (2), 228–38.

Croft, S., Redmond, J., Wyn Rees, G. and Webber, M. (1999) *The Enlargement of Europe*, Manchester, Manchester University Press.

Daly, M. (1997) 'Welfare states under pressure: cash benefits in European welfare states over the last ten years', *Journal of European Social Policy*, 7 (2), 129–46.

Dankert, P. (1998) 'Managing public acceptance of the European Union', in M. Den Boer *et al.* (eds), *Coping with Flexibility and Legitimacy after Amsterdam*, Maastricht, EIPA.

Darby, P. (1973) *British Defence Policy East of Suez, 1947–1963*, Oxford, Oxford University Press/RIIA.

Daugbjerg, C. (1998a) *Policy Networks Under Pressure: Pollution Control, Policy Reforms and the Power of Farmers*, Aldershot, Ashgate.

Daugbjerg, C. (1998b) 'Linking policy networks and environmental policies: nitrate policy making in Denmark and Sweden 1970–1995', *Public Administration*, 76, 275–94.

den Boer, M. (1994) 'The quest for European policing; rhetoric and justification in a disorderly debate', in M. Anderson and M. den Boer, *Policing Across National Boundaries*, London, Pinter.

De Búrca, G. (1998) 'The principle of subsidiarity and the Court of Justice as an institutional actor', *Journal of Common Market Studies*, 36 (2), 217–35.

De Giustino, D. (1996) *A Reader in European Integration*, Harlow, Longman.

Dehousse, R. (1998) *The European Court of Justice*, The European Union Series, Basingstoke, Macmillan.

Delahaye, L. (2000) 'A frozen land of crisis', *Newsweek*, 10 January, pp. 52–3.

Delano, M. (1999) 'La venta de Enersis vuelve a desatar la polemica', *El Pais* (seccion negocios), 24 January, p. 6.

Denny, C. (1999) 'Cyber utopia? Only the usual candidates need apply', *Guardian*, 12 July, p. 23.

Devuyst, Y. (1998) 'Treaty reform in the European Union: the Amsterdam Process', *Journal of European Public Policy*, 5 (4), 615–31.

Dias, H. and Fernandes, M.B. (1993) 'O Surgimento do Servico Social nas Misericórdias Portuguesas', *Revista do Instituto Superior de Servico Social*, III, no. 8, 35–52.

Dicken, P. (1998) *Global Shift: Transforming the World Economy*, 3rd edn, London, Paul Chapman.

Dickenson, D. (1997) 'Counting women in: globalisation, democratization and the women's movement', in A. McGrew (ed.), *The Transformation of Democracy*, Cambridge, Polity Press/Open University.

Dinan, D. (1999) *Ever Closer Union: An Introduction to European Integration*, 2nd edn, The European Union Series, Basingstoke, Macmillan.

Donegani, J.M. and Sadoun, M. (1998) *La Vie Republique: naissance et mort*, Paris, Calmann-Levy.

Doxey, M.P. (1999) *United Nations Sanctions: Current Policy Issues*, revised edn, Centre for Foreign Policy Studies, Dalhouse University.

Duke, S. (1996) 'The second death (or the second coming?) of the WEU', *Journal of Common Market Studies*, 34 (2), 167–90.

Due-Nielsen, C. and Petersen, N. (eds) (1995) *Adaptation and Activism: The Foreign Policy of Denmark 1967–1993*, Copenhagen, DJØ Publishing.

Duff, Andrew (ed.) (1997) *The Treaty of Amsterdam, Text and Commentary*, London, Federal Trust.

Duhamel, A. (1999) *Une ambition française*, Paris, Plon.

Dunlop, J.B. (1999) 'The August coup and its impact on Soviet politics', in M. Kramer (ed.), *The Collapse of the Soviet Union*, Boulder, CO, Westview Press.

Durch, W.J. and Shear, J.A. (1997) 'Faultlines: United Nations operations in the former Yugoslavia,' in W.J. Durch (ed.), *United Nations Peacekeeping: American Politics and the Uncivil Wars of the 1990's*. Basingstoke, Macmillan, pp. 193–275.

Duverger, M. (1987) *La cohabitation des français*, Paris, Presses Universitaires de France.

Dyson, K. (1996) 'The economic order – still *Modell Deutschland*?', in G. Smith, W.E. Paterson and S. Padgett (eds), *Developments in German Politics 2*, London, Macmillan, pp. 194–208.

Dyson, K. (1999) 'The Franco-German relationship and Economic and Monetary Union: Using Europe to "bind Leviathan" ', *West European Politics*, 22 (2), 25–44.

Earnshaw, D. and Judge, D. (1997) 'The life and times of the European Union's cooperation procedure', *Journal of Common Market Studies*, 35 (4), 543–64.

Economist (1990) 'Survey of Italy', *The Economist*, May (supplement).

Economist (1998) 'The Third Way: Goldilocks politics', *The Economist*, 19 December, p. 47.

Economist (1999a) 'Germany survey', *The Economist*, 6 February.

Economist (1999b) *Pocket Europe in Figures*, London, *The Economist* Group/Profile Books.

Economist (1999c) 'Italy and the law: no trust', *The Economist*, 4 September, p. 39.

Economist (1999d) 'Leaving donkey droppings behind', *The Economist*, 17 July, p. 34.

Economist (1999e) 'The complications of clustering', *The Economist*, 2 January, pp. 57–8.

Economist (1999f) 'Virtue's poor reward', *The Economist*, 3 July, p. 97.

Economist (1999g) 'Loyal Italians', *The Economist*, 17 April, p. 53.

Economist (1999h) 'Emerging market indicators', *The Economist*, 25 September, p. 180.

Edgerton, D. (1998) 'Blair's warfare state', *New Left Review*, 230, pp. 123–30.

Edwards, G. (1998) 'Legitimacy and flexibility in post-Amsterdam Europe', in M. den Boer *et al.* (eds), *Coping with Flexibility and Legitimacy after Amsterdam*, Maastricht EIPA.

Edwards, G. and Regelsberger, E. (1990) *Europe's Global Links*, London, Pinter.

Edwards, G. and Wiessala, G. (1998) 'Legitimacy, democracy and identity in post-Amsterdam Europe', in *The European Union: Annual Review of Activities 1997*, Oxford, Blackwell, pp. 1–11.

Edwards, G. and Wiessala, G. (1999) *'Plus ça change* ... ', in G. Edwards and G. Wiessala (eds), *The European Union: Annual Review 1998/9*, Oxford, Blackwell, pp. 1–8.

EIU (The Economist Intelligence Unit) (1998) 'The World in figures', in *The World in 1999*, London, The Economist Group, pp. 87–98.
Eknes, A. (n.d.) *Blue Helmets in a Blown Mission*, Oslo, Norwegian Institute of International Affairs.
Eknes, A. (1995) 'The United Nations predicament in the former Yugoslavia', in T.G. Weiss (ed.), *The United Nations and Civil Wars*, Boulder, CO, Lynne Reinner Publishers, pp. 109–26.
Elder, N., Thomas, A. and Arter, D. (1988) *The Consensual Democracies? The Government and Politics of the Scandinavian States*, Oxford, Blackwell.
Elgey, G. and Colombani, J.M. (1999) *La Cinquième ou la République des phratries*, Paris, Fayard.
Eliassen, K.A. (1998) *Foreign and Security Policy in the European Union*, London, Sage.
Ellman, M. (2000) 'The Russian economy under Yeltsin', Unpublished paper presented to the BASEES Annual conference, Cambridge, 1–3 April.
Elliott, L. (1999) 'East is Eden', G2, *Guardian*, 7 December, pp. 2–3.
Ellworthy, C. and Shea, J. (1999) Debate on the role of NATO and the OSCE in Kosovo, *Woman's Hour*, London, BBC Radio, 27 October.
Epsing-Andersen, G. (1990) *The Three Worlds of Welfare Capitalism*, Cambridge, Polity Press.
Epsing-Andersen, G. (ed.) (1996) *Welfare States in Transition*, London, Sage.
Estes, R.J. (1988) *Trends in World Social Development*, New York, Praeger.
Estes, R.J. (1997) 'Social development trends in Europe, 1970–1994: development prospects for the new Europe', *Social Indicators Research*, 42 (1), 1–19.
Estes, R.J. (1998) 'Trends in world social development, 1970–1995: development challenges for a new century', *Journal of Developing Societies*, 14 (1), 11–39.
European Commission (1977) *Report of the Study Group on the role of public finance in European integration* (The MacDougall Report), Luxembourg, Office for Official Publications of the European Communities.
European Commission (1993a) *European Social Policy: Options for the Union*, Luxembourg, Office for Official Publications of the European Communities.
European Commission (1993b) *Copenhagen European Council*, Luxembourg, Office for Official Publications of the European Communities.
European Commission (1994a) *European Social Policy: A Way Forward for the Union*, Luxembourg, Office for Official Publications of the European Communities.
European Commission (1994b) 'Essen European Council: conclusions of the Presidency', *Bulletin of the European Union*, 27 (12).
European Commission (1995a) *Social Protection in Europe*, Luxembourg, Office for Official Publications of the European Communities.
European Commission (1995b) *White Paper: Preparation of the Associated Countries of Central and Eastern Europe for Integration into the Internal Market of the Union*, COM(95) 163 final, Luxembourg, Office for Official Publications of the European Communities.
European Commission (1997a) 'Agenda 2000: for a stronger and wider Union', *Bulletin of the European Union*, Supplement 5/97.

European Commission (1997b) 'Luxembourg European Council: Presidency conclusions', *Bulletin of the European Union*, No. 12.

European Commission (1998a) 'Agenda 2000 Enlargement. Composite paper 1998. Progress made by the candidate countries towards accession', *Bulletin of the European Union*, Supplement 4/98.

European Commission (1998b) *Central and Eastern Eurobarometer: Public Opinion and the European Union (10 countries survey)*. No. 8, March 1998, Luxembourg, Office for Official Publications of the European Communities.

European Commission (1999a) *Eurobarometer: Public Opinion in the European Union*, Report No. 51, Luxembourg, Office for Official Publications of the European Communities.

European Commission (1999b) *Commission Sets Out an Ambitious Accession Strategy and Proposes to Open Accession Negotiations with Six More Candidate Countries*, IP/99/751, www.europa.eu.int/comm/enlargement/report_10_99/intro/index.

European Commission (1999c) *Report Updating the Commission Opinion on Malta's Application for Membership*, COM (99) 69 final, Luxembourg, Office for Official Publications of the European Communities.

European Commission (1999d) *Composite Paper: Reports on Progress Towards Accession by Each of the Candidate Countries*, COM (99) 500 final, Luxembourg, Office for Official Publications of the European Communities.

European Commission, DG X (1999) *Frontier-Free Newsletter*, June/July, Luxembourg, Office for Official Publications of the European Communities.

European Court of Justice (1999) 'The future of the judicial system of the European Union', ECJ Press Release, No. 36, 28 May.

European Law Journal (1998) *Special Issue on Legal Theory in the European Union*, 4 (4), Oxford, Blackwell.

European Parliament, Working Document (1998) *Towards a European Judicial Area*, Civil Liberties Series, LIBE 101 RN, 5/1998, Brussels, 15–16 April.

European Union (1999a) *The Development of a Common European Security and Defence Policy – The Integration Project of the Next Decade* (speech by J. Solana) 17 December, accessed via www.ue.eu.int/pesc/article.asp?lang = en&id = 4900007.

European Union (1999b) *Conclusions of the European Council Meeting in Helsinki, held on 10 and 11 December 1999*, Document No. 99/253, accessed via wwwarc1.iue.it/iue/efball?nd = 99%2f253.

European Voice (1999a) 'In brief', *European Voice*, 4–10 February, p. 2.

European Voice (1999b) 'Europe in figures', *European Voice*, 9–15 September, p. 23.

Eurostat (1991) *A Social Portrait of Europe*, Luxembourg, Office for Official Publications of the European Communities.

Evans, A. (1997) 'Democratization and human rights', in A. McGrew (ed.), *The Transformation of Democracy*, Cambridge, Polity Press/Open University.

Everson, M. (1998) 'On the necessary cunning of constitutional reasoning', *European Law Journal*, 4 (4), 389–410.

Falkner, G. (1998) *EU Social Policy in the 1990s*, London, Routledge.

Faurby, I. (1995) 'Danish Alliance policy 1967–1993: from quiet adaptation via loud disagreement to cautious involvement', in C. Due-Nielsen and N. Petersen (eds), *Adaptation and Activism: The Foreign Policy of Denmark 1967–1993*, Copenhagen, DJØF Publishing.

Ferrera, M. (1996) 'The "southern model" of welfare in social Europe', *Journal of European Social Policy*, 6 (1), 17–37.

Finer, S.E., Bogdanor, V. and Rudden, B. (1995) *Comparing Constitutions*, Oxford, Clarendon Press.

Fitzmaurice, J. (1996) 'Denmark', in R. Morgan and C. Tame (eds), *Parliaments and Parties: The European Parliament in the Political Life of Europe*, Basingstoke, Macmillan.

Foreign and Commonwealth Office (1999a), 'NATO's fiftieth anniversary summit', *Focus International*, London, June 1999. http://files.fco.gov.uk/info/briefs/1667.pdf.

Foreign and Commonwealth Office (1999b) *Joint Declaration Launching European Defence Capabilities Initiative*, British–Italian summit: 19–20 July, www.fco.gov.uk/news/newsteext.asp?2664.

Foreign and Commonwealth Office (undated), *Human Rights in Foreign Policy*, accessed via http://hrpd.fco.gov.uk.

Forster, A. and Wallace, W. (1996) 'Common Foreign and Security Policy, a new policy or just a new name?' in H. Wallace and W. Wallace (eds), *Policy-Making in the European Union*, Oxford, Oxford University Press, pp. 411–35.

Fossa, G. (1996) *Assemblea annuale Confindustria. Relazione del Presidente*. Rome, Confindustria.

Foster, N. (1998) 'Legal developments', in G. Edwards and G. Wiessala (eds), *The European Union 1997: Annual Review of Activities*, Oxford, Blackwell, pp. 93–110.

Foster, N. (1999a) 'Legal developments', in G. Edwards and G. Wiessala (eds) *The European Union: Annual Review 1998/9*, Oxford, Blackwell, pp. 113–33.

Foster, N. (1999b) *EC Legislation*, 10th edn, London, Blackstone Press.

Fourth Freedom Forum (n.d.) *Making Sanctions Effective: The Case of Yugoslavia* (available from www.fourthfreedom.org/inforum/yugo.

Franchetti, M. (2000) 'Russia's rich await cold hand of President Putin', *Sunday Times*, 26 March, p. 26.

Franco, A. de S. (1997) 'Crescimento sustentado de mãos dadas com o caminho para o Euro', *Europa – Novas Fronteiras*, June, pp. 50–5, Lisbon, Centro de Informação Jacques Delors.

Frankel, J. (1975) *British Foreign Policy 1945–1973*, London, Oxford University Press/RIIA.

Gallagher, T. (1983) *Portugal: A Twentieth-Century Interpretation*, Manchester, Manchester University Press.

Gallagher, T. (1986) 'Twice choosing the unexpected: the Portuguese elections of 1985 and 1986', *West European Politics*, 9 (4), 233–7.

Gallagher, T. (1988) 'Goodbye to revolution: the Portuguese election of July 1987', *West European Politics*, 11 (1), 139–45.

Galloway, D. (1999) 'Agenda 2000: Packaging the deal', in G. Edwards and G. Wiessala (eds), *The European Union: Annual Review*, Oxford, Blackwell, pp. 9–36.

Galtung, J. (1973) *The European Community: A Superpower in the Making*, London, George Allen & Unwin.

Gardner Feldman, L. (1999) 'Reconciliation and legitimacy: foreign relations and enlargement of the EU', in T. Banchoff and M. Smith (eds), *Legitimacy and the European Union: The Contested Polity*, London, Routledge.

Garodkin, I. (1998) *Håndbog I Dansk Politik 98*, Copenhagen, Munksgaard.

Gasteyger, C. (1997) 'The European Union: paper tiger or modern power?', World Affairs, 1 (4), October–December, 94–108.

Gibowski, W. (1999) 'Social change and the electorate: an analysis of the 1998 Bundestagswahl', *German Politics*, 8 (2), 10–32.

Giddens, A. (1999) 'New world without end', Abridged version of the first of the 1999 Reith Lectures published in *Observer*, 11 April.

Gills, B. (1993) 'The hegemonic transition in East Asia, a historical perspective', in S. Gill (ed.), *Gramsci, Historical Materialism and International Relations*, Cambridge, Cambridge University Press, pp. 186–212.

Ginsberg, R. (1989) *Foreign Policy Actions of the European Community: The Politics of Scale*, Boulder, CO, Lynne Rienner Publishers.

Ginsberg, R.H. (1999) 'Conceptualising the European Union as an international actor: narrowing the theoretical capability–expectations gap', *Journal of Common Market Studies*, 37 (3), 429–54.

Giraldes, M. de R. (1995) 'Caracterizacao dos principais recursos humanos de saude em Portugal', *Revista Portuguesa de Saude Publica*, 13 (3).

Glöckler, G. 'A "single voice" for Europe's single currency? EMU and international monetary relations', *Current Politics and Economics of Europe*, 8 (2), 187–206.

Gough, I. (1996) 'Social assistance in Southern Europe', *South European Society & Politics*, 1 (1), 1–23.

Gough, I., Bradshaw, J., Ditch, J., Eardley, T. and Whiteford, P. (1997) 'Social assistance in OECD countries', *Journal of European Social Policy*, 7 (1), 17–43.

Gould, A. (1999) 'The erosion of the welfare state: Swedish social policy and the EU', *Journal of European Social Policy*, 9 (2), 165–74.

Gourlay, C. and Remacle, E. (1998) 'The 1996 IGC: the actors and their interaction', in K.A. Eliassen (ed.), *Foreign and Security Policy in the European Union*, London, Sage, pp. 59–93.

Grabbe, H. and Hughes, K. (1998) *Enlarging the EU Eastwards*, London, Cassell/RIIA.

Graham, T.E., Jr. (1999) 'A world without Russia?', Paper presented to a Jamestown Foundation conference on *Russia: What went wrong? Which way now?*, June. Cited at www.jamestown.org/htm/conf-paper-graham-full.

Gray, J. (1999) *False Dawn*, London, Granta.

Green Cowles, M. (1995) 'Setting the agenda for a new Europe: the ERT and EC 1992', *Journal of Common Market Studies*, 33 (4).

Greve, B. (1996) 'Indications of social policy convergence in Europe', *Social Policy & Administration*, 30 (4), 348–67.

Guardian, (1999a) 'Our unjust society', 3 December, p. 23.

Guardian, (1999b) 'Nato under threat', 24 November, p. 23.

Guay, T.R. (1999) *The United States and the European Union*, Sheffield, Sheffield Academic Press/UACES.

Gundle, S. and Parker, S. (eds) (1996) *The New Italian Republic*, London, Routledge.

Gurov, A. (1992) *Organizatsiia prestupnost' – Ne mif, a real'nost'*, Moscow, Znanie.

Gurov, A. (1995) *Krasnaya Mafia*, Moscow, Komercheskii Vestnik.

Guyomarch, A. (1995) 'The European dynamics of evolving party competition in France'. *Parliamentary Affairs*, 48 (1), 100–23.

Guyomarch, A., Machin, H. and Ritchie, E. (1998) *France in the European Union*, Basingstoke, Macmillan.

Habermas, J. (1976) *Legitimation Crisis*, London, Heinemann.

Haftendorn, H. (1997) 'The post-Cold War Atlantic Alliance' (the Madeleine Feher European Scholar Lecture), Begin-Sadat Center for Strategic Studies, Bar-lian University.

Hampson, J. (1997a) 'Social policy in the Latin rim: the case of Portugal', in M. May, E. Brunsdon and G. Craig (eds), *Social Policy Review 9*, London, Social Policy Association.

Hampson, J. (1997b) 'Social protection and social insurance in Portugal', in J. Clasen (ed.), *Social Insurance in Europe*, Bristol, Policy Press.

Handelman, S. (1994) *Comrade Criminal*, London, Michael Joseph.

Hanson, S.E. and Williams, C. (1999) 'National socialism, left patriotism or super-imperialism? The radical right in Russia', in S.P. Ramet (ed.), *The Radical Right in East-Central Europe*, Pennsylvania, Pennsylvania State University Press, pp. 257–77.

Harding, R. (1999) '*Standort Deutschland* in the globalising economy: an end to the economic miracle?', *German Politics*, 8 (1), 66–88.

Harris, D.J., O'Boyle, M. and Warbrick, C. (1995) *Law of the European Convention on Human Rights*, Oxford, Butterworths.

Hayes-Renshaw, F., Lequesne, C. and Mayor Lopez, P. (1989) 'The Permanent Representations of the member states to the European Communities', *Journal of Common Market Studies*, 28 (2), 119–37.

Hayes-Renshaw, F. and Wallace, H. (1997) *The Council of Ministers*, Basingstoke, Macmillan.

Hayward, J. (1986) *The State and the Market Economy: Industrial Patriotism and Economic Intervention in France*, Oxford, Oxford University Press.

Hedlund, S. (1999) *Russia's 'Market' Economy: A Bad Case of Predatory Capitalism*, London, University College London Press.

Heinz, J.P. *et al.* (1993) *The Hollow Core*, Cambridge, MA, Harvard University Press.

Henderson, K. (ed.) (1999) *Back to Europe: Central and Eastern Europe and the European Union*, London, University College London Press.

Hernando Moreno, J. (1997) 'El comercio exterior español, balance de una década en la Unión Europea', *Información comercial española. Revista de economía*, No. 766, pp. 147–61.

Heywood, P. (1995) *The Government and Politics of Spain*, Basingstoke, Macmillan.

Hill, C. (1993) 'The capabilities–expectations gap or conceptualising Europe's international role', *Journal of Common Market Studies*, 31 (3), 305–28.

Hine, D. (1996) 'Italian political reform in comparative perspective', in S. Gundle and S. Parker (eds), *The New Italian Republic*, London, Routledge, pp. 311–26.

Hirsch, F. (1977) *Social Limits to Growth*, London, Routledge.

Hirst, P. and Thompson, G. (1996) *Globalisation in Question*, Cambridge, Polity Press.

Hix, S. (1998) *The Political System of the European Union*, Basingstoke, Macmillan.

Hockman, B. and Djankov, S. (1997) 'Determinants of the export structure of countries in Central and Eastern Europe', *The World Bank Economic Review*, 2 (3), 471–87.

Hoffmann, S. (1995) *The European Sisyphus: Essays on Europe 1964–1994*, Boulder, CO, Westview.

Holbrooke, R. (1999) *To End a War*, New York, Random House.

Holland, M. (1995) 'Bridging the capability–expectations gap: a case study of the CFSP joint action on South Africa', *Journal of Common Market Studies*, 33 (4), 555–72.

Holland, M. (1997) *Common Foreign and Security Policy: The Record of Reforms*, London, Cassell.

Holland, M. (1999) 'The Common Foreign and Security Policy', in L. Cram, D. Dinan and N. Nugent (eds), *Developments in the European Union*, Basingstoke, Macmillan.

Hoon, G. (1999) 'Britain's role in Europe', Speech to the Mid-Atlantic Club, London, 16 September, www.fco.gov.uk/news/speechtext.asp?2815.

Hough, J.F., Davidheiser, E. and Lehman, S.G. (1996) *The 1996 Presidential Elections*, Washington, DC, Brookings Institute Press.

Hughes, K. and Smith, E. (1998) 'New Labour – new Europe?', *International Affairs*, 74 (1), 93–104.

Hughes, N. (1998) 'The International Development Cooperation Law: The impact of the development community on the Spanish legislative process', *International Journal of Iberian Studies*, 11 (3), 178–88.

Human Rights Watch (1999) World Report: *Croatia – Human Rights Development and the Role of the International Community*, available from www.hrw.org/world_report 99/europe/Croatia3.

Hurd, D. (1994) 'Developing the Common Foreign and Security Policy', *International Affairs*, 70 (3), 1994.

Hutton, W. (1995) *The State We're In*, London, Macmillan.

Hutton, W. (2000) 'Scandal of our betrayed industry', *Observer*, 30 April.

Hyde-Price, A. (1996) *The International Politics of East Central Europe*, Manchester, Manchester University Press.

IFOR, NATO/WEU (1996) *Operation Sharp Guard*, Final Factsheet, 2 October (available from www.nato/ifor/general/shrp-grd).

Illianov, A. (1997) 'Tomorrow's Russia: Adversary, Partner or Ally of the West', *CSIS Russian and European Program Corporate Briefing Series*, 5 March.

Ilynsky, I. (1996) 'Law and order', in C. Williams, V. Chuprov and V. Staroverov (eds), *Russian Society in Transition*, Aldershot, Dartmouth, pp. 219–40.

Intermón (1998) *La Realidad de la Ayuda 1998/99*, Barcelona, Intermón.

International Criminal Tribunal for the Former Yugoslavia (1998) Press Release, The Hague, 20 November.

International Criminal Tribunal for the Former Yugoslavia (1999a) *Making a Difference or Making Excuses*, Judge Gabrielle Kirk McDonald, speech to the Council on Foreign Relations, 12 May, New York.

International Criminal Tribunal for the Former Yugoslavia (1999b) Press Release, The Hague, 13 May.

International Criminal Tribunal for the Former Yugoslavia (1999c) 'President Milosevic and four other senior FRY officials indicted for murder, persecution and deportation in Kosovo', Press Release, The Hague, 27 May.

International Criminal Tribunal for the Former Yugoslavia (1999d) *Factsheet*, 27 October.

International Criminal Tribunal for the Former Yugoslavia (1999e) Press Briefing, United Nations New York, 10 November, by the Chief Prosecutor Carlos Del Ponte and Graham Blewitt, Deputy Prosecutor of the Yugoslavia Tribunal (available from www.un.org.icty.press).

International Criminal Tribunal for the Former Yugoslavia (1999f) Address to the United Nations General Assembly, Judge Gabrielle Kirk McDonald, President of the International Criminal Tribunal for the Former Yugoslavia, 19 November.

International Crisis Group (1996a) Bosnia: *Eastern Slavonia Report*, 27 March.

International Crisis Group (1996b) Bosnia: *Aid and Accountability, Dayton Implementation*, 24 November.

International Crisis Group (1998a) Bosnia: *Whither Bosnia*, 9 September.

International Crisis Group (1998b) Bosnia: *To Build a Peace*, Recommendations for the Madrid Peace Implementation Council Meeting, 15 December.

International Crisis Group (1999a) *Lessons Learned from Bosnia, Models and Methods of International Administration*, Report No 66, 17 May.

International Crisis Group (1999b) *Is Dayton Failing? Bosnia Four Years After the Peace Agreement*, Sarajevo, 28 October. (All available from www.crisisweb.org/)

IPSOS (1998) 'Les français se montrent "europhoriques" ' at www.canalipsos.com/archives_fr/1198/franceurop.

Italian Embassy in Washington (accessed January 2000) *Italy's Military Contribution*, www.italyemb.org.

Jachtenfuchs, M. (1997) 'Ideas and integration: conflicting models of a legitimate European political order', Paper presented at the Fifth Biennial ECSA Conference, Seattle, May–June 1997.

Jacquemin, A. and Wright, D. (eds) (1993) *The European Challenges Post-1992*, Aldershot, Edward Elgar.

Jakobsen, P.V. (1997) 'The Danish approach to UN peace operations after the Cold War: a new model in the making?', Paper presented at the 22nd Annual BISA Conference, Leeds, 15–17 December.

Jakobsen, P.V. (1998) 'The Danish approach to UN peace operations after the Cold War: a new model in the making', *International Peacekeeping*, 5 (3), 106–23.

James, S. (1998) 'Labour markets and social policy in Europe: the case of the European Union', in R. Sykes and P. Alcock (eds), *Developments in European Social Policy*, Bristol, Policy Press.

Jamieson, B. (1993) *Britain Beyond Europe*, London, Duckworth.
Jansen, T. (1997) 'The difficulty of expressing European identity', IEE Doc No. 7, Université catholique de Louvain.
Jeffery, C. (1996) 'The territorial dimension', in G. Smith, W.E. Paterson and S. Padgett (eds), *Developments in German Politics 2*, London, Macmillan, pp. 76–95.
Jervell, S. (1991) 'Norden og samarbeid mellom nordiske land', in J. Sverre (ed.), *Norden I det nye Europa*, Oslo, Utenrikspolitiske Instituttene and the University in Reykjavik, pp. 11-42.
Joenniemi, P. and Stålvant, C.-E. (eds) (1995) *Baltic Sea Politics: Achievements and Challenges*, Stockholm, Nordic Council, Nord, no. 35.
Johnson, W.T. (1995) *NATO Strategy in the 1990s: Reaping the Peace Dividend or the Whirlwind?*, Pennsylvania, US Army War College/Strategic Studies Institute.
Jones, C. (1999) 'Trends and developments in welfare states', in J. Clasen (ed.), *Comparative Social Policy*, Oxford, Blackwell.
Jones, T. (1999) 'A man who enjoys the last laugh', *European Voice*, 1–7 April, p. 9.
Jornal de Noticias (1991) *Eleicoes/91*, 8 October.
Jospin, L. (1999) *Address to the Congress of the Socialist International*, 8 November 1999. Text available at www.premier-ministre.gouv.fr/GB/PM/DGB081199.
Kaase, M. and Newton, K. (1995) *Beliefs in Government*, Oxford, Oxford University Press.
Kaplan, L.S. (1999) 'NATO's first fifty years', *Nato Review*, Special 50th Anniversary Commemorative Issue, pp. 4–19.
Katrougalos, G.S. (1996) 'The south European welfare model: the Greek welfare state, in search of an identity', *Journal of European Social Policy*, 6 (1), 39–60.
Keeler, J.T.S. and Schain, M. (1996a), 'Presidents, premiers, and models of democracy in France', in J.T.S. Keeler and M. Schain (eds), *Chirac's Challenge: Liberalization, Europeanization and Malaise in France*, New York, St Martin's Press, pp. 23–52.
Keeler, J.T.S. and Schain, M. (1996b) 'Introduction: Mitterrand's legacy, Chirac's challenge', in J.T.S. Keeler and M. Schain (eds), *Chirac's Challenge: Liberalization, Europeanization and Malaise in France*, New York, St Martin's Press, pp.1–20.
Kennedy, P. (1989) *The Rise and Fall of the Great Powers*, London, Fontana.
Kennedy-Minott, R. (1992) 'Foreword', in C.E. Zoppo (ed.), *Nordic Security at the Turn of the Twenty-First Century*, New York, Greenwood Press.
Kerremans, B. (1998) 'The political and institutional consequences of widening: capacity and control in an enlarged council', in P. Laurent and M. Maresceau (eds), *The State of the European Union: Volume 4 Deepening and Widening*, Harlow, Longman.
Khan, S. (1996) 'A critical re-evaluation of theories of "globalisation" and "global culture" ', Cambridge, unpublished MPhil dissertation.
Klein, J.P. (1997) 'The prospects for Eastern Croatia: the significance of the United Nations' undiscovered mission', *RUSI Journal*, April, pp. 19–24.
Klein, J.P. (1999) Speech on Dayton by the Principal Deputy High Representative at the Royal Institute of International Affairs, London, 21 April (available from www.ohr.int).

Kleinman, M. and Piachaud, D. (1993) 'European social policy: conceptions and choices', *Journal of European Social Policy*, 3 (1), 1–19.
Kohler Koch, B. (1999) 'Euorpe in search of legitimate governance', ARENA working papers, WP 99/27.
Kolankiewicz, G. (1993) 'The other Europe: different roads to modernity in Eastern and Central Europe', in S. Garcia (ed.), *European Identity and the Search for Legitimacy*, London, Pinter.
Korpi, W. (1980) 'Social policy and distributional conflict in the capitalist democracies', *West European Politics*, 3, 305.
Kucia, M. (1999) 'Public opinion in Central Europe on EU accession: the Czech Republic and Poland', *Journal of Common Market Studies*, 37 (1), 143–52.
Kuenning, H.F. (1999) 'Preventive peacekeeping as a model for the prevention of war: American lessons learned in Macedonia', in W. Biermann and M. Vladset (eds), *United Nations Peacekeeping in Trouble: Lessons Learned from the Former Yugoslavia*, Aldershot, Ashgate.
Kuper, B.-O. (1994) 'The Green and White Papers of the European Union: the apparent goal of reduced social benefits', *Journal of European Social Policy*, 4 (2), 129–37.
Kuper, R. (1998) *The Politics of the European Court of Justice*, London, Kogan Page.
Ladrech, R. (1994) 'Europeanization of domestic politics and institutions: the case of France', *Journal of Common Market Studies*, 32 (1), 69–88.
Laffan, B. (1998) 'Developments in the member states', in G. Edwards and G. Wiessala (eds), *The European Union: Annual Review of Activities 1997*, Oxford, Blackwell, p. 159.
Laffan, B. (1999) 'Developments in the member states', in G. Edwards and G. Wiessala (eds), *The European Union: Annual Review 1998/9*, Oxford, Blackwell, p. 185.
Laursen, F. (1991) 'The European Community in the world context: civilian power or superpower?', *Futures*, September, 747–59.
Laursen, F. (1993) 'The Maastricht Treaty: implications for the Nordic countries', *Cooperation and Conflict*, 28 (2), 115–41.
Lawlor, T. and Rigby, M. (1998) *Contemporary Spain*, Harlow, Longman.
Le Gall, J. (1997) *Les Institutions de la Vie République à l'épreuve de l'alternance: la présidence de François Mitterrand*, Paris, Librairie Générale de Droit et de Jurisdprudence.
Leibfried, S. (1993) 'Towards a European welfare state?', in C. Jones (ed.), *New Perspectives on the Welfare State in Europe*, London, Routledge.
Leibfried, S. and Pierson, P. (1995) 'Semi-sovereign welfare states: social policy in a multitiered Europe', in S. Leibfried and P. Pierson (eds), *European Social Policy: Between Fragmentation and Integration*, Washington, DC, Brookings Institution.
Lenaerts (1991) 'Fundamental rights to be included in a Community Catalogue', *European Law Review*, 16, 367.
Lenzi, G. (ed.) (1998) *WEU at Fifty*, Paris, The Institute for Security Studies, WEU.
Leonard, M. (1998) *Rediscovering Europe*, London, Demos.

Lequesne, C. (1993) *Paris-Bruxelles: comment se fait la politique européenne de la France*, Paris, Presses de la Fondation Nationale des Sciences Politiques.
Lequesne, C. (1996) 'France', in D. Rometsch and W. Wessels (eds), *The European Union and Member States: Towards Institutional Fusion?*, Manchester, Manchester University Press, pp. 185–96.
'Letnye nastroenniya Rossiyan' (1999) *Nezavisimaya Gazeta*, 16 July, p. 8.
Leurdijk, D.A. (1996) *The United Nations and NATO in the Former Yugoslavia 1991–1996, Limits to diplomacy and Force*, Clingendael, Netherlands Atlantic Commission/Netherlands Institute of International Relations.
Leurdijk, D.A. (1998) 'Before and after Dayton, the United Nations and NATO in the Former Yugoslavia', in T.G. Weiss (ed.), *Beyond UN Subcontracting*, Basingstoke, Macmillan, pp. 49–66.
Levi, R. (1999) 'Prodi's voice', *European Voice*, 6–11 May, p. 10.
Lieven, A. (1999) *Chechnya: Tombstone of Russian Power*, New Haven, Yale University Press.
Lijphart, A. (1984) *Democracies: Patterns of Majoritarian and Consensus Government in Twenty-one Countries*, New Haven, Yale University Press.
Lima, L.C. and Afonso, A.J. (1995) 'The promised land: school autonomy, evaluation and curriculum decision-making in Portugal', *Education Review*, 47 (2), 165–72.
Lindström, U. (1993) *Euro-Consent, Euro-Contract, or Euro-Coercion? Scandinavian Social Democracy, the European Impasse, and the Abolition of Things Political*, Oslo, Scandinavia University Press.
Lipietz, A. (1996) 'Social Europe: the post-Maastricht challenge', *Review of International Political Economy*, 3 (3), 369–79.
Lloyd, J. (1999) 'Who lost Russia?', *The Foreign Policy Centre Newsletter*, 1 September.
Lodge, J. (1993) *The European Community and the Challenge of the Future*, London, Pinter.
Lopes, J. da S. (1996) 'A Economia Portuguesa desde 1960', in A. Barreto (ed.), *A Situacao Social em Portugal 1960–1995*, Lisbon, Instituto de Ciencias Sociais, Universidade de Lisboa.
Lord, C. (1998) *Democracy in the European Union*, Sheffield, Sheffield University Press.
Lucas, E. (1998) 'Things fall apart: the centre cannot hold', in *The Economist, The World in 1999*, London, The Economist Group, pp. 58–9.
Lyck, L. and Berg, P.O. (eds) (1997) *The Øresund Region Building*, Copenhagen (New Social Science Monographs), Copenhagen Business School.
MacAskill, E. (1999) 'Cook warns of sidelined UK outside euro zone', *Guardian*, 24 November, p. 12.
McCormick, J. (1999) *Understanding the European Union*, Basingstoke, Macmillan.
McDonagh, B. (1998) *Original Sin in a Brave New World: An Account of the Negotiation of the Treaty of Amsterdam*, Dublin, Institute of European Affairs.
McFaul, M. (1994) *Understanding Russia's 1993 Parliamentary Elections*, Stanford, CA, Hoover Institution Essays in Public Policy.

McFaul, M. (1997) *Russia's 1996 Presidential Election: The End of Polarised Politics*, Washington, Hoover Institution Press.
McGoldrick, D. (1997) *International Relations Law of the European Union*. Harlow, Longman.
McGrew, A. (ed.) (1997) *The Transformation of Democracy*, Cambridge, Polity Press/Open University.
McInnes, C. (1998) 'Labour's Strategic Defence Review', *International Affairs*, 74 (4), 823–45.
McKay, J. (1996) 'Berlin-Brandenburg? Nein Danke! The referendum on the proposed *Länderfusion*', *German Politics*, 5 (3), 485–502.
McKay, J. (2000) 'The Berlin election 1999', *German Politics*, 9 (1) (forthcoming).
MacLean, R.M. (ed.) (1996) *European Union Law*, 6th edn, London, HLT Publications.
McMahon, J.F. (1962) 'The Court of the European Communities', *Journal of Common Market Studies*, 1 (1), 1–21.
Maher, I. (1998) 'EU law in the national legal order: a systems analysis', *Journal of Common Market Studies*, 36 (2), 237–54.
Malo de Molina, J.L. (1993) 'Mercado de trabajo, empleo y salarios. Distorsiones y ajustes', in J.L. Garcia Delgado (ed.), *España economía*, Madrid, Espasa Calpe, pp. 1149–80.
Mangen, S. (1996) 'German welfare and social citizenship', in G. Smith, W.E. Paterson and S. Padgett (eds), *Developments in German Politics*, 2, London, Macmillan, pp. 250–66.
Manicini, F. (1989) 'The making of a Constitution for Europe', *Common Market Law Review*, 24, 595–614.
Marques-Mendes, A.J. (1993) 'The development of the Portuguese economy in the context of the EC', in J. da S. Lopes (ed.), *Portugal and EC Membership Evaluated*, London, Pinter.
Marshall, A. (1994) 'Sweden may join ranks of the EU awkward squad', *The Independent*, 14 November.
Marshall, A. (1999) 'Alliance that held together in a crisis', *The Independent*, 4 June, p. 4.
Martin. P. (1996) 'A sequential approach to regional integration: the European Union and Central and Eastern Europe', *European Journal of Political Economy*, 12, 581–98.
Martinez, L.M. (1998) 'Spain, regulating employment and social fragmentation', in A. Ferner and R. Hyman (eds), *Changing Industrial Relations in Europe*, Oxford, Blackwell, pp. 426–58.
Martins, M. and Guimarães, R. (1993) 'Effects of integration into the EC and the process of industrial adaptation: the 1980s and 1990s in Portugal', in J. da S. Lopes (ed.), *Portugal and EC Membership Evaluated*, London, Pinter.
Maskell, P. (1998) 'Globaliseringsprocessen og danske erhvervspolitiske overvejelser', *Politica*, 30 (1), 24–48.
Mayhew, A. (1998) *Recreating Europe: The European Union's Policy towards Central and Eastern Europe*, Cambridge, Cambridge University Press.

Mazey, S. and Richardson, J. (1997) 'Agenda setting, lobbying and the 1996 IGC', in G. Edwards and A. Pijpers (eds), *The Politics of European Treaty Reform*, London, Cassell.

Medborgerundersøgelsen 1990, conducted by Gallup A/S. Figures for this and surveys of other Nordic countries are quoted from Nordlund, A. (1997), 'Attitudes towards the welfare state in the Scandinavian countries', *Scandinavian Journal of Social Welfare*, 6, 233–46.

Medevdev, D. (2000) Cited in 'Campaign strategy and rhetoric', *RFE/RL Russian Election Report*, No. 3 (11), 17 March.

Menon, A. (1996) 'France and the IGC of 1996', *Journal of European Public Policy*, 3 (2), 231–52.

Menon, R. and Fuller, G.E. (2000) 'Russia's ruinous Chechen war', *Foreign Affairs*, 79 (2), 32–45.

Merlini, C. (1993) 'Italy and Europe', in J. Story (ed.), *The New Europe: Politics, Government and Economy since 1945*, Oxford, Blackwell, pp. 227–44.

Meyer, C. (1999) 'Exploring the EU's communications deficit', *Journal of Common Market Studies*, 37 (4), 617–40.

Minc, A. (1997) *La mondialisation heureuse*, Paris, Pion.

Minc, A. (1998) *Au nom de la loi*, Paris, Gallimard.

Mittelman, J.H. (1996) *Globalisation: Critical Reflections*, International Political Economy Yearbook, Volume 9, London, Lynne Rienner Publishers.

Monar, J. and Morgan, R. (eds) (1994) *The Third Pillar of the European Union*, Brussels, European Interuniversity Press and the College of Europe.

Monnet, J. (1978) *Memoirs*, London, Collins.

Moore, C. (April 1999) *The Kosovo Verification Mission: Withdrawn but not Disgraced*, Truth and Verify, The Verification Technology Information Centre (available from www.vertic.org/tnv/April_1999/kosovo).

Moravcsik, A. (1993) 'Preferences and power in the European Community: a liberal intergovernmentalist approach', *Journal of Common Market Studies*, 31 (4).

Moravcsik, A. (1998) *The Choice for Europe*, London, UCL Press.

Muller, P. (1992) 'Entre le local et l'Europe: la crise du modèle français des politiques publiques', *Revue française de science politique*, 42 (2), 275–97.

Murphy, B. (1998) 'Real and nominal convergence: Spain on the threshold of EMU', *International Journal of Iberian Studies*, 11 (3), 166–77.

Musgrave, R.A. and Musgrave, P.B. (1976) *Public Finance in Theory and Practice*, London, McGraw Hill.

Myant, M. (1999) 'The international financial crisis and the Czech Republic', Paper presented to the BASEES annual conference, March, Cambridge.

NATO (1997a) *NATO's Role in Bringing Peace to the Former Yugoslavia, Basic Fact Sheet*, No. 4, March, Brussels, NATO.

NATO (1997b) *The NATO Led Stabilisation Force (SFOR) in Bosnia and Herzegovina, Basic Fact Sheet*, No. 11, April, Brussels, NATO.

NATO (1999a) *The Alliances Strategic Concept, Approved by the Heads of State and Government, Participating in the Meeting of the North Atlantic Council in Washington D.C. on 23rd and 24th April 1999*, Press Release, 24 April, accessed via www.nato./int/.

NATO (1999b) *Speech of Lord Robertson, NATO Secretary General to the French Institute For International Relations*, 18 May, accessed via www.nato.int/.

NATO (1999c) *The Washington Declaration, Signed and Issued by the Heads of State and Government Participating in the Meeting of the North Atlantic Council in Washington D.C. on 23 and 24 April 1999*, accessed via www.nato.int/ .

NATO (1999d) *Secretary General Javier Solana's Remarks to the Press on His Last Day*, 18 May, accessed via www.nato.int/.

NATO (1999e) *Press Conference on the Kosovo Strike Assessment*, by General Wesley K. Clark and Brigadier General John Corley, NATO speech, Press conference SACEUR, NATO HQ, 27 April 1999 (this date came out on the print-out but appears to be an error).

NATO (1999f) 'Special 50th Anniversary Commemorative Issue', *NATO Review*.

Nelson, R. and Wright, G. (1992) 'The rise and fall of American technological leadership: the postwar era in historical perspective', *Journal of Economic Literature*, 30, pp. 1931–64.

Nichols, T.M. (1999) *The Russian Presidency: Society and Politics in the Second Russian Republic*, New York, St Martin's Press.

Nielsen, H.F. (1998) 'Samarbejde om el skal lukke Barsebäck', *Politiken*, 3 November.

Niemann, A. (1998) 'The PHARE programme and the concept of spillover: neo-functionalism in the making', *Journal of European Public Policy*, 428–46.

Newsnight (1999) BBC Television, 14 September.

Nordlund, A. (1997) 'Attitudes towards the welfare state in the Scandinavian countries', *Scandinavian Journal of Social Welfare*, 6, 233–46.

North Atlantic Assembly (1999) *The OSCE Verification Mission to Kosovo, December 1998–March 1999*, Information Document (May 1999), Personal views by two verifiers, Marc Dickinson and Nicolas Karzorowski, International Secretariat (available from www.naa.be/publications/special/as147gen29-e).

Northedge, F.S. (1974) *Descent from Power*, London, George Allen and Unwin.

Nowak, J. (1999) 'Russia: isolation or co-operation?', Paper presented to a Jamestown Foundation conference on *Russia: What Went Wrong? Which Way Now?*, June, cited at www.jamestown.org/htm/conf-paper-nowak-full.

Nugent, N. (1999) *The Government and Politics of the European Union*, 4th edn, The European Union Series, Basingstoke, Macmillan.

Nuttall, S. (1992) *European Political Cooperation*, Oxford, Clarendon Press.

Oates, W.E. (1972) 'An economist's perspective', in W.E. Oates (ed.), *The Political Economy of Fiscal Federalism*, New York, Harcourt Brace.

Obradovic, D. (1996) 'Policy legitimacy and the European Union', *Journal of Common Market Studies*, 34 (2).

OECD (1993) *OECD Economic Surveys: Portugal*, Paris, OECD.

OECD (1995a) *OECD Economic Surveys: Portugal*, Paris, OECD.

OECD (1995b) *Classification of High-technology Products and Industries*, The Organisation for Economic Co-operation and Development, Directorate for Science, Technology and Industry, Scientific and Technological Policy Committee, Working Party 9 of the Industry Committee on Industrial Statistics Group of National Experts on Science and Technology Indicators, 12–13 October, Paris, OECD.

OECD (1996) *OECD Economic Surveys: Portugal*, Paris, OECD.
OECD (1998a) *OECD Economic Surveys: Portugal*, Paris, OECD.
OECD (1998b) *OECD Economic Surveys, 1997–1998: Russian Federation*, Paris, OECD.
O'Hanlon, M. (1997) 'Transforming NATO: The role of European forces', *Survival*, autumn, pp. 5–15.
Ohmae, K. (1993) 'The rise of the region state', *Foreign Affairs*, 72 (2).
Open Letter (2000) cited at www.putin2000.ru/07/05.
O Publico (1995) *Eleicoes Legislativas*, 2 October.
O Publico (1996) *Portugal tem mais pobres*, 29 October.
OSCE (1996) *Report of, and Annexes to, the Copenhagen Round Table on United Nations Sanctions: The Case of the Former Yugoslavia*, Copenhagen, OSCE.
OSCE (1999a) *What is the OSCE?*, January, accessed via www.osce.org.
OSCE (1999b) *Charter for European Security*, November, Istanbul. Accessed via www.osce.org.
OSCE (1999c) *Seminar on Cooperation among International Organisations and Institutions: Experience and Prospects in South Eastern Europe*, Sofia, Bulgaria, 17–19 May. SEC.GAL/64/99.
Panic, M. (1998) 'Transnational corporations and the nation state', in R. Kozul-Wright and R. Rowthorn (eds), *Transnational Corporations and the Global Economy*, London, Macmillan.
Pappi, F. (1984) 'The West German party system', *West European Politics*, 7 (4), 7–26.
Parker, B. (1998) *Globalisation and Business Practice: Managing Across Boundaries*, London, Sage.
Parker, S. (1996) 'Electoral reform and political change in Italy, 1991–1994', in S. Gundle and S. Parker (eds), *The New Italian Republic*, London, Routledge, pp. 40–59.
Parodi, J.-L. (1997) 'Proportionnalisation périodique, cohabitation, atomisation partisane: un triple défi pour le régime semi-présidentiel de la Cinquième République', *Revue française de science politique*, 37 (3/4), 292–312.
Parott, B. (eds) (1997) *Democratic Changes and Authoritarian Reactions in Russia, Ukraine, Belarus and Moldova*, Cambridge, Cambridge University Press.
Pastor Verdú, J. (1998) 'Democracia y Movimientos Sociales Alternativos', in *12 Visiones de una Politica de Progreso*, Madrid, Acento Editorial, 247–68.
Paterson, W.E. and Southern, D. (1991) *Governing Germany*, Oxford, Blackwell.
Pereira, A. (1991) 'The system of local government in Portugal', in R. Batley and G. Stokes (eds), *Local Government in Europe: Trends and Developments*, Basingstoke, Macmillan.
Pereirinha, J.A. (1997) 'Welfare states and anti-poverty regimes: the case of Portugal', in M. Rhode (ed.), *Southern European Welfare States*, London, Frank Cass.
Peterson, J. (1998) *A Common Foreign Policy for Europe?*, London, Routledge.
Peterson, J. and Sjursen, H. (eds) (1998) *A Common Foreign Policy for Europe? Competing Visions of the CFSP*, London, Routledge.
Peterson, P.J. (1999) 'Gray dawn: the global aging crisis', *Foreign Affairs*, January–February.

Piening, C. (1997) *Global Europe: The European Union in World Affairs*, Boulder, CO, Lynne Rienner Publishers.
Pierson, P. and Leibfried, S. (1995) 'Multitiered institutions and the making of social policy', in S. Leibfried and P. Pierson (eds), *European Social Policy: Between Fragmentation and Integration*, Washington, DC, Brookings Institution.
Pinar Tank, G. (1998) 'Security issues emanating from the Mediterranean Basin', in K.A. Eliassen (ed.), *Foreign and Security Policy in the European Union*. London, Sage, pp. 161–83.
Porter, M.E. (1990) *Competition in Global Industries*, Boston, Harvard Business School Press.
Porto, M. (1984) 'Portugal: twenty years of change', in A. Williams (ed.), *Southern Europe Transformed: Political and Economic Change in Greece, Italy, Portugal and Spain*, London, Harper & Row.
Powell, B. (2000) 'The end of an era', *Newsweek*, 10 January, pp. 50–1.
Pragnell, A. (1985) *Television in Europe*, Manchester, The European Institute for the Media.
Preston, C. (1997) *Enlargement and Integration in the European Union*, London, Routledge.
Putin, V. (2000) *Ot Perrogo Litsa*, Moscow.
Quinn-Judge, P. (1999) 'A family matter', *Time*, 20 September, pp. 42–5.
Quinn-Judge, P. (2000) 'No tears for Boris', *Time*, 1 January, pp. 44–50.
Ramprakash, D. (1994) 'Poverty in the countries of the European Union: a synthesis of Eurostat's statistical research on poverty', *Journal of European Social Policy*, 4 (2), 117–28.
Rasmussen, H. (1986) 'On law and policy in the European Court of Justice: a comparative study', in *Judicial Policy-making*, Dordrecht, Martinus Nijhoff.
Reflection Group (1995) *1996 Intergovernmental Conference: Reflection Group Report*, Brussels, General Secretariat of the Council of the EU.
Regelsberger, E., with de Schoutheete, P. and Wessels, W. (1997) *Foreign Policy of the European Union, from EPC to CFSP and Beyond*, Boulder, CO, Lynne Rienner Publishers.
Remington, T. (1997) 'Democratisation and the new political order in Russia', in K. Dawisha and B. Parott (eds), *Democratic Changes and Authoritarian Reactions in Russia, Ukraine, Belarus and Moldova*. Cambridge, Cambridge University Press.
Rhodes, C. (1998) *The European Union in the World Community*, Boulder, CO, Lynne Rienner Publishers.
Rhodes, M. (1996) 'Globalization and west European welfare states: a critical review of recent debates', *Journal of European Social Policy*, 6 (4), 305–27.
Rhodes, M. (1997) 'Southern European welfare states: identity, problems and prospects for reform', in M. Rhodes (ed.), *Southern European Welfare States*, London, Frank Cass.
Rigby, M. (1998) 'Education and employment in Spain: a labour market in transition', in T. Lawlor and M. Rigby (eds), *Contemporary Spain*, Harlow, Longman, pp. 203–300.
Roberts, A. (1998) 'Portugal prepares to harvest the benefits of monetary union', *The Times*, 16 December.

Robinson, O.F., Fergus, T.D. and Gordon, W.M. (1994) *European Legal History*, 2nd edn, Oxford, Butterworths.

Rodrigues, F. and Monteiro, A. (1998) 'Social work in Portugal', in S. Shardlow and M. Payne (eds), *Contemporary Issues in Social Work: Western Europe*, Aldershot, Arena.

Rosenau, J.N. (1995) 'Distant proximities: The dynamics and dialectics of globalisation', in *International Political Economy – Understanding Global Disorder*. London, Zed Books, pp. 46–64.

Ruggie, J.G. (1995) 'At home abroad, abroad at home: international liberalisation and domestic stability in the new world economy', *Millennium*, 24 (3), 505–26.

Rutland, P. (1999) 'Western policy and the failure of the economic transition in Russia', Paper presented to a Jamestown Foundation conference on *Russia: What Went Wrong? Which Way Now?*, June, cited at www.jamestown.org/htm/conf-paper-rutland-full.

Sakamoto, Y. (1995) 'Democratisation, social movements and world order', in *International Political Economy: Understanding Global Disorder*, London, Zed Books, pp. 129–43.

Sakwa, R. (1999) 'Yeltsin's leadership and Russia's crisis', Unpublished paper presented at BASEES annual conference, Cambridge, 27–29 March.

Salmon, K. (1994) *The Modern Spanish Economy – Transformation and Integration into Europe*, London, Pinter.

Santer, J. (1997) European Parliamentary Debates, *Agence Europe*, 27 June.

Santos, B. de S. (1990) *O Estado e a Sociedade em Portugal (1974–1988)*, Oporto, Edicoes Afrontamento.

Santos, B. de S. (1991) *State, Wage Relations and Social Welfare in the Semiperiphery: The Case of Portugal*, Coimbra, Centro de Estudos Sociais.

Scharpf, F. (1997) 'European integration and welfare states', *Journal of European Public Policy*, 3 (2), 127–43.

Schermers (1990) 'The scales in balance: national constitutional court versus Court of Justice', *CML Review*, 27, 97.

Schioppa Kostoris, F.P. (1996) 'Excesses and limits of the public sector in the Italian economy', in S. Gundle and S. Parker (eds), *The New Italian Republic*, London, Routledge, pp. 273–94.

Schmidt, H. (1999) 'The Transatlantic Alliance in the 21st century', *Nato Review*, Special 50th Anniversary Commemorative Issue, pp. 20–4.

Schmidt, V.A. (1996a) 'Business, the state and the end of dirigisme', in J.T.S. Keeler and M. Schain (eds), *Chirac's Challenge: Liberalization, Europeanization and Malaise in France*, New York, St Martin's Press, pp. 105–42.

Schmidt, V.A. (1996b) *From State to Market? The Transformation of French Business and Government*, Cambridge, Cambridge University Press.

Schmidt, V.A. (1999) 'La France entre l'Europe et le monde: le cas des politiques économiques nationales', *Revue française de science politique*, 49 (1), 51–78.

Schulte, G.L. (1997a) 'Former Yugoslavia and the new NATO', *Survival*, 39, 19–42.

Schulte, G.L. (1997b) 'Bringing peace to Bosnia and change to the alliance', *NATO Review*, No. 2, March, pp. 22–5.

Seguin, P. (1992) *Discours pour la France*, Paris, Grasset.

Seidelin, M., Lauritsen, N. and Borregaard, P. (1999) 'S: Euroafstemning sent å 2000', *Politiken*, 12 September.

Severgnini, B. (1998) 'Who'll be who in Italy?', in *The World in 1999*, London, *The Economist* Publications, pp. 50–1.

Sfikas, T.D. and Williams, C. (eds) (1999) *Ethnicity and Nationalism in East-Central Europe and the Balkans*. Aldershot, Ashgate.

Shonfield, A. (1973) *Europe: Journey to an Unknown Destination*, Harmondsworth, Penguin.

Siune, K. and Svensson, P. (1993) 'The Danes and the Maastricht Treaty: the Danish EC Referendum of June 1992', *Electoral Studies*, 12 (2), 99–111.

Siune, K. Svensson, P. and Tonsgaard, O. (1994) 'The European Union: the Danes said "no" in 1992 but "yes" in 1993', *Electoral Studies*, 13 (2), 107–16.

Sjovaag, M. (1998) 'The Single European Act', in K.A. Eliassen (ed.), *Foreign and Security Policy in the European Union*, London, Sage, pp. 22–42.

Slaughter Burley, A.M. (1993) 'New directions in legal research on the European Community', *Journal of Common Market Studies*, 31 (3), 391–400.

Smith, A. (1993) *Russia in the World Economy*, London, Routledge.

Smith, J. (1999) 'Blair pledges to "tackle poverty everywhere" ', *PA News*, America Online, 7 December.

Smith, Karen, E. (1998) *The Making of EU Foreign Policy*, Basingstoke, Macmillan.

Snyder, F. (1998) 'EMU revisited: Are we making a constitution? What constitution are we making?', European University Institute (EUI)/EUI Working Papers. Paper (Law) No. 6.

Snyder, F. (1998) *General Course on Constitutional Law of the European Union*, Academy of European Law (ed.), *Collected Courses of the Academy of European Law*, Volume VI, Book I, 41–155. Kluwer Law International.

Spicker, P. (1991) 'The principle of subsidiarity and the social policy of the European Community', *Journal of European Social Policy*, 1 (1), 3–14.

Spicker, P. (1996) 'Social policy in a federal Europe', *Social Policy & Administration*, 30 (4), 293–304.

Stavridis, S. (1997) 'The common foreign and security policy of the European Union: why institutional arrangements are not enough', in S. Stavridis, E. Mossialos, R. Morgan and H. Machin (eds), *New Challenges to the European Union, Policies and Policy-Making*. Aldershot, Dartmouth, pp. 87–122.

Steele, J. (1999) 'Clinton's soft words belie hard facts', *Guardian*, 19 November, p. 16.

Stein, E. (1964) 'Assimilation of national laws as a function of European integration', *American Journal of International Law*, 58 (1), 29.

Stein, E. (1981) 'Lawyers, judges and the making of a transnational Constitution', *American Journal of International Law*, 75 (1), 1–27.

Streeck, W. (1995) 'From market making to state building? Reflections on the political economy of European social policy', in S. Leibfried and P. Pierson (eds), *European Social Policy: Between Fragmentation and Integration*, Washington, DC, Brookings Institution.

Strøm, K. (1992) 'Norway, Sweden and the new Europe', *Scandinavian Studies*, 64, 498–528.

Sweden, Permanent Mission to the United Nations (1998), *Sweden Strengthens Its Presence in Kosovo*, Press Release, 11 September (available from www.un.int.sweden/pr980911).

Sykes, R. (1998) 'The future of social policy in Europe?', in R. Sykes and P. Alcock (eds), *Developments in European Social Policy*, Bristol, Policy Press.

Szarka, J. (1998) 'French business in the Mitterrand years: the continuity of change', in M. Maclean (ed.), *The Mitterrand Years: Legacy and Evaluation*. Basingstoke, Macmillan, pp. 151–68.

Taylor, S. (1999a) 'EU list aims to strengthen policing of arms exports', *European Voice*, 9–15 September, p. 4.

Taylor, S. (1999b) 'Stakes rise in enlargement talks', *European Voice*, 20–26 May, p. 9.

Taylor, S. (1999c) 'EU leaders advance on a common defence policy', *European Voice*, 27 May–2 June, p. 7.

Teague, P. (1998) 'Monetary union and social Europe', *Journal of European Social Policy*, 8 (2), 117–37.

Thomsen, B.N. (ed.) (1993) *The Odd Man Out? Denmark and European Integration 1948–1992*, Odense, Odense University Press.

Timonen, V. (1999) 'A threat to social security? The impact of EU membership on the Finnish welfare state', *Journal of European Social Policy*, 9 (3), 253–61.

Tindemans, L. (1976) *European Union: Report by Mr Leo Tindemans to the European Council, Bulletin of the European Communities*, Supplement 1/76.

Titmuss, R. (1974) *Social Policy*, London, Allen & Unwin.

Todd, E. (1998) *L'illusion economique: essai sur la stagnation des sociétés developpées*, Paris, Gallimard.

Togeby, L. (1998) 'Prejudice and tolerance in a period of increasing ethnic diversity and growing unemployment: Denmark since 1970', *Ethnic and Racial Studies*, 21 (6), 1137–54.

Toomey, C. (2000) 'Another reign of terror?', *Sunday Times Magazine*, 26 March, pp. 36–45.

Traynor, I. (2000) 'The spy who would be king', *Guardian*, 25 March, pp. 6–7.

Trifiletti, R. (1999) 'Southern European welfare regimes and the worsening position of women', *Journal of European Social Policy*, 9 (1), 49–64.

Trofimenko, H. (1999) *Russian National Interests and the Current Crisis in Russia*, Aldershot, Ashgate.

Truscott, P. (1997) *Russia First: Breaking with the West*, London, I.B. Taurus.

Tunander, O. (1993) 'The strategic significance of the Nordic-Baltic Region', in M. Kukk, S. Jervell and P. Joenniemi (eds), *The Baltic Sea Area – a Region in the Making*, Oslo, Europa-programmet, pp. 213–30.

United Nations (1994) *Report of the Secretary-General pursuant to Resolution 871 (1993)*, S/1994/300, 16 March.

United Nations (30 May 1995) *Report of the Secretary-General Pursuant to Security Council Resolutions 982 (1995) and 987 (1995)*, S/1995/444.

United Nations (1996) *The Blue Helmets: A Review of United Nations Peace-keeping*, 3rd edn, New York, United Nations.

United Nations (June 1998) *United Nations Report of the Secretary-General on the United Nations Deployment Force pursuant to Security Council Resolution 1142 (1997)*, S/1998/454, 1.

United Nations (1999a) *United Nations Report of the Secretary-General on the United Nations Deployment Force pursuant to Security Council Resolution 1186 (1998)*, February, S/1999/161, 12.

United Nations (1999b) *United Nations Report of the Secretary-General pursuant to General Assembly Resolution 53/55 (1998) Srebrenica Report*, (Advance copy 22 November 1999 available from www.un.org/News/ossg/srebrenica_).

US Department of State (1998) *Background Notes: Italy*, March, obtained via www.italyemb.org.

Vaksberg, A. (1991) *The Soviet Mafia*, London, Weidenfeld and Nicolson.

Valencia, M. (1998) 'Eastern Europe's sad duet', in *The Economist* Intelligence Unit, *The World in 1999*, London, The Economist Group, pp. 53–6.

Valgundersøgelsen (1990), conducted by Gallup Markedsanalyse A/S for Jørgen Goul Andersen, Ole Borre, Steen Sauerberg, Hans Jørgen Nielsen and Torben Worre (Datamateriale DDA-1564. Dansk Data Arkiv, Odense University Munkebjergvænget 48, DK-5230 Odense M, Denmark). Table quoted from Nordlund, A. (1997) 'Attitudes towards the welfare state in the Scandinavian countries', *Scandinavian Journal of Social Welfare*, 6, 233–46.

Verney, D. (1959, 1979) *The Analysis of Political Systems*, London, Routledge.

Villari, L. (1992) *Il capitalismo italiano del novecento*, Rome, bibliotoca Universale Laterza.

Vobruba, G. (1998) 'Social policy for Europe', in W. Beck, L. van der Maesen and A. Walker (eds), *The Social Quality of Europe*, Bristol, Policy Press.

VTsIOM survey of 18–21 August 1999 cited at www.russiavotes.org/Duma_cur.

VTsIOM survey of 5–9 November 1999 cited at www.russiavotes.org/Duma_cur.

VTsIOM survey of 3–6 December 1999 cited at www.russiavotes.org/Duma_cur.

VTsIOM pre-Duma December 1999 survey cited at russiavotes.org/Duma_cur.

VTsIOM survey of 8–10 January 2000 cited at www.russiavotes.org/Yeltsin.

Wæver, O. (1994) 'The European security triangle', *Working Papers 12*, Copenhagen, Centre for Peace and Conflict Research.

Waites, B. (1995) *Europe and the Wider World*, London, Routledge.

Walker, W. (1999) *State Department Briefing*, 8 January, Washington, DC, State Department.

Wallace, H. (1993) 'Deepening and widening: problems of legitimacy for the EC', in S. Garcia (ed.), *European Identity and the Search for Legitimacy*, London, Pinter.

Ward, I. (1996) *A Critical Introduction to European Law*, London, Butterworths.

Ward, I. (1997) 'Law and the other Europeans', *Journal of Common Market Studies*, 35 (1), 79–96.

Weale, A. (1994) 'Social policy and European Union', *Social Policy & Administration*, 28 (1), 5–19.

Weiler, J.H.H. (1992) 'The evolution of mechanisms and institutions for a European foreign policy: reflections on the interaction of law and politics', European University Institute Research Paper No. 85/202, Florence, European University Research Institute.

Weiler, J.H.H. (1993) 'Journey to an unknown destination: a retrospective and prospective of the European Court of Justice in the arena of political integration', *Journal of Common Market Studies*, 31 (4), 417–46.

Weiler, J.H.H. (1997) 'The reformation of European constitutionalism', *Journal of Common Market Studies*, 35 (1), 97–131.

Wellens and Borchard (1989) 'Soft law in EC law', *European Law Review*, 14, 267.

Wendon, B. (1998) 'The Commission and European Union social policy', in R. Sykes and P. Alcock (eds), *Developments in European Social Policy*, Bristol, Policy Press.

Wheeler, N.J. and Dunne, T. (1998) 'Good international citizenship: a third way for British foreign policy', *International Affairs*, 74 (4), 847–87.

Whitman, R. (1998) *From Civilian Power to Superpower: The International Identity of the European Union*, London, Macmillan.

Wiessala, G. (1999a) 'An emerging relationship: the European Union's "new Asia strategy"', *World Affairs*, 3 (1), 96–112.

Wiessala, G. (1999b) 'European Union in a changing world: *trompe l'oeil* or revolution?', *World Affairs*, 3 (4), 36–51.

Wiener, A. and Della Sala, V. (1997) 'Constitution-making and citizenship practice: bridging the democracy gap in the EU', *Journal of Common Market Studies*, 35 (4), 595–614.

Williams, C. (1992) 'Russian views of European integration: an historical perspective', Unpublished paper presented to a New Europe conference, University of Nottingham, April.

Williams, C., Chuprov, V. and Staroverov, V. (eds) (1996) *Russian Society in Transition*, Aldershot, Dartmouth.

Williams, C. and Sfikas, T.D. (1999) *Ethnicity and Nationalism in Russia, the CIS and the Baltic States*, Aldershot, Ashgate.

Williams, S. (1992) *Child Workers in Portugal*, London, Anti-Slavery International.

Wilson, M. (1994) 'The Balkans', in K. Clements and R. Ward (eds), *Building International Community*, London, Allen & Unwin, pp. 140–62.

Wincott, D. (1995) 'Institutional interaction and European integration: towards an everyday critique of liberal intergovernmentalism', *Journal of Common Market Studies*, 33 (4), 598–610.

Wolf, M. (1999) 'Caught in the transition gap', *Financial Times*, 30 June, p. 11.

World Bank (1996) *From Plan to Market*, Washington, DC, World Bank.

Worre, T. (1993) 'Denmark and the European Union: public opinion in the 1980s and the referendum of June 1992', in B.N. Thomsen (ed.), *The Odd Man Out? Denmark and European Integration 1948–1992*, Odense, Odense University Press.

Woodall, P. (1998) 'How bad will it get?', in The Economist Intelligence Unit, *The World in 1999*, London, The Economist Group, p. 105.

Wright, V. and Elgie, R. (1996) 'The French presidency: the changing public policy environment', in R. Elgie (ed.), *Electing the French President: The 1995 Presidential Election*, Basingstoke, Macmillan, pp. 172–94.

Young, O.R. (1997) *Global Governance: Drawing Insights from the Environmental Experience*, Cambridge, MA, MIT Press.
Yost, D.S. (1998) 'The new NATO and collective security', *Survival*, 40 (2), 135–60.
Yurlov, F.N. (1999) 'Russia – a lost decade', *World Affairs*, 3 (3), 81–95.

Index